Hands-On Enterprise Automation on Linux

Efficiently perform large-scale Linux infrastructure automation with Ansible

James Freeman

BIRMINGHAM - MUMBAI

Hands-On Enterprise Automation on Linux

Copyright © 2020 Packt Publishing

Commissioning Editor: Vijin Boricha
Acquisition Editor: Rohit Rajkumar
Content Development Editor: Alokita Amanna
Senior Editor: Rahul Dsouza
Technical Editor: Prachi Sawant
Copy Editor: Safis Editing
Project Coordinator: Vaidehi Sawant
Proofreader: Safis Editing
Indexer: Pratik Shirodkar
Production Designer: Nilesh Mohite

First published: January 2020

Production reference: 1240120

Published by Packt Publishing Ltd.
Livery Place
35 Livery Street
Birmingham
B3 2PB, UK.

ISBN 978-1-78913-161-1

www.packt.com

*This book is dedicated to everyone who has inspired me to follow my dreams,
my passions, and live my truth, especially Lyndon Rees, Eleonora Guantini, Elane Slade,
and the late Sirdar Khan.*

`Packt.com`

Subscribe to our online digital library for full access to over 7,000 books and videos, as well as industry leading tools to help you plan your personal development and advance your career. For more information, please visit our website.

Why subscribe?

- Spend less time learning and more time coding with practical eBooks and Videos from over 4,000 industry professionals

- Improve your learning with Skill Plans built especially for you

- Get a free eBook or video every month

- Fully searchable for easy access to vital information

- Copy and paste, print, and bookmark content

Did you know that Packt offers eBook versions of every book published, with PDF and ePub files available? You can upgrade to the eBook version at `www.packt.com` and as a print book customer, you are entitled to a discount on the eBook copy. Get in touch with us at `customercare@packtpub.com` for more details.

At `www.packt.com`, you can also read a collection of free technical articles, sign up for a range of free newsletters, and receive exclusive discounts and offers on Packt books and eBooks.

Foreword

Few would disagree when I say that the world of technology has grown ever more complex over the last couple of decades since the internet came to prominence. More and more products have arrived, promising us solutions to tame the growing complexity. Along with the promises come a raft of experts, there to help us through what is actually yet more complexity.

2012 saw the first release of Ansible. By 2013, it was gaining significant traction since its promise of power through simplicity was not an empty one. Here was a technology rooted in a simple truth—solving problems with technology really means solving problems for people. Therefore, people matter. A tool that is easy to pick up and learn? What an amazing thought! Early adopters were those who saw through the functionality list to realize that here was a people-pleasing game changer.

I first met James at one of his technical Ansible talks a few years ago. It was still relatively early days for Ansible, although we'd just been acquired by Red Hat. At that first meeting, I realized that here was a fellow who understood the link between people and Ansible's powerful simplicity. I've been lucky enough to see James speak on a number of occasions since, with two standout talks coming to mind.

At AnsibleFest 2018 in Austin, Texas, James gave a great talk about a client engagement where he presided over a business-critical database upgrade—on a Friday afternoon. What's the golden rule we all tout in tech? Don't make business-critical changes on a Friday! Yet James's charismatic storytelling had the audience enthralled. The second occasion was more recent, at an Ansible London meetup. Taking a very different approach to the usual tech-heavy talks, James presented the audience with a tale of positive psychology, a story that had Ansible as the underlying tool supporting people. It turned out to be a great success, sparking a lively interaction across the audience during the Q&A session that followed.

Scalability isn't just about a technology; it is about people. If you want a technology to scale, it must be easy for people to adopt, to master, and to share. James is a model of scalability himself, as he so readily shares his knowledge. He also shows in this book that Ansible is an orchestrator, a conductor of the symphony if you like, with the ability to span an enterprise. I'm sure you'll enjoy reading it as much as I've enjoyed every interaction I've had with James.

Mark Phillips
Product Marketing Manager, Red Hat Ansible

I've worked alongside James for several years and consider him to be one of the foremost Ansible experts in the world. I've been witness to his help in the digital modernization efforts of large and small organizations with the help of automation and DevOps practices.

In *Hands-On Enterprise Automation on Linux*, James generously shares his experience with a practical, no-nonsense approach to managing heterogeneous Linux environments. If you learn best through a hands-on approach, then this is the book for you. James provides plenty of in-depth examples in each chapter so that you can cement your understanding and feel prepared to take Ansible into a live environment.

Ready to become an automation rockstar and revolutionize your IT ops team? Then read on!

Ben Strauss
Security Automation Manager, MindPoint Group

Contributors

About the author

James Freeman is an accomplished IT consultant and architect with over 20 years' experience in the technology industry. He has more than 7 years of first-hand experience of solving real-world enterprise problems in production environments using Ansible, frequently introducing Ansible as a new technology to businesses and CTOs for the first time. He has a passion for positive psychology and its application in the world of technology and, in addition, has authored and facilitated bespoke Ansible workshops and training sessions, and has presented at both international conferences and meetups on Ansible.

About the reviewers

Gareth Coffey is an automation consultant for Cachesure, based in London, developing bespoke solutions to enable companies to migrate services to public and private cloud platforms. Gareth has been working with Unix/Linux-based systems for over 15 years. During that time, he has worked with a multitude of different programming languages, including C, PHP, Node.js, and various automation and orchestration tool sets. As well as consulting, Gareth runs his own start-up – Progressive Ops, developing cloud-based services aimed at helping start-up companies deploy resources across multiple cloud providers, with a focus on security.

Thanks to my wife and daughter for putting up with the late nights and early mornings.

Iain Grant is a senior engineer with over 20 years' experience as an IT professional, in both small and enterprise companies, where he has held a wide variety of positions, including trainer, programmer, firmware engineer, and system administrator. During this time, he has worked on multiple operating systems, ranging from OpenVMS, through Windows, to Linux, where he has also contributed to the Alpha Linux kernel. He currently works in an enterprise environment looking after over 300 Linux servers, with responsibility for their automation and management.

I would recommend this book as standard reading for any professional or senior engineer working with Linux. The areas covered provide you with excellent guidance and examples of a controlled build, as well as a managed and secure environment, resulting in an easier life for anyone looking after small or large Linux estates.

Packt is searching for authors like you

If you're interested in becoming an author for Packt, please visit `authors.packtpub.com` and apply today. We have worked with thousands of developers and tech professionals, just like you, to help them share their insight with the global tech community. You can make a general application, apply for a specific hot topic that we are recruiting an author for, or submit your own idea.

Table of Contents

Preface

Welcome to *Hands-On Enterprise Automation on Linux*, your guide to a collection of the most valuable processes, methodologies, and tools for streamlining and efficiently managing your Linux deployments at enterprise scale. This book will provide you with the knowledge and skills required to standardize your Linux estate and manage it at scale, using open source tools including Ansible, AWX (Ansible Tower), Pulp, Katello, and OpenSCAP. You will learn about the creation of standard operating environments, and how to define, document, manage, and maintain these standards using Ansible. In addition, you will acquire knowledge of security hardening standards, such as the CIS Benchmarks. Throughout the book, practical, hands-on examples will be provided for you to try for yourself, on which you can build your own code, and to demonstrate the principles being covered.

Who this book is for

This book is for anyone who has a Linux environment to design, implement, and care for. It is intended to appeal to a wide range of open source professionals, from infrastructure architects through to system administrators, including professionals up to C level. Proficiency in the implementation and maintenance of Linux servers and familiarity with the concepts involved in building, patching, and maintaining a Linux server infrastructure are assumed. Prior knowledge of Ansible and other automation tools is not essential but may be beneficial.

What this book covers

Chapter 1, *Building a Standard Operating Environment on Linux*, provides a detailed introduction to standardized operating environments, a core concept that will be referred to throughout this hands-on book, and which is essential understanding in order for you to embark on this journey.

Chapter 2, *Automating Your IT Infrastructure with Ansible*, provides a detailed, hands-on breakdown of an Ansible playbook, including inventories, roles, variables, and best practices for developing and maintaining playbooks; a crash course enabling you to learn just enough Ansible to begin your automation journey.

Chapter 3, *Streamlining Infrastructure Management with AWX*, explores, with the help of practical examples, the installation and utilization of AWX (also available as Ansible Tower) so as to build good business processes around your Ansible automation infrastructure.

Chapter 4, *Deployment Methodologies*, enables you to understand the various methods available in relation to large-scale deployments in Linux environments, and how to leverage these to the best advantage of the enterprise.

Chapter 5, *Using Ansible to Build Virtual Machine Templates for Deployment*, explores the best practices for deploying Linux by building virtual machine templates that will be deployed at scale on a hypervisor in a practical and hands-on manner.

Chapter 6, *Custom Builds with PXE Booting*, looks at the process of PXE booting for when the templated approach to server builds may not be possible (for example, where bare-metal servers are still being used), and how to script this to build standard server images over the network.

Chapter 7, *Configuration Management with Ansible*, provides practical examples of how to manage your build once it enters service, so as to ensure that consistency remains a byword without limiting innovation.

Chapter 8, *Enterprise Repository Management with Pulp*, looks at how to perform patching in a controlled manner to prevent inconsistencies re-entering even the most carefully standardized environment through the use of the Pulp tool.

Chapter 9, *Patching with Katello*, builds on our work involving the Pulp tool by introducing you to Katello, providing even more control over your repositories whilst providing a user-friendly graphical user interface.

Chapter 10, *Managing Users on Linux*, provides a detailed look at user account management using Ansible as the orchestration tool, along with the use of centralized authentication systems such as LDAP directories.

Chapter 11, *Database Management*, looks at how Ansible can be used both to automate deployments of databases, and to execute routine database management tasks, on Linux servers.

Chapter 12, *Performing Routine Maintenance with Ansible*, explores some of the more advanced on-going maintenance that Ansible can perform on a Linux server estate.

Chapter 13, *Using CIS Benchmarks*, provides an in-depth examination of the CIS server hardening benchmarks and how to apply them on Linux servers.

Chapter 14, *CIS Hardening with Ansible*, looks at how a security hardening policy can be rolled out across an entire estate of Linux servers in an efficient, reproducible manner with Ansible.

Chapter 15, *Auditing Security Policy with OpenSCAP*, provides a hands-on look at the installation and use of OpenSCAP to audit Linux servers for policy violations on an on-going basis, since security standards can be reversed by either malicious or otherwise well-meaning end users.

Chapter 16, *Tips and Tricks*, explores a number of tips and tricks to keep your Linux automation processes running smoothly in the face of the ever-changing demands of the enterprise.

To get the most out of this book

To follow the examples in this book, it is recommended that you have access to at least two Linux machines for testing on, though more may be preferable to develop the examples more fully. These can be either physical or virtual machines—all examples were developed on a set of Linux virtual machines, but should work just as well on physical ones. In Chapter 5, *Using Ansible to Build Virtual Machine Templates for Deployment*, we make use of nested virtualization on a KVM virtual machine to build a Linux image. The exact hardware requirements for this are listed at the beginning of this chapter. This will require either access to a physical machine with the appropriate CPU to run the examples on, or a hypervisor that supports nested virtualization (for example, VMware or Linux KVM).

Please be aware that some examples in this book could be disruptive to other services on your network; where there is such a risk, this is highlighted at the beginning of each chapter. I recommend you try out the examples in an isolated test network unless/until you are confident that they will not have any impact on your operations.

Although other Linux distributions are mentioned in the book, we focus on two key Linux distributions—CentOS 7.6 (though if you have access to it, you are welcome to use Red Hat Enterprise Linux 7.6, which should work just as well in most examples), and Ubuntu Server 18.04. All test machines were built from the official ISO images, using the minimal installation profile.

As such, where additional software is required, we take you through the steps needed to install it so that you can complete the examples. If you choose to complete all the examples, you will install software such as AWX, Pulp, Katello, and OpenSCAP. The only exception to this is FreeIPA, which is mentioned in Chapter 10, *Managing Users on Linux*. Installing a directory server for your enterprise is a huge topic that sadly requires more space than we have in this book—hence, you may wish to explore this topic independently.

The text assumes that you will run Ansible from one of your Linux test machines, but Ansible can actually be run on any machine with Python 2.7 or Python 3 (versions 3.5 and higher) installed (Windows is supported for the control machine, but only through a Linux distribution running in the **Windows Subsystem for Linux** (**WSL**) layer available on newer versions of Windows. Supported operating systems for Ansible include (but are not limited to) Red Hat, Debian, Ubuntu, CentOS, macOS, and FreeBSD.

This book uses the Ansible 2.8.x.x series release, although a few examples are specific to Ansible 2.9.x.x, which was released during the course of writing. Ansible installation instructions can be found at `https://docs.ansible.com/ansible/intro_installation.html`.

Download the example code files

You can download the example code files for this book from your account at `www.packt.com`. If you purchased this book elsewhere, you can visit `www.packtpub.com/support` and register to have the files emailed directly to you.

You can download the code files by following these steps:

1. Log in or register at `www.packt.com`.
2. Select the **Support** tab.
3. Click on **Code Downloads**.
4. Enter the name of the book in the **Search** box and follow the onscreen instructions.

Once the file is downloaded, please make sure that you unzip or extract the folder using the latest version of:

- WinRAR/7-Zip for Windows
- Zipeg/iZip/UnRarX for Mac
- 7-Zip/PeaZip for Linux

The code bundle for the book is also hosted on GitHub at `https://github.com/PacktPublishing/Hands-On-Enterprise-Automation-on-Linux`. In case there's an update to the code, it will be updated on the existing GitHub repository.

We also have other code bundles from our rich catalog of books and videos available at `https://github.com/PacktPublishing/`. Check them out!

Download the color images

We also provide a PDF file that has color images of the screenshots/diagrams used in this book. You can download it here: `https://static.packt-cdn.com/downloads/9781789131611_ColorImages.pdf`.

Conventions used

There are a number of text conventions used throughout this book.

`CodeInText`: Indicates code words in text, database table names, folder names, filenames, file extensions, pathnames, dummy URLs, user input, and Twitter handles. Here is an example: "To start with, let's create a role called `loadmariadb`."

A block of code is set as follows:

```
- name: Ensure PostgreSQL service is installed and started at boot time
  service:
    name: postgresql
    state: started
    enabled: yes
```

Any command-line input or output is written as follows:

```
$ mkdir /var/lib/tftpboot/EFIx64/centos7
```

Bold: Indicates a new term, an important word, or words that you see on screen. For example, words in menus or dialog boxes appear in the text like this. Here is an example: "Select **System info** from the **Administration** panel."

Warnings or important notes appear like this.

Tips and tricks appear like this.

Get in touch

Feedback from our readers is always welcome.

General feedback: If you have questions about any aspect of this book, mention the book title in the subject of your message and email us at customercare@packtpub.com.

Errata: Although we have taken every care to ensure the accuracy of our content, mistakes do happen. If you have found a mistake in this book, we would be grateful if you would report this to us. Please visit www.packtpub.com/support/errata, selecting your book, clicking on the Errata Submission Form link, and entering the details.

Piracy: If you come across any illegal copies of our works in any form on the internet, we would be grateful if you would provide us with the location address or website name. Please contact us at copyright@packt.com with a link to the material.

If you are interested in becoming an author: If there is a topic that you have expertise in, and you are interested in either writing or contributing to a book, please visit authors.packtpub.com.

Reviews

Please leave a review. Once you have read and used this book, why not leave a review on the site that you purchased it from? Potential readers can then see and use your unbiased opinion to make purchase decisions, we at Packt can understand what you think about our products, and our authors can see your feedback on their book. Thank you!

For more information about Packt, please visit packt.com.

Section 1: Core Concepts 1

The objective of this section is to understand the systems administration fundamentals and techniques that will be covered in this book. First, we will cover a hands-on introduction to Ansible, the tool that will be used throughout this book for automation and purposes such as package management and advanced systems administration en masse.

This section comprises the following chapters:

- Chapter 1, *Building a Standard Operating Environment on Linux*
- Chapter 2, *Automating Your IT Infrastructure with Ansible*
- Chapter 3, *Streamlining Infrastructure Management with AWX*

Building a Standard Operating Environment on Linux

1

This chapter provides a detailed exploration of the **Standard Operating Environment** (henceforth, **SOE** for short) concept in Linux. Although we will go into much greater detail later, in short, an SOE is an environment where everything is created and modified in a standard way. For example, this would mean that all Linux servers are built in the same way, using the same software versions. This is an important concept because it makes managing the environment much easier and reduces the workload for those looking after it. Although this chapter is quite theoretical in nature, it sets the groundwork for the rest of this book.

We will start by looking at the fundamental definition of such an environment, and then proceed to explore why it is desirable to want to create one. From there, we will look at some of the pitfalls of an SOE to give you a good perspective on how to maintain the right balance in such an environment, before finally discussing how an SOE should be integrated into day-to-day maintenance processes. The effective application of this concept enables efficient and effective management of Linux environments at very large scales.

In this chapter, we will cover the following topics:

- Understanding the challenges of Linux environment scaling
- What is an SOE?
- Exploring SOE benefits
- Knowing when to deviate from standards
- Ongoing maintenance of SOEs

Understanding the challenges of Linux environment scaling

Before we delve into the definition of an SOE, let's explore the challenges of scaling a Linux environment without standards. An exploration of this will help us to understand the definition itself, as well as how to define the right standards for a given scenario.

Challenges of non-standard environments

It is important to consider that many challenges experienced by enterprises with technology estates (whether Linux or otherwise) do not start out as such. In the early stages of growth, in fact, many systems and processes are entirely sustainable, and in the next section, we will look at this early stage of environment growth as a precursor to understanding the challenges associated with large-scale growth.

Early growth of a non-standard environment

In a surprisingly large number of companies, Linux environments begin life without any form of standardization. Often, they grow organically over time. Deployments start out small, perhaps just covering a handful of core functions, and as time passes and requirements grow, so does the environment. Skilled system administrators often make changes by hand on a per-server basis, deploying new services and growing the server estate as business demands dictate.

This organic growth is the path of least resistance for most companies—project deadlines are often tight and in addition both budget and resource are scarce. Hence, when a skilled Linux resource is available, that resource can assist in just about all of the tasks required, from simple maintenance tasks to commissioning complex application stacks. It saves a great deal of time and money spent on architecture and makes good use of the skillset of staff on hand as they can be used to address immediate issues and deployments, rather than spending time on architectural design. Hence, quite simply, it makes sense, and the author has experienced this at several companies, even high-profile multi-national ones.

Impacts of non-standard environments

Let's take a deeper look at this from a technical standpoint. There are numerous flavors of Linux, numerous applications that perform (at a high level) the same function, and numerous ways to solve a given problem. For example, if you want to script a task, do you write it in a shell script, Perl, Python, or Ruby? For some tasks, all can achieve the desired end result. Different people have different preferred ways of approaching problems and different preferred technology solutions, and often it is found that a Linux environment has been built using a technology that was *the flavor of the month* when it was created or that was a favorite of the person responsible for it. There is nothing wrong with this in and of itself, and initially, it does not cause any problems.

If organic growth brings with it one fundamental problem, it is this: scale. Making changes by hand and always using the latest and greatest technology is great when the environment size is relatively small, and often provides an interesting challenge, hence keeping technical staff feeling motivated and valued. It is vital for those working in technology to keep their skills up to date, so it is often a motivating factor to be able to employ up-to-date technologies as part of the day job.

Scaling up non-standard environments

When the number of servers enters the hundreds, never mind thousands (or even greater!), this whole *organic* process breaks down. What was once an interesting challenge becomes laborious and tedious, even stressful. The learning curve for new team members is steep. A new hire may find themselves with a disparate environment with lots of different technologies to learn, and possibly a long period of training before they can become truly effective. Long-serving team members can end up being silos of knowledge, and should they depart the business, their loss can cause continuity issues. Problems and outages become more numerous as the non-standard environment grows in an uncontrolled manner, and troubleshooting becomes a lengthy endeavor—hardly ideal when trying to achieve a 99.99% service uptime agreement, where every second of downtime matters! Hence, in the next section, we will look at how to address these challenges with an SOE.

Addressing the challenges

From this, we realize our requirement for standardization. Building a suitable SOE is all about the following:

- Realizing economies of scale
- Being efficient in day-to-day operations
- Making it easy for all involved to get up to speed quickly and easily
- Being aligned with the growing needs of the business

After all, if an environment is concise in its definition, then it is easier for everyone involved in it to understand and work with. This, in turn, means tasks are completed quicker and with greater ease. In short, standardization can bring cost savings and improved reliability.

It must be stressed that this is a concept and not an absolute. There is no right or wrong way to build such an environment, though there are best practices. Throughout this chapter, we will explore the concept further and help you to identify core best practices associated with SOEs so that you can make informed decisions when defining your own.

Let's proceed to explore this in more detail. Every enterprise has certain demands of their IT environments, whether they are based on Linux, Windows, FreeBSD, or any other technology. Sometimes, these are well understood and documented, and sometimes, they are simply implicit—that is to say, everyone assumes the environment meets these *standards*, but there is no official definition. These requirements often include the following:

- Security
- Reliability
- Scalability
- Longevity
- Supportability
- Ease of use

These, of course, are all high-level requirements, and very often, they intersect with each other. Let's explore these in more detail.

Security

Security in an environment is established by several factors. Let's look at some questions to understand the factors involved:

- Is the configuration secure?
- Have we allowed the use of weak passwords?
- Is the superuser, root, allowed to log in remotely?
- Are we logging and auditing all connections?

Now, in a non-standard environment, how can you truly say that these requirements are all enforced across all of your Linux servers? To do so requires a great deal of faith they have all been built the same way, that they had the same security parameters applied, and that no-one has ever revisited the environment to change anything. In short, it requires fairly frequent auditing to ensure compliance.

However, where the environment has been standardized, and all servers have been built from a common source or using a common automation tool (we shall demonstrate this later in this book), it is much easier to say with confidence that your Linux estate is secure.

A standards-based environment isn't implicitly secure, of course—if there is an issue that results in a vulnerability in the build process for this environment, automation means this vulnerability will be replicated across the entire environment! It is important to be aware of the security requirements of your environment and to implement these with care, maintaining and auditing your environment continuously to ensure security levels are maintained.

Security is also enforced by patches, which ensure you are not running any software with vulnerabilities that could allow an attacker to compromise your servers. Some Linux distributions have longer lives than others. For example, Red Hat Enterprise Linux (and derivatives such as CentOS) and the Ubuntu LTS releases all have long, predictable life cycles and make good candidates for your Linux estate.

As such, they should be part of your standards. By contrast, if a *bleeding edge* Linux distribution such as Fedora has been used because, perhaps, it had the latest packages required at the time, you can be sure that the life cycle will be short, and that updates would cease in the not too distant future, hence leaving you open to potential unpatched vulnerabilities and the need to upgrade to a newer release of Fedora.

Even if the upgrade to a newer version of Fedora is performed, sometimes packages get *orphaned*—that is to say, they do not get included in the newer release. This might be because they have been superseded by a different package. Whatever the cause, upgrading one distribution to another could cause a false sense of security and should be avoided unless thoroughly researched. In this way, standardization helps to ensure good security practices.

Reliability

Many enterprises expect their IT operations to be up and running 99.99% of the time (or better). Part of the route to achieving this is robust software, application of relevant bug fixes, and well-defined troubleshooting procedures. This ensures that in the worst case scenario of an outage, the downtime is as minimal as possible.

Standardization again helps here—as we discussed in the preceding section on security, a good choice of underlying operating system ensures that you have ongoing access to bug fixes and updates, and if you know that your business needs a vendor backup to ensure business continuity, then the selection of a Linux operating system with a support contract (available with Red Hat or Canonical, for example) makes sense.

Equally, when servers are all built to a well-defined and understood standard, making changes to them should yield predictable results as everyone knows what they are working with. If all servers are built slightly differently, then a well-meaning change or update could have unintended consequences and result in costly downtime.

Again with standardization, even if the worst-case scenario occurs, everyone involved should know how to approach the problem because they will know that all servers have been built on a certain base image and have a certain configuration. This knowledge and confidence reduce troubleshooting times and ultimately downtime.

Scalability

All enterprises desire their business to grow and most times, this means that IT environments need to scale up to deal with increased demand. In an environment where the servers are built in a non-standard manner, scaling up an environment becomes more of a challenge.

For example, if scaling horizontally (adding more identical servers to an existing service), the new servers should all have the same configuration as the existing ones. Without standards, the first step is to work out how the initial set of servers was built and then to clone this and make the necessary changes to produce more unique servers.

This process is somewhat cumbersome whereas, with a standardized environment, the investigative step is completely unnecessary, and horizontal scaling becomes a predictable, repeatable, *business-as-usual* task. It also ensures greater reliability as there should be no unintended results from the new servers in the case that a non-standard configuration item was missed. Human beings are incredible, intelligent beings capable of sending a man to the moon, and yet they are equally capable of overlooking a single line in a configuration file. The idea of standardization is to mitigate this risk, and hence make it quick and efficient to scale an environment either up or out using a well-thought-out operating system template, the concept of which we will explore as we proceed through this chapter.

Longevity

Sometimes when deploying a service, a particular software version is needed. Let's take the example of a web application that runs on PHP. Now, suppose that your particular enterprise has, for historical reasons, standardized on CentOS 6 (or RHEL 6). This operating system only ships with PHP 5.3, meaning that if you suddenly take on an application that only supports PHP 7.0 and above, you need to figure out how to host this.

One apparently obvious solution to this would be to roll out a Fedora virtual machine image. After all, it shares similar technologies to CentOS and RHEL and has much more up-to-date libraries included with it. The author has direct experience of this kind of solution in several roles! However, let's take a look at the bigger picture.

RHEL (and CentOS, which is based upon this) has a lifespan of around 10 years, depending on the point at which you purchased it. In an enterprise, this is a valuable proposition—it means that you can guarantee that any servers you build will have patches and support for up to 10 years (and possibly longer with extended life cycle support) from the point at which you built them. This ties in nicely with our previous points around security, reliability, and supportability (in the following section).

However, any servers that you build on Fedora will have a lifespan of somewhere in the region of 12-18 months (depending on the Fedora release cycle)—in an enterprise setting, having to redeploy a server after, say, 12-18 months is a headache that is not needed.

This is not to say there is never a case for deploying on Fedora or any other fast-moving Linux platform—it is simply to state that in an enterprise where security and reliability are vitally important, you are unlikely to want a Linux platform with a short life cycle as the short term gain (newer library support) would be replaced in 12-18 months with the pain of a lack of updates and the need to rebuild/upgrade the platform.

Of course, this does depend very much on your approach to your infrastructure—some enterprises take a very container-like approach to their servers and re-deploy them with every new software release or application deployment. When your infrastructure and build standards are defined by code (such as Ansible), then it is entirely possible to do this with a fairly minimal impact on your day-to-day operations, and it is unlikely that any single server would be around for long enough for the operating system to become outdated or unsupported.

At the end of the day, the choice is yours and you must establish which path you feel provides you with the most business benefit without putting your operations at risk. Part of standardization is to make sound, rational decisions on technology and to adopt them wherever feasible, and your standard could include frequent rebuilds such that you can use a fast-moving operating system such as Fedora. Equally, you might decide that your standard is that servers will have long lives and be upgraded in place, and in this case, you would be better choosing an operating system such as an Ubuntu LTS release or RHEL/CentOS.

In the following section, we will look in greater detail at how an SOE benefits the concept of supportability in the next section.

Supportability

As we have already discussed, having a standardized environment brings with it two benefits. The first is that a well-chosen platform means a long vendor support life cycle. This, in turn, means long support from either the vendor (in the case of a product such as RHEL) or the community (in the case of CentOS). Some operating systems such as Ubuntu Server are available with either community support or a paid contract directly from Canonical.

Supportability doesn't just mean support from the vendor or the Linux community at large, however. Remember that, in an enterprise, your staff is your front line support before anyone external steps in. Now, imagine having a crack team of Linux staff, and presenting them with a server estate comprised of Debian, SuSe, CentOS, Fedora, Ubuntu, and Manjaro. There are similarities between them, but also a huge number of differences. Across them, there are four different package managers for installing and managing software packages, and that's just one example.

Whilst entirely supportable, it does present more of a challenge for your staff and means that, for anyone joining the company, you require both a broad and a deep set of Linux experience—either that or an extensive on-boarding process to get them up to speed.

With a standardized environment, you might end up with more than one operating system, but nonetheless, if you can meet all of your requirements with, say, CentOS 7 and Ubuntu Server 18.04 LTS (and know that you are covered for the next few years because of your choices), then you immediately reduce the workload on your Linux team and enable them to spend more time creatively solving problems (for example, automating solutions with Ansible!) and less time figuring out the nuances between operating systems. As we have also discussed, in the event of an issue, they will be more familiar with each OS and hence need to spend less time debugging, reducing downtime.

This brings us nicely into the subject of ease of use at scale, and we will provide an overview of this in the next section.

Ease of use

This final category overlaps heavily with the last two—that is to say that, quite simply, the more standardized your environment, the easier it is for a given set of employees to get to grips with it. This automatically promotes all of the benefits we have discussed so far around reducing downtime, easier recruitment and on-boarding of staff, and so on.

Having set out the challenges that an SOE helps to address, we will proceed in the next section to look at the anatomy of such an environment to understand it from a technical standpoint.

What is an SOE?

Now that we've explored the reasons why an SOE is important to the enterprise and understood at a high level the solutions for these problems, let's look in detail at an SOE. We will begin by defining the SOE itself.

Defining the SOE

Let's take a quick look at this from a more practical standpoint. As we have already said, an SOE is a concept, not an absolute. It is, at its simplest level, a common server image or build standard that is deployed across a large number of servers throughout a company. Here, all required tasks are completed in a known, documented manner.

To start with, there is the base operating system—and, as we have discussed, there are hundreds of Linux distributions to choose from. Some are quite similar from a system administration perspective (for example, Debian and Ubuntu), whilst some are markedly different (for example, Fedora and Manjaro). By way of a simple example, let's say you wanted to install the Apache Web Server on Ubuntu 18.04 LTS—you would enter the following commands:

```
# sudo apt-get update
# sudo apt-get install apache2
```

Now, if you wanted to do the same thing but on CentOS 7, you would enter the following:

```
# sudo yum install httpd
```

As you can see, there is nothing in common between these commands—not even the name of the package, even though the end result in both cases is an installation of Apache. On a small scale, this is not an issue, but when servers are numerous and as server count goes up, so does the complexity of managing such an environment.

The base operating system is just the start. Our example above was installing Apache, yet we could also install nginx or even lighttpd. They are, after all, also web servers.

Then, there is configuration. Do you want users to be able to log in as root over SSH? Do you need a certain level of logging for audit or debug purposes? Do you need local or centralized authentication? The list is myriad, and as you can see, if left unchecked could grow into a massive headache.

This is where the SOE comes in. It is effectively a specification, and at a high level, it might say the following:

- Our standard base operating system is Ubuntu 18.04 LTS.
- Our standard web server will be Apache 2.4.
- SSH logins are enabled, but only for users with SSH keys and not root.
- All user logins must be logged and archived for audit purposes.
- Except for a few local *break glass* accounts, all accounts must be centrally managed (for example, by LDAP or Active Directory).
- Our corporate monitoring solution must be integrated (for example, the Nagios NCPA agent must be installed and configured to communicate with our Nagios server).
- All system logs must be sent to the corporate central log management system.
- Security hardening must be applied to the system.

The preceding is simply an example, and it is by no means complete; however, it should begin to give you an idea of what an SOE looks like at a high level. As we proceed through this chapter, we will delve deeper into this subject and give more examples to build up a clear definition.

Knowing what to include

Before we proceed, let's take a look in a little more detail at what to include in the environment. We have outlined in the previous section a very simplistic definition for an SOE. Part of any good SOE operating process is to have a pre-defined operating system build that can be deployed at a moment's notice. There are multiple ways this might be achieved and we will discuss these later in this book—however, for the time being, let's assume that a base image of Ubuntu 18.04 LTS as suggested previously has been built. What do we integrate into this *standard* build?

We know, for example, that our login policy is going to be applied throughout the organization—hence, when the build is created, `/etc/ssh/sshd_config` must be customized to include `PermitRootLogin no` and `PasswordAuthentication no`. There is no point in performing this step in the post-deployment configuration, as this would have to be performed on each and every single deployment. Quite simply, this would be inefficient.

There are also important automation considerations for our operating system image. We know that Ansible itself communicates over SSH, and so we know that we are going to require some kind of credentials (it is quite likely this will be SSH key-based) for Ansible to run against all of the deployed servers. There is little point in having to manually roll out Ansible credentials to every single machine before you can actually perform any automation, and so it is important to consider the kind of authentication you want Ansible to use (for example, password- or SSH key-based), and to create the account and corresponding credentials when you build the image. The exact method for doing this will depend upon your corporate security standards, but I would advocate as a potential solution the following:

- Creating a local account on the standard image for Ansible to authenticate against
- Giving this account appropriate sudo rights to ensure all desired automation tasks can be performed
- Setting the local password for this account, or adding the SSH public key from an Ansible key-pair to the `authorized_keys` file for the local Ansible account you created

Doing this, of course, does present some security risks. It is most likely that Ansible will need full access to root on your servers for it to effectively perform all of the automation tasks you might ask of it, and so this Ansible account could become a backdoor if the credentials were ever compromised. It is recommended that as few people as possible have access to the credentials and that you make use of a tool such as AWX or Ansible Tower (which we shall explore in `Chapter 3`, *Streamlining Infrastructure Management with AWX*) to manage your credentials, hence preventing people from getting hold of them inappropriately. You will also almost certainly want to enable auditing of all activities performed by the Ansible account and have these logged to a central server somewhere so that you can inspect them for any suspicious activity and audit them as required.

Moving on from user accounts and authentication, consider also **Nagios Cross-Platform Agent** (**NCPA**). We know in our example that all deployed servers are going to need to be monitored, and so it is a given that NCPA agent must be installed, and the token defined such that it can communicate with the Nagios server. Again, there is no point doing this on every single server after the standard image is deployed.

What about the web server though? It is sensible to have a standard, as it means all who are responsible for the environment can become comfortable with the technology. This makes administration easier and is especially beneficial for automation, as we shall see in the next section. However, unless you only ever deploy web servers running on Linux, this probably shouldn't be included as part of the standard build.

As a sound principle, the standard builds should be as simple and lightweight as possible. There is no point in having additional services running on them, taking up memory and CPU cycles, when they are redundant. Equally, having unconfigured services increases the attack surface for any potential attacker and so for security reasons, it is advisable to leave them out.

In short, the standard build should only include configuration and/or services that are going to be common to every server deployed. This approach is sometimes referred to as **Just enough Operating System** or **JeOS** for short, and it is the best starting point for your SOE.

Having understood the basic principles of an SOE, we will proceed in the next section to look in more detail at the benefits an SOE brings to your enterprise.

Exploring SOE benefits

By now, you should have some idea of what an SOE is, and how it brings economies of scale and greater efficiency to a Linux environment. Now, let's build on that and look in more detail at an example of the importance of standardization.

Example benefits of an SOE in a Linux environment

To say that there are commonalities in a Linux environment is to say that the servers that comprise it all share attributes and features. For example, they might all be built upon Ubuntu Linux, or they might all have Apache as their web server.

We can explore this concept with an example. Suppose that you have 10 Linux web servers behind a load balancer and that they are all serving simple static content. Everything is working fine, but then a configuration change is mandated. Perhaps this is to change the document root of each web server to point to a new code release that has been deployed to them by another team.

As the person responsible, you know that because the overall solution is load balanced, all servers should be serving the same content. Therefore, the configuration change is going to be required on each and every one. That means 10 configurations changes to make if you do it by hand.

You could, of course, do this by hand, but this would be tedious and certainly isn't the best use of time for a skilled Linux admin. It is also error-prone—a typo could be made on one of the 10 servers and not spotted. Or the admin could be interrupted by an outage elsewhere and only a subset of the server configurations changed.

The better solution would be to write a script to make the change. This is the very basis of automation and it is almost certainly going to be a better use of time to run a single script once against 10 servers than to manually make the same change 10 times over. Not only is it more efficient, but if the same change became required in a month, the script could be reused with just minimal adjustment.

Now, let's throw a spanner into the works. What if, for reasons unknown, someone built five of the web servers using Apache on CentOS 7, and the other five using nginx on Ubuntu 18.04 LTS? The end result would, after all, be the same—at a basic level, they are both web servers. However, if you want to change the document root in Apache on CentOS 7, you would need to do the following:

1. Locate the appropriate configuration file in `/etc/httpd/conf.d`.
2. Make the required change to the `DocumentRoot` parameter.
3. Reload the web server with `systemctl reload httpd.service`.

If you had to do the same thing for nginx on Ubuntu 18.04 LTS, you would do the following:

1. Locate the correct configuration file in `/etc/nginx/sites-available`.
2. Make the required change to the `root` parameter.
3. Ensure that the site configuration file is enabled using the `a2ensite` command—otherwise, Apache will not actually see the configuration file.
4. Reload the web server with `systemctl reload apache2.service`.

As you can see from this rather simplistic (albeit contrived) example, a lack of commonality is the enemy of automation. To cope with the case, you would need to do as follows:

1. Detect the operating system on each server. This in itself is non-trivial—there is no one way to detect a Linux operating system, so your script would have to walk through a series of checks, including the following:
   1. The contents of `/etc/os-release`, if it exists
   2. The output of `lsb_release`, if it is installed
   3. The contents of `/etc/redhat-release`, if it exists
   4. The contents of `/etc/debian_version`, if it exists
   5. Other OS-specific files as required, if none of the preceding produce meaningful results
2. Run different modification commands in different directories to effect the change as discussed previously.
3. Run different commands to reload the web server, again as detailed previously.

Hence, the script becomes complex, more difficult to write and maintain, and certainly more difficult to make reliable.

Although this particular example is unlikely to occur in real life, it does serve to make an important point—automation is much easier to implement when the environment is built to a given standard. If a decision is made that all web servers are to be based on CentOS 7, to run Apache 2, and have the site configuration named after the service name, then our automation becomes so much easier. In fact, you could even run a simple `sed` command to complete the change; for example, suppose the new web application was deployed to `/var/www/newapp`:

```
# sed -i 's!DocumentRoot.*!DocumentRoot /var/www/newapp!g'
/etc/httpd/conf.d/webservice.conf
# systemctl reload httpd.service
```

No environment detection was necessary at all—just two simple shell commands. This could be the basis of a really simple automation script to be run either on each of the 10 servers in turn or remotely over SSH. Either way, our automation task is now very simple and shows how important commonality is. Importantly, an SOE by its very nature provides this commonality. Lack of commonality doesn't just make automation difficult though—it also hampers testing, often distorting test results as they may not be representative if environments are different.

In the next section of this chapter, we will build on this knowledge to demonstrate how an SOE benefits the process of software testing.

Benefits of SOE to software testing

A common problem I have seen in many environments is that of a new software deployment having been successfully tested in an isolated pre-production environment and yet not working correctly when it is released into the production environment. More often than not, this problem is traced back to fundamental differences between the production and pre-production environments, and so it is clear that for testing to be valid, both environments must be as similar as possible.

Indeed, one of the problems containerization platforms such as Docker set out to solve was exactly this, and hence portability is a core feature of container environments. Code deployed on Docker is built on top of a container image that is, in simple terms, a stripped-down operating system image (remember JeOS?). This, in effect, is a really tiny SOE, just running in a container rather than on a bare metal server or virtual machine. However, it is worth considering that if portability through environment standardization is a key feature of container technology, then should we not try to achieve this across the board regardless of our infrastructure.

After all, if the configuration of the production servers is different from the pre-production ones, then how valid is the testing? If the pre-production environment was built on CentOS 7.6, but the production environment lags behind it on CentOS 7.4, then can you really ensure that a successful test result in one environment will guarantee it in the other? On paper, it should work, but with fundamental differences in software and library versions between the environments, this can never be guaranteed. This is before we even consider possible differences in configuration files and installed software.

Hence, SOEs can help here—if all environments are built to the same standards, then in theory, they should all be identical. Those of you who are eagle-eyed will notice the use of the word *should* in the previous sentence and it is there for a good reason. SOEs are a great step forward in defining the solution for testing failures, but they are not the whole story.

An environment is only standard as long as no-one modifies it, and if all users have administration-level privileges, then it is very easy for someone (well-meaning or otherwise) to log in and make changes that mean the environment deviates from the standard.

The answer to this issue is automation—not only do SOEs promote and enable automation, they also rely on it to maintain the level of standardization that they were required for in the first place. The two support each other directly and should ideally be inseparable partners—the SOE being the definition for the environment itself, and the automation providing the implementation, enforcement, and auditing of the standard. Indeed, this is the very premise of this book—that environments should be standardized as far as possible, and that as many changes as possible should be automated.

The focus of this book will be on the automation aspect of this equation, as other than adhering to the principles outlined in this chapter, the standards adopted will be unique for every environment and it is not the goal of this book to determine them at a low level. Working with our earlier example, both Apache and nginx have their benefits, and what fits one use case may not fit another.

The same is true with operating systems—some organizations may rely on the support package provided with Red Hat Enterprise Linux, whilst others don't need this but need the bleeding edge technologies provided by, say, Fedora. There is no right or wrong way to define a standard, as long as it meets the needs of the services it underpins. So far, we have focused very much on commonality and standards; however, there will always be edge cases where an alternative solution is required. In the next section, we will establish how to know when you should deviate from your standards.

Knowing when to deviate from standards

It would be easy to oversell the benefits of standardization, and they are certainly a requirement for automation to be effective. However, like anything, it can be taken too far. There is no point, for example, building servers on top of Red Hat Enterprise Linux 5.7 in 2019 simply because this was once defined as a standard (it is now End of Life and no longer supported or updated). Similarly, from time to time, software vendors will have qualified their product on certain specific Linux distributions or application stacks and will not provide support unless their software is run within that ecosystem.

These are cases when deviations from the SOE are necessary, but they should be performed in a controlled manner. For example, if a business has built up its Linux server estate on Ubuntu 18.04 LTS, and then a new software stack is purchased that is only qualified on RHEL 7, it is clear that builds of RHEL 7 are going to be required. These should, however, be part of a new set of standards if possible and become a secondary SOE.

For example, if the CIS security hardening benchmark is applied to the Ubuntu SOE, then the equivalent one should be applied to the RHEL too. Similarly, if the business has standardized on nginx, then this should be used on the environment unless there is a compelling reason not to (hint: a compelling reason is not that it's new and sexy—it is that it solves a real problem or somehow improves something in a tangible way).

This results in the business going from one Linux SOE to two, which is still entirely manageable and certainly better than returning to organic growth methodologies that hamper effective automation.

In short, expect deviations, and don't fear them. Instead, handle them and use the requirements to expand your standards, but stick with them where you can. SOEs present a balancing act for everyone—on the one hand, they bring advantages of scale, make automation easier, and reduce the training time for new staff (as all servers are more or less the same in build and configuration), but if applied too rigidly, they could hamper innovation. They must not be used as an excuse to do things a certain way *because that's how it has always been done.*

There will always be a good reason to deviate from a standard; simply look for the business benefit it brings, whether it's vendor support, lower resource requirements (hence saving power and money), a longer support window, or otherwise. Try and avoid doing so just because a new technology is *shiny.* As long as you are mindful of this fact, you will make good decisions regarding deviation from your standards. In the next section of this chapter, we will explore the ongoing maintenance of SOEs.

Ongoing maintenance of SOEs

Although we will look at patching and maintenance in much greater detail later in this book, it deserves a mention here as it dovetails nicely into the discussion on commonality and deviations.

If nothing else, you are going to have to patch your Linux environment. For security reasons alone, this is a given and good practice, even in an air-gapped environment. Let's say that your environment is made up entirely of virtual machines and that you decided to standardize on CentOS 7.2 some time ago. You built a virtual machine, performed all of the required configuration steps to turn it into your SOE image, and then converted it into a template for your virtualization environment. This becomes your *gold build*. So far, so good.

However, CentOS 7.2 was released in December 2015, nearly 4 years ago at the time of writing, and if you were to deploy such an image today, the first thing you would have to do is patch it. This would, depending on the build definition (and the number of packages included in it), possibly involve downloading a gigabyte or more of packages to bring it up to the latest standard and ensure you were running with all discovered vulnerabilities patched, and all of the requisite bug fixes in place.

Obviously, if you are doing this at scale, this is inefficient—each new server is going to pull all that data down over the network (or worse, the internet, if you don't have an internal mirror), and then consume a great deal of I/O time and CPU time applying the patches, during which the server can't be used for anything meaningful. If you only deploy one server every few months, you can probably put up with this. If you deploy them on a more regular basis, then this is going to waste a lot of valuable time and resources.

Hence, as well as performing ongoing maintenance of your environment itself, it is important to perform ongoing maintenance of your standards. In 2019, it makes sense to update your CentOS build to 7.6. At the very least, your ongoing maintenance schedule should involve updating the *gold build* regularly.

We will go into much greater detail on how this might be performed later in this book. However, for those who are eager to know now, this might be as simple as booting the virtual machine image up, performing the updates, sanitizing it (for example, removing SSH host keys that would be duplicated when the template is cloned), and then creating a new template from it. Obviously, if any other changes to the SOE have been made since the last maintenance cycle, then these can be incorporated too.

You should expect your SOE to evolve over time—it would be easy perhaps to labor this point—but there is an important balance between creating and maintaining standards, and being overly rigid with them. You must accept that there are times when you will need to deviate from them as we discussed in the previous section and that, over time, they will evolve.

In short, SOEs should become a part of your regular IT processes; if employed correctly, they don't hinder innovation— instead, they actively support it by giving back time to those working with them and ensuring they spend less time performing mundane, repetitive tasks and hence have more time for evaluating new technologies and finding better ways of doing things. This, after all, is one of the key benefits of automation, which SOEs support directly.

Summary

SOEs are a valuable addition to technology processes in almost any environment. They require some time to be spent upfront on design work and defining standards, but this time is more than offset later on as it supports efficient and effective automation of the environments, and in this manner, actually gives time back to those responsible for the environment, giving them more time to work on evaluating new technologies, finding more efficient ways to do things, and being innovative in general.

In this chapter, you learned the fundamental definition of an SOE. You explored the benefits that they bring to just about any Linux environment where scale is important, how they support automation, and when and how to make deviations from the standards to ensure that they do not become overly rigid and hamper growth. Finally, you learned about the importance of ongoing maintenance, including maintenance of your standards as part your ongoing maintenance cycles.

In the next chapter, we will explore how to make use of Ansible as an effective automation framework for your Linux environment.

Questions

1. What does the acronym SOE stand for?
2. Why would you choose an operating system with a long support cycle, such as CentOS, rather than one with a more rapid release cycle, such as Fedora?
3. Should you ever deviate from the standards you have defined for your environment?
4. List three challenges of scaling Linux environments up to enterprise scale.
5. Name three benefits that SOEs bring to Linux in the enterprise.
6. How does an SOE help to reduce the training requirements in an enterprise?
7. Why does an SOE benefit the security of your Linux environment?

Further reading

- To learn more about SOEs from a Red Hat perspective, refer to this article: `https://servicesblog.redhat.com/2016/11/03/standard-operating-environment-part-i-concepts-and-structures/`.

2
Automating Your IT Infrastructure with Ansible

While there are numerous ways to automate tasks on Linux, there is one technology that stands out above the rest for automation at scale, and that is Ansible. Although it is entirely possible to automate a task (or tasks) easily with a shell script, there are a number of disadvantages to this, the most significant being that shell scripting does not scale up well in large environments. It should be said that there are other automation tools, but Ansible makes use of native communication protocols (for example, SSH on Linux, and WinRM on Windows) and hence is completely agentless! This makes deploying it into existing environments simple. While automation with Ansible is a huge, in-depth subject, this chapter is intended to cover the basics and get you up and running rapidly so that, even if you have no prior experience, you can follow the automation examples in this book. Indeed, this is one of the reasons for the rapid and widespread adoption of Ansible over the last few years—although it is incredibly powerful, getting started and automating your first tasks is extremely simple.

In this chapter, we will cover the following Ansible topics:

- Exploring the Ansible playbook structure
- Exploring inventories in Ansible
- Understanding roles in Ansible
- Understanding Ansible variables
- Understanding Ansible templates
- Bringing Ansible and the SOE together

Technical requirements

This chapter includes examples based on the following technologies:

- Ubuntu Server 18.04 LTS
- CentOS 7.6
- Ansible 2.8

To run through these examples, you will need access to a server or virtual machine running one of the operating systems listed here, and also access to Ansible. Note that the examples given in this chapter may be destructive in nature (for example, they involve installing files and packages) and, if run as is, are only intended to be run in an isolated test environment.

Once you are satisfied that you have a safe environment in which to operate, let's get started on looking at the installation of new software packages with Ansible.

All example code discussed in this chapter is available from GitHub at: `https://github.com/PacktPublishing/Hands-On-Enterprise-Automation-on-Linux/tree/master/chapter02`.

Exploring the Ansible playbook structure

Getting up and running with Ansible is a straightforward endeavor, and packages are available for most major Linux distributions, FreeBSD, and just about any platform where Python runs. If you have a recent version of Microsoft Windows installed that supports the **Windows Subsystem for Linux** (**WSL**), Ansible even installs and runs under this.

Note, though, that there are no native Windows packages at the time of writing.

The official Ansible documentation provides installation documentation for all major platforms. Please refer to `https://docs.ansible.com/ansible/latest/installation_guide/intro_installation.html`.

In this chapter, our examples will be run on Ubuntu Server 18.04.2. However, as Ansible works across multiple different platforms, most examples should work on other operating systems too (or, at most, require minimal adaptation).

Following the official installation documentation, the following commands are executed to install the latest version of Ansible on our demonstration system:

```
$ sudo apt-get update
$ sudo apt-get install software-properties-common
$ sudo apt-add-repository --yes --update ppa:ansible/ansible
$ sudo apt-get install ansible
```

If all goes well, you should be able to query the Ansible binary for its version by running the following command:

```
$ ansible --version
```

The output should look something like this:

```
● ● ●            james@automation-01: ~/hands-on-automation/chapter02/example01 (ssh)
~/hands-on-automation/chapter02/example01> ansible --version
ansible 2.7.10
  config file = /etc/ansible/ansible.cfg
  configured module search path = [u'/home/james/.ansible/plugins/modules', u'/u
sr/share/ansible/plugins/modules']
  ansible python module location = /usr/lib/python2.7/dist-packages/ansible
  executable location = /usr/bin/ansible
  python version = 2.7.15rc1 (default, Nov 12 2018, 14:31:15) [GCC 7.3.0]
~/hands-on-automation/chapter02/example01>
```

Congratulations! Now that Ansible is installed, let's take a look at the fundamentals of running your first set of Ansible tasks, called a **playbook**. To get one of these to run, you actually need to have the following three things in place:

1. A configuration file
2. An inventory
3. The playbook itself

When Ansible is installed, a default configuration file is normally installed in /etc/ansible/ansible.cfg. There are many advanced features that can be changed through this file, and it can be overridden using a number of methods. For this book, we will work almost exclusively with the default settings, meaning that for now, it is sufficient to acknowledge the existence of this file.

 To find out more about the Ansible configuration file, this document is a good starting point, available at https://docs.ansible.com/ansible/latest/installation_guide/intro_configuration.html

Nothing happens on Ansible without an inventory. The inventory is a text file (or script) that provides the Ansible binaries with a list of hostnames to operate against, even if it is just the localhost. We will look at inventories in more detail in the next part of the chapter, as they are going to be important in our automation journey. For now, you will find that on most Linux platforms, a sample inventory file is installed in /etc/ansible/hosts as part of the Ansible installation. When the inventory file is empty (or contains only comments, as in the case of the sample one), Ansible implicitly operates against the localhost only.

Last, but by no means least, you must actually have a playbook to run against a server (or servers). Let's now work through an example to get a very simple playbook to run with Ansible. Ansible playbooks are written in YAML (a recursive acronym, meaning **YAML Ain't Markup Language**) and, as this is very easy to read—indeed, this is one of the core strengths of Ansible—playbooks can very easily be picked up by someone with minimal Ansible skills, and yet be easily understood, for either application or modification.

If you are not used to writing code in Python or YAML, then the one thing you need to know about writing YAML for playbooks is this: indentation matters. Rather than using brackets or braces to define blocks of code, and semicolons to denote line ends (as is common in many high-level languages), YAML uses the indentation level itself to determine where in the code you are, and how it relates to the surrounding code. Indentation is always created using spaces—never use tabs. Even if the indentation looks the same to the naked eye, the YAML parser will not see it as the same.

Consider the following block of code:

```
---
- name: Simple playbook
  hosts: localhost
  become: false
```

This is the beginning of an Ansible playbook. Ansible YAML files always start with three dashes (---), with no indentation. Next, we have a single line that defines the start of the play, denoted by the single dash (-), with no indentation. Note that an Ansible playbook can consist of one or more plays, with each play being (at a basic level) a set of tasks to be performed on a given set of hosts. This particular line of the playbook specifies the name for the play. Although the name keyword is optional in most places and can be omitted, it is strongly recommended to include it for all play definitions (just as we have here), and also, for each and every task. This, quite simply, aids the readability of the playbook and the speed at which someone new can pick it up, thus promoting efficiency and a low barrier to entry for newcomers, as we discussed in the preceding chapter.

The third line of this block tells Ansible which `hosts` the tasks included in the play should be run against. In this instance, we are only going to run against `localhost`. The fourth line tells Ansible not to `become` the superuser (root), as it is not required for this task. Some tasks—for example, restarting a system service—must be performed as the superuser and, in this case, you would specify `become: true`. Note the two-space indentation on both the third and fourth lines in the preceding code—this tells the YAML parser that the lines are part of the play, defined on the second line.

Now, let's add two tasks to our playbook by appending the following block of code under the previous one:

```
tasks:
  - name: Show a message
    debug:
      msg: "Hello world!"

  - name: Touch a file
    file:
      path: /tmp/foo
      state: touch
```

The `tasks` keyword defines the end of the play definition, and the start of the actual tasks we wish to execute. Note that it is still indented by two spaces, which tells the parser it is part of the play we defined previously. We then increase the indentation again for the next line, to denote that this is part of the `tasks` block.

By now, you will see a familiar pattern building up. Every time a line of code forms part of a preceding statement, we increase the indentation by two spaces. Each new item starts with a single dash (–), thus our preceding block of code contains two tasks.

The first one uses the `name` keyword with the value `Show a message` by way of documentation (think of comments in other programming languages) and uses something called an **Ansible module**. Modules are predefined blocks of code that Ansible uses to perform given tasks. The `debug` module, included here, is used largely for displaying messages or variable contents and, hence, playbook debugging. We pass the `msg` parameter to the `debug` module by indenting `msg` by a further two spaces, telling the module which message we want to be printed when the playbook is run.

The second task has the `name` and `Touch a file` keyword and uses the `file` module to touch a file located in `/tmp/foo`. When we run this playbook, the output should look something like this:

```
james@automation-01: ~/hands-on-automation/chapter02/example02 (ssh)

~/hands-on-automation/chapter02/example02> ansible-playbook simple.yml
 [WARNING]: provided hosts list is empty, only localhost is available. Note
that the implicit localhost does not match 'all'


PLAY [Simple playbook] *****************************************************

TASK [Gathering Facts] *****************************************************
ok: [localhost]

TASK [Show a message] ******************************************************
ok: [localhost] => {
    "msg": "Hello world!"
}

TASK [Touch a file] ********************************************************
changed: [localhost]

PLAY RECAP *****************************************************************
localhost                  : ok=3    changed=1    unreachable=0    failed=0

~/hands-on-automation/chapter02/example02> ls -l /tmp/foo
-rw-rw-r-- 1 james james 0 May 20 16:53 /tmp/foo
~/hands-on-automation/chapter02/example02> █
```

As a rule of thumb for most simple playbooks, tasks are run sequentially from top to bottom, making the order of execution predictable and easy to manage. That's it! You have written and executed your first Ansible playbook. You will note how easy that was, and how little work was involved in integrating it with a single test system. Now, for such a simple example, a valid question would be: *Why go to all that trouble with Ansible when two lines of shell scripting could achieve the same thing?* An example of shell scripting can be seen in the following code block:

```
echo "Hello World!"
touch /tmp/foo
```

The first reason to use Ansible is that, while this example is very simple and easy to understand, as the required tasks for a script become more complex, they become much harder to read and require someone who understands shell scripting to debug or modify them. With the Ansible playbook, you can see that the code is incredibly readable, and each part has an associated `name`. The enforced indentation also serves to make the code more readable, and while both comments and indentation are supported in a shell script, neither is enforced, and they are commonly left out. On top of this, all modules must have documentation to be accepted into the core Ansible distribution—thus, you are guaranteed to have good-quality documentation on hand for your playbook. Module documentation can be found on the official Ansible website, or as part of the installed Ansible package. For example, if we wanted to learn how to use the `file` module we used earlier, we would simply enter the following command in the shell of our system:

```
$ ansible-doc file
```

When invoked, this command will give you the complete documentation for the file module, which incidentally is the same as the documentation on the official Ansible web site. Thus you always have the Ansible module documentation at your fingertips, even if the system you are working on is disconnected from the Internet. The following screenshot shows a page of the output from the command we just ran:

The next reason is that the Ansible modules (mostly) offer support for idempotent changes. What this means is, if a change has already been made, we won't make it a second time. This is especially important for some changes that might be destructive in nature. It also saves time and compute resources, and even helps in auditing systems. On top of this, Ansible offers flow control and robust error handling and, where a shell script will continue even after an error, unless you integrate your own error-handling code (possibly causing unpredictable or undesirable results), Ansible will stop all further execution and require you to fix the problem before running the playbook again.

It is worth mentioning that while modules form a core part of the strength of Ansible, there could be times when the functionality you need is not handled by any of the available modules. The beauty of Ansible being **open source software** (**OSS**) is that you can write and integrate your own modules. This is beyond the scope of this book but is well worth exploring as you develop your Ansible skills. In instances where existing modules just don't have the required functionality, and you don't have the time or resources to write your own module, Ansible can also send raw shell commands to the system being automated. In fact, there are two modules—shell and command—that can send raw commands to remote systems. Thus, you can even mix shell scripting with Ansible if the need arises, although you should always use native Ansible modules before resorting to the use of shell or command. Ansible is incredibly flexible in this way—the built-in functionality is extensive, but in the event that it ever falls short, it is incredibly easy to extend the functionality yourself.

These benefits are just the tip of the iceberg, and we will explore some of the others as we proceed through this chapter. As stated earlier, this chapter is not intended to be exhaustive, but to serve as an introductory guide to Ansible, to get you started and help you understand the examples in this book.

In the next section, we will explore probably one of the biggest reasons to use Ansible over a simple shell script.

Exploring inventories in Ansible

As we have already touched upon, one of the key reasons for the rapid uptake of Ansible is the fact that it can integrate, without an agent, into most major operating systems. For example, a single Ansible host can automate commands on just about any other Linux (or BSD) host to which it can connect over SSH. It can even automate tasks on Windows hosts that have had remote WinRM enabled, and it is here that we start to uncover the real power of Ansible.

In the previous section of this chapter, we only looked at Ansible running against the implicit localhost, without using SSH. Ansible supports two different kinds of inventories: static and dynamic. Throughout this book, we will mostly work with static inventories, as they serve the examples we are working with. Indeed, static inventories are perfect for small environments, where the workload of keeping the list of servers to be automated (which, in essence, is what an Ansible inventory is) is small. However, as inventories grow in scale, or remain small but change rapidly (for example, cloud compute resources or Docker containers), the work required to keep an Ansible inventory file up to date becomes much larger and prone to error.

Ansible offers a number of ready-made dynamic inventory solutions that integrate with popular public cloud platforms such as Microsoft Azure and Amazon Web Services, on-premise compute platforms such as OpenStack and VMware, and infrastructure management solutions such as Katello. It is even possible to write your own dynamic inventory scripts, and as your environment scales, you will most likely find yourself going down this path.

For now, let's focus on static inventories. Suppose that we want to take our example playbook from earlier in the chapter, and run it against two remote hosts rather than the localhost. First of all, let's create an inventory file that contains the names/addresses of the two hosts. A static inventory is written in INI format (as opposed to the YAML used in the playbooks) and, at its simplest level, consists of one host per line. Note that hosts can be specified either by DNS entry or by IP address.

Here is the inventory file for our demo environment:

```
[test]
testhost1
testhost2
```

As you can see, the file is very simple. The first line, with square brackets around it, is the name of a group in which the servers below it are placed. Servers can live in more than one group, and this aids greatly in the day-to-day management of servers. For example, if you have a playbook to apply security updates to all Linux servers, then you would probably want a group called something like [linux-servers] that contains the addresses of all such servers. If you then had a playbook to deploy a web application, you would probably want to put all the web servers in a group called [web-servers]. This makes it easy to target the correct set of servers when running a given playbook—remember the hosts: line at the top of our playbook in the earlier example?

Groups can even be children of other groups. Thus, if you know your web servers are all based on Linux, you could specify the `web-servers` group as a child of the `linux-servers` group, thus including all web servers for security patching, without the need for duplication in the inventory.

We need to make a slight modification to our earlier playbook. The first four lines should now contain the following:

```
---
- name: Simple playbook
  hosts: all
  become: false
```

As you can see, we have now changed the `hosts` parameter from `localhost` to `all` (`all` is a special keyword, meaning all hosts in the inventory, regardless of group). If we had wanted to just specify the `test` group, we would have put in `hosts: test`, or even `hosts: testhost1`, for the playbook to run only against a single host.

Now, we know that Ansible uses SSH to connect to remote Linux hosts in the inventory and, at this stage, we have not set up key-based SSH authentication. Thus, we need to tell Ansible to prompt for the SSH password (by default, it does not, meaning it will fail if key-based authentication is not set up). Similar to the SSH command-line utility, unless you tell Ansible otherwise, it will initiate an SSH connection to the remote system, using the username of the current session user on the local machine. Thus, in my example, the user `james` exists on my Ansible server and my two test systems, and all tasks are performed as this user. I can run the following command to run my playbook against my two remote systems:

```
$ ansible-playbook -i hosts --ask-pass simple.yml
```

This looks a little different from the last time we ran it—note the following new parameters:

- `-i hosts`: Tells Ansible to use the file called `hosts` in the current working directory for the inventory
- `--ask-pass`: Tells Ansible to stop and prompt for the SSH password for access to the remote systems (it is assumed the password is the same on all systems)
- `simple.yml`: Tells Ansible the name of the playbook to run

Let's see this in action, as follows:

```
● ● ●                james@automation-01: ~/hands-on-automation/chapter02/example04 (ssh)

~/hands-on-automation/chapter02/example04> ansible-playbook -i hosts --ask-pass
simple.yml
SSH password:

PLAY [Simple playbook] *******************************************************

TASK [Gathering Facts] *******************************************************
ok: [testhost1]
ok: [testhost2]

TASK [Show a message] ********************************************************
ok: [testhost1] => {
    "msg": "Hello world!"
}
ok: [testhost2] => {
    "msg": "Hello world!"
}

TASK [Touch a file] **********************************************************
changed: [testhost2]
changed: [testhost1]

PLAY RECAP *******************************************************************
testhost1                  : ok=3    changed=1    unreachable=0    failed=0
testhost2                  : ok=3    changed=1    unreachable=0    failed=0

~/hands-on-automation/chapter02/example04>
```

Here, you can see that both the tasks we created earlier in the chapter have been run—only this time, they have been run on a pair of remote systems using the native SSH communication protocol. As SSH is normally enabled on most Linux servers, this immediately gives us massive scope for expanding our automation—this example has been performed on an inventory containing just two hosts, but it could just have easily contained 200 or more hosts.

Note that the tasks are still run in sequential order as before—only this time, each task is now run to completion on all hosts in the inventory before the next task is attempted, again making our playbook flow very predictable and easy to manage.

If we set up SSH keys for the remote hosts, then the `--ask-pass` parameter is no longer necessary, and the playbook runs without any interaction from the user, which is most desirable for many automation scenarios:

> SSH keys, while more secure than passwords, do bring their own risks, especially if the keys are not encrypted with a password. In this case, anyone who gets hold of an unencrypted private key will be able to gain remote access to any system with the matching public key, without any further prompt or challenge. If you do go down the route of setting up SSH keys, be sure you understand the security implications.

Let's run through a simple process to generate an SSH key and configure it on our test systems for Ansible to authenticate against:

1. To set up a very simple SSH key-based access on our test hosts, we could run the following command from the Ansible host to create the key pair (do not do this if you already have a key pair, as you could overwrite it!):

    ```
    $ ssh-keygen -b 2048 -t rsa -f ~/.ssh/id_rsa -q -N ''
    ```

2. This command silently creates a 2048-bit RSA key in the file at `~/.ssh/id_rsa`, with no passphrase (hence unencrypted). The corresponding public key to be copied to remote systems will be created as `~/.ssh/id_rsa.pub` (that is, the same filename and path specified by `-f`, with `.pub` appended). Now, copy it to the two remote hosts, using the following commands (you will be prompted for your SSH password both times):

    ```
    $ ssh-copy-id testhost1
    $ ssh-copy-id testhost2
    ```

3. Finally, we can run our playbook just as we did before, but without the `--ask-pass` flag, as shown in the following screenshot:

```
● ● ●                james@automation-01: ~/hands-on-automation/chapter02/example05 (ssh)

~/hands-on-automation/chapter02/example05> ansible-playbook -i hosts simple.yml


PLAY [Simple playbook] ********************************************************

TASK [Gathering Facts] ********************************************************
ok: [testhost1]
ok: [testhost2]

TASK [Show a message] *********************************************************
ok: [testhost1] => {
    "msg": "Hello world!"
}
ok: [testhost2] => {
    "msg": "Hello world!"
}

TASK [Touch a file] **********************************************************
changed: [testhost2]
changed: [testhost1]

PLAY RECAP *******************************************************************
testhost1                  : ok=3    changed=1    unreachable=0    failed=0
testhost2                  : ok=3    changed=1    unreachable=0    failed=0

~/hands-on-automation/chapter02/example05> █
```

The difference, as you can see, is subtle but hugely important—no user intervention was required, meaning our simple playbook suddenly has massive scale across an environment of virtually any size.

Although here, we have taken advantage of the fact that Ansible will read (by default) the SSH private keys that are found in the .ssh directory for the user account in question, you are not limited to using these keys. You can specify a private key file manually by using the `ansible_ssh_private_key_file` host variable in the inventory, or you can use `ssh-agent` to make different private SSH keys available to Ansible in the current shell session.

Doing this is left as an exercise for you to complete, and the following pages from the official Ansible documentation will assist you with this:

- For an introduction to using `ssh-agent` with Ansible, please refer to `https://docs.ansible.com/ansible/latest/user_guide/connection_details.html`.
- For an introduction to the inventory host variables available in Ansible, including `ansible_ssh_private_key_file`, please refer to `https://docs.ansible.com/ansible/latest/user_guide/intro_inventory.html`.

Of course, you don't need to perform all tasks on remote systems as the current user—you can use the `--user` (or `-u`) flag with `ansible-playbook` to specify a user to be used across all hosts in the inventory, or you can even use the `ansible_user` host variable within the inventory itself to specify user accounts on a per-host basis. Obviously, you should try to avoid a scenario such as this, as it goes against the principle of commonality that we discussed in Chapter 1, *Building a Standard Operating Environment on Linux*, but the important thing to note is that Ansible offers huge flexibility and opportunity to customize. It scales incredibly well in SOEs, but where there are deviations, it is easy to get Ansible to adapt without difficulty.

We will go into variables in greater detail later in this chapter, but it is worth mentioning at this stage that inventories can also contain variables. These can either be user-created variables or special variables, such as the aforementioned `ansible_user`. Extending our simple inventory from this chapter, if we wanted to set the SSH user to `bob` and create a new user-defined variable called `http_port` for use later in a playbook, our inventory might look like this:

```
[test]
testhost1
testhost2

[test:vars]
ansible_user=bob
http_port=8080
```

That covers the basics of inventories that you will need to know to get started with Ansible and to proceed with this book. Hopefully, you are starting to get an idea of the low barrier to entry presented to new users by Ansible that has made it so popular.

Understanding roles in Ansible

As easy as Ansible is to get started with, and as readable as a playbook is when it is short, it does get more complex, as do the requirements. In addition, there are certain functions that may well be needed repeatedly in different scenarios. For example, you might need to deploy a MariaDB database server as a common task in your environment. A module called `apt` is used for managing packages on Ubuntu servers, and so, if we wanted to install the `mariadb-server` package on our test system, the playbook to perform this task could look like this:

```
---
- name: Install MariaDB Server
  hosts: localhost
  become: true

  tasks:
    - name: Install mariadb-server package
      apt:
        name: mariadb-server
        update_cache: yes
```

Note that this time, we have set `become` to `true`, as we need root privileges to install packages. This is, of course, a very simple example, as installing a database server normally requires a great deal more configuration work, but it serves as a starting point. We could run this on our test system, and yield the desired result, as follows:

```
● ● ●              james@automation-01: ~/hands-on-automation/chapter02/example07 (ssh)
~/hands-on-automation/chapter02/example07> ansible-playbook install-db.yml
 [WARNING]: provided hosts list is empty, only localhost is available. Note
that the implicit localhost does not match 'all'


PLAY [Install MariaDB Server] ********************************************************

TASK [Gathering Facts] ***************************************************************
ok: [localhost]

TASK [Install mariadb-server package] ***********************************************
changed: [localhost]

PLAY RECAP **************************************************************************
localhost                  : ok=2    changed=1    unreachable=0    failed=0

~/hands-on-automation/chapter02/example07>
```

So far, so good. If you had to do this on a routine basis, though, in different playbooks for different hosts, would you really want to be writing (or, indeed, copying and pasting) that tasks block from this example over and over again? Also, this example is simplistic, and in reality, the database deployment code would be far more complex. If someone makes a fix or improvement in the code, how do you ensure that this new revision of code is propagated into all the right places?

This is where roles come in, and an Ansible role, while in essence nothing more than a structured set of directories and YAML, enables efficient and effective reuse of code. It also makes the initial playbook easier to read, as we shall see shortly. Once roles are created, they can be stored in a central location, such as a version control repository (for example, GitHub), and then, the latest version can always be accessed whenever a playbook needs to install MariaDB.

Roles are (by default) run from a subdirectory called `roles/`, in the same directory as your playbook. Throughout this book, we will use this convention, though it must be stated that Ansible will also search for roles in `/etc/ansible/roles` and the paths specified by the `roles_path` parameter in the Ansible configuration file (which, by default, can be found in `/etc/ansible/ansible.cfg`, though there are ways to override this). Each role then has its own subdirectory under this, and that directory name forms the name of the role. Let's explore this through a simple example, as follows:

1. We will get started by creating a `roles/` directory, and an `install-mariadb/` directory under this, for our first role:

   ```
   $ mkdir -p roles/install-mariadb
   ```

2. Each role has a fixed directory structure under it; however, for our simple example, we are only interested in one: `tasks/`. The `tasks/` subdirectory of a role contains the main list of tasks that will be run when the role is called, in a file called `main.yml`. Let's create that directory now, as follows:

   ```
   $ cd roles/install-mariadb
   $ mkdir tasks
   $ vi tasks/main.yml
   ```

3. Naturally, you can use your preferred editor in place of `vi`. In the `main.yml` file, enter the following code—note that it is essentially the tasks block from the original playbook, but the indentation level has now changed:

```
---
- name: Install mariadb-server package
  apt:
    name: mariadb-server
    update_cache: yes
```

4. Once we have created this file, we then edit our original `install-db.yml` playbook so that it looks like this:

```
---
- name: Install MariaDB Server
  hosts: localhost
  become: true

  roles:
    - install-mariadb
```

Notice how much more compact the playbook is now! It is also a great deal easier to read, and yet if we run it, we can see that it performs the same function. Note how the state of the MariaDB server installation task was `changed` last time we ran it but is now `ok`. This means that Ansible detected that the `mariadb-server` package was already installed, and hence no further action was required. This is an example of the previously mentioned idempotent change in action, as can be seen in the following screenshot:

```
james@automation-01: ~/hands-on-automation/chapter02/example08 (ssh)
~/hands-on-automation/chapter02/example08> ansible-playbook install-db.yml
 [WARNING]: provided hosts list is empty, only localhost is available. Note
that the implicit localhost does not match 'all'


PLAY [Install MariaDB Server] ***************************************************

TASK [Gathering Facts] *********************************************************
ok: [localhost]

TASK [install-mariadb : Install mariadb-server package] ************************
ok: [localhost]

PLAY RECAP *********************************************************************
localhost                  : ok=2    changed=0    unreachable=0    failed=0

~/hands-on-automation/chapter02/example08>
```

Well done! You have created and executed your first role. If you want to read more about roles and the required directory structure, please refer to `https://docs.ansible.com/ansible/latest/user_guide/playbooks_reuse_roles.html`.

There's even more to roles than this—not only are they invaluable in structuring your playbooks and enabling reuse of code; there is also a central repository for community-contributed roles, called **Ansible Galaxy**. If you search Ansible Galaxy for MariaDB-related roles, you will find (at the time of writing) 277 different roles, all designed to perform various database installation tasks. This means that you don't even have to write your own roles for common tasks—you can either make use of community-contributed ones or fork them, and modify them to your own ends. Most common server automation tasks have already been solved somewhere along the way by the Ansible community, and so it is very likely you will find exactly what you are looking for.

Let's test this now, as follows:

1. First, install a role from Ansible Galaxy that installs MariaDB server on Ubuntu:

```
$ ansible-galaxy install -p roles/ mrlesmithjr.mariadb-mysql
```

2. Now, we will modify our playbook to reference this role instead:

```
---
- name: Install MariaDB Server
  hosts: localhost
  become: true

  roles:
    - mrlesmithjr.mariadb-mysql
```

3. That's all that is required—if we run it, we can see that this playbook performs many more tasks than our simple one, including a lot of the security setup that is good practice when installing a new database, as can be seen in the following screenshot:

```
• • •            james@automation-01: ~/hands-on-automation/chapter02/example09 (ssh)
~/hands-on-automation/chapter02/example09> ansible-playbook install-db.yml
 [WARNING]: provided hosts list is empty, only localhost is available. Note
that the implicit localhost does not match 'all'


PLAY [Install MariaDB Server] *********************************************

TASK [Gathering Facts] ****************************************************
ok: [localhost]

TASK [mrlesmithjr.mariadb-mysql : include_tasks] *************************
included: /home/james/hands-on-automation/chapter02/example09/roles/mrlesmithjr.
mariadb-mysql/tasks/debian.yml for localhost

TASK [mrlesmithjr.mariadb-mysql : debian | installing pre-reqs] *********
changed: [localhost]

TASK [mrlesmithjr.mariadb-mysql : debian | adding mariadb repo keys] ***
skipping: [localhost]

TASK [mrlesmithjr.mariadb-mysql : debian | adding mariadb repo keys] ***
ok: [localhost]

TASK [mrlesmithjr.mariadb-mysql : debian | adding mariadb repo] ********
changed: [localhost]

TASK [mrlesmithjr.mariadb-mysql : include] ****************************
```

The end result, however, is that the `mariadb-server` package is installed on our test system—and this time, we barely even had to write any code! It is advisable, of course, to check what a role from Ansible Galaxy is going to do before blindly running it on your systems, in case it makes changes that you hadn't expected (or wanted!). Nonetheless, roles, in conjunction with Ansible Galaxy, form a powerful addition to the value that Ansible has to offer.

With an understanding of roles under our belts, in the next section, we will look at an important concept to help you get the most out of your playbooks and roles by making their content dynamic: Ansible variables.

Understanding Ansible variables

Most of the examples we have looked at so far have been static in nature. This is fine for the simplest playbook examples, but in many cases, it is desirable to be able to either store values or define them easily in a central place, rather than having to go hunting through a playbook (and tree of roles) for a specific hardcoded value. As in other languages, it is also desirable to capture values somehow, for reuse later.

There are many different types of variables in Ansible, and it is important to know that they have a strict order of precedence. Although we won't encounter this much in this book, it is important to be aware of this, as you might otherwise receive unexpected results from your variables.

 More details on variable precedence can be found at `https://docs.ansible.com/ansible/latest/user_guide/playbooks_variables.html#variable-precedence-where-should-i-put-a-variable`

In short, variables can be defined in a number of locations, and the right location for a given scenario will be driven by the objective of the playbook. For example, if a variable is common to an entire group of servers, it would be logical to define it in the inventory as a group variable. If it applies to every host a specific playbook runs against regardless, then you would almost certainly define it in the playbook. Let's take a quick look at this by modifying our `simple.yml` playbook from earlier in this chapter, this time, defining a play variable called `message` for our `debug` statement to display when the playbook is run, as follows:

```
---
- name: Simple playbook
  hosts: localhost
  become: false

  vars:
    message: "Life is beautiful!"

  tasks:
    - name: Show a message
      debug:
        msg: "{{ message }}"
    - name: Touch a file
      file:
        path: /tmp/foo
        state: touch
```

Note that we have now defined a `vars` section before the `tasks` one and that the variable is accessed by placing it in pairs of curly braces. Running this playbook yields the following results:

```
james@automation-01: ~/hands-on-automation/chapter02/example10 (ssh)

~/hands-on-automation/chapter02/example10> ansible-playbook simple.yml
 [WARNING]: provided hosts list is empty, only localhost is available. Note
that the implicit localhost does not match 'all'


PLAY [Simple playbook] **************************************************

TASK [Gathering Facts] **************************************************
ok: [localhost]

TASK [Show a message] ***************************************************
ok: [localhost] => {
    "msg": "Life is beautiful!"
}

TASK [Touch a file] *****************************************************
changed: [localhost]

PLAY RECAP **************************************************************
localhost                  : ok=3    changed=1    unreachable=0    failed=0

~/hands-on-automation/chapter02/example10>
```

If you refer to the variable precedence order list, you will note that variables passed to the `ansible-playbook` binary on the command line are top of the list, and override all other variables. Thus, if we want to override the contents of our message variable without editing the playbook, we can do so as follows:

```
$ ansible-playbook simple.yml -e "message=\"Hello from the CLI\""
```

Note the special quoting and escaping required to handle the spaces in the variable content, and the effects of this on the operation of the playbook:

```
● ● ●            james@automation-01: ~/hands-on-automation/chapter02/example10 (ssh)
~/hands-on-automation/chapter02/example10> ansible-playbook simple.yml -e "messa
ge=\"Hello from the CLI\""
 [WARNING]: provided hosts list is empty, only localhost is available. Note
that the implicit localhost does not match 'all'


PLAY [Simple playbook] ****************************************************

TASK [Gathering Facts] ****************************************************
ok: [localhost]

TASK [Show a message] *****************************************************
ok: [localhost] => {
    "msg": "Hello from the CLI"
}

TASK [Touch a file] *******************************************************
changed: [localhost]

PLAY RECAP ****************************************************************
localhost                  : ok=3    changed=1    unreachable=0    failed=0

~/hands-on-automation/chapter02/example10>
```

Variables can also be passed to roles, and are a simple yet powerful way of creating generic roles that can be used in a multitude of scenarios, without using identical configuration data. For example, in the previous section, we explored installing a MariaDB server. While this is a good candidate for a role, you certainly don't want the same root database password to be configured on every server. It thus makes sense to define a variable for the password, and pass this to the role from the calling playbook (or another appropriate source, such as a host or group variable).

As well as user-defined variables, Ansible also has a number of built-in variables, referred to as special variables. These can be accessed from anywhere in the playbook, and are useful for obtaining certain details pertaining to the state of the play.

For example, if you needed to know the hostname currently being acted upon for a specific task, this is available through the `inventory_hostname` variable. A full list of these variables is available at `https://docs.ansible.com/ansible/latest/reference_appendices/special_variables.html`

Many readers will, by now, have noticed that the output from all our example playbooks contains a line that says `Gathering Facts`. Although this can be turned off, it is, in fact, incredibly useful, and populates a wide array of variables with useful key system data. To get an idea of the kind of data gathered during this phase, run the following code from the command line:

```
$ ansible -m setup localhost
```

This command, rather than running a playbook, instructs Ansible to run the `setup` module directly on the `localhost`—the `setup` module is the one that is run behind the scenes, during the `Gathering Facts` stage. The output will look something like this, and goes on for pages—this is just the first few lines:

```
● ● ●                james@automation-01: ~/hands-on-automation/chapter02/example11 (ssh)
~/hands-on-automation/chapter02/example11> ansible -m setup localhost
 [WARNING]: provided hosts list is empty, only localhost is available. Note
that the implicit localhost does not match 'all'

localhost | SUCCESS => {
    "ansible_facts": {
        "ansible_all_ipv4_addresses": [
            "192.168.81.142"
        ],
        "ansible_all_ipv6_addresses": [
            "fe80::20c:29ff:fe8d:21ab"
        ],
        "ansible_apparmor": {
            "status": "enabled"
        },
        "ansible_architecture": "x86_64",
        "ansible_bios_date": "04/13/2018",
        "ansible_bios_version": "6.00",
        "ansible_cmdline": {
            "BOOT_IMAGE": "/vmlinuz-4.15.0-50-generic",
            "maybe-ubiquity": true,
            "ro": true,
            "root": "/dev/mapper/ubuntu--vg-ubuntu--lv"
        },
        "ansible_date_time": {
            "date": "2019-05-21",
            "day": "21",
```

We can immediately see there is some really useful information there, such as the IP addresses of the host, the root volume, and so on. Remember our discussion about commonality in Chapter 1, *Building a Standard Operating Environment on Linux*, and the difficulty in detecting the operating system you are running against? Well, Ansible makes this easy, as that data is all readily available in the gathered facts. We can modify our debug statement to display the Linux distribution we are running against, simply by specifying the appropriate fact, accessible from the output from the last command, as follows:

```
- name: Show a message
  debug:
    msg: "{{ ansible_distribution }}"
```

Now, when we run the playbook, we can easily tell we are running on Ubuntu, as can be seen in the following screenshot:

```
● ● ●          james@automation-01: ~/hands-on-automation/chapter02/example11 (ssh)
~/hands-on-automation/chapter02/example11> ansible-playbook simple.yml
 [WARNING]: provided hosts list is empty, only localhost is available. Note
that the implicit localhost does not match 'all'


PLAY [Simple playbook] ***********************************************************

TASK [Gathering Facts] ***********************************************************
ok: [localhost]

TASK [Show a message] ************************************************************
ok: [localhost] => {
    "msg": "Ubuntu"
}

TASK [Touch a file] **************************************************************
changed: [localhost]

PLAY RECAP ***********************************************************************
localhost                  : ok=3    changed=1    unreachable=0    failed=0
```

Ansible enables you to conditionally run individual tasks, roles, or even entire blocks of tasks, and hence having access to facts makes it straightforward to write robust playbooks that can be run against multiple platforms and perform the correct actions on each platform.

It is also worth noting that variables do not need to be stored in unencrypted text. Occasionally, it might be necessary to store a password in a variable (as discussed earlier—perhaps the root password for our MariaDB server install). Storing those details in plain text format presents a big security risk, but fortunately, Ansible includes a technology called **Vault**, which is capable of storing variable data encrypted using AES256. These encrypted vaults can be referenced by any playbook, provided the vault password is passed to the playbook when it is run. Vaults are beyond the scope of this chapter, but if you would like to read more about them, please see `https://docs.ansible.com/ansible/latest/user_guide/playbooks_vault.html`. In this book, we will not use them extensively, simply to keep the example code concise. However, it is strongly recommended that in a production environment, you use vaults wherever sensitive data for a playbook needs to be stored.

Now that we have introduced the concept of variables in Ansible, and the various types available, let's take a look at an important means for managing configuration files in Ansible—the use of templates.

Understanding Ansible templates

A common automation requirement is to set a value in a configuration file, or even to deploy a new configuration file, based on some given parameters. Ansible provides modules that can perform similar functions to the venerable `sed` and `awk` utilities, and of course, these are valid ways to modify an existing configuration file. Let's suppose we have a small Apache virtual host configuration file, containing the following code:

```
<VirtualHost *:80>
    DocumentRoot "/var/www/automation"
    ServerName www.example.com
</VirtualHost>
```

We want to deploy this configuration, but customize the `DocumentRoot` parameter for each host. Naturally, we could just deploy the preceding file, exactly as it is, to every host, and then use a regular expression, in conjunction with the Ansible `replace` module, to find the `DocumentRoot` line and modify it (similar to using the `sed` command-line utility). The resulting playbook might look like this:

```
---
- name: Deploy and customize an Apache configuration
  hosts: localhost
  become: true

  vars:
```

```
    docroot: "/var/www/myexample"

  tasks:
    - name: Copy static configuration file to remote host
      copy:
        src: files/vhost.conf
        dest: /etc/apache2/sites-available/my-vhost.conf

    - name: Replace static DocumentRoot with variable contents
      replace:
        path: /etc/apache2/sites-available/my-vhost.conf
        regexp: '^(\s+DocumentRoot)\s+.*$'
        replace: '\1 {{ docroot }}'
```

If we create our sample static virtual host configuration file in `files/vhost.conf` with the preceding contents shown and run this playbook, we can see that it works, as follows:

```
● ● ●              james@automation-01: ~/hands-on-automation/chapter02/example12 (ssh)
~/hands-on-automation/chapter02/example12> ansible-playbook apache-conf.yml
 [WARNING]: provided hosts list is empty, only localhost is available. Note
that the implicit localhost does not match 'all'


PLAY [Deploy and customize an Apache configuration] ****************************

TASK [Gathering Facts] *********************************************************
ok: [localhost]

TASK [Copy static configuration file to remote host] ***************************
changed: [localhost]

TASK [Replace static DocumentRoot with variable contents] **********************
changed: [localhost]

PLAY RECAP *********************************************************************
localhost                  : ok=3    changed=2    unreachable=0    failed=0

~/hands-on-automation/chapter02/example12> cat /etc/apache2/sites-available/my-v
host.conf
<VirtualHost *:80>
    DocumentRoot /var/www/myexample
    ServerName www.example.com
</VirtualHost>
~/hands-on-automation/chapter02/example12>
```

However, this is an inelegant solution. First of all, we're using two tasks, and if we wanted to customize `ServerName` as well, we'd need even more. Secondly, those who are familiar with regular expressions will know it wouldn't take much to trip up the simple one used here. Writing good robust regular expressions for tasks such as this is an art in itself.

Luckily, Ansible has inherited from the Python in which it is written a technology called **Jinja2 templating**. This is perfect for scenarios such as this (and many other deployment-related automation scenarios). Instead of a cumbersome multistep approach such as this, we now define our starting virtual host configuration file as a template in `templates/vhost.conf.j2`, as follows:

```
<VirtualHost *:80>
    DocumentRoot {{ docroot }}
    ServerName www.example.com
</VirtualHost>
```

As you can see, this is almost identical to our original configuration file, except that we have now replaced one of the static values with one of our variables, surrounded by pairs of curly braces, just as we would do in the playbook itself. Before we proceed with this example, it is worth mentioning that Jinja2 is an incredibly powerful templating system that goes far beyond simple variable substitution into a flat file. It is capable of conditional statements, such as `if...else` and `for` loops, and includes a wide array of filters that can be used to manipulate content (for example, to convert a string to uppercase, or to join the members of a list together to form a string).

With that said, this book is not intended as a complete language reference for either Ansible or Jinja2—rather, it is intended as a practical guide to show you how to build up your SOE using Ansible. Please refer to the *Further reading* section at the end of this chapter for some references, which will give you a more complete overview of both Ansible and Jinja2.

Returning to our example, we will modify the playbook to deploy this example, as follows:

```
---
- name: Deploy and customize an Apache configuration
  hosts: localhost
  become: true

  vars:
    docroot: "/var/www/myexample"

  tasks:
    - name: Copy across and populate the template configuration
      template:
        src: templates/vhost.conf.j2
        dest: /etc/apache2/sites-available/my-vhost.conf
```

Notice how much more elegant this playbook is—the `template` module copies the configuration template to the remote host, just as the `copy` module did in the prior example, and also populates any variables we have specified. This is an incredibly powerful way to deploy configuration files in a repeatable, common manner, and it is highly recommended that you adopt this approach where possible. When human beings edit files, they often do so in an inconsistent manner, and that can be the enemy of automation, as you have to build a really robust regular expression to ensure you catch all possible edge cases. Deploying from templates with Ansible creates repeatable, reliable results that can easily be validated in a production environment. Running this playbook yields identical results to our previous, more complex example, as follows:

```
james@automation-01: ~/hands-on-automation/chapter02/example12 (ssh)
~/hands-on-automation/chapter02/example12> ansible-playbook apache-template-conf
.yml
 [WARNING]: provided hosts list is empty, only localhost is available. Note
that the implicit localhost does not match 'all'


PLAY [Deploy and customize an Apache configuration] ****************************

TASK [Gathering Facts] *********************************************************
ok: [localhost]

TASK [Copy across and populate the template configuration] *********************
changed: [localhost]

PLAY RECAP *********************************************************************
localhost                  : ok=2    changed=1    unreachable=0    failed=0

~/hands-on-automation/chapter02/example12> cat /etc/apache2/sites-available/my-v
host.conf
<VirtualHost *:80>
    DocumentRoot /var/www/myexample
    ServerName www.example.com
</VirtualHost>
~/hands-on-automation/chapter02/example12>
```

That concludes our look at variables for now, and indeed, our crash course in Ansible. In the next section, we tie up everything we have learned, before drawing this chapter to a close.

Bringing Ansible and the SOE together

We have already worked through a number of end-to-end examples with Ansible. Although simple, they showcase the fundamental building blocks of automation with Ansible, on which this book is based. A big part of achieving automation in a Linux environment at scale is having both good standards and robust processes. Hence, not only should your operating environment be standardized; so should your deployment and configuration processes.

As discussed in the previous chapter, although a well-defined SOE will be consistent at the point of deployment, this consistency can soon be lost if administrators are allowed to make changes at will, using whatever their preferred method is. Just as it is desirable to deploy an SOE to achieve success in automation, so it is also desirable to make automation your go-to for as many (ideally all) administrative tasks as possible.

Ideally, there should be one single source of truth for playbooks (for example, a central Git repository) and a single source of truth for inventories (this might be in the form of a centrally stored static inventory, or the use of a dynamic inventory).

The goal of any well-written Ansible playbook (or role) is that the results from running it are repeatable and predictable. Take, for example, the playbook we ran at the end of the previous section, where we were deploying a simple Apache `vhost.conf` file using a playbook that we wrote. Every time you run this playbook on any server, the contents of `/etc/apache2/sites-available/my-vhost.conf` will be the same, as the playbook deploys this file using a template, and overwrites the target file if it exists.

This, of course, is but a microcosm of the standard operating environment, but such an environment will be built up of hundreds—if not thousands—of these tiny building blocks. After all, if you can't get your Apache configurations to be consistent across your infrastructure, how can you be confident that any other parts of it have been built in accordance with your standards?

The repeatable nature of well-written playbooks is important to mention here too—just because you deployed a consistent Apache configuration doesn't mean it will remain consistent. Five minutes after you deploy the configuration, someone with the required privileges could log in to the server and change the configuration. Thus, your environment could deviate from your SOE definition almost immediately. Running your Ansible playbooks repeatedly across your infrastructure is actually an important part of your ongoing processes, as the nature of these playbooks will be to bring the configuration back into line with your original standards. Thus Ansible playbooks are a vital component of not only defining and deploying your SOE but also in the ongoing enforcement of the standards.

No fixes should be manually deployed, if at all possible. Suppose someone manually tweaks the configuration in `/etc/apache2/sites-available/my-vhost.conf` to overcome an issue. This in itself is not a problem, but it is vital that these changes are placed back into the playbook, role, or template. If deploying or enforcing your SOE through Ansible somehow breaks it, then something is wrong with your processes.

Indeed, by implementing processes such as we have discussed so far, and will continue to explore throughout this book, successful automation across an enterprise can be achieved. The introduction to Ansible automation given in this chapter, while brief, serves as one part of these suggested processes.

There is much more to learn about Ansible and, in short, I would like to propose a bold statement: If you can conceive it as a server deployment or configuration task, Ansible can help. Thanks to its open source nature, Ansible is very extensible, and its wide adoption means that many of the common automation challenges have already been solved, and relevant features included. It is hoped that this chapter has given you a head start on your journey into Linux automation with Ansible.

Summary

Ansible is a robust, powerful, open source tool that, once you have mastered a few simple concepts, can help you to achieve automation on a very large scale in your Linux environment. Ansible is agentless, and so requires no configuration on Linux client machines for you to begin your automation journey, and a robust community behind the project means that easy answers are available to most of the challenges you may wish to solve with it.

In this chapter, you learned the fundamentals of playbook structure and some of the key files required to run a simple playbook. You learned about the importance of inventories and how to use them, and how to efficiently reuse code with roles (and indeed, how to leverage code from the community to save you time and effort). You learned about variables and facts, and how to reference them in playbooks, and how to make use of Jinja2 templating to aid your automation journey. Throughout this journey, you built and ran a number of complete playbooks, demonstrating the use of Ansible.

In the next chapter, you'll discover how to streamline infrastructure management, and further refine your automation processes with AWX.

Questions

1. What is Ansible, and how is it different from running a simple shell script?
2. What is an Ansible inventory?
3. Why is it generally beneficial to code your tasks into roles rather than single large playbooks?
4. Which templating language does Ansible make use of?
5. Can you override variables in Ansible?
6. Why would you use the Ansible template module in place of a simple search and replace operation?
7. How might you make use of Ansible facts to improve the flow of your playbook?

Further reading

- For an in-depth understanding of Ansible and Jinja2 templating, please refer to *Mastering Ansible, Third Edition—James Freeman* and *Jesse Keating* (`https://www.packtpub.com/gb/virtualization-and-cloud/mastering-ansible-third-edition`).

3
Streamlining Infrastructure Management with AWX

As we have discussed so far in this book, effective enterprise automation on Linux involves several key elements, including standardization of both tools and technologies, and implementing processes and tools that make the management of the environment more efficient. Ansible is a great first step in this journey and can be supplemented with a complementary technology called AWX to further streamline its application.

AWX is, in short, a GUI-driven tool for the management of Ansible jobs. It does not replace Ansible functionality, but rather adds to it by providing a multi-user GUI-driven frontend that allows for the simple management and orchestration of playbooks. When managing large Linux environments such as those in an enterprise, AWX is the perfect complement to Ansible automation and is an important step in effective and efficient management. In this chapter, we will cover the following topics:

- Introduction to AWX
- Installing AWX
- Running your playbooks from AWX
- Automating routine tasks with AWX

Technical requirements

This chapter includes examples based on the following technologies:

- Ubuntu Server 18.04 LTS
- CentOS 7.6
- Ansible 2.8

To run through these examples, you will need access to a server or virtual machine running one of the aforementioned operating systems and Ansible. Note that the examples given in this chapter may be destructive in nature (for example, they involve installing Docker and running services on the server) and, if run as is, are only intended to be run in an isolated test environment.

Once you are satisfied that you have a safe environment to operate in, let's get started by looking at the installation of new software packages with Ansible.

All example code discussed in this book is available from GitHub at: `https://github.com/ PacktPublishing/Hands-On-Enterprise-Automation-on-Linux`.

Introduction to AWX

AWX sets out to solve the problems associated with Ansible automation in an enterprise environment. To maintain our hands-on focus, let's consider the organic growth scenario we discussed in `Chapter 1`, *Building a Standard Operating Environment on Linux*. In a small environment where Ansible has been implemented, you might have just one or two key people responsible for writing and running playbooks against the environment. In this small scenario, it is reasonably easy to know who has run which playbooks and what the latest versions are, and the training requirements for Ansible are low as only a small number of key people are responsible for its use.

As the environment scales to enterprise sizing, so do the number of Ansible operators. If all of those responsible for running Ansible have it installed on their own machines, and all have local copies of the playbooks, suddenly the management of that environment becomes a nightmare! How can you ensure that everyone is using the latest versions of the playbooks? How do you know who ran what and what the outcome was? What if a change needs to be run out of hours? Can you pass the Ansible job off to a **Network Operations Center** (**NOC**) team, or is that not possible because they would need training on how to use Ansible?

AWX sets out to address all of these challenges, as we shall see subsequently, starting in the next section, where we look at how AWX can reduce your staff training costs.

AWX reduces training requirements

Ansible is very easy to get up and running. It still needs a little training, though. For example, IT admins and operators who haven't received training may not be comfortable with running a playbook on the command line. This is demonstrated in the following example. Although fairly simple in Ansible terms, anyone unfamiliar with the tool will find that it isn't very user-friendly:

```
$ ansible-playbook -i hosts --ask-pass simple.yml
```

Although it isn't a complex command, those unfamiliar with it might be reluctant to run it for fear of causing damage to production systems, let alone interpret the pages of output that a sizeable playbook can produce.

To alleviate this, AWX provides a web GUI-based interface that is quite literally point and click. Although many advanced features can be used by those familiar with it, a playbook can be run with literally a few clicks of the mouse, and the results are shown using a simple *traffic light* system (red indicating that the playbook run failed, while green shows that it passed). In this way, AWX provides an interface from which even those with no prior Ansible experience can launch a playbook and pass the results on to another team for analysis.

AWX offers benefits for security teams and managers too, by logging detailed results of all actions and jobs performed, and we shall provide an overview of this in the next section.

AWX enables auditability

Although the Ansible command-line tools provide logging options, these are not enabled by default and as a result, the run output of playbooks can be lost as soon as a terminal session is closed. This is not great in an enterprise scenario, particularly when an issue or outage occurs and a root cause analysis is required.

AWX addresses this in two ways. First of all, every user must log in to the GUI before any actions can be performed. AWX can integrate with centralized accounting systems such as LDAP or Active Directory, or users can be defined locally on the AWX host. All actions in the UI are then tracked, and as such, it is possible to trace back playbook runs to specific users and indeed configuration changes. In an enterprise environment, this level of accountability and this kind of audit trail is a *must-have*.

Beyond this, AWX captures all of the output of every playbook run, along with key pieces of information such as which inventory the playbook was run against, what variables were passed to it (if any), and the date and time of the run. This means that if an issue occurs, AWX can provide a complete audit trail to help you find out what happened and when.

Not only can AWX assist with auditing your automation, but it can also help with ensuring version control of your playbooks, as we shall discuss in the next section.

AWX supports version control

In an enterprise scenario, individuals storing playbooks locally could be a problem waiting to happen. For example, if user A updates a playbook with a critical fix, how do you ensure that user B has access to that code? Ideally, the code should be stored in a version control system (for example, GitHub) and the local copy updated for every single run.

Good processes are an important component of enterprise automation of Linux and while user B should update their local playbooks before running them, you cannot enforce this. Again, AWX addresses this issue by allowing playbooks to be sourced from a version control repository, with the local copy of the playbooks on the AWX server being updated automatically.

 Although AWX can help you, especially when it comes to ensuring the latest version of code has been pulled from the repository, it cannot help with other errant behaviors such as someone not committing their code in the first place. The intention, however, of enforcing the use of AWX for Ansible playbook runs is that anyone who makes changes must commit them for AWX to run them. Local access to the AWX server should be tightly restricted to prevent people from making code changes on the local filesystem, and in this way, you can have confidence that everyone is actively and effectively using your version control system.

These updates can be event-driven so that, for example, local playbooks can be updated every single time a playbook from that store is run. They can also be updated on a scheduled basis or manually, as per the decisions of the AWX administrators.

AWX can help with the security of your automation too. We shall explore this in the next section by looking at credential management in AWX.

AWX helps with credential management

For Ansible to effectively manage an Enterprise Linux environment, it must have some form of credentials to access all of the servers it is managing. SSH authentication is normally secured with either SSH keys or passwords, and in a large team of Ansible operators, this can mean everyone has access to those passwords and SSH private keys since they are required for Ansible to be run. Needless to say, this presents a security risk!

As stated previously, from a security standpoint, this is less than desirable as it would be too easy for someone to copy and paste credentials and use them in a manner for which they were not intended. AWX also handles this by storing required credentials in its database, encrypted with a passphrase chosen at installation time. The GUI stores all the credentials using reversible encryption so that they can be passed to Ansible when playbooks are run later on. However, the GUI does not let you see any previously entered sensitive data (such as passwords or SSH private keys)—that is to say that they can be entered and changed, but you cannot show a password or SSH key in the GUI, and hence operators can't easily make use of the AWX frontend to obtain credential information for use elsewhere. In this way, AWX helps enterprises keep their credentials under lock and key and ensures that they are only used for Ansible deployments and are not leaked or used for any other unintended purposes.

Ansible Vault is an excellent tool for encrypting any sensitive data that a playbook needs to operate on, be that for playbook data in the form of variables or storing server credentials themselves, such as an SSH private key. Although Vault is highly secure, it is easy to see the vault contents if you have the vault password (here, you would need to run a playbook that uses the Vault). As a result, AWX provides unique functionality to supplement Ansible and ensure security in an enterprise environment.

In these ways, AWX helps to address many of the challenges that enterprises face when deploying Ansible in a large-scale environment. Before we complete this section of this chapter, we will touch very briefly on how AWX can help you to integrate with other services.

Integrating AWX with other services

There is a myriad of tools that AWX can integrate with—for example, both Red Hat's Satellite 6 and CloudForms products (and their open source Katello and ManageIQ counterparts) provide native integration with both AWX and Ansible Tower. These are just two examples, and this is all possible because everything that we will explore as we progress through this chapter is also accessible through an API and a command-line interface.

This enables AWX to be integrated with a wide variety of services, or you could even write your own that would run a playbook from AWX as a result of some other action, just by calling the API. The command-line interface (called `tower-cli`, after the commercial Ansible Tower product) is also incredibly useful, especially when it comes to programmatically populating data in AWX. For example, if you wanted to add a host to a static inventory, you could do this through the web user interface (as we shall demonstrate later), the API, or using the CLI. The latter two methods lend themselves incredibly well to integration with other services—for example, a **Configuration Management Database (CMDB)** could push new hosts into an inventory using the API, without the need for any manual action by the user.

To explore these two integration points further, you can refer to the following official documentation sources:

- The AWX API is documented here: `https://docs.ansible.com/ansible-tower/latest/html/towerapi/index.html`.
- The `tower-cli` command is documented here: `https://tower-cli.readthedocs.io/en/latest/`.

Given the wide and varied nature of such integrations, they are beyond the scope of this book—however, it is important to mention them here because it is hoped that, as you read this chapter, you will see opportunities for integration with other services and hence be able to explore this topic further. In the next section of this chapter, we shall get hands-on with AWX and look at a simple deployment. Later in this chapter, this will be followed up with some example use cases.

Installing AWX

Installing AWX is a straightforward affair once you put the right prerequisites in place. In fact, one of the prerequisites for AWX is Ansible, proving the complementary nature of this technology. Most of the AWX code runs in a set of Docker containers, which makes it straightforward to deploy in most Linux environments.

The use of Docker containers means that it is possible to run AWX in OpenShift or other Kubernetes environments—however, for the sake of simplicity here, we will get started by installing it on a single Docker host. Before you proceed any further, you should ensure that your chosen host has the following:

- Docker, fully installed and working
- The `docker-py` module for your version of Python

- Access to Docker Hub (internet access)
- Ansible 2.4 or newer
- Git 1.8.4 or newer
- Docker Compose

These prerequisites are normally readily available for most Linux systems. Now, we will perform the following steps to begin our installation:

1. Continuing our example of the Ubuntu system we used in the previous chapter, we will run the following command to install the AWX requirements:

   ```
   $ sudo apt-get install git docker.io python-docker docker-compose
   ```

2. Once these have been installed, the next task is to clone the AWX code from its repository on GitHub:

   ```
   $ git clone https://github.com/ansible/awx.git
   ```

   The Git tool will faithfully clone the latest and greatest version of the AWX source code—note that this project is under active development and there is a possibility that the latest release might have bugs in it.

 If you want to clone one of the stable AWX releases, browse the **Releases** section of the repository and check out the desired version: https://github.com/ansible/awx/releases.

3. We have cloned the repository, and it is now time for us to define the configuration for our installation of AWX, especially security details such as a password. To get started on this, change into the `installer` directory under the cloned repository:

   ```
   $ cd awx/installer
   ```

   Hopefully, the contents of this directory will look familiar to you after reading the previous chapter. There is an `inventory` file, a playbook for us to run called `install.yml`, and a `roles/` directory. However, don't go and run the `install.yml` playbook just yet as there are some variables in the inventory file that we must set before we proceed.

If you take a look through the inventory file, you will see there is a great deal of configuration that can occur inside it. Some variables are commented out, while others are set to default values. There is a minimum of six variables that I recommend that you set before installing AWX, and these are as follows:

Variables name	Recommended value
admin_password	This is the default password for the admin user—you will need this the first time you log in, so be sure to set it to something memorable and secure!
pg_password	This is the password for the backend PostgreSQL database—be sure to set it to something unique and secure.
postgres_data_dir	This is the directory on the local filesystem where the PostgreSQL container will store its data—it defaults to a directory under /tmp, which, on most systems, will be automatically cleaned up regularly. This often destroys the PostgreSQL database, so set it to something AWX-specific (for example, /var/lib/awx/pgdocker).
project_data_dir	For uploading playbooks manually to AWX without the need for a version control system, the playbooks must sit somewhere on the filesystem. To prevent having to copy them into a container, this variable maps the local folder specified to the required one inside a container. For the examples in this book, we will use the default (the /var/lib/awx/projects folder).
rabbitmq_password	This is the password for the backend RabbitMQ service—be sure to set it to something unique and secure.
secret_key	This is the secret key used to encrypt credentials in the PostgreSQL database. It must be the same between upgrades of AWX, so be sure to store it somewhere secure as it will need to be set in future AWX inventories. Make this something long and secure.

4. You will observe that in this inventory file there is a great deal of secret information that is in plaintext. While we can tolerate this for the duration of the installation process, this file should not be left lying around on the filesystem when the installation is complete as it could give a potential attacker all of the details they need to easily compromise your systems. Once the installation phase is complete, be sure to either copy this file into a password manager of some kind or simply store the individual passwords—either way, do not leave the file unencrypted!

5. Once the inventory is customized, it is time to run the installation itself—this is launched by running the following command:

```
$ sudo ansible-playbook -i inventory install.yml
```

From our work on Ansible in the previous chapter, you will recognize this command—it is using the `ansible-playbook` command to run the `install.yml` playbook, while also using the inventory file called `inventory` that we edited in *step 1*. Pages of output will pass by in the Terminal, and if the installation is successful, you should see something like this:

```
● ● ●                      james@automation-01: ~/awx/installer (ssh)

TASK [local_docker : Create /tmp/awxcompose directory] **************************
ok: [localhost]

TASK [local_docker : Create Docker Compose Configuration] ***********************
ok: [localhost] => (item=environment.sh)
ok: [localhost] => (item=credentials.py)
ok: [localhost] => (item=docker-compose.yml)

TASK [local_docker : Render SECRET_KEY file] ************************************
ok: [localhost]

TASK [local_docker : Start the containers] *************************************
changed: [localhost]

TASK [local_docker : Update CA trust in awx_web container] *********************
changed: [localhost]

TASK [local_docker : Update CA trust in awx_task container] ********************
changed: [localhost]

PLAY RECAP *********************************************************************
localhost                  : ok=11    changed=3    unreachable=0    failed=0

~/awx/installer>
```

6. Once the installation completes, it takes a few minutes for the Docker containers to actually start up and for the backend database to be created. However, once this is done, you should be able to navigate to the IP address of your chosen AWX host in your browser and see the login page, an example of which is shown in the following screenshot:

7. Log in as the admin user using the password you set in the `admin_password` variable in the inventory file earlier. You should then be taken to the dashboard page of AWX:

That's it—you have successfully installed and logged in to AWX! Of course, there are many
more advanced installation parameters you can define, and equally, in an enterprise, you
would not rely on just a single AWX host with no backup (or high availability).

Note that when you log in to AWX, the connection is not SSL-secured,
which could result in sensitive data such as machine credentials being
transmitted over your network in the clear.

There is no one solution to out-of-the-box high availability and SSL issues that will suit
every enterprise, and so we leave the actual solution for this as an exercise for you. For
example, if you have an OpenShift environment with multiple hosts, then installing AWX
in this environment will enable it to keep running, even if the host it runs on fails. There are
of course ways to achieve high availability without OpenShift too.

Applying secure HTTP to AWX is also going to be solved in a different manner in different environments. Most Docker environments will have some kind of load balancer in front of them to help to handle their multi-host nature, and as a result, the SSL encryption could be offloaded onto this. It is also possible to secure a single Docker host, such as the one we have built here, but installing something capable of reverse proxying (for example, nginx) and configuring that to handle the SSL encryption.

In short, there is no one-size-fits-all solution to this, but it is recommended that you address these in the manner best suited to your enterprise. For this reason, we will not discuss them further here, other than to recommend that you take them into account when deploying AWX for production use.

Now that you have an AWX instance running, we must configure it so that we can successfully replicate how we ran playbooks from the command line in the previous chapter. For example, we must define an inventory just as we did previously and ensure we have set up SSH authentication so that Ansible can perform the automated tasks on the remote computer. In the next part of this chapter, we will walk through all of the setup that's required to run your first playbook through AWX.

Running your playbooks from AWX

When we ran an example playbook from the command line, we created our inventory file and then our playbook and then ran it using the `ansible-playbook` command. All of this, of course, assumed that we had already set up connectivity to the remote system by way of either specifying a password interactively or through the setup of SSH keys.

Although the end result in AWX is very similar—playbooks are run against an inventory—the terminology and naming are rather different. In this part of this chapter, we will walk through the process of getting your first playbook up and running from AWX. Although we don't have space in this book to give a complete rundown on every feature AWX has to offer, this section intends to give you sufficient knowledge and confidence to start managing your playbooks from AWX, and to explore further on your own.

Before you can run your first playbook from AWX, there are several prerequisite setup stages that must be completed. In the next section, we will complete the first of these—creating the credentials that will be used to authenticate over SSH with our target machine.

Setting up credentials in AWX

When you log in to AWX, you will notice a menu bar down the left-hand side of the screen. To define a new set of credentials that we will use to allow Ansible to log into our target machine, perform the following steps:

1. Click on **Credentials** in the left-hand menu bar.
2. Click on the green + icon to create a new credential.
3. Give the credential a name and select **Machine** from the **CREDENTIAL TYPE** field. There are many types of credentials that enable AWX to interact with a wide variety of services, but for now, we are only interested in this particular type.
4. There are many other fields available for specifying parameters for more advanced use cases—however, for our demonstration purposes, this is sufficient.

Your end result should look something like the following screenshot. Note that I have specified the login password for my demo machine, but you could equally have specified the SSH private key in the larger text box on the screen. You will also observe the presence of the **Prompt on launch** checkbox—there are many options in AWX that it can prompt the user for at the time a playbook is run, which can lend itself to a really rich interactive user experience. However, in this demo, we won't do this as we want to demonstrate playbooks running without user intervention:

When you have a credential defined, the next step is to define the inventory to run our playbook against. We'll explore this in the next section.

Creating inventories in AWX

Just like on the command line, AWX requires an inventory to be created for playbooks to be executed against. Here, we are going to make use of one of the official, publicly available Ansible example playbooks, which requires an inventory with two groups in it. In a larger setup, we would specify a different server for each group, but for this small demo, we can reuse the same server for both roles.

The code in question is used to install a simple LAMP stack on an RHEL or CentOS 7 machine and is available to view here: `https://github.com/ansible/ansible-examples/tree/master/lamp_simple_rhel7`.

To run this demo, you will need a CentOS 7 machine. My demo host is called `centos-testhost`, and if I were defining an inventory file on the command line, it would look like this:

```
[webservers]
centos-testhost

[dbservers]
centos-testhost
```

To replicate this in the AWX GUI, run through the following sequence:

1. Click on **Inventories** on the left-hand menu bar.
2. Click on the green + icon to create a new inventory.
3. Select **Inventory** from the drop-down menu.
4. Give the inventory a suitable name and click **SAVE**.

Your screen should look something like the one shown here once you have completed this process:

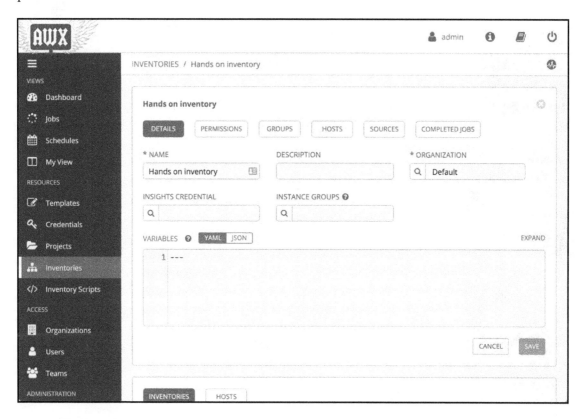

When complete, we can create our first group and put our test host into it. To do this, follow these steps:

1. Click on the **GROUPS** button at the top of the pane.
2. Click the green + icon to create a new group.
3. Enter the name webservers into the **NAME** field.
4. Click the green **SAVE** button.
5. Click the **HOSTS** button at the top.
6. Click the green + icon button to add a new host.
   1. Select **New Host** from the drop-down list.
7. Enter the name centos-testhost into the **HOST NAME** field.
8. Click the green **SAVE** button.

Once you have completed these steps, your screen should look something like the following screenshot:

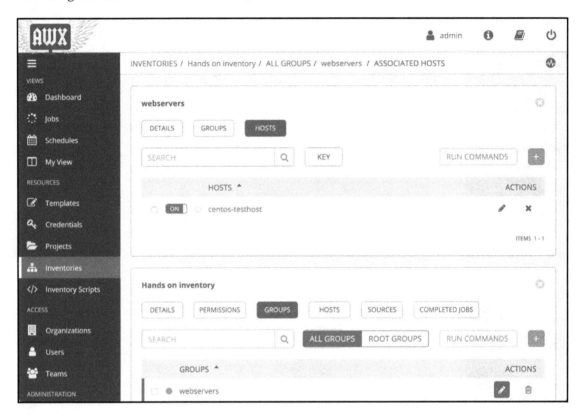

Repeat this process to define the dbservers group. Take care not to create this group as a subgroup of the webservers group, which is easy to do. You will note the breadcrumb trail at the top of the preceding screenshot—use that to navigate back to the top level of our new inventory by clicking on Hands on Inventory (or your name, if you chose a different one).

From here, the process is almost identical, except that when you come to adding the host to the newly created group (*step 6* onward from the preceding steps), choose **Existing Host** as we are reusing our single host for both groups in this example. Your resulting screen should look something like the following screenshot:

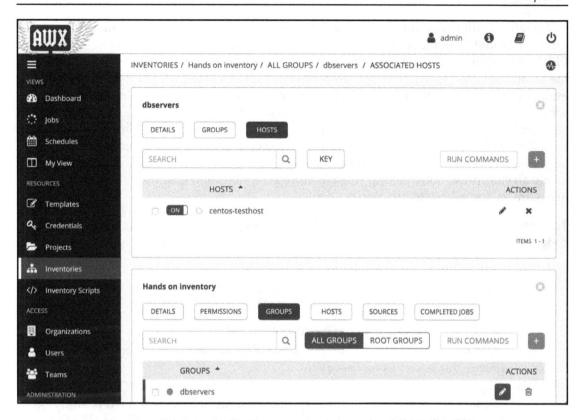

With those steps complete, our inventory complete with groupings is complete in AWX, and we can move on to the next stage in defining our configuration—the creation of an AWX project. We will do exactly this in the next section of this chapter.

Creating a project in AWX

If you were working with Ansible on the command line, it is unlikely you would store all of your playbooks and roles in one directory for very long as it would get unmanageable and very difficult to work out which file was which. This is the purpose of a project in AWX—it is quite simply a logical grouping of playbooks and is used to make organization easier and simpler.

Although we will not go into **Role-Based Access Control** (**RBAC**) in this book, projects also serve a role in this. In the screenshots provided so far, you may have noticed a **PERMISSIONS** button at the top of a number of the panes. These are present throughout the UI and are used to define which users have access to which configuration items. For example, if you have a team of **Database Administrators** (**DBAs**) who should only have access to run playbooks relevant to database servers against those servers, you could create an inventory of database servers and only give the DBAs access to this. Similarly, you could put all of the DBA-related playbooks into one project, and again only give that team permission to access that project. In this way, AWX forms a part of the good processes inside an enterprise, both making Ansible more accessible, and ensuring that the right items are only available to the correct people.

To continue our simple example, let's create a new project to reference our example Ansible code:

1. Click on **Projects** on the left-hand menu bar.
2. Click on the green **+** icon to create a new project.
3. Give the project a suitable name.
4. Select **Git** from the **SCM TYPE** drop-down list.
5. Enter the following URL into the **SCM URL** field: `https://github.com/ansible/ansible-examples.git`.
6. Optionally, you could also populate the **SCM BRANCH/TAG/COMMIT** field if you wanted to only work with a specific commit or branch in the repository. In this simple example, we will use the latest commit, known in Git as **HEAD**.
7. No other credentials are necessary as this is a publicly available GitHub example—however, if you were using a password-protected repository, you would create an SCM credential to the machine credential we created in the *Setting up credentials in AWX* section of this chapter.
8. Check the **UPDATE REVISION ON LAUNCH** checkbox—this causes AWX to pull the latest version of the code from our **SCM URL** every time a playbook from this project is run. If this is unchecked, you must manually update the local copy of the code before AWX will see the latest version.
9. Click on the green **SAVE** button.

When complete, the resulting screen should look something like the following screenshot:

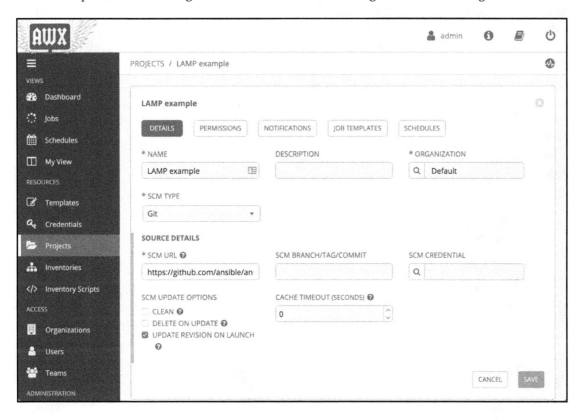

Before we can proceed to the final step of configuring our playbook for its first run, we need to manually pull the contents from the GitHub repository. To do this, click on the two semicircular arrows to the right of your newly created project—this forces a manual sync of the project from the upstream repository. An example of this is shown in the following screenshot for your reference:

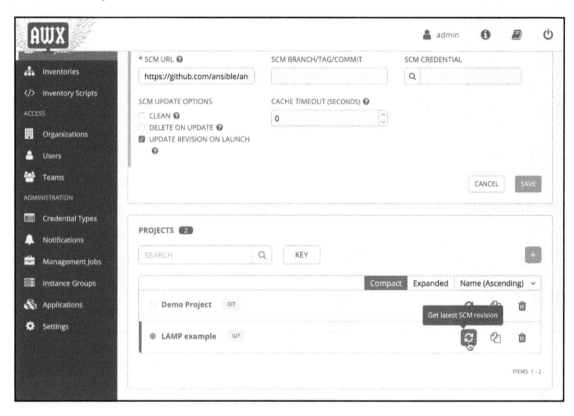

The green dot to the left of the project title (as seen in the preceding screenshot) will pulsate during the sync. Once this completes successfully, it will turn a static green, whereas if something goes wrong, it will turn red. Assuming all is well, we can proceed to the final stage of preparing to run our playbook.

With our project defined in AWX, the next task required as we head toward running our first playbook from it is to create a template, and we will do exactly that in the next section.

Creating a template in AWX

Templates in AWX pull together all of the other configuration items you have created so far—in essence, a template is the AWX definition of all of the parameters you would specify on the command line following the `ansible-playbook` command.

Let's walk through the process of creating a template so that we can run our playbook:

1. Click on **Templates** on the left-hand menu bar.
2. Click on the green + icon to create a new template.
3. Select **Job Template** from the drop-down list.
4. Give the template a suitable name.
5. In the **INVENTORY** field, select the inventory we created earlier in this chapter.
6. In the **PROJECT** field, select the project we created earlier.
7. In the **PLAYBOOK** field, note that the drop-down list has automatically been populated with a list of all of the viable playbooks that are available in the GitHub repository we specified in our **PROJECT** definition. Choose `lamp_simple_rhel7/site.yml` from the list.
8. Finally, select the credential we defined earlier in the **CREDENTIAL** field.
9. Click the green **SAVE** button.

The end result should look something like the following screenshot, which shows all of the fields filled in:

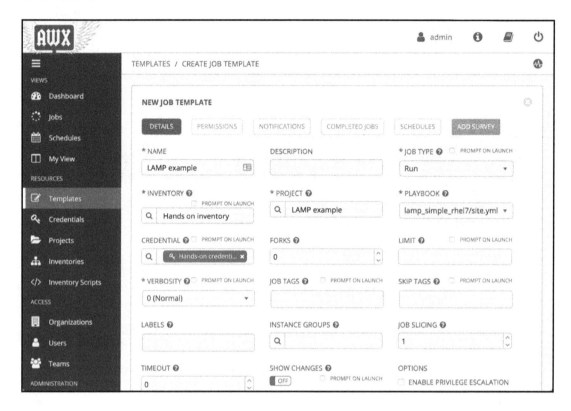

With those steps complete, we have now completed everything required to run our first ever job from AWX. Hence, we shall proceed to do exactly that in the next section and observe the results.

Running a playbook from AWX

When we run a playbook from AWX, what we're actually doing is running a template. Hence, to do this interactively, we will navigate our way back to the **Templates** screen, which should present a list of available templates. Note that when you are employing role-based access control, you can only see the templates (and inventories and other configuration items) that you have permission to see—if you don't have permission, it is invisible. This helps make AWX more manageable when using it across different teams.

We are using an administrator account, so we can see everything. To launch our newly
created template, follow these instructions:

1. Click on the rocket ship icon on the right of the template name, as shown in the
   following screenshot, which shows our newly created **Templates** with the option
   to execute it highlighted:

When you do this, the screen automatically reloads and you will see details of the run on your screen. Don't worry if you navigate away from this—you can always find it again later by clicking on **Jobs** on the left-hand menu bar. Since we have defined this job, it fails in the first instance. Luckily, the **Jobs** pane shows you all of the same details and output that you would get when you run Ansible from the command line, only in AWX, it is archived in the database so that you can always go back to it at a later date or so that another user can analyze it simply by logging into AWX (assuming they have the required permissions).

2. Looking at the job output, we can see the problem is some kind of permissions issue, and a screenshot showing what this might look like is shown for your reference:

Taking a look at the playbook source code on GitHub, we can see that the original author hardcoded the use of the root user account for this playbook (note the `remote_user: root` statements in `site.yml`). Normally, you wouldn't do this—it is generally better practice to get Ansible to log in using an unprivileged account, and then to use `sudo` as required by putting the `become: true` statement in the play headers (we'll see this in action later in this book).

3. To work around this, for now, we'll simply allow root logins over SSH on our CentOS 7 server, and then modify the credential in AWX to be for the root account. Note that you could also define a new credential and change the credential linked to the template—either are acceptable solutions. Once you have changed the credential, run the template again—this time, the output should look somewhat different, as we can see in the following screenshot, which is showing now a successful run of the playbook:

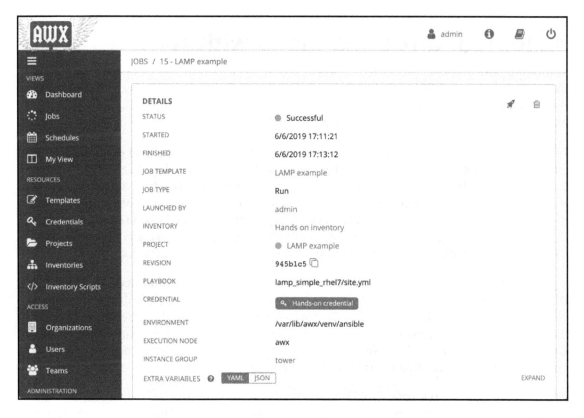

As we can see from the preceding screenshot, we have a successful playbook run, along with all of the relevant details about which user launched it, which revision on GitHub was used, which credentials were used, which inventory, and so on. Scrolling down this pane gives the output from `ansible-playbook` that we saw in the error screenshot previously; if we wish to, we can further analyze the playbook run to see whether there were any warnings, what was changed, and so on. Hence, with AWX we really achieve a nice simple user interface to Ansible, which integrates all of the good practices that should be present when automating Linux in an enterprise environment such as security, auditability, and centralized control of Ansible (and indeed playbook code through source control integration).

We have seen how AWX can assist us with running tasks manually—but what if we want a truly *hands-off* approach to task automation? We will explore scheduling tasks in the next section of this chapter.

Automating routine tasks with AWX

Although there are many facets to AWX that would require much more space than we have in this book, one particular one stands out—the automation of routine tasks. Routine tasks that Ansible could handle might include patching of servers, running some kind of compliance check or audit, or enforcing a security policy.

For example, you could write an Ansible playbook to ensure that the SSH daemon does not allow remote root logins as this is considered a good security practice. It is, of course, easy for any system administrator with root privileges to log in and turn this back on; however, running an Ansible playbook regularly to turn this off enforces it and ensures no-one (well-meaning or otherwise) turns it back on. The idempotent nature of Ansible changes means that where the configuration is already in place, Ansible will not make any changes, and hence running the playbook is safe, light on system resources, and non-disruptive.

If you wanted to do this with Ansible on the command line, you would need to create a cron job to run the `ansible-playbook` command regularly, along with all of the required parameters. This would mean having the SSH private keys installed on the server handling the automation, and means you have to keep track of which servers are running Ansible on a routine basis. This is not ideal for an enterprise where good practice is the byword of automation and ensures that everything keeps running smoothly.

Luckily, AWX can help us out here, too. To keep this example concise, we will reuse the LAMP stack example from the previous section of this chapter. In this scenario, we might want to schedule a one-off installation of the LAMP stack for a time when things are quiet, whereas for a routine task, it would be on an ongoing basis.

To set a schedule for this template, follow these steps:

1. Click on **Templates** on the left-hand menu bar.
2. Click on the template we created earlier.
3. Click on the **SCHEDULES** button at the top of the pane.
4. Click on the green + icon to add a new schedule to it.
5. Set the appropriate start date and time—I will set mine a few minutes from now to demonstrate it in action.
6. Also, set the appropriate timezone.
7. Finally, select the **REPEAT FREQUENCY**—in this example, I will choose **None (run once)**, but note that other ongoing options are available from the drop-down list.
8. Click on the green **SAVE** button to activate the schedule.

When you have completed the preceding steps, the resulting configuration screen should look something like the following:

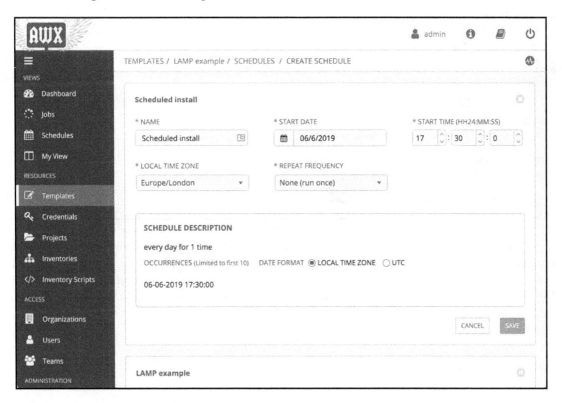

Now, if you watch the **Jobs** pane, you should see your template start to run at the scheduled time. When you analyze the completed (or indeed running) job, you should see that it was launched by the name of the schedule you created earlier, rather than by the name of a user account such as admin (as we saw when we launched it manually). A screenshot is provided here that shows an example of a completed job that was launched by our **Scheduled install** schedule that we created earlier in this section:

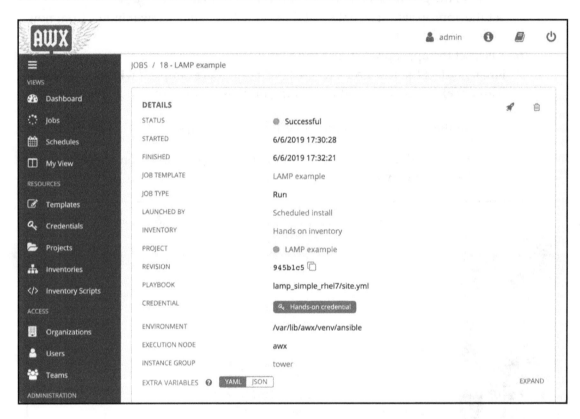

If you want to see all scheduled jobs that are forthcoming on your AWX instance, you can simply click on the **Schedules** menu item on the left-hand menu bar, and a screen will load that lists all configured schedules in your AWX instance. For those of you familiar with Linux administration, this is akin to listing cron jobs. An example of such a screen is shown in the following screenshot:

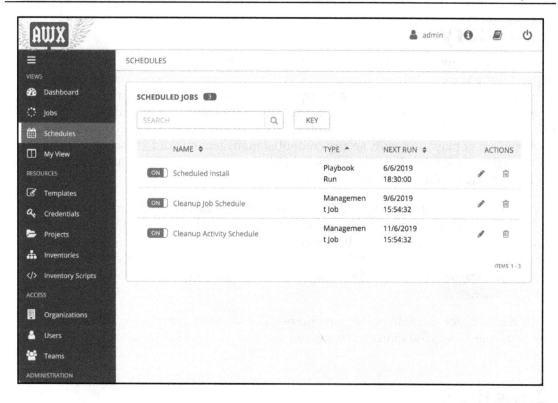

This gives you a concise overview of all of the schedules you have created, without having to go into the individual configuration items themselves to edit them.

In this way, AWX supports not just interactive automation of your Linux environment, but also hands-off scheduled automation tasks too, hence increasing the power and flexibility of your automation solution.

It is hoped that this overview gives you an idea of the benefits that a tool such as AWX or Ansible Tower can bring to your enterprise, and why it is beneficial to supplement your Ansible automation with this.

Summary

Ansible offers a great deal of power with just a small amount of learning, yet when deployed at a large scale in an enterprise, it can become more difficult to keep track of everything, especially which users have the latest versions of playbook code and who ran what playbook when. AWX supplements Ansible in the enterprise by bringing with it key benefits such as role-based access control, auditability, integrated source control management of playbook code, secure credential management, and job scheduling. It achieves this while providing an easy to use point and click interface, which further lowers the barrier to entry for all staff responsible for the Linux environment.

In this chapter, you learned why AWX is important to an Enterprise Linux environment and how to leverage a number of its key features. You then carried out a hands-on installation of a single AWX node before completing a practical end-to-end example of running a playbook directly from GitHub to install a LAMP stack on a CentOS 7 server. Finally, you learned about job scheduling to automate routine maintenance tasks using Ansible.

In the next chapter, we will look at the different deployment methodologies that are relevant to an Enterprise Linux environment and how to leverage these.

Questions

1. What is a key advantage of using AWX to store your credentials over the methods available to you on the command line?
2. Why is it important to make good use of a version control system such as Git to store your playbooks?
3. How is AWX advantageous over Ansible on the command line when it comes to dynamic inventories?
4. What is a project in AWX?
5. What is a template in AWX analogous to on the command line?
6. How does AWX tell you which commit to a Git repository a playbook run was performed against?
7. Why is it advisable to restrict access to the server that hosts AWX, especially the shell and local filesystem?
8. If you need to programmatically launch playbook runs, how can AWX help you?

Further reading

- For an in-depth understanding of Ansible including AWX, please refer to *Mastering Ansible, Third Edition* by *James Freeman* and *Jesse Keating* (`https://www.packtpub.com/gb/virtualization-and-cloud/mastering-ansible-third-edition`).
- To achieve a greater understanding of version control with Git and best practices associated with its use, please refer to *Git Best Practices Guide* by *Eric Pidoux* (`https://www.packtpub.com/application-development/git-best-practices-guide`).
- To understand how to access and work with the AWX API, please refer to `https://docs.ansible.com/ansible-tower/latest/html/towerapi/index.html`.
- If you wish to explore the control of AWX with the `tower-cli` tool, please refer to the official documentation here: `https://tower-cli.readthedocs.io/en/latest/`.

Section 2: Standardizing Your Linux Servers

2

This section presents a hands-on look at how to ensure that consistency and repeatability remain core facets of your Linux server environment, promoting best practices such as scalability, reproducibility, and efficiency.

This section comprises the following chapters:

- Chapter 4, *Deployment Methodologies*
- Chapter 5, *Using Ansible to Build Virtual Machine Templates for Deployment*
- Chapter 6, *Custom Builds with PXE Booting*
- Chapter 7, *Configuration Management with Ansible*

Deployment Methodologies

4

So far in this book, we have set the groundwork for a stable foundation for your Enterprise Linux environment. We have discussed in detail how to ensure your Linux environment lends itself well to automation through standardization and how to leverage Ansible and AWX to support you on your automation journey. Before we get started on the really detailed technical work in this chapter, we must take a look at one final piece of detail—your deployment methodology.

We have already established a need for a small number of consistent Linux builds for your environment. There is now a decision-making process for you to go through—how to deploy these builds across your enterprise. Most enterprises have several choices available to them, ranging from the easiest—downloading publicly available template images—through building their own templates, to perhaps the most complex—building from scratch using a pre-boot environment. Alternatively, the best approach might be some hybrid of these approaches. In this chapter, we will explore these options and understand how to ensure you are selecting the best one for your enterprise that supports you in your automation journey and is efficient and easy to implement. In subsequent chapters, we will then go into greater technical depth on each approach.

The following topics will be covered in this chapter:

- Knowing your environment
- Keeping builds efficient
- Ensuring consistency across Linux images

Technical requirements

This chapter assumes that you have access to a virtualization capable environment running Ubuntu 18.04 LTS. Some examples are also performed on CentOS 7. In either of these cases, the examples can be run on either a physical machine (or laptop) running one of the aforementioned operating systems, with a process that has virtualization extensions enabled, or a virtual machine with nested virtualization enabled.

Ansible 2.8 is also used later in this chapter and it is assumed you have this installed on the Linux host you are using.

All example code discussed in this book is available from GitHub at: `https://github.com/PacktPublishing/Hands-On-Enterprise-Automation-on-Linux`.

Knowing your environment

No two enterprise environments are the same. Some businesses still rely heavily on bare-metal servers, whilst others now rely on one of a myriad of virtualization or cloud providers (either private or public). Knowing which environments are available to you is a key part of the decision-making process.

Let's explore the various environments and the relevant build strategies for each.

Deploying to bare-metal environments

Bare-metal environments are without a doubt the grandfather of all enterprise environments. Before the revolution in virtualization and then cloud technologies throughout the 21st century, the only way to build an environment was on bare metal.

These days it is unusual to find an entire environment which is run on bare metal, though it is common to find ones where certain key components are run on physical hardware, especially databases or computational tasks that require certain physical hardware assistance (for example, GPU acceleration or hardware random number generation).

When building servers from bare metal, two fundamental approaches are suitable in most environments. The first is to build the servers manually using either optical media or, more commonly now, a USB drive. This is a slow, interactive process that is not repeatable at scale, and hence it is not recommended for any environments other than those containing just a handful of physical servers, where the requirement to build new machines is minimal and infrequent.

The other most viable option for building at scale in the repeatable, consistent manner that we have advocated throughout this book so far is to boot physical servers over the network, using a **Pre-eXecution Environment** (**PXE**). This involves loading a tiny boot environment from a network server, and then using this to load the Linux kernel and associated data. In this manner, it is possible to bring up an installation environment without the need for any form of physical media. Once the environment is up, we would use an unattended installation method to allow the installation to complete without any intervention from the user.

We will cover these methods in detail later in this book, as well as repeatable techniques for configuring the servers once they are built. In the meantime, however, it will suffice to simply state that, for building out physical Linux servers in an enterprise, PXE booting coupled with an unattended installation is the route that is easiest to automate and will produce the most repeatable results.

Deploying to traditional virtualization environments

Traditional virtualization environments are those that predate what we know today as cloud environments—that is to say, they are straightforward hypervisors on which operating systems are run. Commercial examples such as VMware are common, as well as their open source counterparts such as Xen and KVM (and frameworks built off of these, such as oVirt).

As these technologies were originally built to supplement traditional physical environments, they present several possible options for building out your Enterprise Linux estate. For example, most of these platforms support the same network-booting capabilities as their bare-metal counterparts, and hence we could actually just pretend they are bare metal and continue with a network booting methodology.

However, virtualized environments introduced something that was difficult to achieve in physical environments because of the differences in hardware between the bare-metal devices on which they all ran—templates. A templated virtual machine is quite simply a deployable snapshot of a preconfigured virtual machine. Hence, you might build out the perfect CentOS 7 image for your enterprise, integrate your monitoring platform, perform all of the security hardening required, and then, using tools built into the virtualization platform itself, turn it into a template. The following is a screenshot of the CentOS 7 templates in the author's lab environment:

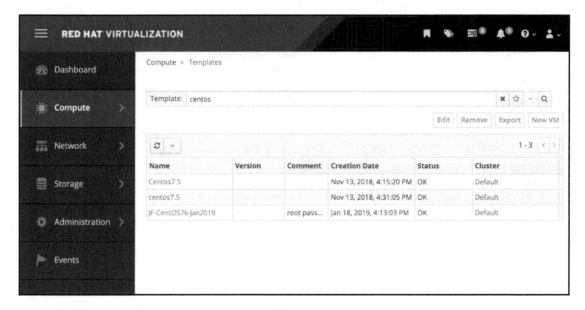

Each of these templates is a fully configured CentOS 7 base image ready to be deployed, with all pre-deployment work such as removal of SSH host keys completed. As a result, all an administrator has to do is to select the appropriate template and click on the **New VM** button—the process will be similar in platforms other than RHV, as most mainstream virtualization solutions provide this functionality in some guise.

 Note that, to keep the examples accessible, I have used the GUI as the primary process for creating a new VM. Nearly all virtualization and cloud platforms have APIs, command-line interfaces, and even Ansible modules that can be used to deploy virtual machines, and in an enterprise setting, these would scale far better than the GUI itself. Given the wide variety of environments available, this is left as an exercise for you to explore.

This is in itself a fairly straightforward process, but it requires a little care and attention. For example, nearly all Linux servers these days have SSH turned on, and the SSH daemon on each server has a unique host identification key that is used to prevent (amongst other things) man-in-the-middle attacks. If you template a preconfigured operating system, you will also template these keys, which means a distinct possibility of duplicates across your environment. This reduces security quite considerably. It is hence very important to perform several steps to prepare your virtual machine before turning it into a template, and one such common step is to delete the SSH host keys.

Servers created using the PXE method do not suffer from this problem, as they are all installed from scratch and hence there are no historic log entries to clean up and no duplicate SSH keys.

In Chapter 5, *Using Ansible to Build Virtual Machine Templates for Deployment*, we will go into detail on creating virtual machine templates suitable for templating using Ansible. Although both the PXE boot and template deployment methodologies are equally valid for virtualized environments, most people find the templated route to be more efficient and easier to manage, and for this reason, I also advocate it (for example, most PXE boot environments need to know the MAC address of the network interface used on the physical or virtual server being deployed—this is not a necessary step in template deployment).

Deploying to cloud environments

The most recent incumbent to Enterprise Linux architectures (barring of course containers, which is another discussion entirely) is the cloud provisioning environment. This might be through a *public cloud* solution such as **Amazon Web Services** (**AWS**), Microsoft Azure, **Google Cloud Platform** (**GCP**), or one of the myriad of smaller providers that have sprung up in recent years. It might equally be through an on-premise solution such as one of the variants of the OpenStack project or a proprietary platform.

These cloud environments have radically changed the life cycle of Linux machines in the enterprise. Whereas on bare-metal or traditional virtualized architectures, Linux machines were cared for, nurtured, and repaired if ever they failed, cloud architectures are built on the premise that each machine is more or less expendable, and that if it fails, a new one is simply deployed in its place.

As a result, PXE deployment methodologies are not even possible in such environments, and instead they rely on pre-built operating system images. These are in essence just a template either created by a third-party vendor or prepared by the enterprise.

Whether you go with a commercial provider or build an on-premise OpenStack architecture, you will find a catalog of available operating system images for you to choose from. Generally, those provided by the cloud provider themselves are trustworthy, though depending on your security requirements, you may find those provided by external parties suitable as well.

For example, here is a screenshot of the recommended operating system images available for OpenStack:

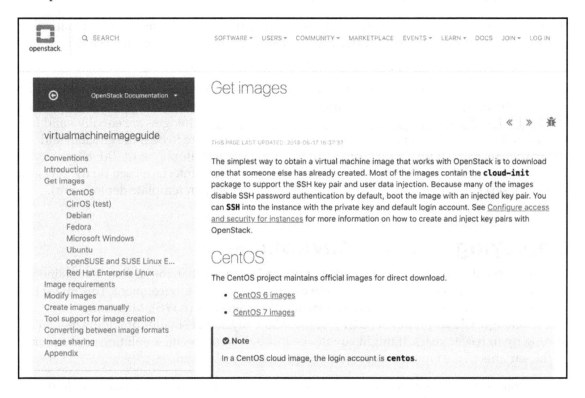

As you can see from the table of contents, most of the major Linux distributions are represented here, which immediately saves you the task of building the basic operating system itself. The same is true of AWS:

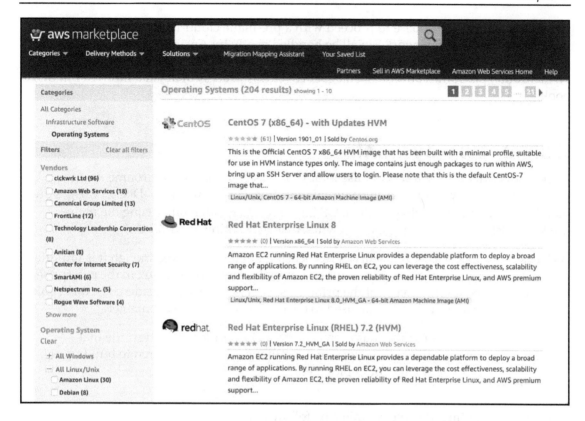

In short, if you are using a cloud environment, you will be spoiled for choice for base operating system images from which to get started. Even so, it is unlikely this choice will be sufficient for all enterprises. For example, using a pre-built, cloud-ready image does not negate requirements for things such as enterprise security standards, monitoring, or log forwarding agent integration, and a myriad of other things that are so important for the enterprise. Before we proceed, it is worth noting that you can, of course, create your own images for your chosen cloud platforms. In the interests of efficiency though, why re-invent the wheel? If someone has already completed this step for you, this is something that you can effectively delegate elsewhere.

Although most ready-made operating system images are trustworthy, you should always exercise caution when selecting a new one, especially if it has been created by an author you are unfamiliar with. There is no way to know for sure what the image comprises and you should always carry out due diligence when selecting an image to work with.

Assuming that you do choose to proceed with a pre-made cloud-ready image, the post-installation configuration work can all be handled neatly by Ansible. In fact, the steps required are almost identical to those required to build templates for traditional virtualization platforms, and we shall again cover this process in detail a little later in this book.

Docker deployments

Docker deployments are a special case in our discussion on Linux environments. In practical terms, they share a lot in common with cloud environments—Docker images are built based upon pre-existing minimal OS images and are often built using the native Docker toolchains, though automation with Ansible is entirely possible.

As Docker is a special case, we will not be focusing on it in this book, though it is important to note that Docker, being a recent incumbent into the presence of Linux in the enterprise, is actually designed around many of the principles we have already considered in this book. Let's briefly consider the Dockerfile used to create the official nginx container.

 For those not familiar with Docker, a Dockerfile is a flat text file that contains all the directives and commands that are required to build up a container image for deployment.

At the time of writing, this file contains the following:

```
#
# Nginx Dockerfile
#
# https://github.com/dockerfile/nginx
#

# Pull base image.
FROM ubuntu:bionic

# Install Nginx.
RUN \
  add-apt-repository -y ppa:nginx/stable && \
  apt-get update && \
  apt-get install -y nginx && \
  rm -rf /var/lib/apt/lists/* && \
  echo -e "\ndaemon off;" >> /etc/nginx/nginx.conf && \
  chown -R www-data:www-data /var/lib/nginx
```

Although not based on Ansible, we can see the following in the preceding code block:

1. The FROM line near the top defines a minimal Ubuntu base image on which to perform the rest of the configuration—this can be thought of as your SOE Linux image that we have discussed for other platforms.
2. The RUN command then performs the steps necessary to install the nginx package and perform some housekeeping to keep the image tidy and minimal (reducing space requirements and clutter).

The code then continues as follows:

```
# Define mountable directories.
VOLUME ["/etc/nginx/sites-enabled", "/etc/nginx/certs",
"/etc/nginx/conf.d", "/var/log/nginx", "/var/www/html"]

# Define working directory.
WORKDIR /etc/nginx

# Define default command.
CMD ["nginx"]

# Expose ports.
EXPOSE 80
EXPOSE 443
```

Continuing our analysis of this file, we can see the following:

1. The VOLUME line defines which directories from the host filesystem can be mounted within the container.
2. The WORKDIR directive tells Docker which directory to run the CMD that follows it in—think of it as a boot-time configuration.
3. The CMD line defines the command to run when the container starts—a microcosm of the process of defining which services will start at boot time in a full Linux system image.
4. Finally, the EXPOSE lines define which ports the container should expose to the network—perhaps a little like a firewall might allow certain ports through.

In short, the native process to build a Docker container is very much aligned with our defined build process for an Enterprise Linux environment—hence, we can proceed in confidence with this process. With this in mind, we will now explore the process of ensuring our builds are as tidy and efficient as possible.

Keeping builds efficient

Knowing the fundamentals of your Linux environment, as we discussed in the last section, is vital to working out your deployment methodology. Although there exist some similarities between the build processes themselves (especially between traditional hypervisors and cloud environments), knowing these differences enables you to make informed decisions about how to deploy Linux throughout your enterprise.

Once you have chosen the methodologies most appropriate to your environment, it's important to consider a few principles to ensure your process is streamlined and efficient (again, bywords of Enterprise Linux deployments). We will cover these here to proceed into the real in-depth, hands-on work in the remainder of this book. Let's get started by looking at the need for simplicity in our builds.

Keeping your builds simple

Let's start to put some practical application of our earlier discussion on the importance of SOEs to our Linux build processes. Whatever route you choose and whatever your environment looks like, one key facet you should consider is to keep your build standard as simple and concise as possible.

No two enterprise environments are the same, and hence the build requirements for each enterprise will certainly be different. Nonetheless, a common set of example requirements is given here to demonstrate the kinds of things that will be needed in the build process:

- Monitoring agents
- Log forwarding configuration
- Security hardening
- Core enterprise software requirements
- NTP configuration for time synchronization

This list is just a start, and every enterprise will be different, but it gives you an idea of the kinds of things that will go into a build. However, let's start to look at some of the edge cases to your build process. It is fair to say that each Linux server will be built with a purpose in mind and, as such, will run some form of application stack.

Again, the application stack is certain to vary between enterprises, but examples of the kinds of applications that might commonly be required are as follows:

- A web server such as Apache or nginx
- The OpenJDK environment for Java workloads

- A MariaDB database server
- A PostgreSQL database server
- NFS file-sharing tools and kernel extensions

Now, in your standardization process, when you originally defined your SOE, you may even have gone to the lengths of already specifying the use of (just as an example) OpenJDK 8 and MariaDB 10.1. Does this mean you should actually include these in your build process?

The answer is almost always, *no*. Quite simply, adding these applications adds to the complexity of the build and to post-install configuration and debugging. It also reduces security—but more on that shortly.

Let's suppose we standardize on MariaDB 10.1 and include that in our base operating system image (and hence every single Linux machine deployed contains it), knowing that only a subset of the machines in operation will actually ever use it.

There are several reasons for not including MariaDB in the base image:

- An install of just the server components of MariaDB 10.1 takes around 120 MB, depending on your operating system and packaging—there will also be dependency packages but let's just start with this. Although storage is cheap and plentiful these days, if you deploy 100 servers across your environment (actually a small number for most enterprises), that's approximately 11.7 GB of space dedicated to a package you don't need. The actual figure will be far higher as there will be dependency packages to install and so on.
- This may also have a knock-on effect on backups and the storage required for these, and indeed any virtual machine snapshots if you use that in the enterprise.
- If an application arrives that requires MariaDB 10.3 (or indeed, the business decides to update its standard to 10.3), then the images need to be upgraded or possibly version 10.1 uninstalled before 10.3 is installed. This is an unnecessary level of complexity when a minimal Linux image could just have received an updated MariaDB workload.
- You need to ensure that MariaDB is turned off and firewalled off when not required to as to prevent any misuse—this is an additional auditing and enforcement requirement that again is unnecessary on many servers where MariaDB isn't used.

There are other security considerations too, but the key message here is that it is wasteful on resources and time. This doesn't, of course, only apply to MariaDB 10.1—that is simply an example, but it serves to show that, as a rule, application workloads should not be included in the base operating system definition. Let's take a more detailed look at the security requirements for our builds now.

Making your builds secure

We have already touched on security and not installing or running unnecessary packages. Any running service provides a potential attack vector for an intruder, and whilst hopefully, you will never have one inside your enterprise network, it is still good practice to build the environment in a manner that is as secure as possible. This is especially true of services that come configured with default passwords (and in some cases, with no password configured at all—though this is thankfully becoming rare now).

These principles apply when defining the build itself too. Don't create a build with weak static passwords, for example. Ideally, every build should be configured to obtain even initial credentials from an external source, and although there are a myriad of ways to achieve this, you are encouraged to look up `cloud-init` if this is a new concept to you. There are cases, especially in legacy environments, where you may need some initial credentials to allow access to the newly built server, but reusing weak passwords is dangerous and opens up the possibility of the newly built server being intercepted before it is configured and some kind of malware planted on it.

In short, the following list provides some sound guidance on ensuring secure builds:

- Don't install applications or services that are not required.
- Do ensure services that are common to all builds but require post-deployment configuration are disabled by default.
- Don't re-use passwords even for initial access and configuration if at all possible.
- Do apply your enterprise security policy as early as possible in the process—in the build process of the image or server if possible, but if not, as soon as possible after installation.

These principles are simple yet fundamental, and it is important to adhere to them. Hopefully, a situation will never arise where it matters that they have been applied, but if it does, they might just stop or sufficiently impede an intrusion or attack on your infrastructure. This, of course, is a topic that deserves its own book, but it is hoped these pointers, along with the examples in Chapter 13, *Using CIS Benchmarks*, will point you in the right direction. Let's take a brief look now at ensuring our build processes are efficient.

Creating efficient processes

Efficient processes are supported heavily by automation, as this ensures minimal human involvement and consistent, repeatable end results. Standardization also supports this, as it means that much of the decision-making process has already been completed, and so all people involved know exactly what they are doing and how it should be done.

In short, stick to these principles outlined in this book and your build processes will, by their very nature, be efficient. Some degree of manual intervention is inevitable, even if it involves choosing a unique hostname (though this can be automated) or perhaps the process of a user requesting a Linux server in the first place. However, from here, you want to automate and standardize wherever possible. We will follow this mantra throughout this book. For now, though, we will take a look at the importance of consistency in our build processes.

Ensuring consistency across Linux images

In `Chapter 1`, *Building a Standard Operating Environment on Linux*, we discussed the importance of commonality in SOE environments. Now that we are actually looking at the build process itself, this comes back to the fore as we are, for the first time, looking at how to actually implement commonality. Assuming Ansible is your tool of choice, consider the following task. We are writing playbooks for our image build process and have decided that our standard image is to synchronize its time with our local time server. Suppose that our base operating system of choice is Ubuntu 16.04 LTS for historic reasons.

Let's create a simple role to ensure NTP is installed and to copy across our corporate standard `ntp.conf`, which includes the addresses of our in-house time servers. Finally, we need to restart NTP to pick up the changes.

 The examples in this chapter are purely hypothetical and given to demonstrate what Ansible code for a given purpose might look like. We will expand on the tasks performed (such as deploying configuration files) in detail in later chapters and provide hands-on examples for you to try out.

This role could look like the following:

```
---
- name: Ensure ntpd and ntpdate is installed
  apt:
    name: "{{ item }}"
    update_cache: yes
```

```
    loop:
      - ntp
      - ntpdate
  - name: Copy across enterprise ntpd configuration
    copy:
      src: files/ntp.conf
      dest: /etc/ntp.conf
      owner: root
      group: root
      mode: '0644'
  - name: Restart the ntp service
    service:
      name: ntp
      state: restarted
      enabled: yes
```

This role is simple, concise, and to the point. It always ensures the `ntp` package is installed, and also ensures we are copying across the same version of our configuration file, making sure it is the same on every server. We could improve this further by checking this file out of a version control system, but that is left as an exercise for you.

Instantly, you can see the power of writing an Ansible role for this one simple step—there is great consistency to be achieved from including this role in a playbook, and if you scale this approach up to your entire enterprise, then all configured services will be consistently installed and configured.

However, it gets better. Let's say that the business decides to rebase the standard operating system to Ubuntu 18.04 LTS to make use of newer technologies and increase the supported lifespan of the environment. The `ntp` package is still available on Ubuntu 18.04, though by default, the `chrony` package is now installed. To proceed with NTP, the role would need only minor tweaks to simply ensure that `chrony` is removed first (or you could disable it if you prefer)—after this, it is identical, for example, consider the following role code that ensures the correct packages are absent and present:

```
  ---
  - name: Remove chrony
    apt:
      name: chrony
      state: absent
  - name: Ensure ntpd and ntpdate is installed
    apt:
      name: "{{ item }}"
      update_cache: yes
    loop:
      - ntp
      - ntpdate
```

We would then continue this code by adding two further tasks that copy across the configuration and restart the service to ensure it picks up the new configuration:

```
- name: Copy across enterprise ntpd configuration
  copy:
    src: files/ntp.conf
    dest: /etc/ntp.conf
    owner: root
    group: root
    mode: '0644'
- name: Restart the ntp service
  service:
    name: ntp
    state: restarted
    enabled: yes
```

Alternatively, we could decide to embrace this change and make use of chrony on the new base image. Hence, we would simply need to create a new chrony.conf to ensure it talks to our enterprise NTP servers, and then proceed exactly as before:

```
---
- name: Ensure chrony is installed
  apt:
    name: chrony
    update_cache: yes
- name: Copy across enterprise chrony configuration
  copy:
    src: files/chrony.conf
    dest: /etc/chrony.conf
    owner: root
    group: root
    mode: '0644'
- name: Restart the chrony service
  service:
    name: chrony
    state: restarted
    enabled: yes
```

Notice how similar these roles all are? Only minor changes are required even when supporting a change in the base operating system or even underlying service.

Although these three roles differ in places, they are all performing the same basic tasks, which are as follows:

1. Ensure that the correct NTP service is installed.
2. Copy across the standard configuration.
3. Ensure the service is enabled at boot time and has started.

Hence, we can be sure that, using this approach, we have consistency.

Even when changing the platform entirely, the high-level approach can still be applied. Let's say that the enterprise has now taken on an application that is only supported on CentOS 7. This means an accepted deviation to our SOE, however, even our new CentOS 7 build will need to have the correct time, and as NTP is a standard, it will still use the same time servers. Hence, we can write a role to support CentOS 7:

```
---
- name: Ensure chrony is installed
  yum:
    name: chrony
    state: latest
- name: Copy across enterprise chrony configuration
  copy:
    src: files/chrony.conf
    dest: /etc/chrony.conf
    owner: root
    group: root
    mode: '0644'
- name: Restart the chrony service
  service:
    name: chronyd
    state: restarted
    enabled: yes
```

Again, the changes are incredibly subtle. This is a significant part of the reason for embracing Ansible as our automation tool of choice for enterprise automation—we can build and adhere to our standards with great ease, and our operating system builds are consistent if we change the version or even the entire distribution of Linux we are using.

Summary

At this stage, we have defined our requirement for standardization, established which tools to use in our journey toward automation, and now taken a practical look at the fundamental types of environments into which enterprises can expect to deploy an operating system. This has set the groundwork for our automation journey and has provided us with the context for the rest of this book—a hands-on journey through the process of building and maintaining a Linux environment in the enterprise.

In this chapter, we learned about the different types of environments into which Linux might be deployed and the different build strategies available to each. We then looked at some practical examples of ensuring that our builds are of a high standard and can be completed efficiently and repeatably. Finally, we started to look at the benefits of automation and how it can ensure consistency across builds, even when we change the entire underlying Linux distribution.

In the next chapter, we will begin our hands-on journey into Enterprise Linux automation and deployments, looking at how Ansible can be employed to build out virtual machine templates, whether from cloud environment images or from scratch.

Questions

1. What are the similarities between building a Docker container and an SOE?
2. Why would you not include MariaDB in your base build if it is only required on a handful of servers?
3. How would you ensure your base operating system image is as small as possible?
4. Why should you be careful about embedding passwords in your base operating system image?
5. How would you ensure all Linux images send their logs to your centralized logging server?
6. When would you not use a base image provided by a cloud provider and build your own instead?
7. How would you secure your SSH daemon configuration using Ansible?

Further reading

- For an in-depth understanding of Ansible, please refer to *Mastering Ansible, Third Edition* by *James Freeman* and *Jesse Keating* (`https://www.packtpub.com/gb/virtualization-and-cloud/mastering-ansible-third-edition`).
- To gain an understanding of the Docker code and discussion in this chapter, please refer to *Mastering Docker, Third Edition* by *Russ McKendrick* and *Scott Gallagher* (`https://www.packtpub.com/gb/virtualization-and-cloud/mastering-docker-third-edition`).

5
Using Ansible to Build Virtual Machine Templates for Deployment

So far in this book, we have covered in detail the groundwork for the remainder—that is to say, we have set the rationale for what we intend to do next and provided a *crash course* in our automation tool of choice, Ansible. From the preceding chapter, we know that, in an enterprise-scale environment, there are two fundamental methods for deploying Linux, and which of these to use is determined by the technologies in use in your environment and your intended goals.

In this chapter, we will cover in detail how to build virtual machine images that will serve on most virtualization and cloud platforms. The differences between these two platforms are subtle but distinct as we shall find out, and by the end of this chapter, you will know how to handle both environments with ease. We will start with a discussion on the initial build requirements, and then move on to configure and prepare the images for use in your chosen environment.

The following topics will be covered in this chapter:

- Performing the initial build
- Using Ansible to build and standardize the template
- Cleaning up the build with Ansible

Technical requirements

This chapter assumes that you have access to a virtualization-capable environment running Ubuntu 18.04 LTS. Some examples are also performed on CentOS 7. In either of these cases, the examples can be run on either a physical machine (or laptop) running one of the aforementioned operating systems, with a process that has virtualization extensions enabled or a virtual machine with nested virtualization enabled.

Ansible 2.8 is also used later in this chapter and it is assumed you have this installed on the Linux host you are using.

All example code discussed in this chapter is available from GitHub at: `https://github.com/PacktPublishing/Hands-On-Enterprise-Automation-on-Linux/tree/master/chapter05`.

Performing the initial build

As discussed in `Chapter 4`, *Deployment Methodologies*, whether you are using a traditional virtualization platform such as oVirt or VMware or a cloud-based one such as OpenStack or Amazon's EC2, your starting point for any Linux deployments (and hence further automation) will be a templated image.

In terms of the SOE we defined in `Chapter 1`, *Building a Standard Operating Environment on Linux*, the templated image is the very real initial manifestation of this. It is usually a small virtual machine image, with just enough software installed and configuration completed that it is useful in almost all scenarios it might be deployed in for the enterprise. As long as the image boots up cleanly with a unique hostname, SSH host keys, and such, then it can be customized almost immediately using further automation as we shall discover from `Chapter 7`, *Configuration Management with Ansible*, later in this book. Let's dive into the build process by taking a ready-made template image (provided by a third party) as our starting point.

Using ready-made template images

For most platforms, there are a large number of readily available images for you to download, and again, we discussed a few of these in the previous chapter. For many enterprises, these images will be sufficient. However, what if you absolutely need full control over your image definition? Perhaps you are adopting a new standard (at the time of writing, Red Hat Enterprise Linux 8 has just been released, and CentOS 8 will surely follow in due course), and you want to implement it early to gain experience and test workloads. What if you operate in a secure environment (perhaps payment card industry-compliant), and you absolutely have to have 100% confidence in how the image was built and there can be no risk of compromise?

This, of course, is not to say that any publicly available images are compromised or even likely to be, but historically there have been a handful of *man-in-the-middle* or *supply chain* attacks where attackers have compromised services not directly, but rather indirectly by attacking common components that are used as building blocks.

Most publicly available images come from trustworthy sources that have put in place a variety of checks and controls to ensure their integrity. Provided you make use of these checks, and perform due diligence on any images you download, most enterprises will find little need to create their own images from scratch, as automation tools such as Ansible will take care of all post-deployment configuration.

Let's take a practical example: suppose that, for a new set of deployments, we have decided to create an SOE based upon the Fedora 30 server image, and we will be running this on an OpenStack infrastructure:

1. We would download the cloud image from the official Fedora project web site—details can be found here, though note that the version number will change over time as new releases of Fedora arrive, at https://alt.fedoraproject.org/cloud/.

   Upon establishing the correct Fedora cloud image for our environment, we can download our required image with a command such as this:

   ```
   $ wget
   https://download.fedoraproject.org/pub/fedora/linux/releases/30/Clo
   ud/x86_64/images/Fedora-Cloud-Base-30-1.2.x86_64.qcow2
   ```

2. Simple enough—now, let's verify it. Verification instructions are normally provided with all major Linux releases, whether for ISOs or complete images, and those for our Fedora image download can be found at https://alt.fedoraproject.org/en/verify.html.

Let's run through the process and validate our image. First of all, we will import the official Fedora GPG key to validate the checksum file to make sure it hasn't been tampered with:

```
$ curl https://getfedora.org/static/fedora.gpg | gpg --import
```

3. Now we will download the checksum file for the cloud base images and verify it:

```
$ wget
https://alt.fedoraproject.org/en/static/checksums/Fedora-Cloud-30-1
.2-x86_64-CHECKSUM
$ gpg --verify-files *-CHECKSUM
```

4. Although you may get a warning about the key not being certified by a trusted signature (this is a facet of the way GPG key trust is established), the important thing is that the signature of the file is validated as good—see the following screenshot for an example of the output:

```
● ● ●                          james@automation-01: ~ (ssh)
~>  wget https://alt.fedoraproject.org/en/static/checksums/Fedora-Cloud-30-1.2-x
86_64-CHECKSUM
--2019-06-27 10:20:57--  https://alt.fedoraproject.org/en/static/checksums/Fedor
a-Cloud-30-1.2-x86_64-CHECKSUM
Resolving alt.fedoraproject.org (alt.fedoraproject.org)... 209.132.181.16, 8.43.
85.67, 85.236.55.6, ...
Connecting to alt.fedoraproject.org (alt.fedoraproject.org)|209.132.181.16|:443.
.. connected.
HTTP request sent, awaiting response... 200 OK
Length: 1799 (1.8K)
Saving to: ‛Fedora-Cloud-30-1.2-x86_64-CHECKSUM’

Fedora-Cloud-30-1.2 100%[====================>]   1.76K  --.-KB/s     in 0s

2019-06-27 10:20:58 (67.9 MB/s) - ‛Fedora-Cloud-30-1.2-x86_64-CHECKSUM’ saved [1
799/1799]

~> gpg --verify-files *-CHECKSUM
gpg: Signature made Fri 26 Apr 2019 07:38:05 PM UTC
gpg:                using RSA key EF3C111FCFC659B9
gpg: Good signature from "Fedora (30) <fedora-30-primary@fedoraproject.org>" [un
known]
gpg: WARNING: This key is not certified with a trusted signature!
gpg:          There is no indication that the signature belongs to the owner.
Primary key fingerprint: F1D8 EC98 F241 AAF2 0DF6  9420 EF3C 111F CFC6 59B9
```

5. As long as the signature verifies successfully, the last step is to validate the actual image against the checksums themselves, with the following command:

```
$ sha256sum -c *-CHECKSUM
```

You will get errors for any files that are in the `*-CHECKSUM` file that you haven't downloaded, but as you can see in the following screenshot, our downloaded image matches the checksum in the file and so we can proceed to use it:

```
● ● ●                          james@automation-01: ~ (ssh)
~> sha256sum -c *-CHECKSUM
Fedora-Cloud-Base-30-1.2.x86_64.qcow2: OK
sha256sum: Fedora-Cloud-Base-30-1.2.x86_64.raw.xz: No such file or directory
Fedora-Cloud-Base-30-1.2.x86_64.raw.xz: FAILED open or read
```

With these steps completed, we can proceed to use the downloaded image in our OpenStack platform. You may, of course, want to customize this image after deployment, and we will look at ways to do this later in this book. Just because you have chosen an *off-the-shelf* image does not mean it has to remain that way. Note that these steps will vary slightly for each Linux distribution, but the high-level procedure should be the same. The important thing is to validate all downloaded images.

There is also an issue of trust surrounding the use of publicly available operating system images. How do you know that the author removed all redundant services and sysprepped the image correctly? How do you know that there are no back doors or other vulnerabilities? Although there are many excellent publicly available images out there, you should always perform due diligence on any that you download and ensure they are fit for your environment.

What if you absolutely have to generate your own image, however? We will explore this in the next part of this chapter.

Creating your own virtual machine images

The preceding process described will be fine for many enterprises, but sooner or later, the requirement will come about to create your own completely customized virtual machine image. Fortunately, modern Linux distributions make it easy to achieve this, and you don't need to even be on the same platform as you are building.

Let's take a look at building a CentOS 7.6 virtual machine image using an Ubuntu 18.04 Server host:

1. The first step before we begin is to ensure that the build host is capable of running virtual machines—this is normally a set of CPU extensions that are included with most modern x86 systems. It is also possible to build virtual machine images using nested virtualization, that is, to create a virtual machine within another virtual machine. However, to do this, you will have to enable virtualization support in your build VM. The process for this varies from one hypervisor to another, and so we will not go into detail on this here.

 If you are using a VMware hypervisor to perform nested virtualization, you will need to enable **code profiling** support for the CPU as well as enabling **hypervisor applications**—some of the steps in this process will fail otherwise.

2. Once you have your build host up and running, you will need to install the Linux **Kernel-based Virtual Machine** (**KVM**) toolset—the commands to do this will vary depending upon your build host version of Linux, but on our Ubuntu host, we need to run the following commands:

```
$ sudo apt-get install libvirt-bin libvirt-doc libvirt-clients
virtinst libguestfs-tools libosinfo-bin
$ sudo gpasswd -a <your account> libvirt
$ sudo gpasswd -a <your account> kvm
$ logout
```

Note the need to add your user account to two KVM-related groups—you will also need to log out and back in again for these group changes to take effect.

3. Once this is complete, you will also need to download a local copy of the ISO image for your chosen Linux image. I use the following command to download an ISO image as it is sufficient for the CentOS 7.6 SOE image I am going to create:

```
$ wget
http://vault.centos.org/7.6.1810/isos/x86_64/CentOS-7-x86_64-Minima
l-1810.iso
```

4. With all of these pieces in place, you will now create an empty virtual machine disk image. The best format to choose for this is the **Quick Copy On Write** (**QCOW2**) format, which is compatible with OpenStack and most public cloud platforms. Hence, we will make this image as generic as possible to enable the widest array of support possible.

To create a blank 20 GB QCOW2 image in the current directory, we would run the following command:

```
$ qemu-img create -f qcow2 centos76-soe.qcow2 20G
```

Note that other image formats are available. If, for example, you were building exclusively for VMware, it would make sense to use the VMDK format instead:

```
$ qemu-img create -f vmdk centos76-soe.vmdk 20G
```

Note that both these commands create sparse images—that is, they are only as big as the data and metadata they contain. They can be turned later into pre-allocated images by your chosen hypervisor platform if you wish:

```
● ● ●                      james@automation-01: ~ (ssh)
~> qemu-img create -f qcow2 centos76-soe.qcow2 20G
Formatting 'centos76-soe.qcow2', fmt=qcow2 size=21474836480 cluster_size=65536 l
azy_refcounts=off refcount_bits=16
~> qemu-img create -f vmdk centos76-soe.vmdk 20G
Formatting 'centos76-soe.vmdk', fmt=vmdk size=21474836480 compat6=off hwversion=
undefined
~> ls -lh centos76-soe.*
-rw-r--r-- 1 james james 193K Jun 28 15:39 centos76-soe.qcow2
-rw-r--r-- 1 james james 2.6M Jun 28 15:39 centos76-soe.vmdk
~>
```

With the empty disk images created, it's time to install the VM image:

1. We will use the `virt-install` command to achieve this, which basically runs up a temporary VM for OS installation. Don't worry about parameters such as CPU and memory—as long as these are sufficient for the OS installation to be run, they will be fine—they do not have any bearing on the deployed virtual machine.

   Note the use of VNC in the `--graphics vnc,listen=0.0.0.0` option—we will use this to remotely control the virtual machine and complete the installation. You can choose another graphics option, such as SPICE, if you prefer.

2. The following command is an example of how to use `virt-install` to create a CentOS 7 image from the ISO we downloaded earlier, using the preceding 20 GB QCOW2 disk image we created:

```
$ virt-install --virt-type kvm \
--name centos-76-soe \
--ram 1024 \
```

```
--cdrom=CentOS-7-x86_64-Minimal-1810.iso \
--disk path=/home/james/centos76-soe.qcow2,size=20,format=qcow2 \
--network network=default \
--graphics vnc,listen=0.0.0.0 \
--noautoconsole \
--os-type=linux \
--os-variant=centos7.0 \
--wait=-1
```

Most of these parameters are self-explanatory, but pay particular attention to your environment. For example, if you have edited or removed the default network, the preceding command will fail. Similarly, ensure the correct paths for all files referenced.

To see the list of supported --os-variant parameters, run the osinfo-query os command.

Naturally, you would vary these parameters according to the operating system you are installing, your disk image name, and so on.

3. For now, let's run this command—when successful, it should inform you that you can connect to the virtual machine console to continue:

```
● ● ●                          james@automation-01: ~ (ssh)
~> virt-install --virt-type kvm \
> --name centos-76-soe \
> --ram 1024 \
> --cdrom=CentOS-7-x86_64-Minimal-1810.iso \
> --disk path=/home/james/centos76-soe.qcow2,size=20,format=qcow2 \
> --network network=default \
> --graphics vnc,listen=0.0.0.0 \
> --noautoconsole \
> --os-type=linux \
> --os-variant=centos7.0 \
> --wait=-1

Starting install...
Domain installation still in progress. Waiting for installation to complete.
```

4. We will now connect to it from another shell using the virt-viewer utility:

```
$ virt-viewer centos-76-soe
```

From here, you will install the operating system in the normal way. As we have discussed in `Chapter 4`, *Deployment Methodologies*, try to go for the most minimal install that you can. Don't worry too much about hostname and such, as these should get set later as part of the deployment process; specify the following:

1. Choose **KEYBOARD** and **LANGUAGE SUPPORT** most relevant to your locale.
2. Choose the appropriate **DATE & TIME** settings for your country.
3. Ensure **SOFTWARE SELECTION** is **Minimal Install** (this is the default).
4. Set **INSTALLATION DESTINATION**—there will only be one virtual hard drive attached to this VM using the preceding `virt-install` command, so this is simply a matter of selecting it.
5. Enable or disable **KDUMP** as appropriate.
6. Ensure networking is enabled under **NETWORK & HOST NAME**.

The resulting CentOS 7 installation settings screen should look something like the following screenshot:

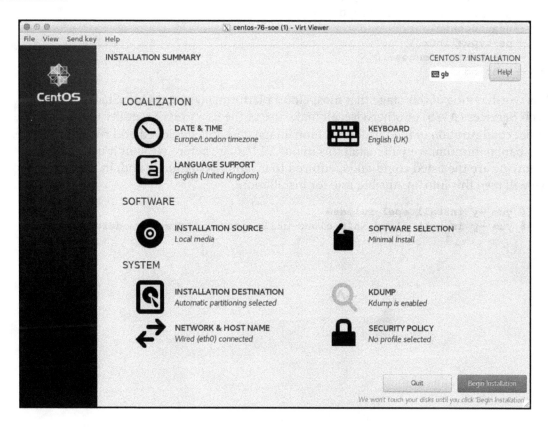

Allow the installation to complete as normal, and then log into the VM you have just created. Once logged into the running VM, you should perform any and all customization that you want to appear in the final version of the VM template. In the next section of this chapter, we will go into the use of Ansible for configuring deployed virtual machines, and using it to build templates is no different—hence, to prevent overlap with later chapters, we will not go into details of Ansible configuration work here.

When your VM goes to reboot after the initial installation, you may find that it shuts down. If it does, you will need to undefine it using the `virsh` utility, and then run it again using a slight variant on our previous `virt-install` command, telling `virt-install` to boot this time from the hard drive image rather than the CD:

```
$ virsh undefine centos-76-soe
$ virt-install --virt-type kvm \
--name centos-76-soe \
--ram 1024 \
--disk path=/home/james/centos76-soe.qcow2,size=20,format=qcow2 \
--network network=default \
--graphics vnc,listen=0.0.0.0 \
--noautoconsole \
--os-type=linux \
--os-variant=centos7.0 \
--boot=hd
```

It is worth noting at this stage that most cloud platforms, whether OpenStack, **Amazon Web Services** (**AWS**) or otherwise, all make use of the `cloud-init` utility to perform the initial configuration of the virtual machine image once it is deployed and running. Hence, as a bare minimum, we will install this in our VM image before we shut it down. The following are the listed commands required to install this manually and, in the next section, we will turn this into an Ansible role for installation:

```
$ yum -y install epel-release
$ yum -y install cloud-init cloud-utils-growpart dracut-modules-growroot
```

When you have completed these commands successfully, you will probably need to customize /etc/cloud/cloud.cfg to configure cloud-init for the environment you will use it in, although the default configuration serves as a good start for many environments.

 Configuring cloud-init is left as an exercise for you, given the wide variety of cloud platforms.

Finally, when you have performed any other customization you need, you can now shut the virtual machine down. Make sure to shut it down cleanly rather than simply powering it off, as this is going to become a template to be deployed at scale.

Once the virtual machine has been shut down, the next step is to run **system preparation** (**sysprep**) on the image, and then to compact the sparse image file to make it as small as possible for distribution and archival.

The process of sysprepping is to prepare an image for deployment at scale. Hence, all uniquely identifiable parameters will be wiped to produce a clean image for deployment at scale, such as the following:

- SSH host keys
- History files
- Local session configuration
- Log files
- MAC address references in network configuration

The preceding list is not exhaustive though—there are numerous items to clean up for an image to be considered truly clean and ready for deployment, and it would warrant an entire chapter by itself to explain them all. Fortunately for us, there are two commands in the suite of KVM tools that perform exactly these tasks for us:

```
$ sudo virt-sysprep -a centos76-soe.qcow2
$ sudo virt-sparsify --compress centos76-soe.qcow2 centos76-soe-final.qcow2
```

Although the output from the first command is too lengthy to fit in a single screenshot, it shows the wide variety of tasks that are considered necessary as part of sysprep, and if you find yourself running through this process either manually or with Ansible, the virt-sysprep utility should give you a good guideline as to the tasks you should perform:

```
●  ●  ●                    james@automation-01: ~ (ssh)

~> sudo virt-sysprep -a centos76-soe.qcow2
[   0.0] Examining the guest ...
[   5.8] Performing "abrt-data" ...
[   5.8] Performing "backup-files" ...
[   7.1] Performing "bash-history" ...
[   7.1] Performing "blkid-tab" ...
[   7.2] Performing "crash-data" ...
[   7.2] Performing "cron-spool" ...
[   7.2] Performing "dhcp-client-state" ...
[   7.2] Performing "dhcp-server-state" ...
[   7.2] Performing "dovecot-data" ...
[   7.2] Performing "logfiles" ...
[   7.2] Performing "machine-id" ...
[   7.2] Performing "mail-spool" ...
[   7.2] Performing "net-hostname" ...
[   7.2] Performing "net-hwaddr" ...
[   7.3] Performing "pacct-log" ...
[   7.3] Performing "package-manager-cache" ...
[   7.3] Performing "pam-data" ...
[   7.3] Performing "passwd-backups" ...
[   7.3] Performing "puppet-data-log" ...
[   7.3] Performing "rh-subscription-manager" ...
[   7.3] Performing "rhn-systemid" ...
[   7.3] Performing "rpm-db" ...
[   7.3] Performing "samba-db-log" ...
[   7.3] Performing "script" ...
[   7.3] Performing "smolt-uuid" ...
[   7.3] Performing "ssh-hostkeys" ...
[   7.3] Performing "ssh-userdir" ...
[   7.3] Performing "sssd-db-log" ...
[   7.3] Performing "tmp-files" ...
[   7.3] Performing "udev-persistent-net" ...
[   7.3] Performing "utmp" ...
```

Finally, we re-sparsify the disk image, effectively compacting it for efficient storage. Note that if you get any free space warnings when running this tool (it requires a great deal of space in /tmp by default—the exact amount will be determined by the size of your virtual disk image), you should generally not ignore them, as there is a chance the utility will fill up your partition, hence stopping your build host from working correctly:

```
james@automation-01: ~ (ssh)
~> sudo virt-sparsify --compress centos76-soe.qcow2 centos76-soe-final.qcow2
[   0.0] Create overlay file in /tmp to protect source disk
[   0.0] Examine source disk
[   3.2] Fill free space in /dev/centos/root with zero
 100% ⣿⣿⣿⣿⣿⣿⣿⣿⣿⣿⣿⣿⣿⣿⣿⣿⣿⣿⣿⣿⣿⣿⣿⣿⣿⣿⣿⣿⣿⣿⣿⣿⣿⣿⣿⣿⣿⣿⣿⣿⣿⣿⣿⣿⣿⣿⣿⣿⣿⣿⣿⣿⣿⣿⣿⣿⣿⣿⣿⣿⣿ 00:00
[  32.2] Clearing Linux swap on /dev/centos/swap
 100% ⣿⣿⣿⣿⣿⣿⣿⣿⣿⣿⣿⣿⣿⣿⣿⣿⣿⣿⣿⣿⣿⣿⣿⣿⣿⣿⣿⣿⣿⣿⣿⣿⣿⣿⣿⣿⣿⣿⣿⣿⣿⣿⣿⣿⣿⣿⣿⣿⣿⣿⣿⣿⣿⣿⣿⣿⣿⣿⣿⣿⣿ 00:00
[  36.2] Fill free space in /dev/sda1 with zero
[  37.8] Copy to destination and make sparse
[ 103.2] Sparsify operation completed with no errors.
virt-sparsify: Before deleting the old disk, carefully check that the
target disk boots and works correctly.
~>
```

The steps performed in this part of this chapter should work for just about any Linux distribution, being built on just about any Linux host. As ever, refer to the documentation for your preferred distribution for guidance on package names. Nonetheless, by following this process, you have now successfully built yourself a completely bespoke cloud image, which you should be able to upload to many of the popular cloud and hypervisor platforms.

From here, we will take a more detailed look at customizing the template with Ansible, rather than entering commands manually as we did in this section.

Using Ansible to build and standardize the template

You should, by now, have a base Linux image for deployment in your enterprise. If you chose to download a ready-made template (or indeed, to make use of one provided by a public cloud provider), then your image will be very much a blank template, ready for customization. If you chose to build your own, then you may have already chosen to perform a small amount of customization such as the installation of cloud-init that we performed earlier. You will note, however, that we did this by hand, which is hardly along the line of the scalable, repeatable, auditable processes that we have lauded throughout the early parts of this book. As we proceed through this section of this chapter, we will take a look at how to customize a base template, regardless of its origin, using Ansible.

There is no one-size-fits-all Linux image that will suit everyone, and as a result, this chapter is not definitive. We will, however, look at some of the more common tasks that might be associated with customizing as an image for deployment, such as the following:

- Transferring files into the image
- Installing packages
- Editing configuration files
- Validating the image

Through a combination of these examples, most readers should be able to customize their own images to their requirements with ease. Let's start exploring this in greater depth with a look at how to transfer files into the virtual machine image we created previously using Ansible.

Transferring files into the image

It is commonplace, in the experience of the author, to need to *inject* files into an operating system image to ensure it meets a given set of requirements. These files might be a simple text file, such as an enterprise-standard *message of the day*, a configuration file for an existing package, or perhaps even a binary file that is not available in a package. Ansible can handle all of these with ease, so let's look at some specific examples. As it is generally good practice to write your Ansible code in roles to support reuse and readability, we will define a role for our example here. In this example, I am making the following assumptions:

- We have downloaded/built our Linux template as outlined in the previous section of this chapter.
- We are running this bare template in a virtual machine.
- The IP address of this virtual machine is `192.168.81.141`.
- The virtual machine has a user account already set up with the following credentials:
    - Username: `imagebuild`.
    - Password: `password`.
    - This account is sudo-enabled.

Naturally, we would not distribute a cloud image with a sudo-enabled account that uses a weak password like this, so we are assuming we will use this account during the build phase only and then will remove it during the cleanup phase. Ansible needs to be able to connect to a remote host to perform its magic, but the account it uses can be transient in nature and removed after use:

1. Under our example, we would create an inventory file that looks like this—yours will undoubtedly be different and customizing it for your image and environment is left as an exercise for you:

```
[imagesetup]
192.168.81.141

[imagesetup:vars]
ansible_user=imagebuild
ansible_password=password
ansible_sudo_pass=password
```

This is a very simple example; in many ways, it is the bare minimum needed for this process when we do not have SSH key authentication configured. Often SSH keys are the best way to handle SSH authentication as they offer several benefits, not least that tasks can run without a password prompt.

Although this inventory file is intended to be transient in nature, it is still best practice to use `ansible-vault` to store passwords and this is recommended here. For the sake of simplicity in this chapter and to reduce the number of steps that you need to complete, we will leave the passwords unencrypted (in cleartext).

2. Next, we'll create the basic directory structure for our role:

```
$ mkdir -p roles/filecopyexample/tasks
$ mkdir -p roles/filecopyexample/files
```

3. Now, let's create a few sample files to copy across. First of all, create a customized message to append to the message of the day in `roles/filecopyexample/files/motd`:

```
------------------------
Enteprise Linux Template
Created with Ansible
------------------------
```

4. Let's also create a new configuration file for the `chrony` service to synchronize time to our corporate time servers in `roles/filecopyexample/files/chrony.conf`:

```
pool ntp.example.com iburst maxsources 4

keyfile /etc/chrony/chrony.keys

driftfile /var/lib/chrony/chrony.drift

logdir /var/log/chrony

maxupdateskew 100.0

rtcsync

makestep 1 3
```

We intend to copy these two files across to the remote server. However, Ansible is not limited to copying files from the Ansible host—it can also download files from a remote server directly to the target host:

1. Let's suppose your build is going to need `docker-compose`—we could download this from an internal server, or even directly from the internet if your image machine has access to the internet. Suppose we want to install `docker-compose` 1.18.0 into our images, we can instruct Ansible to download this directly from `https://github.com/docker/compose/releases/download/1.18.0/docker-compose-Linux-x86_64`.

2. Now, let's build our role to copy across our two files and download `docker-compose` into our image—this must be written in `roles/filecopyexample/tasks/main.yml`. The first part of this role is shown in the following code, and serves to copy across the two configuration files we discussed earlier:

```
---
- name: Copy new MOTD file, and backup any existing file if it
exists
  copy:
    src: files/motd
    dest: /etc/motd
    owner: root
    group: root
    mode: '0644'
    backup: yes
- name: Copy across new chrony configuration, and backup any
```

```
existing file if it exists
  copy:
    src: files/chrony.conf
    dest: /etc/chrony.conf
    owner: root
    group: root
    mode: '0644'
    backup: yes
```

The role then continues, with the task of installing `docker-compose` on the VM image:

```
- name: Install docker-compose 1.18.0
  get_url:
    url:
https://github.com/docker/compose/releases/download/1.18.0/docker-c
ompose-Linux-x86_64
    dest: /usr/local/bin/docker-compose
    mode: 0755
    owner: root
    group: root
```

Hence, our role is now complete, though be sure to customize it correctly for your environment. For example, it is likely a newer version of `docker-compose` might be available and this will mean a change to the `url` parameter of the preceding `get_url` module.

The path of the `chrony` configuration file may vary depending on your operating system—check this before running the preceding playbook. The path shown in the example is suitable for a CentOS 7 system like the one we built earlier.

3. Finally, we will create a file in the top-level directory (where the `roles/` directory was created) called `site.yml` to call and run this role. This should contain the following:

```
---
- name: Run example roles
  hosts: all
  become: yes

  roles:
    - filecopyexample
```

4. Finally, let's run our example with the `ansible-playbook -i hosts site.yml` command and see what happens:

```
● ● ●                   james@automation-01: ~/hands-on-automation/chapter05/example01 (ssh)
~/hands-on-automation/chapter05/example01> ansible-playbook -i hosts site.yml

PLAY [Run example roles] ************************************************************

TASK [Gathering Facts] *************************************************************
ok: [192.168.81.141]

TASK [filecopyexample : Copy new MOTD file, and backup any existing file if it e
xists] ***
changed: [192.168.81.141]

TASK [filecopyexample : Copy across new chrony configuration, and backup any exi
sting file if it exists] ***
changed: [192.168.81.141]

TASK [filecopyexample : Install docker-compose 1.18.0] *************************
changed: [192.168.81.141]

PLAY RECAP ************************************************************************
192.168.81.141              : ok=4     changed=3     unreachable=0     failed=0

~/hands-on-automation/chapter05/example01> docker-compose
Define and run multi-container applications with Docker.

Usage:
  docker-compose [-f <arg>...] [options] [COMMAND] [ARGS...]
  docker-compose -h|--help
```

As we can see, the `changed` statuses tell us that all three of our files were transferred or downloaded successfully, and by way of example, we can see that it is now possible to run `docker-compose`, which was installed during the playbook run (though this would require Docker to run correctly, which we have not installed as part of this example).

Obviously this example has made a fundamental assumption—that the `chrony` package was installed on our example image during the build phase. Although it makes sense to start with a minimal operating system image for the reasons we have discussed previously, there is almost certainly going to be a requirement to install a few supplemental packages on the basic build, and we will explore this in the next section.

Installing packages

We have looked at how to install a standalone binary such as `docker-compose` in the previous section—but what if we need to actually install some additional operating system packages that were not installed in our base image? For example, `cloud-init` is incredibly useful in most cloud environments but was not included in our minimal CentOS 7 install that we performed earlier.

Here, again, Ansible can help—this time, we will define a role to install the packages we require. We'll reuse the inventory file from the previous section and create a new role called `packageinstall` in the same manner that we did before:

1. Now, the preceding example on copying files would work on all Linux distributions—the only thing you need to be mindful of is where destination files might life. For example, our CentOS 7 VM image will have the `chrony` configuration file installed in `/etc/chrony.conf`, whilst an Ubuntu 18.04 LTS server would have it in `/etc/chrony/chrony.conf`. Apart from this small change to the `dest:` parameter of the `copy` module, the code would remain the same.

   Unfortunately, it gets a little more complex with package installation.

2. Let's suppose we want to install `cloud-init` and `docker` on our CentOS 7 example image—the role required to do this might look like this:

   ```
   ---
   - name: Install the epel-release package
     yum:
       name: epel-release
       state: present

   - name: Install cloud-init and docker
     yum:
       name: "{{ item }}"
       state: present
     loop:
       - cloud-init
       - docker
   ```

3. We must install the EPEL repository first, and then we can install the required packages. When we run it, the output should look something like this:

```
● ● ●                    james@automation-01: ~/hands-on-automation/chapter05/example02 (ssh)
~/hands-on-automation/chapter05/example02> ansible-playbook -i hosts site.yml

PLAY [Run example roles] ********************************************************

TASK [Gathering Facts] **********************************************************
ok: [192.168.81.144]

TASK [packageinstall : Install the epel-release package] ************************
changed: [192.168.81.144]

TASK [packageinstall : Install cloud-init and docker] **************************
changed: [192.168.81.144] => (item=cloud-init)
changed: [192.168.81.144] => (item=docker)

PLAY RECAP **********************************************************************
192.168.81.144             : ok=3    changed=2    unreachable=0    failed=0

~/hands-on-automation/chapter05/example02>
```

If you are using a different Linux distribution, then you need to vary the package manager accordingly. For example, on distributions that use the apt package manager such as Debian or Ubuntu, the equivalent Ansible role would look like the following block of code:

```
---
- name: Install cloud-init and docker
  apt:
    name: "{{ item }}"
    state: present
  loop:
    - cloud-init
    - docker.io
```

Note the change in module from yum to apt, and the different package name used for the Docker container service. Other than that, the playbook is almost identical.

We can improve on this further—this different results in the need to maintain two different roles for two different operating system bases—but what if we could intelligently combine them into one? Fortunately, the facts that Ansible gathers when it first runs can be used to identify the operating system and, as such, run the correct code.

We will repurpose our earlier example code to combine both of these installations into one Ansible role:

1. The first part of the code is almost identical to the preceding example, except that we have now specified the `when` clause to ensure it is only run on Debian- or Ubuntu-based Linux distributions:

```
---
- name: Install cloud-init and docker
  apt:
    name: "{{ item }}"
    state: present
  loop:
    - cloud-init
    - docker.io
  when: ansible_distribution == 'Debian' or ansible_distribution ==
'Ubuntu'
```

2. We then add two further tasks that perform the required steps to install Docker on CentOS or Red Hat Enterprise Linux:

```
- name: Install the epel-release package
  yum:
    name: epel-release
    state: present
  when: ansible_distribution == 'CentOS' or ansible_distribution ==
'Red Hat enterprise Linux'

- name: Install cloud-init and docker
  yum:
    name: "{{ item }}"
    state: present
  loop:
    - cloud-init
    - docker
  when: ansible_distribution == 'CentOS' or ansible_distribution ==
'Red Hat enterprise Linux'
```

Notice again the when clauses under each task—these specific examples are used to determine whether the tasks should be run depending on the facts that Ansible obtained during the initial part of the run. Hence, if we now run this role on an Ubuntu system, we see the following:

```
● ● ●               james@automation-01: ~/hands-on-automation/chapter05/example04 (ssh)

~/hands-on-automation/chapter05/example04> ansible-playbook -i hosts site.yml

PLAY [Run example roles] ************************************************************

TASK [Gathering Facts] **************************************************************
ok: [192.168.81.141]

TASK [packageinstall : Install cloud-init and docker] ***************************
ok: [192.168.81.141] => (item=cloud-init)
ok: [192.168.81.141] => (item=docker.io)

TASK [packageinstall : Install the epel-release package] *********************
skipping: [192.168.81.141]

TASK [packageinstall : Install cloud-init and docker] ***************************
skipping: [192.168.81.141] => (item=cloud-init)
skipping: [192.168.81.141] => (item=docker)

PLAY RECAP **************************************************************************
192.168.81.141              : ok=2    changed=0    unreachable=0    failed=0

~/hands-on-automation/chapter05/example04>
```

3. As you can see, the first task related to apt was run, but the two following ones based on yum were skipped because the conditions of the when clause were not met. Now, if we run it on a CentOS 7 target instead, we see this:

```
● ● ●          james@automation-01: ~/hands-on-automation/chapter05/example04 (ssh)
~/hands-on-automation/chapter05/example04> ansible-playbook -i hosts site.yml

PLAY [Run example roles] ********************************************************

TASK [Gathering Facts] **********************************************************
ok: [192.168.81.144]

TASK [packageinstall : Install cloud-init and docker] ***************************
skipping: [192.168.81.144] => (item=cloud-init)
skipping: [192.168.81.144] => (item=docker.io)

TASK [packageinstall : Install the epel-release package] ************************
ok: [192.168.81.144]

TASK [packageinstall : Install cloud-init and docker] ***************************
ok: [192.168.81.144] => (item=cloud-init)
ok: [192.168.81.144] => (item=docker)

PLAY RECAP **********************************************************************
192.168.81.144             : ok=3    changed=0    unreachable=0    failed=0

~/hands-on-automation/chapter05/example04>
```

The inverse is now true: the `apt` task was skipped, but the two `yum` related tasks were run. In this way, it is possible to maintain a single role for installing a common set of package requirements, even when dealing with several different base operating systems. Combining `when` clauses with Ansible facts is a very powerful way to ensure the correct behavior of a single code base across a variety of systems, and hence if your SOE does extend to both Debian and Red Hat-based systems, you can still maintain code with ease and simplicity.

Once supplemental packages have been installed, they often must be configured for them to be useful. In the next section, we will explore the use of Ansible in editing configuration files.

Editing configuration files

So far, all of the configuration work we have performed has been very black and white—we are either installing something (be that a file or a package), or we could equally and just as easily delete it (more on this in the section on cleaning up). However, what if something more subtle is required? Earlier in this chapter, in the section entitled *Transferring files into the image*, we replaced the entire `chrony.conf` file with our own version. This, however, might be a bit too much brute force—for example, we might only need to change one line in a file, and replacing the entire file to change one line is a bit heavy-handed, especially when you consider that the configuration file might get updated in a future package version.

Let's take another common operating system image configuration requirement: SSH daemon security. By default, CentOS 7 installations like the one we created earlier allow remote logins from the root account. This is not desirable for security reasons, so the question is, how do we update the SSH daemon configuration without having to replace the entire file? Luckily, Ansible has modules for just such a task.

To perform this task, the `lineinfile` module will come in handy. Consider the following role, which we'll call `securesshd`:

```
---
- name: Disable root logins over SSH
  lineinfile:
    dest: /etc/ssh/sshd_config
    regexp: "^PermitRootLogin"
    line: "PermitRootLogin no"
    state: present
```

Here, we are using the `lineinfile` module to process the `/etc/ssh/sshd_config` file. We are telling it to look for lines beginning with `PermitRootLogin` (this prevents us from accidentally editing commented-out lines), and then to replace this line with `PermitRootLogin no`.

Let's try that against a CentOS 7 test system:

```
● ● ●              james@automation-01: ~/hands-on-automation/chapter05/example05 (ssh)
~/hands-on-automation/chapter05/example05> ansible-playbook -i hosts site.yml

PLAY [Run example roles] ********************************************************

TASK [Gathering Facts] **********************************************************
ok: [192.168.81.144]

TASK [securesshd : Disable root logins over SSH] ********************************
changed: [192.168.81.144]

PLAY RECAP **********************************************************************
192.168.81.144              : ok=2    changed=1    unreachable=0    failed=0

~/hands-on-automation/chapter05/example05>
```

This works just as desired. Regular expressions require a great deal of care though. For example, the SSH daemon will process configuration lines that contain whitespace at the beginning of the line. However, our simple regular expression in the preceding code does not take account of whitespace, and so could easily miss an otherwise valid SSH configuration directive. To craft regular expressions that take account of all possible situations and permutations of a file is an art in itself and so caution is most definitely advised in their creation and use.

TIP

> Note that, on a live system, you would also need to restart the SSH service
> to make this change effective; however, as this is an image that we will
> clean up and then shut down for future deployment, there is no need to
> do this here.

A halfway house between uploading an entire file and editing an existing one is the use of templates. Ansible Jinja2 templating is incredibly powerful and very useful where files might have to have contents that vary with some variable parameter.

Consider again our `chrony` configuration example from earlier—here, we transferred a static file with a hardcoded NTP server address. This is fine if your enterprise relies on a static NTP server (or a set of them), but some will rely on different NTP servers depending on where the image is to be deployed.

Let's demonstrate this with a new role called `templatentp`. For this, we will define a templates directory in `roles/templatentp/templates` and place into it a file called `chrony.conf.j2` with the following contents:

```
pool {{ ntpserver }} iburst maxsources 4

keyfile /etc/chrony/chrony.keys

driftfile /var/lib/chrony/chrony.drift

logdir /var/log/chrony

maxupdateskew 100.0

rtcsync

makestep 1 3
```

Notice that the file is almost identical to the previous example, except that we now have an Ansible variable name in place of the static hostname on the first line of the file.

Let's create the `main.yml` file for the role as follows:

```
---
- name: Deploy chrony configuration template
  template:
    src: templates/chrony.conf.j2
    dest: /etc/chrony.conf
    owner: root
    group: root
    mode: '0644'
    backup: yes
```

Notice how similar it is to the `copy` example. Our `site.yml` is also only slightly different—in it, we will define the variable with the NTP server hostname. There are many places in Ansible where this variable could be defined, and it is left to the user to figure out the best place for them to define it:

```
---
- name: Run example roles
  hosts: all
  become: yes

  vars:
    ntpserver: time.example.com

  roles:
    - templatentp
```

Finally, we can run the playbook and see the results:

```
● ● ●              james@automation-01: ~/hands-on-automation/chapter05/example06 (ssh)
~/hands-on-automation/chapter05/example06> ansible-playbook -i hosts site.yml

PLAY [Run example roles] ************************************************************

TASK [Gathering Facts] *************************************************************
ok: [192.168.81.144]

TASK [templatentp : Deploy chrony configuration template] **************************
changed: [192.168.81.144]

PLAY RECAP *************************************************************************
192.168.81.144              : ok=2     changed=1     unreachable=0     failed=0

~/hands-on-automation/chapter05/example06>
```

In this way, Ansible provides you with powerful tools to not only copy or download entire configurations into place, but also to manipulate existing ones to suit your environment. Let's suppose that our image is now complete. We could take this on faith, but good practice suggests we should always test the result of any build process, especially an automated one. Thankfully, Ansible can help us to validate the image we have created according to our requirements, and we will explore this in the next section.

Validating the image build

As well as installing and configuring your image, you might also wish to verify that certain components that are critical, and that you assume to be present, are actually present. This is especially true when you download an image that was created by someone else.

There are many ways to perform this task in Ansible—let's take a simple example. Suppose you have an archival script that makes use of the `bzip2` compression utility to compress files. This is just a small tool but if you rely on it for certain purposes, your scripts would break if it was not present. It is also a pertinent example, as the minimal install of CentOS 7 (as we performed earlier) does not actually include it!

How can Ansible solve this problem? There are two approaches we can take. First of all, we know from our earlier background work on Ansible that most modules are idempotent—that is, they are designed to achieve a desired state on the target host and not repeat actions that have already been performed.

Hence, we could have very easily included a role such as this in our configuration playbook:

```
---
- name: Ensure bzip2 is installed
  yum:
    name: bzip2
    state: present
```

When this role is run and `bzip2` is not installed, it will perform the installation and return the result `changed`. When it detects that `bzip2` is installed, it will return `ok` and perform no further actions. However, what if we truly want to check for something rather than just perform an action, perhaps as a post-build step? Later in this book, we'll look at more detailed ways of auditing systems, but for now, let's further this example with Ansible.

If you were using shell commands, you would check for the presence of `bzip2` in one of two ways, that is, query the RPM database to see whether the `bzip2` package is installed or check for the presence of `/bin/bzip2` on the filesystem.

1. Let's look at the latter example in Ansible. The Ansible `stat` module can be used to verify the existence of a file. Consider the following code, which we'll create in a role called `checkbzip2` in the usual manner:

   ```
   ---
   - name: Check for the existence of bzip2
     stat:
       path: /bin/bzip2
     register: bzip2result
     failed_when: bzip2result.stat.exists == false

   - name: Display a message if bzip2 exists
     debug:
       msg: bzip2 installed.
   ```

Here, we are using the `stat` module to tell us about the `/bin/bzip2` file (if it exists). We `register` the result of the module run in a variable called `bzip2result`, and then we define a custom failure condition on the task that will cause it to fail (and hence fail the entire the playbook run) if the file does not exist. Note that when a failure condition is encountered, Ansible halts the entire playbook run, forcing you to address the issue before continuing. Obviously, this may or may not be the behavior you desire, but it is easy to vary the failure condition accordingly.

2. Let's take a look at this in action:

```
● ● ●          james@automation-01: ~/hands-on-automation/chapter05/example07 (ssh)
~/hands-on-automation/chapter05/example07> ansible-playbook -i hosts site.yml

PLAY [Run example roles] ************************************************************

TASK [Gathering Facts] **************************************************************
ok: [192.168.81.144]

TASK [checkbzip2 : Check for the existence of bzip2] ********************************
fatal: [192.168.81.144]: FAILED! => {"changed": false, "failed_when_result": tru
e, "stat": {"exists": false}}

PLAY RECAP **************************************************************************
192.168.81.144             : ok=1    changed=0    unreachable=0    failed=1

~/hands-on-automation/chapter05/example07>
```

As you can see, the debug statement was never run because of the failure encountered. Hence, we can be absolutely sure when running this role that our image is going to have `bzip2` installed—if it doesn't, our playbook will fail.

3. Once `bzip2` is installed, the run looks quite different:

```
● ● ●          james@automation-01: ~/hands-on-automation/chapter05/example07 (ssh)
~/hands-on-automation/chapter05/example07> ansible-playbook -i hosts site.yml

PLAY [Run example roles] ************************************************************

TASK [Gathering Facts] **************************************************************
ok: [192.168.81.144]

TASK [checkbzip2 : Check for the existence of bzip2] ********************************
ok: [192.168.81.144]

TASK [checkbzip2 : Display a message if bzip2 exists] ******************************
ok: [192.168.81.144] => {
    "msg": "bzip2 installed."
}

PLAY RECAP **************************************************************************
192.168.81.144             : ok=3    changed=0    unreachable=0    failed=0

~/hands-on-automation/chapter05/example07>
```

This is quite definitive in its behavior, which is exactly what we would want. Ansible is not just limited to checking for files though—we could also check that our `sshd_config` file has the `PermitRootLogin no` line we looked at earlier:

1. We could do this with a role as follows:

```
---
- name: Check root login setting in sshd_config
  command: grep -e "^PermitRootLogin no" /etc/ssh/sshd_config
  register: grepresult
  failed_when: grepresult.rc != 0

- name: Display a message if root login is disabled
  debug:
    msg: root login disabled for SSH
```

2. Now, running this when the setting is not in place again yields a failure:

```
james@automation-01: ~/hands-on-automation/chapter05/example08 (ssh)
~/hands-on-automation/chapter05/example08> ansible-playbook -i hosts site.yml

PLAY [Run example roles] ***********************************************

TASK [Gathering Facts] *************************************************
ok: [192.168.81.144]

TASK [checksshdroot : Check root login setting in sshd_config] *********
fatal: [192.168.81.144]: FAILED! => {"changed": true, "cmd": ["grep", "-e", "^Pe
rmitRootLogin no", "/etc/ssh/sshd_config"], "delta": "0:00:00.003986", "end": "2
019-07-02 09:36:10.801677", "failed_when_result": true, "msg": "non-zero return
code", "rc": 1, "start": "2019-07-02 09:36:10.797691", "stderr": "", "stderr_lin
es": [], "stdout": "", "stdout_lines": []}

PLAY RECAP *************************************************************
192.168.81.144             : ok=1    changed=0    unreachable=0    failed=1

~/hands-on-automation/chapter05/example08>
```

3. Yet if we put this setting in place, we see the following:

```
● ● ●                james@automation-01: ~/hands-on-automation/chapter05/example08 (ssh)
~/hands-on-automation/chapter05/example08> ansible-playbook -i hosts site.yml

PLAY [Run example roles] ***************************************************

TASK [Gathering Facts] *****************************************************
ok: [192.168.81.144]

TASK [checksshdroot : Check root login setting in sshd_config] *************
changed: [192.168.81.144]

TASK [checksshdroot : Display a message if root login is disabled] *********
ok: [192.168.81.144] => {
    "msg": "root login disabled for SSH"
}

PLAY RECAP *****************************************************************
192.168.81.144             : ok=3    changed=1    unreachable=0    failed=0

~/hands-on-automation/chapter05/example08> █
```

Again, it's very definitive. Note the `changed` status in the preceding output—this is so because we used the `command` module, which successfully ran `command`—hence, it always returns `changed`. We could alter this behavior with a `changed_when` clause to this task if we wanted.

In this manner, Ansible playbooks can be put together that not only customize your build but also validate the end result. This is especially useful for testing purposes, and where security is a consideration.

Before completing this chapter, let's take a look, in the next section, at how we pull together all of the disparate roles and pieces of code we have discussed so far to form a cohesive automated solution.

Putting it all together

Throughout this section of this chapter, you will note that we have used roles for all of our examples. Naturally, when it comes to building out your final image, you don't want to end up running lots of playbooks individually as we have done here. Luckily, if we were to combine everything, all we would need to do is put all of the roles together in the `roles/` subdirectory, and then reference them all in the `site.yml` playbook. The `roles` directory should look something like this:

```
~/hands-on-automation/chapter05/example09/roles> tree -d
.
├── checkbzip2
```

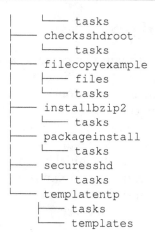

```
    │        └── tasks
    ├── checksshdroot
    │        └── tasks
    ├── filecopyexample
    │        ├── files
    │        └── tasks
    ├── installbzip2
    │        └── tasks
    ├── packageinstall
    │        └── tasks
    ├── securesshd
    │        └── tasks
    └── templatentp
             ├── tasks
             └── templates
```

Then, our `site.yml` file will look like this:

```
---
- name: Run example roles
  hosts: all
  become: yes

  roles:
    - filecopyexample
    - packageinstall
    - templatentp
    - installbzip2
    - securesshd
    - checkbzip2
    - checksshdroot
```

Running this code is left as an exercise for the reader, as we have already run all of the component parts earlier in this chapter. However, if all goes well then, when all roles have completed, there should be no `failed` statuses—just a mixture of `changed` and `ok`.

If you have run through the process of post-build customization, as detailed in this chapter, the resulting image will likely need cleaning up a second time. We could resort to the `virt-sysprep` command again, however, Ansible can help us here too. In the next section, we will explore the use of Ansible for cleaning up images for large scale deployment.

Cleaning up the build with Ansible

By now, you should have a pretty good idea of how to build or validate a base image, and then customize it with Ansible. Before we close this chapter, it is worth revisiting the task of cleaning up your image for deployment. Whether you have built an image from scratch or downloaded a ready-made one, if you have booted it up and run commands on it, either manually or using Ansible, you are likely to have a whole load of items that you really don't want present every time you deploy the image. For example, do you really want all of the system log files from every configuration task you performed and the initial boot to be present on every single virtual machine deployed? If you had to run any commands by hand (even if it was to set up authentication to allow Ansible to run), do you want those commands in the `.bash_history` file of the account you ran them in on every deployment?

The answer to these is, of course, no. Then there are those files that could actually cause problems if cloned—for example, duplicate SSH host keys or MAC address-specific configurations such as `udev` configuration data. All of this should be cleaned out before you consider the image ready for distribution.

Ansible can help with this task too, although it is recommended that you use the `virt-sysprep` tool that we demonstrated earlier in this chapter, as this takes care of all of these steps for you. There might be a reason why you don't want to use this tool—perhaps you don't have access to it in your environment, or there isn't a build for your preferred distribution of Linux. In this instance, you can use Ansible to perform the final cleanup. The great thing about Ansible is that you can use the built-in modules, as we have demonstrated so far in this chapter, but you can equally use raw shell commands—this can be especially useful when you need to perform wildcard operations across a filesystem.

The following is an example of a role that relies on raw shell commands to clean up an image in preparation for deployment. It is not as complete as the job performed by `virt-sysprep`, but does serve as a good example of how this could be performed using Ansible. Note that this example is specific to CentOS 7—if using a different operating system, then it will be necessary to change paths, package database cleanup commands, and so on. Hence, this playbook is presented to the reader very much as a practical example of how the cleanup could be performed in Ansible, though it is intended that the reader takes this further depending on their own requirements. First of all, we clean out the package database, as this data need not be replicated across deployments:

```
---
- name: Clean out yum cache
  shell: yum clean all
```

We then continue by clearing out the logs—this is achieved by stopping the logging daemon, forcing a rotation of the logs, and then recursively deleting the directory containing them:

```
- name: Stop syslog
  shell: service rsyslog stop

- name: Force log rotation
  shell: /sbin/logrotate -f /etc/logrotate.conf
  ignore_errors: yes

- name: Clean out logs
  shell: /bin/rm -f /var/log/*-???????? /var/log/*.gz /var/log/*.[0-9]
/var/log/**/*.gz /var/log/**/*.[0-9]

- name: Truncate log files
  shell: truncate -s 0 /var/log/*.log

- name: Truncate more logs
  shell: truncate -s 0 /var/log/**/*.log

- name: Clear the audit log
  shell: /bin/cat /dev/null > /var/log/audit/audit.log

- name: Clear wtmp
  shell: /bin/cat /dev/null > /var/log/wtmp
```

We then clear our hardware and MAC address-specific configurations that would be invalid on a deployed VM image:

```
- name: Remove the udev persistent device rules
  shell: /bin/rm -f /etc/udev/rules.d/70*

- name: Remove network related MAC addresses and UUID's
  shell: /bin/sed -i '/^\(HWADDR\|UUID\)=/d' /etc/sysconfig/network-
scripts/ifcfg-*
```

Following this, we clear out /tmp and remove any history files from user home directories. The following example is not complete, but does show some pertinent examples:

```
- name: Clear out /tmp
  shell: /bin/rm -rf /tmp/* /var/tmp/*

- name: Remove user history
  shell: /bin/rm -f ~root/.bash_history /home/**/.bash_history

- name: Remove any viminfo files
  shell: rm -f /root/.viminfo /home/**/.viminfo
```

```
  - name: Remove .ssh directories
    shell: rm -rf ~root/.ssh m -rf /home/**/.ssh
```

Finally, we perform our final task—in this case, the removal of the SSH host keys. Note that following this, we also shut down the VM—this is performed as part of this command to prevent accidental creation of any additional history or logging data. Note also the `ignore_errors` clause, which prevents the playbook from failing when the shutdown occurs and the SSH connection is terminated:

```
  - name: Remove SSH keys and shut down the VM (this kills SSH connection)
    shell: /bin/rm -f /etc/ssh/*key* && shutdown -h now
    ignore_errors: yes
```

Running this code on a CentOS 7 VM will result is a fairly well-cleaned image, but there are specifics not covered here. For example, we have cleared out all bash history, but if any alternate shells were used, their data would not be cleaned. Similarly, we have cleaned out VIM application data from root's home directory, but not any other applications that may or may not have been used during the image creation. Hence, it is up to you to extend this role as you require in your environment.

By this stage, you will have run through the entire process, end-to-end, of creating, customizing, and cleaning up a Linux operating system for our proposed SOE. Effective use of Ansible means that the entire process can be automated, and hence enables us to make a strong start toward automation in the enterprise. All that remains is to deploy the template we have created into your environment, and from here, you can clone it and build on it to your heart's content.

Summary

We have seen several hands-on examples of how to obtain or build Linux virtual machine images for use in a wide variety of scenarios and environments. We have seen how Ansible lends itself to automating this process, and hence how it complements the image build process to support the good practices we have previously discussed for automation in the enterprise and, in particular, the creation and management of an SOE.

In this chapter, you learned how to build Linux images for templating purposes and indeed obtain and verify ready-made ones. You then learned through practical examples how to customize these template images with Ansible, covering key concepts such as package installation and configuration file management. Finally, you learned how to ensure that image builds are clean and tidy and do not contain data that would either be wasteful or harmful to replicate across and infrastructure.

In the next chapter of this book, we will look at how to create standardized images for use on bare metal servers and in some traditional virtualization environments.

Questions

1. What is the purpose of system preparation (sysprep)?
2. When would you need to make use of Ansible facts in your roles?
3. How would you deploy a new configuration file to a virtual machine image using Ansible?
4. Which Ansible module is used to download a file from the internet directly into a virtual machine image?
5. How would you write a single Ansible role that will install packages on both Ubuntu and CentOS?
6. Why would you wish to validate an ISO image you have downloaded?
7. How does the use of Ansible roles at this stage benefit the environment once it is deployed?

Further reading

- For an in-depth understanding of Ansible, please refer to *Mastering Ansible, Third Edition* by *James Freeman* and *Jesse Keating*, available at https://www.packtpub.com/gb/virtualization-and-cloud/mastering-ansible-third-edition
- For more details on the use of KVM for virtualization on Linux, please refer to *Mastering KVM Virtualization* by *Prasad Mukhedkar, Anil Vettathu, Humble Devassy Chirammal*, available at https://www.packtpub.com/gb/networking-and-servers/mastering-kvm-virtualization

6
Custom Builds with PXE Booting

When working with physical hardware, it is not a given that you could simply clone a virtual machine template to the hard drive and expect it to work. It is, of course, entirely possible to do this with the right tools, but it is tricky, and there is no guarantee the resulting system will run.

For example, cloud-ready images will only have the kernel modules installed for the common virtualized network adapters, and so, may not run (or not have network connectivity) when installed on a modern piece of hardware.

In spite of this, it is still entirely possible to perform automated, standardized builds on physical hardware, and this chapter provides a complete hands-on approach to doing so. In conjunction with the preceding chapter, by the end of this one, you will have practical experience of the automated build process for standardizing images for all your platforms, whether they are virtual, cloud-based, or physical.

The following topics will be covered in this chapter:

- PXE booting basics
- Performing unattended builds
- Adding custom scripts to unattended boot configurations

Technical requirements

In this chapter, we are going to look at the process of PXE booting, for physical and virtual servers. You will require two servers on the same network, and it is recommended that the network be isolated, as some of the steps performed in this chapter could be disruptive and, even, destructive if performed in a live operational network.

You will need one server (or virtual machine) to be pre-installed with your choice of Linux distribution—in our examples, we will use Ubuntu Server 18.04 LTS. The other server (or virtual machine) should be blank, and suitable for reinstalling.

All example code discussed in this chapter is available from GitHub at: `https://github.com/PacktPublishing/Hands-On-Enterprise-Automation-on-Linux/tree/master/chapter06`.

PXE booting basics

Before the widespread adoption of virtualization and cloud platforms, there was a requirement to generate a standardized operating system build on physical servers, without the need to visit a data center and insert some form of installation media. PXE booting was created, as one of the common solutions to this requirement, and the name comes from the **Pre-eXecution Environment** (think of a tiny, minimal operating system) that is loaded so that an operating system installation can occur.

At a high level, when we talk about the PXE build of a given server, the following process is occurring:

1. The server must be configured to use one (or all) of its network adapters for network booting. This is commonly a factory default setting for most new hardware.
2. Upon power-up, the server brings up the network interfaces, and on each, in turn, attempts to contact a DHCP server.
3. The DHCP server sends back IP address configuration parameters, along with further information on where the pre-execution environment should be loaded from.
4. The server then retrieves the pre-execution environment, typically, using the **Trivial File Transfer Protocol** (TFTP).

5. The PXE environment runs and looks in a known, well-defined location on the TFTP server for configuration data.

6. The configuration data is loaded, and instructs the PXE environment how to proceed. Normally, with Linux, this involves loading a kernel and initial RAMDisk image from the TFTP server, which contains just enough Linux to proceed with the installation, and pulling further installation sources from another network service (often HTTP).

Although this all sounds rather complex, it is, in fact, quite straightforward when broken down into a step-by-step process. As we proceed through this chapter, we will walk through the process of building out a PXE boot server that is capable of performing an unattended installation of either CentOS 7 or Ubuntu 18.04 Server. This will serve as a good hands-on example, and also demonstrates how we can script our build processes even on physical hardware, where the VM template processes we discussed in the last chapter are not readily available.

Before any process of PXE booting can commence, we must first set up some supporting services that provide the necessary network services. In the next section, we will look at how these may be set up and configured.

Installing and configuring PXE-related services

As with just about any Linux setup, the exact way to do this will depend upon the Linux distribution on which you are performing the installation, and also, the software packages you are going to use. Here, we are going to make use of the ISC DHCP server, the venerable TFTP daemon, and nginx. However, you could just as feasibly use dnsmasq and Apache.

In many enterprises, these decisions will have already been made—most will have some form of DHCP infrastructure already in place, and many businesses with IP telephony systems will have a TFTP server too. Thus, this chapter serves to provide an example only—real-world implementations will likely be driven by long-established corporate standards.

 There is no safety mechanism to prevent you from running two DHCP servers on the same network. DHCP relies on broadcast messages, and so any DHCP clients on the network will receive an answer from whichever server answers them faster. As a result, it is entirely possible to stop a network from functioning by setting up a second DHCP server. If you follow the process outlined in this chapter, be sure you are performing it on an isolated network, suitable for testing.

For this setup, we are going to assume that we have an isolated network. Our PXE server will have the IP address 192.168.201.1, and the subnet mask will be 255.255.255.0. These details will be important in setting up our DHCP server. Let's now walk through the process of setting up your server to support PXE booting:

1. We need to install the following list of required packages:
   - DHCP server
   - TFTP server
   - Web server

   Assuming an Ubuntu 18.04 host, as discussed earlier, run this command to install the packages we will need for this part of the chapter:

   ```
   $ apt-get install isc-dhcp-server tftpd-hpa nginx
   ```

2. With these installed, the next step is to configure our DHCP server, with which the preceding package is configured through the /etc/dhcp/dhcpd.conf file. The configuration file shown in the following code block is a good, if basic, example for our PXE boot network, though naturally, you'll need to edit the subnet definition to match your own test network. The first part of the file contains some important global directives and the subnet definition for the network:

   ```
   allow bootp;
   # https://www.syslinux.org/wiki/index.php?title=PXELINUX#UEFI
   # This one line must be outside any bracketed scope
   option architecture-type code 93 = unsigned integer 16;


   subnet 192.168.201.0 netmask 255.255.255.0 {
       range 192.168.201.51 192.168.201.99;
       option broadcast-address 192.168.201.255;
       option routers 192.168.201.1;
       option domain-name-servers 192.168.201.1;
   ```

   The next part of the file then contains configuration directives, to ensure that we load the correct pre-execution binary, depending on the type of system being used. It is common at the time of writing to find a mix of both BIOS- and UEFI-based systems, so the following configuration is important:

   ```
   class "pxeclients" {
       match if substring (option vendor-class-identifier, 0, 9) =
   "PXEClient";

       if option architecture-type = 00:00 {
   ```

```
            filename "BIOS/pxelinux.0";
        } else if option architecture-type = 00:09 {
            filename "EFIx64/syslinux.efi";
        } else if option architecture-type = 00:07 {
            filename "EFIx64/syslinux.efi";
        } else if option architecture-type = 00:06 {
            filename "EFIia32/syslinux.efi";
        } else {
            filename "BIOS/pxelinux.0";
        }
    }
}
```

Most of this is fairly self-explanatory if you have worked with DHCP servers before. However, the block of text headed class "pxeclients" deserves a special mention. Some years ago, server hardware relied on the BIOS to boot, and thus PXE boot configurations were simple, as there was only one pre-boot environment that you needed to load. Most new server hardware now is configured with firmware that can operate in either *Legacy BIOS* or *UEFI modes*, and most default to UEFI, unless configured otherwise. The pre-execution binary is different, depending on the type of firmware in use, and hence, the if statements in this block make use of a DHCP option, returned to the server when the client makes its DHCP request.

3. With this configuration in place, enable the DHCP server, and restart it, as follows:

```
$ systemctl enable isc-dhcp-server.service
$ systemctl restart isc-dhcp-server.service
```

4. The default configuration for the TFTP server will suffice for this example, so, let's also enable this and ensure it is running as follows:

```
$ systemctl enable tftpd-hpa.service
$ systemctl restart tftpd-hpa.service
```

5. Finally, we'll use the default configuration of nginx, and serve all the files we need from /var/www/html—obviously, in an enterprise environment, you would want to do something a bit more advanced, but for the following practical example here, this will suffice:

```
$ systemctl enable nginx.service
$ systemctl restart nginx.service
```

That's our server infrastructure configured, but one last task remains. We need the pre-execution environment binaries for our TFTP server, to send to the clients.

Although these are readily available for most Linux distributions (and Ubuntu 18.04 is no exception), these packages are often quite old (the last stable release of PXELINUX was in 2014), and I have run into known bugs with these, especially when working with UEFI hardware. Although you are welcome to try newer snapshots, the author has achieved the most success with the release tagged 6.04-pre2, and so, we will explain how to build this and copy the files into the correct places for our TFTP server, as follows:

1. First of all, download and unpack the required release of SYSLINUX (which contains the PXELINUX code) by entering the following code:

    ```
    $ wget
    https://www.zytor.com/pub/syslinux/Testing/6.04/syslinux-6.04-pre2.
    tar.gz
    $ tar -xzf syslinux-6.04-pre2.tar.gz
    $ cd syslinux-6.04-pre2/
    ```

2. Next, we need to install a few build tools to successfully compile the code, as follows:

    ```
    $ sudo apt-get install nasm uuid-dev g++-multilib
    ```

3. Finally, we'll make sure the build directory is clean, and then build the code, as follows:

    ```
    $ make spotless
    $ make
    ```

When the build is complete, the final step is to copy the files into the correct places. Recalling our DHCP server configuration from earlier, we know that we need to separate out the files related to Legacy BIOS boots, and those released to newer UEFI boots. Here, we will step through the process of setting up your server for both BIOS and UEFI network boots:

1. The default root directory for the TFTP server is /var/lib/tftpboot on Ubuntu 18.04. Under this path, we will create the two directories referenced by the DHCP server configuration, as follows:

    ```
    $ mkdir -p /var/lib/tftpboot/{EFIx64,BIOS}
    ```

2. Then, we will run this set of commands, to gather up and copy all BIOS-related boot files into the newly created `BIOS` directory:

```
$ cp bios/com32/libutil/libutil.c32
bios/com32/elflink/ldlinux/ldlinux.c32 bios/core/pxelinux.0
/var/lib/tftpboot/BIOS
$ mkdir /var/lib/tftpboot/BIOS/pxelinux.cfg
$ mkdir /var/lib/tftpboot/BIOS/isolinux
$ find bios -name *.c32 -exec cp {} /var/lib/tftpboot/BIOS/isolinux
\;
```

3. We then repeat this step, except this time, we specify the UEFI-related boot files, as follows:

```
$ cp efi64/com32/elflink/ldlinux/ldlinux.e64
efi64/com32/lib/libcom32.c32 efi64/com32/libutil/libutil.c32
efi64/efi/syslinux.efi /var/lib/tftpboot/EFIx64
$ mkdir /var/lib/tftpboot/EFIx64/pxelinux.cfg
$ mkdir /var/lib/tftpboot/EFIx64/isolinux
$ find efi64/ -name *.c32 -exec cp {}
/var/lib/tftpboot/EFIx64/isolinux \;
```

With those steps completed, we now have a completed, functional PXE server. We have not downloaded any operating system images yet, so the boot process wouldn't proceed very far, but if you were to execute a test at this point, your server firmware should report that it has obtained an IP address from the DHCP server, and should present you with some boot-related messages. However, we will build this out further before going into any detailed testing in this book, and, in the next section, we will look at how to obtain the correct network installation images for your chosen Linux distribution.

Obtaining network installation images

The next step in our PXE boot setup process is to build out the images required. Luckily, obtaining the boot images is quite easy—the kernel and packages are normally contained on the DVD ISO images for your chosen Linux distribution. Obviously, this can vary from distribution to distribution, so you will need to check this. In this chapter, we will show examples for Ubuntu Server and CentOS 7—these principles could also be applied to many Debian derivatives, Fedora, and Red Hat Enterprise Linux.

The installation images required for network booting, along with the required installation packages, are normally found on the full DVD images—*live* images are often not sufficient because they lack either a sufficiently complete set of packages to perform the installation, or the network boot-capable kernel is missing.

Let's make a start with the CentOS 7 image, as follows:

1. First of all, download the latest DVD image from your nearest mirror—for example, the one shown in the following code block:

```
$ wget
http://mirror.netweaver.uk/centos/7.6.1810/isos/x86_64/CentOS-7-x86
_64-DVD-1810.iso
```

2. Once downloaded, mount the ISO image to a suitable location so that the files can be copied from it, as follows:

```
$ mount -o loop CentOS-7-x86_64-DVD-1810.iso /mnt
```

3. Now, the network boot-capable kernel and initial RAMDisk image should be copied to a location of our choosing, under the TFTP server root.

Note that in the following example, we are only doing this for UEFI booting. To set up for **Legacy BIOS booting**, follow exactly the same process, but place all files to be served by TFTP in /var/lib/tftpboot/BIOS instead. This applies throughout the rest of this chapter.

The commands to achieve this on our test system are as follows:

```
$ mkdir /var/lib/tftpboot/EFIx64/centos7
```

```
$ cp /mnt/images/pxeboot/{initrd.img,vmlinuz}
/var/lib/tftpboot/EFIx64/centos7/
```

4. Finally, we need the web server we installed earlier to serve out the files for the installer—once the kernel and initial RAMDisk environment load, the rest of the environment will be served over HTTP, which is better suited to large data transfers. Again, we'll create a suitable subdirectory for our CentOS content, as follows:

```
$ mkdir /var/www/html/centos7/

$ cp -r /mnt/* /var/www/html/centos7/

$ umount /mnt
```

That's all there is to it! Once these steps have been completed, we'll repeat this process for our Ubuntu 18.04 Server boot image, as follows:

```
$ wget
http://cdimage.ubuntu.com/releases/18.04/release/ubuntu-18.04.2-ser
ver-amd64.iso

$ mount -o loop ubuntu-18.04.2-server-amd64.iso /mnt

$ mkdir /var/lib/tftpboot/EFIx64/ubuntu1804

$ cp /mnt/install/netboot/ubuntu-installer/amd64/{linux,initrd.gz}
/var/lib/tftpboot/EFIx64/ubuntu1804/

$ mkdir /var/www/html/ubuntu1804

$ cp -r /mnt/* /var/www/html/ubuntu1804/

$ umount /mnt
```

With these steps complete, we just have one more configuration stage to go before we can perform a network boot of our chosen operating system.

> The process is almost identical—the only difference is that the NetBoot-capable kernel and RAMDisk were sourced from a different directory on the ISO image.

In the next section, we will configure the PXE boot server we have built so far, so as to boot from these installation images.

Performing your first network boot

Thus far, we have configured our server to give our clients an IP address on boot, and have even built two installation trees, such that we can install either CentOS 7 or Ubuntu 18.04 Server, without the need for any physical media. However, when our target machine boots over the network, how does it know what to boot?

The answer to this comes in the form of the PXELINUX configuration. This is very similar in nature to the **GRand Unified Bootloader** (**GRUB**) configuration that most Linux installations use, to define their boot options and parameters when they boot from disk. Using the installation we have built so far, these configuration files are expected to be in `/var/lib/tftpboot/EFIx64/pxelinux.cfg` (or `/var/lib/tftpboot/BIOS/pxelinux.cfg` for Legacy BIOS machines).

Now, a word on file naming. You might want all devices that boot off a network interface to perform a network boot. However, consider a server where a valid Linux installation is on the local disk, but through some error (perhaps misconfiguration of the boot order in the firmware, or a missing boot loader), it boots from the network interface instead of the local disk. If you have a full, unattended installation configured on your PXE server, this would wipe the local disks, with potentially disastrous consequences.

If you want all servers to perform a network boot regardless, you create a special configuration file, called `default`.

However, if you want to be more targeted, you instead create a configuration file with the name based on the MAC address. Suppose we have a server with the MAC address `DE:AD:BE:EF:01:23`, and our DHCP server is going to assign it the IP address `192.168.10.101/24` (this would most likely be through a static DHCP mapping so that we can ensure that this server always gets this IP address). When this server network boots using UEFI, it will look initially for `/var/lib/tftpboot/EFIx64/pxelinux.cfg/01-de-ad-be-ef-01-23`.

If this file is not present, it will look for a file named after the hex-encoded IP address. If this does not exist, it then takes one digit off the hexadecimal IP address at a time, until it finds a matching file. In this manner, our server would look for `/var/lib/tftpboot/EFIx64/pxelinux.cfg/C0A80A65`. If it doesn't find it, it cycles through the ever-shortening IP address representations, until it runs out of options. If no appropriately named file is found, it finally reverts to the `default` file, and if that file isn't present, a boot failure is reported by the client.

Thus, the full search sequence for configuration files is as follows:

1. `/var/lib/tftpboot/EFIx64/pxelinux.cfg/01-de-ad-be-ef-01-23`
2. `/var/lib/tftpboot/EFIx64/pxelinux.cfg/C0A80A65`
3. `/var/lib/tftpboot/EFIx64/pxelinux.cfg/C0A80A6`
4. `/var/lib/tftpboot/EFIx64/pxelinux.cfg/C0A80A`
5. `/var/lib/tftpboot/EFIx64/pxelinux.cfg/C0A80`
6. `/var/lib/tftpboot/EFIx64/pxelinux.cfg/C0A8`
7. `/var/lib/tftpboot/EFIx64/pxelinux.cfg/C0A`
8. `/var/lib/tftpboot/EFIx64/pxelinux.cfg/C0`
9. `/var/lib/tftpboot/EFIx64/pxelinux.cfg/C`
10. `/var/lib/tftpboot/EFIx64/pxelinux.cfg/default`

The idea of shortening the IP address filename is to enable you to create a subnet-wide configuration—for example, if all machines in the `192.168.10.0/24` subnet needed the same boot configuration, you could create a single file called `/var/lib/tftpboot/EFIx64/pxelinux.cfg/C0A80A`. Pay special attention to the case of the letters in the filename—the MAC address-based filename requires lowercase letters, while the IP address requires uppercase letters.

There are numerous permutations of configuration for the contents of this configuration file, and looking into all the possibilities for this is left as an exercise for the reader—there is ample documentation, and examples, available for PXELINUX. However, with the specific aim of booting our network install images, let's consider the following file. Initially, we define the header for the menu, with a simple title and timeout, as follows:

```
default isolinux/menu.c32
prompt 0
timeout 120

menu title --------- Enterprise Automation Boot Menu ---------
```

We then proceed to define the entries for our two operating system install images that we have built, as follows:

```
label 1
menu label ^1. Install CentOS 7.6 from local repo
kernel centos7/vmlinuz
append initrd=centos7/initrd.img method=http://192.168.201.1/centos7
devfs=nomount ip=dhcp inst.vnc inst.vncpassword=password

label 2
menu label ^2. Install Ubuntu Server 18.04 from local repo
kernel ubuntu1804/linux
append initrd=ubuntu1804/initrd.gz vga=normal locale=en_US.UTF-8
mirror/country=manual mirror/http/hostname=192.168.201.1
mirror/http/directory=/ubuntu1804 mirror/http/proxy="" live-installer/net-
image=http://192.168.201.1/ubuntu1804/install/filesystem.squashfs
```

As with other examples in this book, these are real-world, tested examples that will work in their own right. However, they should be customized to your own requirements, and you should endeavor to read and understand the code before applying it in a production environment.

 In these preceding examples, `192.168.201.1` is the IP address of my PXE server in my test setup. Be sure to replace this wherever you see it with the IP address of your PXE server.

This is, in fact, a very simple example—here, we are defining a simple text mode menu with two entries, one for each of our operating systems. Each menu entry has a `label`, a title that appears in the menu, and then, a `kernel` and `append` line. The `kernel` line tells the client from where to source the kernel on our TFTP server, while the `append` line is used to specify the path of the RAMDisk image and all supplementary boot parameters.

These boot parameters, as you can see, are greatly different for different Linux distributions, as are the capabilities of the installers. For example, the CentOS 7 installer is graphical (though a text mode option is available) and supports a VNC server, which we are configuring in the first menu item, enabling a remote installation using a VNC console, using the parameters `inst.vnc` and `inst.vncpassword=password`. The other parameters used are the following:

- `method=http://192.168.201.1/centos7`: Sets the address from where our CentOS 7 repo will be served
- `devfs=nomount`: Tells the kernel not to mount the devfs filesystem

- `ip=dhcp`: Tells the pre-boot environment to obtain an IP address using DHCP, to then be able to reach the HTTP server

The Ubuntu installer is, by contrast, normally run in text mode, and so does not support a VNC server, so a different remote access technology would be required to perform an interactive installation, such as **Serial-Over-LAN** (**SOL**). Nonetheless, this menu file would be sufficient for us to perform an interactive installation of either OS as we choose, and is provided as a template for the reader to build on and develop, as they see fit. The parameters in use are the following:

- `vga=normal`: Tells the installer to use the standard VGA mode
- `locale=en_US.UTF-8`: Sets the locale—adjust this to suit your environment
- `mirror/country=manual`: Tells the installer we are manually defining the repository mirror
- `mirror/http/hostname=192.168.201.1`: Sets the hostname of the repository mirror we created previously
- `mirror/http/directory=/ubuntu1804`: Sets the path on the repository mirror host that is serving the repository content
- `mirror/http/proxy=""`: Tells the installer we are not using a proxy
- `live-installer/net-image=http://192.168.201.1/ubuntu1804/install/filesystem.squashfs` : The URL from where the installer disk image can be downloaded

Of course, in an unattended boot scenario, you would not want to present the server with a choice of operating system—you simply want it to boot the one you want to install. In this instance, simply remove the menu items that are not needed.

Let's take a look at this in action. Upon a successful network boot of a test machine, we should be presented with the following menu, as defined previously:

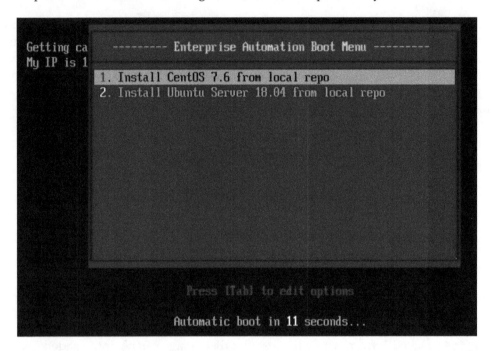

1. If we select the CentOS image as our boot target, you will see the kernel and base system load, and then ultimately, a screen asking you to connect to the installer using a VNC client, as shown in the following screenshot:

```
Starting installer, one moment...
anaconda 21.48.22.147-1 for CentOS 7 started.
 * installation log files are stored in /tmp during the installation
 * shell is available on TTY2
 * if the graphical installation interface fails to start, try again with the
   inst.text bootoption to start text installation
 * when reporting a bug add logs from /tmp as separate text/plain attachments
17:27:41 Starting VNC...
17:27:44 The VNC server is now running.
17:27:44

You chose to execute vnc with a password.


17:27:44 Please manually connect your vnc client to 192.168.201.56:1 to begin the install.
17:27:44 Attempting to start vncconfig


 [anaconda] 1:main* 2:shell  3:log  4:storage-log  5:program-log     Switch tab: Alt+Tab | Help: F1
```

2. Connecting with a VNC viewer, as instructed, yields the familiar interactive CentOS 7 graphical installer, as shown in the following screenshot:

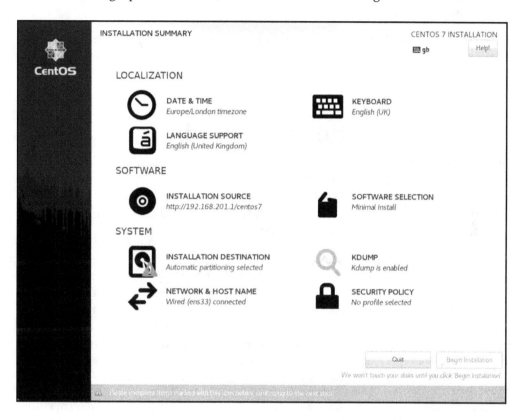

3. Thus, a complete remote installation is possible, without the need to visit the location of the server, or connect a keyboard and mouse! The same is almost true if we boot our Ubuntu Server image, only this time, the console is on the host screen, rather than available over VNC, as can be seen in the following screenshot:

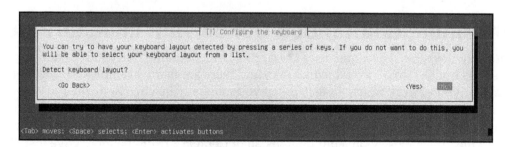

This lends itself well to either redirecting the console over an SOL implementation or a remove KVM option. Neither of these is particularly convenient, especially as the goal of this book is automation!

Thus, in the next section, we will look at performing automated installations, using the concept of *unattended builds*—that is to say, builds where no human needs to intervene for the installation to take place.

Performing unattended builds

The ultimate goal of this process is to have a server boot over the network and configure itself completely, rather than having to have someone interact with it. Although this is not a process controlled by Ansible, it is still a vital component in our **Standard Operating Environment (SOE)** architecture to ensure consistency of builds, and that build standards can be well documented and version controlled.

Fortunately, both CentOS (Red Hat-based) and Ubuntu (Debian-based) installers provide the capability for unattended installs to be completed in a programmatic manner. Sadly, there is no common standard for this process and, as you will see in this section, the language used for this process is wholly different between the two Linux types we are discussing here. Nevertheless, by covering off these two technologies, we are giving a good grounding that will enable you to perform remote, unattended installations on a wide variety of Linux systems.

Note that the examples in this chapter are complete and working, and thus are provided as hands-on examples—however, they are really just scratching the surface in terms of what these unattended installation technologies can do. It is left as an exercise for you to expand on these examples, and build them out to your own requirements.

Let's get started by looking in the next section at how we perform unattended builds on Red Hat-based platforms such as CentOS using kickstart files.

Performing unattended builds with kickstart files

The Red Hat installer, Anaconda, uses a scripting language called **kickstart** to define unattended builds. This is well documented, and there are many examples available on the internet for you to work from—in fact, when you manually install a Red Hat derivative such as CentOS 7, you will find a kickstart file in `/root/anaconda-ks.cfg`, which could be employed to automate future builds! In the following, we will build up our own simple kickstart file, based loosely on a minimal install of CentOS 7 from the interactive installer.

1. Let's start building up our example kickstart file for use in this chapter. Consider this block of code:

```
auth --enableshadow --passalgo=sha512
url --url="http://192.168.201.1/centos7/"
graphical
firstboot --enable
ignoredisk --only-use=sda
keyboard --vckeymap=gb --xlayouts='gb'
lang en_GB.UTF-8
reboot
```

Much of the kickstart file is very readable—in the preceding code block, you can see the following: we are defining `sha512` for the password hashing algorithm; our repository server is available at `http://192.168.201.1/centos7/`; we are performing a `graphical` install, using only `/dev/sda`, and with some GB specific locale settings. We also tell the installer to `reboot` automatically once the install completes successfully.

2. We then build on this by setting up the network (note that you must know the network device name in advance of creating this file, so you might find it useful to boot into a live environment to check this first) by running the following code:

```
network --bootproto=dhcp --device=ens33 --ipv6=auto --activate
network --hostname=ksautomation
```

This sets the hostname of our newly built server to `ksautomation`, and enables IPv6 and IPv4 DHCP on the network device called `ens33`.

3. We then define the root account password, and—optionally—any additional accounts we want to be added as part of the build, by running the following code:

```
rootpw --iscrypted
$6$cUkXdOxB$o8uxoU6arUj0g9SXqMGnigBYDH4rCkkQt9z/qYPm.1UYNwaZChCz2ep
QMUlbHUg8IVzN9lei9i/rschw1HydU.
user --groups=wheel --name=automation --
password=$6$eCIJyrjn$Vu30KX//UntsM0h..MLT6ik.m1GL8ayILBFWjbDrKSXowl
i5/hycMaiFzGI926YXEMfXXjAuwOFLIdANZ09/g1 --iscrypted --
gecos="Automation User"
```

Note that the password hashes must be used in this file—there are many ways to generate these. I used the following snippet of Python to generate unique hashes for the `password` string (you would obviously want to choose a more secure password!):

```
$ python -c "import random, string, crypt;
pwsalt = ''.join(random.sample(string.ascii_letters,8));
print crypt.crypt('password', '\$6\$%s\$' % pwsalt)"
```

Running the preceding three lines of code in the shell of any Linux server that has Python installed will generate the password hash needed for your kickstart file, which you can copy and paste into your installation.

 The preceding code is used only to generate the password hashes—do not include it in your kickstart file!

4. Finally, we set the time zone appropriately, and enable the `chrony` time synchronization service. We initialize the disk label on our chosen boot device, `sda`, and make use of Anaconda's automated partitioning (designated by the `autopart` directive), to set up the disk.

Note that `clearpart --none` does not actually clear the partition table—and if you run through this example with the kickstart file as defined here, the installation will only complete if there is space on the target disk to install CentOS 7. To have the kickstart file wipe the target disk and perform a fresh installation of CentOS 7 (which may be desirable to avoid having to manually wipe old machines before reuse), perform the following changes to the kickstart file:

1. Insert the `zerombr` directive above the `clearpart` statement to ensure the boot sector is cleared.
2. Change the `clearpart` line to read `clearpart --drives=sda --initlabel --all`—be sure to only specify the drives you want clearing in the `--drives=` parameter!

The fragment of following code does not include these changes as they are destructive—however, you are free to experiment with them as you wish in your test environment:

```
services --enabled="chronyd"
timezone Europe/London --isUtc
```

```
bootloader --location=mbr --boot-drive=sda
autopart --type=lvm
clearpart --none --initlabel
```

We then define our packages to be installed by default. Here, we are installing the `core` package group, the `minimal` system package set, and the `chrony` package. We are also disabling `kdump` for our test server, as shown in the following code block:

```
%packages
@^minimal
@core
chrony

%end

%addon com_redhat_kdump --disable --reserve-mb='auto'

%end
```

Finally, we can perform additional customization, such as setting a strong password policy—the following lines are actually the defaults from the interactive installer, and should be customized to your requirements:

```
%anaconda
pwpolicy root --minlen=6 --minquality=1 --notstrict --nochanges --
notempty
pwpolicy user --minlen=6 --minquality=1 --notstrict --nochanges --
emptyok
pwpolicy luks --minlen=6 --minquality=1 --notstrict --nochanges --
notempty
%end
```

When you have built your complete kickstart file, it's time to test the boot process. Remember the PXELINUX boot configuration we used in the last section? Well, that is reused almost in its entirety, except this time, we need to tell it where to find the kickstart file. I am storing the file we have just created in `/var/www/html/centos7-config/centos7unattended.cfg`—thus, it can be downloaded from our HTTP server, just like with the packages for the installer. In this case, our PXELINUX configuration would look like this:

```
default isolinux/menu.c32
prompt 0
timeout 120

menu title --------- Enterprise Automation Boot Menu ---------

label 1
```

```
menu label ^1. Install CentOS 7.6 from local repo
kernel centos7/vmlinuz
append initrd=centos7/initrd.img
method=http://192.168.201.1/centos7 devfs=nomount ip=dhcp inst.vnc
inst.vncpassword=password
inst.ks=http://192.168.201.1/centos7-config/centos7unattended.cfg
```

Let's run through the installation process, and see what happens. Initially, the process will look identical to the interactive installation we performed earlier in this chapter.

> The preceding PXE boot configuration shown is identical to before, save for the `inst.ks` parameter at the end, telling Anaconda where to download our kickstart file from.

Indeed, when you connect to the VNC console of your machine as it is being built, things will initially look the same—the graphical installer for CentOS 7 loads, as shown in the following screenshot:

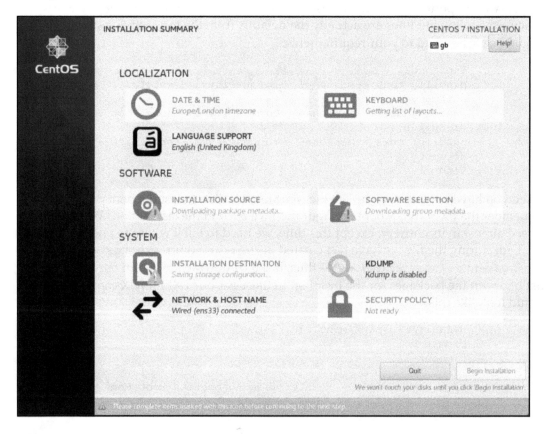

So far, everything looks like an ordinary interactive installation. However, once the installer finishes the various tasks listed (for example, **Saving storage configuration...**), you will note that you are presented with a screen that looks complete, save for the **Begin Installation** button being grayed out (as shown in the following screenshot):

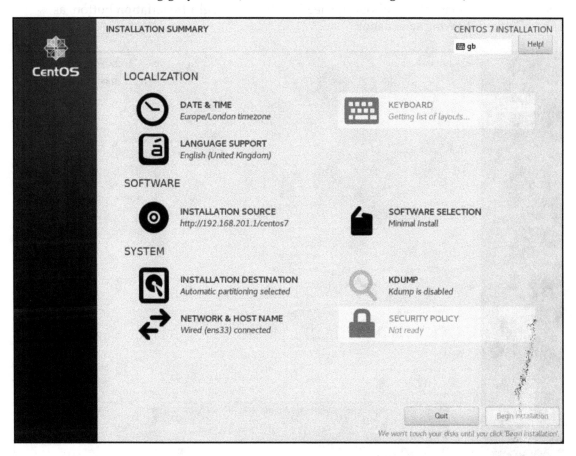

Note the differences here—the installation source has now been set to the HTTP server we set up for our installation process. All other items that are usually completed manually, such as disk selection, have been completed automatically, using the configuration in our kickstart script. In fact, if we wait a short while longer, you will see that the installation commences automatically, without the need to click the **Begin Installation** button, as shown in the following screenshot:

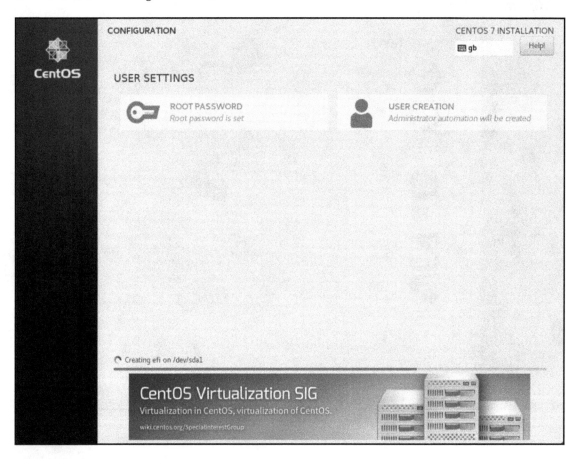

The installation now proceeds, using the parameters from our kickstart file. Note that the root password and initial user account creation has been completed, using the parameters from the kickstart script, and so, these buttons are again grayed out. In short, although the installation process appears very similar to a normal interactive installation, the user is not able to interact with the process in any way.

There are only two times when a user will be expected to interact with a kickstart installation, as follows:

1. A configuration is incomplete or incorrect—in this instance, the installer will pause and expect the user to intervene, and (if possible) correct the issue.
2. If the `reboot` keyword has not been specified in the kickstart file.

In the latter case, the installation will complete, but the installer will wait for the **Reboot** button to be clicked, as shown in the following screenshot:

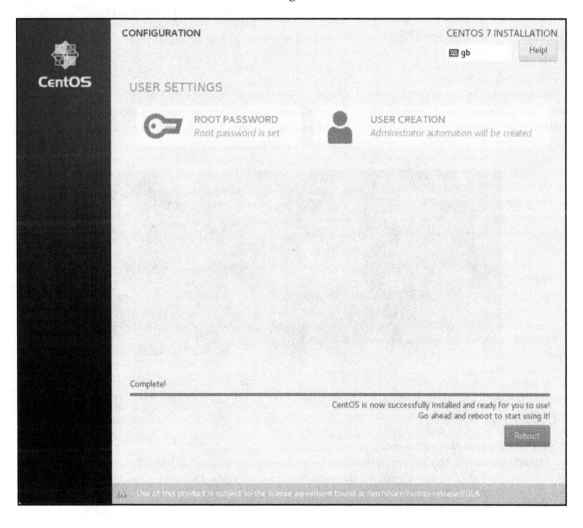

Rebooting automatically at the end of a kickstart installation is often desirable, as it saves the need to connect to the console. However, there are times when it is not—perhaps you don't actually want the newly built server to be running on the network at the present time. Or, perhaps you are building an image for templating purposes, and so don't want the first boot to complete, as it will mean log files and other data that subsequently need to be cleaned up.

The exact path the installation takes is up to you—the important thing to note is that you can connect to the VNC console, as shown in the preceding screenshots, and see exactly how the installation is going. If there are any errors or issues, you will be alerted.

Test this out, and see how the build performs for you. In the event of any issues, the installer runs up several consoles on the physical server that contain logging information—you can switch between these using *Alt + Tab*, or *Alt + F<n>*, where *F<n>* is one of the function keys—each of the first six corresponds to a different console, which will contain useful logging information. These can be queried, to debug any issues that might arise. The instructions are actually shown at the bottom of the text mode console screen—see the following screenshot for an example:

```
Starting installer, one moment...
anaconda 21.48.22.147-1 for CentOS 7 started.
 * installation log files are stored in /tmp during the installation
 * shell is available on TTY2
 * if the graphical installation interface fails to start, try again with the
   inst.text bootoption to start text installation
 * when reporting a bug add logs from /tmp as separate text/plain attachments
17:27:41 Starting VNC...
17:27:44 The VNC server is now running.
17:27:44

You chose to execute vnc with a password.


17:27:44 Please manually connect your vnc client to 192.168.201.56:1 to begin the install.
17:27:44 Attempting to start vncconfig

[anaconda] 1:main* 2:shell  3:log  4:storage-log  5:program-log    Switch tab: Alt+Tab | Help: F1
```

In the preceding screenshot, we can see we are on console 1, entitled `main`. Console 2 has a `shell` for debugging purposes, and consoles 3 through 5 show `log` files specific to the installation process.

However, if all of this goes well, you will see the installer run without any intervention required, and then, the server will reboot and present you with a login prompt. From there, you should be able to log in, using the password you defined via the password hash earlier.

That concludes the process of building a CentOS 7 server over the network using a kickstart file. The same high-level process can be followed for Ubuntu and other Debian derivatives through the use of pre-seed files, as we shall explore in the next section.

Performing unattended builds with pre-seed files

Broadly speaking, Ubuntu Server builds (and indeed, other Debian derivative operating systems) function exactly the same way. You specify a script file to tell the installer what actions to take, in place of a human being selecting options. With Ubuntu Server, this is called a pre-seed file. Let's go through this now, and build one up.

The pre-seed files are very powerful, and there is lots of documentation around—however, they can sometimes appear more complex to the naked eye. Starting with the following lines of code, we set the appropriate locale and keyboard layout for our server:

```
d-i debian-installer/locale string en_GB
d-i console-setup/ask_detect boolean false
d-i keyboard-configuration/xkb-keymap select gb
```

We then configure the following network parameters:

```
d-i netcfg/choose_interface select auto
d-i netcfg/get_hostname string unassigned-hostname
d-i netcfg/get_domain string unassigned-domain
d-i netcfg/hostname string automatedubuntu
d-i netcfg/wireless_wep string
```

Here, you will note that we don't actually need to know the interface name in advance—rather, we can get Ubuntu to guess it, using its automated detection algorithm. We are setting the hostname to `automatedubuntu`; however, note that the other parameters are used to prevent the installer from prompting for a hostname from the user, thus meaning the installation is not truly unattended. Next, we add some details about where the installer can download its packages from, as shown in the following code block:

```
d-i mirror/country string manual
d-i mirror/http/hostname string 192.168.201.1
d-i mirror/http/directory string /ubuntu1804
d-i mirror/http/proxy string
```

These should naturally be adjusted to suit your network, HTTP server setup on your PXE server, and so on.

 Many of these are also set in the kernel parameters, as we saw in our PXELINUX configuration earlier—we just need to confirm a few of them here.

We then set up the root account password, and any additional user accounts, as follows:

```
d-i passwd/root-password password password
d-i passwd/root-password-again password password
d-i passwd/user-fullname string Automation User
d-i passwd/username string automation
d-i passwd/user-password password insecure
d-i passwd/user-password-again password insecure
d-i user-setup/allow-password-weak boolean true
d-i user-setup/encrypt-home boolean false
```

Note here that I have specified the passwords in plain text, to highlight the possibility to do this here—there are alternative parameters you can specify that will accept a password hash, which is far more secure when creating configuration files. Here, the root password is set to `password`, and a user account called `automation` is set up, with the password `insecure`. As before, our password policy is quite weak and could be strengthened here, or later, using Ansible. We then set the time zone as appropriate, and turn on NTP synchronization, as follows:

```
d-i clock-setup/utc boolean true
d-i time/zone string Etc/UTC
d-i clock-setup/ntp boolean true
```

The most complex block of code in our otherwise simplistic example is the following one, which is used to partition and set up the disk:

```
d-i partman-auto/disk string /dev/sda
d-i partman-auto/method string lvm
d-i partman-lvm/device_remove_lvm boolean true
d-i partman-md/device_remove_md boolean true
d-i partman-lvm/confirm boolean true
d-i partman-lvm/confirm_nooverwrite boolean true
d-i partman-auto-lvm/guided_size string max
d-i partman-auto/choose_recipe select atomic
d-i partman/default_filesystem string ext4
d-i partman-partitioning/confirm_write_new_label boolean true
d-i partman/choose_partition select finish
d-i partman/confirm boolean true
d-i partman/confirm_nooverwrite boolean true
d-i partman-md/confirm boolean true
d-i partman-partitioning/confirm_write_new_label boolean true
d-i partman/choose_partition select finish
d-i partman/confirm boolean true
d-i partman/confirm_nooverwrite boolean true
```

Although verbose, this section of the file basically says to automatically partition the disk /dev/sda, set up LVM, use automated calculations to determine the filesystem layout, and then create ext4 filesystems. As you can see, there are many safeguards and confirmation prompts that we have flagged as true as otherwise, the installer would stop and wait for user input to proceed. If this were to happen, our installation would again not be truly unattended. From here, we specify the package set we want to be installed, as follows:

```
tasksel tasksel/first multiselect standard
d-i pkgsel/include string openssh-server build-essential
d-i pkgsel/update-policy select none
```

The preceding lines of code essentially set up a minimal server build with the openssh-server package and build-essential packages on it. The automated update policy is configured to not automatically update. Finally, to finish off the file, we tell it where to install the boot loader, and to reboot upon successful completion, as follows:

```
d-i grub-installer/only_debian boolean true
d-i grub-installer/with_other_os boolean true
d-i finish-install/reboot_in_progress note
```

As with our CentOS example, we will serve this file from our web server, and thus, the PXELINUX boot configuration needs adjusting, to make sure we incorporate this file—an appropriate example is shown as follows:

```
default isolinux/menu.c32
prompt 0
timeout 120

menu title --------- Enterprise Automation Boot Menu ---------

label 1
menu label ^1. Install Ubuntu Server 18.04 from local repo
kernel ubuntu1804/linux
append initrd=ubuntu1804/initrd.gz
url=http://192.168.201.1/ubuntu-config/ubuntu-unattended.txt vga=normal
locale=en_US.UTF-8 console-setup/ask_detect=false console-
setup/layoutcode=gb keyboard-configuration/layoutcode=gb
mirror/country=manual mirror/http/hostname=192.168.201.1
mirror/http/directory=/ubuntu1804 mirror/http/proxy="" live-installer/net-
image=http://192.168.201.1/ubuntu1804/install/filesystem.squashfs
netcfg/get_hostname=unassigned-hostname
```

Note the following new options in use this time:

- `url`: Tells the installer from where to obtain our pre-seed file.
- `console-setup/layoutcode` and `keyboard-configuration/layoutcode`: Prevents the installer from asking about keyboard settings when it is first run.
- `netcfg/get_hostname`: Although we have set the hostname in the pre-seed file, we have to specify this parameter here, otherwise the installer will stop, and prompt the user to enter a hostname.

Again, if you test this by booting a server over the network using the preceding configuration, you should see the server build complete. Unlike the CentOS 7 installation, you will not see any menu options—these will only be presented to you if your pre-seed configuration file is incorrect, or is missing some important details. Instead, you will simply see a series of progress bars flash by, as the various stages of the installation are completed. For example, the following screenshot shows that the base system is installed to the disk after the partitions and logical volumes have been set up:

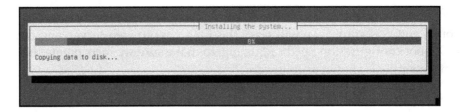

Assuming all goes well, this process will continue until you are presented with a final progress bar, which shows the final tidy-up being completed before the server is rebooted. In the following screenshot, the filesystems are being unmounted, in preparation for a reboot:

When this final progress bar completes, your server will reboot, and you will be presented with a login prompt, from where you can log in with the credentials specified in the pre-seed file `d-i passwd` parameters shown previously. Note that if you use different credentials for your build, you must use these here, and not those specified previously.

At this stage, you should be able to perform an unattended build of either CentOS or Ubuntu Server over the network and perform basic changes, such as selecting the required packages and setting credentials. In the next section, we will explore methods of additional bespoke customization, beyond the original OS.

Adding custom scripts to unattended boot configurations

As you will have seen from the examples in this chapter, the kickstart and pre-seed files are quite prescriptive in what they can do. For most purposes, they should be perfectly adequate, allowing you to build a machine suitable for further customization with Ansible. Indeed, much of the rest of this book is dedicated to how you would manage and automate configuration management across an estate of servers, built per the details in this and the preceding chapters.

However, what if your enterprise has a task (or tasks) that absolutely has to be performed at build time—perhaps for security compliance (which we shall explore in Chapter 13, *Using CIS Benchmarks*), for example? Luckily, both of the technologies we have discussed here provide an option for that. Let's first take a look at how you might perform custom commands in a kickstart-unattended installation.

Customized scripting with kickstart

As discussed previously, it is recommended for most tasks that you perform the post-build configuration with Ansible. However, let's take a simple and hypothetical example—suppose that, for security reasons, you need to disable root SSH logins immediately when the server is built, for security compliance. There is no directive in kickstart that can perform this task, and leaving the server with this enabled while it waits for Ansible to run against it may not be acceptable to a corporate security team, as there is a window of opportunity for a potential attacker. Luckily, at the bottom of our kickstart file, we can put a %post block in that runs any shellcode you put into it. Thus, we could run the sed utility from within the following code block:

```
%post --log=/root/ks.log

/bin/sed -i 's/#PermitRootLogin yes/PermitRootLogin no/'
/etc/ssh/sshd_config

%end
```

This very simple block of code runs after the installation process has finished (but before the reboot), and logs its output into `/root/ks.log`. You could customize this as you see fit—however, here, for the sake of our simple example, we are performing a search and replace operation on the default SSH daemon configuration, to ensure that even on first boot, root logins over SSH are disabled.

In the next section, we'll see how the same thing is achieved in an Ubuntu pre-seed file.

Customized scripting with pre-seed

Suppose we want to perform the same customization with Ubuntu. Ubuntu pre-seed files run a single line of commands rather than a block as used in kickstart; hence, they lend themselves better to either simple tasks, or indeed to downloading a script for more complex operations. We could embed the `sed` command in our pre-seed file by adding the following line at the bottom:

```
d-i preseed/late_command string in-target /bin/sed -i
's/#PermitRootLogin.*/PermitRootLogin no/' /etc/ssh/sshd_config
```

Suppose, however, we have a much more complex script to run, and that trying to write it all on one line would make it difficult both to read and manage—instead, we could change the preceding command, to download a script from a chosen place and run it, as follows:

```
d-i preseed/late_command string in-target wget -P /tmp/
http://192.168.201.1/ubuntu-config/run.sh; in-target chmod +x /tmp/run.sh;
in-target sh -x /tmp/run.sh
```

Note here that we are using `wget` (which was installed earlier in the build process) to download a file called `run.sh` from the `/ubuntu-config/` path on our web server. We then make it executable and run it. In this way, far more complex command sequences can be run at the end of the build process, just prior to the first reboot.

In this manner, incredibly complex, bespoke operating system builds can be installed remotely, over the network, without any human intervention at all. The use of kickstart and pre-seed files also means that the process is scripted and repeatable, which is an important principle for us to adhere to.

Summary

Even when using bare-metal servers (and some virtualization platforms), it is entirely possible to script the installation process, to ensure that all builds are consistent and thus adhere to the SOE principle we set out earlier in this book. By following the processes set out in this chapter, you will ensure that all your servers are built in a consistent manner, regardless of the platform on which they are running.

Specifically, you gained experience of performing an interactive Linux installation environment, using PXE network booting. You then learned how to fully automate the build process, using kickstart and pre-seed scripts, to ensure that builds are completely unattended (and, hence, automated). Finally, you learned how to further customize the builds, by adding custom scripts to the build definition.

In the next chapter, we will proceed to look at the use of Ansible to customize servers, both when they are newly built, and on an ongoing basis.

Questions

1. What does PXE stand for?
2. Which basic services are required for a PXE boot?
3. Where would you obtain the installation sources for a network boot?
4. What is an unattended installation?
5. What is the difference between a kickstart file and a pre-seed file?
6. Why would you need to use a `%post` block in a kickstart file?
7. What is the purpose of the `BIOS` and `EFIx64` directories under the TFTP server root?
8. How would you create a separate partition for `/home` in a pre-seed file?

Further reading

- To see all the possible pre-seed file options, please visit `https://help.ubuntu.com/lts/installation-guide/example-preseed.txt`.
- To learn more about kickstart files (also works on CentOS), please visit `https://access.redhat.com/documentation/en-us/red_hat_enterprise_linux/7/html/installation_guide/sect-kickstart-howto`.
- To see a syntax reference for kickstart file commands, please visit `https://access.redhat.com/documentation/en-us/red_hat_enterprise_linux/7/html/installation_guide/sect-kickstart-syntax#sect-kickstart-commands`.

Configuration Management with Ansible
7

So far in this book, we have established a solid framework for our Enterprise Linux infrastructure, one that lends itself well to the large-scale deployments typical in an enterprise, and to automated management with Ansible at this scale. In this chapter, we now proceed to go into depth on the automated management aspect of this infrastructure, starting with the installation and configuration of software packages.

In just about every enterprise, one task is almost guaranteed to be required during the lifespan of a standardized Linux system—the installation and configuration of a service. This might simply involve the configuration of an existing system service, or possibly even the installation of the service itself, followed by post-configuration work.

We will cover the following topics in this chapter, to explore Ansible configuration management in greater depth:

- Installing new software
- Making configuration changes with Ansible
- Managing configuration at an enterprise scale

Technical requirements

This chapter includes examples based on the following technologies:

- Ubuntu Server 18.04 LTS
- CentOS 7.6
- Ansible 2.8

To run through these examples, you will need access to two servers or virtual machines running one of each of the operating systems listed here, and also Ansible. Note that the examples given in this chapter may be destructive in nature (for example, they install and uninstall software packages and make changes to server configuration), and if run as-is, they are only intended to be run in an isolated test environment.

Once you are satisfied that you have a safe environment in which to operate, let's get started on looking at the installation of new software packages with Ansible.

All example code discussed in this chapter is available from GitHub, at the following URL: `https://github.com/PacktPublishing/Hands-On-Enterprise-Automation-on-Linux/tree/master/chapter07`.

Installing new software

Depending on your requirements, it is quite possible that your SOE operating system build has sufficient software installed, and requires only configuration work. However, for many people, that will not be the case, so we will begin this chapter with a section covering the installation of software. As with all our work so far, our desire is that anything we do here is repeatable and lends itself well to automation, and thus, even if new software is required, it is desirable that we do not install it by hand.

Let's start by looking at the simplest possible case here—installing a native operating system package.

Installing a package from operating system default repositories

Suppose that you are rolling out a new service that requires a database server—for example, MariaDB. It is unlikely that you will have installed and enabled MariaDB in all of your SOE images, and hence, the first task before you do anything else will be to install the software package.

Both of our example operating systems in this book (and indeed, many of their derivatives) include native packages for MariaDB, so we could quite easily make use of these. When it comes to package installation, there is, of course, a need to understand what is going on behind the scenes in our target operating system. For example, on Ubuntu, we know that we would normally install our chosen software by using the APT package manager. Thus, if we wanted to install this manually, including the matching client for management purposes, we would issue the following command:

```
# sudo apt install mariadb-server mariadb-client
```

Of course, on CentOS, things are quite different—even though packages are available for MariaDB, the command to install them would instead be the following one:

```
# sudo yum install mariadb mariadb-server
```

Although Ansible can automate a great deal of your Enterprise Linux requirements, it cannot abstract away some of the fundamental differences between different Linux operating systems. Fortunately, though, Ansible makes everything else quite straightforward. Consider the following inventory:

```
[servers]
ubuntu-testhost
centos-testhost
```

We have advocated building a standard operating environment throughout this book, so this inventory is rather unlikely to occur in real life—however, it serves as a good example here as we can demonstrate how to install a MariaDB server on two differing platforms. As with earlier examples in this book, we'll complete this task by making use of roles.

Building on our work on templates from earlier in this book, consider the following role:

```
---
- name: Install MariaDB Server on Ubuntu or Debian
  apt:
    name: "{{ item }}"
    state: present
```

```
    loop:
      - mariadb-server
      - mariadb-client
    when: ansible_distribution == 'Debian' or ansible_distribution ==
'Ubuntu'

  - name: Install MariaDB Server on CentOS or RHEL
    yum:
      name: "{{ item }}"
      state: present
    loop:
      - mariadb-server
      - mariadb
    when: ansible_distribution == 'CentOS' or ansible_distribution == 'Red
Hat Enterprise Linux'
```

This neatly packaged role will operate correctly on both Ubuntu and CentOS (and, indeed, **Red Hat Enterprise Linux** (**RHEL**) and Debian, if required), and takes account of both the differing package managers and different package names. Naturally, if you are fortunate enough to have an environment that is completely unified (for example, only Ubuntu Server-based), then the code can be simplified even further.

There exists an Ansible module called `package` that attempts to detect the correct package manager to use, based on the operating system the playbook is run against. Although this removes the need for separate yum- and apt- based tasks, such as the ones we used previously, you still need to take into account the different package naming between different Linux operating systems, so you may still require a `when` clause.

We will define a simple playbook to call the role, as follows:

```
  ---
  - name: Install MariaDB
    hosts: all
    become: yes

    roles:
      - installmariadb
```

Now, we can run the playbook and observe what happens, as follows:

```
● ● ●                james@automation-01: ~/hands-on-automation/chapter07/example01 (ssh)
~/hands-on-automation/chapter07/example01> ansible-playbook -i hosts site.yml

PLAY [Install MariaDB] *******************************************************

TASK [Gathering Facts] *******************************************************
ok: [ubuntu-testhost]
ok: [centos-testhost]

TASK [installmariadb : Install MariaDB Server on Ubuntu or Debian] ***********
skipping: [centos-testhost] => (item=mariadb-server)
skipping: [centos-testhost] => (item=mariadb-client)
changed: [ubuntu-testhost] => (item=mariadb-server)
changed: [ubuntu-testhost] => (item=mariadb-client)

TASK [installmariadb : Install MariaDB Server on CentOS or RHEL] *************
skipping: [ubuntu-testhost] => (item=mariadb-server)
skipping: [ubuntu-testhost] => (item=mariadb)
changed: [centos-testhost] => (item=mariadb-server)
ok: [centos-testhost] => (item=mariadb)

PLAY RECAP *******************************************************************
centos-testhost            : ok=2    changed=1    unreachable=0    failed=0
ubuntu-testhost            : ok=2    changed=1    unreachable=0    failed=0

~/hands-on-automation/chapter07/example01>
```

From the preceding output, you can see how the tasks that are irrelevant to each system are skipped, while the successful installation of our desired package results in a `changed` status. Also, note that the task status returned was `ok` when installing the MariaDB client package called `mariadb` on our CentOS test system. The reason for this is that the `loop` defined in our `role` iterates over each listed package in turn, installing it; on CentOS, the `mariadb` package is a dependency of the `mariadb-server` package, and so it was installed when that particular task was run.

Although specifying this manually could be seen as redundant, it does no harm to keep it in our role as it ensures that whatever happens, the client package is present. It is also a form of self-documentation—in a few years, someone could come back to this playbook and understand that both the MariaDB client and server packages were required, even if they were unaware of this nuance of the CentOS 7 operating system.

Before we build on this example, a note on package removal. Ansible tasks are, as we have discussed previously, idempotent. For example, if we run our playbook a second time, we will see that the results returned are all `ok`. In the following instance, Ansible has detected that our chosen packages are already installed, and doesn't attempt a second installation:

```
● ● ●              james@automation-01: ~/hands-on-automation/chapter07/example01 (ssh)
~/hands-on-automation/chapter07/example01> ansible-playbook -i hosts site.yml

PLAY [Install MariaDB] ************************************************************

TASK [Gathering Facts] ************************************************************
ok: [ubuntu-testhost]
ok: [centos-testhost]

TASK [installmariadb : Install MariaDB Server on Ubuntu or Debian] ************
skipping: [centos-testhost] => (item=mariadb-server)
skipping: [centos-testhost] => (item=mariadb-client)
ok: [ubuntu-testhost] => (item=mariadb-server)
ok: [ubuntu-testhost] => (item=mariadb-client)

TASK [installmariadb : Install MariaDB Server on CentOS or RHEL] **************
skipping: [ubuntu-testhost] => (item=mariadb-server)
skipping: [ubuntu-testhost] => (item=mariadb)
ok: [centos-testhost] => (item=mariadb-server)
ok: [centos-testhost] => (item=mariadb)

PLAY RECAP ***********************************************************************
centos-testhost            : ok=2    changed=0    unreachable=0    failed=0
ubuntu-testhost            : ok=2    changed=0    unreachable=0    failed=0

~/hands-on-automation/chapter07/example01>
```

However, what if you need to tidy something up? Perhaps a package that features in the standard image has become obsolete or needs removing, for security reasons. In this instance, it is not sufficient simply to remove the playbook or role. While the presence of our example role ensures the installation of packages, the removal of the role does not reverse this. In short, we must manually uninstall or remove changes if they are not required. Backing out of our installation would require a role such as this:

```
---
- name: Uninstall MariaDB Server on Ubuntu or Debian
  apt:
    name: "{{ item }}"
    state: absent
  loop:
    - mariadb-server
    - mariadb-client
  when: ansible_distribution == 'Debian' or ansible_distribution ==
'Ubuntu'
```

```
  - name: Uninstall MariaDB Server on CentOS or RHEL
    yum:
      name: "{{ item }}"
      state: absent
    loop:
      - mariadb-server
      - mariadb
    when: ansible_distribution == 'CentOS' or ansible_distribution == 'Red
Hat Enterprise Linux'
```

Notice the almost identical nature of the role, except that we are now using `state: absent` instead of `state: present`. This is common to most Ansible tasks you might run—if you want to define a procedure for backing out or otherwise reverting a change, you will need to write that separately. Now, when we run the preceding role by calling it from a suitable playbook, we can see that the packages are cleanly uninstalled, as shown in the following screenshot:

```
● ● ●              james@automation-01: ~/hands-on-automation/chapter07/example03 (ssh)
~/hands-on-automation/chapter07/example03> ansible-playbook -i hosts site.yml

PLAY [Install Duplicati] ***********************************************************

TASK [Gathering Facts] *************************************************************
ok: [ubuntu-testhost]
ok: [centos-testhost]

TASK [installduplicati : Install Duplicati beta on Ubuntu] *************************
skipping: [centos-testhost]
changed: [ubuntu-testhost]

TASK [installduplicati : Install Duplicati beta on CentOS or RHEL] *************
skipping: [ubuntu-testhost]
changed: [centos-testhost]

PLAY RECAP *************************************************************************
centos-testhost            : ok=2    changed=1    unreachable=0    failed=0
ubuntu-testhost            : ok=2    changed=1    unreachable=0    failed=0

~/hands-on-automation/chapter07/example03>
```

Sometimes, of course, the packages we want to install are not available as part of the default operating system package repositories.

In the next section, we will look at how to handle this in accordance with the automation principles we have set out so far.

Installing non-native packages

Thankfully, the installation of non-native packages is not significantly more difficult with Ansible than with native ones. Ideally, in an enterprise environment, all required packages would be served out of an internal repository, and indeed, we will cover this later in the book. In this instance, the enterprise repository would be used in conjunction with Ansible roles, such as those from the previous section.

Occasionally, though, this may not be possible, or desirable. Take, for instance, a development or test system where a new package is being evaluated—here, you would probably not want to upload a test package to an enterprise repository server when it is not known whether there will be a requirement for the package moving forward. Nonetheless, we wish to adhere to our principles of automation and ensure that we perform our testing in a repeatable, self-documenting manner.

Suppose you are evaluating the Duplicati backup software for your enterprise and need to install the latest beta version to perform some testing. Obviously, you could download this manually from their releases page, copy it across to your target server, and install it by hand. However, this is inefficient, and certainly not a repeatable process. Luckily, the apt and yum modules we used earlier support the installation of packages, both from a local path and a remote URL.

Thus, to test the installation of Duplicati beta version 2.0.4.23, you could write a role such as this:

```
---
- name: Install Duplicati beta on Ubuntu
  apt:
    deb:
https://github.com/duplicati/duplicati/releases/download/v2.0.4.23-2.0.4.23
_beta_2019-07-14/duplicati_2.0.4.23-1_all.deb
  when: ansible_distribution == 'Debian' or ansible_distribution ==
'Ubuntu'

- name: Install Duplicati beta on CentOS or RHEL
  yum:
    name:
https://github.com/duplicati/duplicati/releases/download/v2.0.4.23-2.0.4.23
_beta_2019-07-14/duplicati-2.0.4.23-2.0.4.23_beta_20190714.noarch.rpm
    state: present
  when: ansible_distribution == 'CentOS' or ansible_distribution == 'Red
Hat Enterprise Linux'
```

As you can see from this role, the installation proceeds without needing to separately download the package first, as shown in the following screenshot:

```
james@automation-01: ~/hands-on-automation/chapter07/example05 (ssh)
~/hands-on-automation/chapter07/example05> ansible-playbook -i hosts site.yml

PLAY [Configure MariaDB] ***********************************************

TASK [Gathering Facts] *************************************************
ok: [ubuntu-testhost]

TASK [configuremariadb : Reconfigure MariaDB Server to listen for external conne
ctions] ***
changed: [ubuntu-testhost]

TASK [configuremariadb : Restart MariaDB to pick up configuration changes] *****
changed: [ubuntu-testhost]

PLAY RECAP ************************************************************
ubuntu-testhost            : ok=3    changed=2    unreachable=0    failed=0

~/hands-on-automation/chapter07/example05> grep bind-address /etc/mysql/mariadb.
conf.d/50-server.cnf
bind-address = 0.0.0.0
~/hands-on-automation/chapter07/example05>
```

Thus, in this way, whether for testing or production purposes, you can install packages that are not available in the default package repositories of your chosen operating system, and maintain the benefits of automation. In the next section, we will explore how Ansible can install software that is not packaged at all and that requires manual installation.

Installing unpackaged software

Some software, of course, doesn't come neatly packaged and requires a more manual approach to installation. Take, for example, the hosting control panel software **Virtualmin**. This, at the time of writing, normally requires the user to download a shell script and execute it to perform the installation.

Fortunately, once again, Ansible can help here—consider the following role:

```
---
- name: download virtualmin install script
  get_url:
    url: http://software.virtualmin.com/gpl/scripts/install.sh
    dest: /root/install.sh
    mode: 0755

- name: virtualmin install (takes around 10 mins) you can see progress
using: tail -f /root/virtualmin-install.log
    shell: /root/install.sh --force --hostname {{ inventory_hostname }} --
```

```
minimal --yes
  args:
    chdir: /root
```

Here, we are making use of the Ansible `get_url` module to download the installation script and then using the `shell` module to run it. Notice also how we can put helpful instructions into the task names—although no substitute for good documentation, this is incredibly helpful as it tells anyone running the script how to check on the progress of the installation using the `tail` command.

 Note that the `shell` module requires some care in its use—as it cannot possibly know whether the shell task you have given it has been run before, it runs the command every time the playbook is run. Thus, if you run the preceding role a second time, it will attempt to install Virtualmin again. You should use a `when` clause under your `shell` task to ensure it only runs under certain conditions—perhaps in the preceding example, when `/usr/sbin/virtualmin` (which is installed by `install.sh`) is not present.

This method could be extended to almost any software you can imagine—you could even download a source code tarball and extract it and build the code using a series of `shell` module calls in Ansible. This is an unlikely case, of course, but the emphasis here is that Ansible can help you create repeatable installations, even if you don't have access to pre-packaged software in an RPM or DEB format.

In this manner, almost any software can be installed—after all, the process of software installation is to download a file (or archive), put it into the right location, and configure it. This is, in essence, what package managers such as `yum` and `apt` are doing behind the scenes, and Ansible can handle this kind of activity just as well, as we have demonstrated here. In the next section, we will explore the use of Ansible to make configuration changes on systems on which you have built and/or installed software.

Making configuration changes with Ansible

When it comes to configuring a new service, the task is rarely completed by simply installing the required software. There is almost always a configuration stage required after the installation.

Let's consider in detail some fundamental examples of the myriad of configuration changes that might be required.

Making small configuration changes with Ansible

When it comes to making configuration changes, the `lineinfile` Ansible module is often your first port of call and can handle a lot of the small-scale changes that might be required. Consider the example of deploying a MariaDB server that we started earlier in this chapter. Although we successfully installed the packages, they will have been installed with their default configuration, and this is unlikely to suit all but the most basic of use cases.

For example, the default bind address for the MariaDB server is `127.0.0.1`, meaning that it is not possible to make use of our MariaDB installation from an external application. We have well established the need to make changes in a reliable, repeatable manner, so let's take a look at how we might change this using Ansible.

In order to change this configuration, the first thing we need to do is establish where the default configuration is located and what it looks like. From here, we will define an Ansible task, to rewrite the configuration.

Taking our Ubuntu server by way of example, the service bind-address is configured in the `/etc/mysql/mariadb.conf.d/50-server.cnf` file—the default directive looks like this:

```
bind-address            = 127.0.0.1
```

Thus, in order to change this, we might employ a simple role, like this:

```
---
- name: Reconfigure MariaDB Server to listen for external connections
  lineinfile:
    path: /etc/mysql/mariadb.conf.d/50-server.cnf
    regexp: '^bind-address\s+='
    line: 'bind-address = 0.0.0.0'
    insertafter: '^\[mysqld\]'
    state: present

- name: Restart MariaDB to pick up configuration changes
  service:
    name: mariadb
    state: restarted
```

Let's break the `lineinfile` task down and look at it in more detail:

- `path`: Tells the module which configuration file to modify.
- `regexp`: Used to locate an existing line to modify if there is one so that we don't end up with two conflicting `bind-address` directives.
- `line`: The line to replace/insert into the configuration file.

- `insertafter`: If the `regexp` is not matched (that is, the line is not present in the file), this directive ensures that the `lineinfile` module inserts a new line after the `[mysqld]` statement, thus ensuring it is in the correct part of the file.
- `state`: Setting this to `present` state ensures that the line is present in the file, even if the original `regexp` is not matched—in this instance, a line is added to the file in accordance with the value of `line`.

Following on from this modification, we know that the MariaDB server will not pick up any configuration changes unless we restart it, so we do exactly that at the end of the role. Now, if we run this, we can see that it has the desired effect, as shown in the following screenshot:

For simple configuration adjustments such as this, on a small number of systems, this achieves exactly the result that we desire. There are, however, drawbacks to this approach that need to be addressed, especially when it comes to not just the point in time where the change is made, but also to the long-term integrity of the system. Even with the best automation strategies in the world, someone making manual changes can remove the consistency and standardization that is core to good automation practice, and hence there is a real need to ensure that future playbook runs will still yield the desired end result. We will explore this issue in the next section.

Maintaining configuration integrity

The issue with making changes in this manner is that they do not scale well. Tuning a MariaDB server for a production workload often requires setting perhaps half a dozen, or more, parameters. Thus, that simple role that we wrote previously could well grow to become a tangle of regular expressions and directives that are difficult to decipher, let alone manage.

Regular expressions themselves are not foolproof and are only as good as they are written to be. In our previous example, we used the following line to look for the bind-address directive, with a view to changing it. The regular expression `^bind-address\s+=` means to look for lines in the file that have the following:

- Have the bind-address literal string at the start of the line (denoted by the ^)
- Have one or more spaces after the `bind-address` literal string
- Have a = sign after these spaces

The idea behind this regular expression is to ensure that we ignore comments such as the following one:

```
#bind-address = 0.0.0.0
```

However, MariaDB is quite tolerant of whitespace in its configuration files, and the regular expression we have defined here will fail to match the following permutations of this line, all of which are equally valid:

```
bind-address=127.0.0.1
  bind-address = 127.0.0.1
```

In these instances, since the `regexp` parameter didn't match, our role will add a new line to the configuration file with the `bind-address = 0.0.0.0` directive. As MariaDB treats the preceding examples as valid configuration, we end up with two configuration directives in the file which, may well give you unexpected results. Different software packages will handle this differently too, adding to the confusion. There are other complexities to consider too. Many Linux services feature highly complex configurations that are often broken down across multiple files to make them easier to manage. The documentation that comes with the native MariaDB server package on our test Ubuntu system states the following:

```
# The MariaDB/MySQL tools read configuration files in the following order:
# 1. "/etc/mysql/mariadb.cnf" (this file) to set global defaults,
# 2. "/etc/mysql/conf.d/*.cnf" to set global options.
# 3. "/etc/mysql/mariadb.conf.d/*.cnf" to set MariaDB-only options.
# 4. "~/.my.cnf" to set user-specific options.
```

However, this configuration order is dictated by
the `/etc/mysql/mariadb.cnf` file, which at the bottom has directives to include the files
listed on lines 2 and 3 in the preceding code block. It is entirely possible for someone (well-
meaning or otherwise) to simply come along and
overwrite `/etc/mysql/mariadb.cnf` with a new version that removes the include
statements for these subdirectories, and instead includes the following:

```
[mysqld]
bind-address = 127.0.0.1
```

As our role that makes use of `lineinfile` is completely unaware of this file, it will
faithfully set the parameter in `/etc/mysql/mariadb.conf.d/50-server.cnf`, without
understanding that this configuration file is no longer being referenced, and again, the
results on the server will—at best—be unpredictable.

While the goal of enterprise automation is that all systems should have their changes
managed centrally with a tool such as Ansible, the reality is that you cannot always
guarantee that this will occur. Occasionally, things will break, and people who are in a
hurry to fix them may be forced to bypass processes to save time. Equally, new staff
members who are unfamiliar with systems may make changes in a manner such as we have
suggested here.

Alternatively, take—for example—our proposed SSH daemon configuration from Chapter
5, *Using Ansible to Build Virtual Machine Templates for Deployment*. Here, we proposed a
simple role (shown again in the following code block, for reference) that would disable root
logins over SSH, one of a number of recommended security parameters for the SSH
daemon:

```
---
- name: Disable root logins over SSH
  lineinfile:
    dest: /etc/ssh/sshd_config
    regexp: "^PermitRootLogin"
    line: "PermitRootLogin no"
    state: present
```

Note that our `regexp` has the same weaknesses as our other role when it comes to
whitespace. When `sshd` has two duplicate parameters in its configuration file, it takes the
first value as the correct one. Thus, if I knew that the role listed in the previous code block
was being run against a system, all I would have to do is put these lines at the *very top*
of `/etc/ssh/sshd_config`:

```
# Override Ansible roles
PermitRootLogin yes
```

Thus, our Ansible role will run faithfully against this server and report that it has successfully managed the SSH daemon configuration, while in reality, we have overridden it and enabled root logins.

These examples show us two things. First of all, be very careful when working with regular expressions. The more thorough you can be, especially when dealing with whitespace, the better. Obviously, in an ideal world, this would not even be necessary, but unexpected changes such as this have brought down many systems. To prevent the preceding SSH daemon example from being possible, we might try the following regular expression:

```
^\s*PermitRootLogin\s+
```

This will take account of zero or more spaces before the `PermitRootLogin` keyword, and then take account of one or more spaces afterward, all while taking account of the whitespace tolerance built into `sshd`. However, regular expressions are very literal, and we haven't even taken account of tabs yet!

Ultimately, this brings us to the second factor demonstrated through these examples—that to maintain configuration and, hence, system integrity at enterprise scale, and ensure that you have a high degree of confidence in both your automation and the systems it produces, another approach might be required for configuration management. This is exactly what we go on to explore in the next section—techniques for reliably managing configuration at large, enterprise scales.

Managing configuration at an enterprise scale

Clearly, from these examples, another approach is required for the management of configuration at an enterprise scale. There is nothing wrong with the `lineinfile` approach we discussed previously when it comes to making small numbers of changes in a well-controlled environment, yet let us consider a more robust approach to configuration management, better suited to a large organization.

We will start by considering scalable methods for simple static configuration changes (that is, those that are the same across all servers) in the next section.

Making scalable static configuration changes

It is vital that the configuration changes that we make are version controlled, repeatable, and reliable—thus, let's consider an approach that achieves this aim. Let's start with a simple example by revisiting our SSH daemon configuration. On most servers, this is likely to be static, as requirements such as restricting remote root logins and disabling password-based logins are likely to apply across an entire estate. Equally, the SSH daemon is normally configured through one central file—/etc/ssh/sshd_config.

On an Ubuntu server, the default configuration is very simple, consisting of just six lines if we remove all the whitespace and comments. Let's make some modifications to this file so that remote root logins are denied, X11Forwarding is disabled, and only key-based logins are allowed, as follows:

```
ChallengeResponseAuthentication no
UsePAM yes
X11Forwarding no
PrintMotd no
AcceptEnv LANG LC_*
Subsystem sftp /usr/lib/openssh/sftp-server
PasswordAuthentication no
PermitRootLogin no
```

We will store this file within our roles/ directory structure and deploy it with the following role tasks:

```
---
- name: Copy SSHd configuration to target host
  copy:
    src: files/sshd_config
    dest: /etc/ssh/sshd_config
    owner: root
    group: root
    mode: 0644

- name: Restart SSH daemon
  service:
    name: ssh
    state: restarted
```

Here, we use the Ansible `copy` module to copy the `sshd_config` file we have created and stored within the role itself to our target host and ensure it has the ownership and mode that's suitable for the SSH daemon. Finally, we restart the SSH daemon to pick up the changes (note that this service name is valid on Ubuntu Server and may vary on other Linux distributions). Thus, our completed `roles` directory structure looks like this:

```
roles/
└── securesshd
    ├── files
    │   └── sshd_config
    └── tasks
        └── main.yml
```

Now, we can run this to deploy the configuration to our test host, as follows:

```
● ● ●            james@automation-01: ~/hands-on-automation/chapter07/example06 (ssh)
~/hands-on-automation/chapter07/example06> ansible-playbook -i hosts site.yml

PLAY [Secure SSH configuration] *********************************************

TASK [Gathering Facts] ******************************************************
ok: [ubuntu-testhost]

TASK [securesshd : Copy SSHd configuration to target host] ******************
ok: [ubuntu-testhost]

TASK [securesshd : Restart SSH daemon] **************************************
changed: [ubuntu-testhost]

PLAY RECAP ******************************************************************
ubuntu-testhost            : ok=3    changed=1    unreachable=0    failed=0

~/hands-on-automation/chapter07/example06> ▌
```

Now, deploying the configuration through this means gives us a number of advantages over the methods we have explored previously, as listed here:

- The role itself can be committed to a version control system, thus implicitly bringing the configuration file itself (in the `files/` directory of the role) under version control.
- Our role tasks are very simple—it is very easy for someone else to pick up this code and understand what it does, without the need to decipher the regular expressions.

- It doesn't matter what happens to our target machine configuration, especially in terms of whitespace or configuration format. The pitfalls discussed at the end of the previous section are avoided completely because we simply overwrite the file on deployment.
- All machines have an identical configuration, not just in terms of directives, but in terms of order and formatting, thus ensuring it is easy to audit configuration across an enterprise.

Thus, this role represents a big step forward in terms of enterprise-scale configuration management. However, let's see what happens if we run the role against the same host a second time. The resulting output can be seen in the following screenshot:

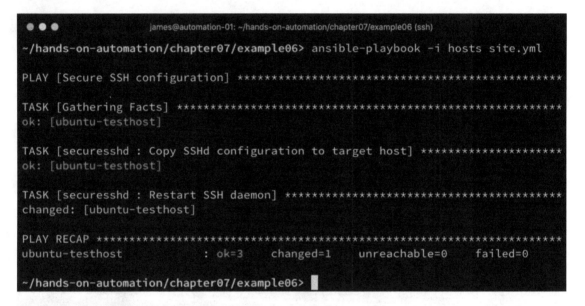

From the preceding screenshot, we can see that Ansible has determined that the SSH configuration file is unmodified from the last run, and hence, the `ok` status is returned. However, in spite of this, the `changed` status of the `Restart SSH daemon` task indicates that the SSH daemon has been restarted, even though no configuration change was made. Restarting system services is normally disruptive, and so it should be avoided unless absolutely necessary. In this case, we would not wish to restart the SSH daemon unless a configuration change is made.

The recommended way to handle this is with a `handler`. A `handler` is an Ansible construct that is much like a task, except that it only gets called when a change is made. Also, when multiple changes are made to a configuration, the handler can be notified multiple times (once for each applicable change), and yet the Ansible engine batches up all handler calls and runs the handler once, only after the tasks complete. This ensures that when it is used to restart a service, such as in this example, the service is only restarted once, and only then when a change is made. Let's test this now, as follows:

1. First of all, remove the service restart task from the role and add a `notify` clause to notify the handler (we shall create this in a minute). The resulting role tasks should look like this:

```
---

- name: Copy SSHd configuration to target host
  copy:
    src: files/sshd_config
    dest: /etc/ssh/sshd_config
    owner: root
    group: root
    mode: 0644
  notify:
    - Restart SSH daemon
```

2. Now, we need to create a `handlers/` directory in the role and add our previously removed handler code to it so that it looks like this:

```
---

- name: Restart SSH daemon
  service:
    name: ssh
    state: restarted
```

3. The resulting `roles` directory structure should now look like this:

```
roles/
└── securesshd
    ├── files
    │   └── sshd_config
    ├── handlers
    │   └── main.yml
    └── tasks
        └── main.yml
```

4. Now, when we run the playbook twice on the same server (having initially reverted the SSH configuration to the original one), we see that the SSH daemon is only restarted in the instance where we have actually changed the configuration, as shown in the following screenshot:

```
● ● ●            james@automation-01: ~/hands-on-automation/chapter07/example07 (ssh)
~/hands-on-automation/chapter07/example07> ansible-playbook -i hosts site.yml

PLAY [Secure SSH configuration] ************************************************

TASK [Gathering Facts] *********************************************************
ok: [ubuntu-testhost]

TASK [securesshd : Copy SSHd configuration to target host] *********************
changed: [ubuntu-testhost]

RUNNING HANDLER [securesshd : Restart SSH daemon] ******************************
changed: [ubuntu-testhost]

PLAY RECAP *********************************************************************
ubuntu-testhost            : ok=3    changed=2    unreachable=0    failed=0

~/hands-on-automation/chapter07/example07> ansible-playbook -i hosts site.yml

PLAY [Secure SSH configuration] ************************************************

TASK [Gathering Facts] *********************************************************
ok: [ubuntu-testhost]

TASK [securesshd : Copy SSHd configuration to target host] *********************
ok: [ubuntu-testhost]

PLAY RECAP *********************************************************************
ubuntu-testhost            : ok=2    changed=0    unreachable=0    failed=0

~/hands-on-automation/chapter07/example07> █
```

To further demonstrate handlers before we move on, let's consider this enhancement to the role tasks:

```
---
- name: Copy SSHd configuration to target host
  copy:
    src: files/sshd_config
    dest: /etc/ssh/sshd_config
    owner: root
    group: root
```

```
      mode: 0644
    notify:
      - Restart SSH daemon

  - name: Perform an additional modification
    lineinfile:
      path: /etc/ssh/sshd_config
      regexp: '^\# Configured by Ansible'
      line: '# Configured by Ansible on {{ inventory_hostname }}'
      insertbefore: BOF
      state: present
    notify:
      - Restart SSH daemon
```

Here, we deploy our configuration file and perform an additional modification. We are putting a comment into the head of the file, which includes an Ansible variable, with the hostname of the target host.

This will result in two changed statuses on our target host, and yet, if we revert to the default SSH daemon configuration and then run our new playbook, we see the following:

```
● ● ●              james@automation-01: ~/hands-on-automation/chapter07/example08 (ssh)

~/hands-on-automation/chapter07/example08> ansible-playbook -i hosts site.yml

PLAY [Secure SSH configuration] ********************************************

TASK [Gathering Facts] *****************************************************
ok: [ubuntu-testhost]

TASK [securesshd : Copy SSHd configuration to target host] *****************
changed: [ubuntu-testhost]

TASK [securesshd : Perform an additional modification] *********************
changed: [ubuntu-testhost]

RUNNING HANDLER [securesshd : Restart SSH daemon] **************************
changed: [ubuntu-testhost]

PLAY RECAP *****************************************************************
ubuntu-testhost              : ok=4    changed=3    unreachable=0    failed=0

~/hands-on-automation/chapter07/example08>
```

Pay careful attention to the preceding output and the sequence in which the tasks are run. You will note that the handler is not run in sequence and is actually run once at the end of the play.

Even though our tasks both changed and hence would have notified the handler twice, the handler was only run at the end of the playbook run, minimizing restarts, just as required.

In this manner, we can make changes to static configuration files at large scales, across many hundreds—if not thousands—of machines. In the next section, we will build on this to demonstrate ways of managing configuration where dynamic data is required—for example, configuration parameters that might change on a per-host or per-group basis.

Making scalable dynamic configuration changes

While the preceding examples resolve many of the challenges of making automated configuration changes at scale in an enterprise, it is noticeable that our final example was somewhat inefficient. We deployed a static, version-controlled configuration file, and made a change to it using the lineinfile module again.

This allowed us to insert an Ansible variable into the file, which in many instances is incredibly useful, especially when configuring more complex services. However, it is—at best—inelegant to split this change across two tasks. Also, reverting to the use of the lineinfile module again exposes us to the risks we discussed earlier and means we would need one lineinfile task for every variable we wish to insert into a configuration.

Thankfully, Ansible includes just the answer to such a problem. In this case, the concept of Jinja2 templating comes to our rescue.

Jinja2 is a templating language for Python that is incredibly powerful and easy to use. As Ansible is coded almost entirely in Python, it lends itself well to the use of Jinja2 templates. So, what is a Jinja2 template? At its most fundamental level, it is a static configuration file, such as the one we deployed for the SSH daemon earlier, but with the possibility of variable substitutions. Of course, Jinja2 is far more powerful than that—it is, in essence, a language in its own right, and features common language constructs such as for loops and if...elif...else constructs, just as you would find in other languages. This makes it incredibly powerful and flexible, and entire sections of a configuration file (for example) can be omitted, depending on how an if statement evaluates.

As you can imagine, Jinja2 deserves a book of its own to cover the detail of the language—however, here, we will provide a practical hands-on introduction to Jinja2 templating for the automation of configuration management in an enterprise.

Let's go back to our SSH daemon example for a minute, where we wanted to put the target hostname into a comment at the head of the file. While this is a contrived example, progressing it from the `copy/lineinfile` example to a single `template` task will show the benefits that templating brings. From here, we can progress to a more comprehensive example. To start with, let's define our Jinja2 template for the `sshd_config` file, as follows:

```
# Configured by Ansible {{ inventory_hostname }}
ChallengeResponseAuthentication no
UsePAM yes
X11Forwarding no
PrintMotd no
AcceptEnv LANG LC_*
Subsystem sftp /usr/lib/openssh/sftp-server
PasswordAuthentication no
PermitRootLogin no
```

Notice that the file is identical to the file we deployed using the copy module earlier, only now, we have included the comment in the file header and used the Ansible variable construct (denoted by pairs of curly braces) to insert the `inventory_hostname` variable.

Now, for the sake of our sanity, we will call this file `sshd_config.j2` to ensure we can differentiate templates from flat configuration files. Templates are normally placed into a `templates/` subdirectory within the role, and so are subject to version control in the same way that playbook, roles, and any associated flat configuration files are.

Now, rather than copying the flat file and then performing substitutions with one or more `lineinfile` tasks, we can use the Ansible `template` module to deploy this template and parse all Jinja2 constructs.

Thus, our tasks now look like this:

```
---
- name: Copy SSHd configuration to target host
  template:
    src: templates/sshd_config.j2
    dest: /etc/ssh/sshd_config
    owner: root
    group: root
    mode: 0644
  notify:
    - Restart SSH daemon
```

Notice that the task is almost identical to our earlier `copy` task and that we call our handler, just as before.

The completed module directory structure now looks like this:

```
roles
└── securesshd
    ├── handlers
    │   └── main.yml
    ├── tasks
    │   └── main.yml
    └── templates
        └── sshd_config.j2
```

Let's run this and evaluate the results, which can be seen in the following screenshot:

```
● ● ●                james@automation-01: ~/hands-on-automation/chapter07/example09 (ssh)

~/hands-on-automation/chapter07/example09> ansible-playbook -i hosts site.yml

PLAY [Secure SSH configuration] ********************************************

TASK [Gathering Facts] *****************************************************
ok: [ubuntu-testhost]

TASK [securesshd : Copy SSHd configuration to target host] *****************
changed: [ubuntu-testhost]

RUNNING HANDLER [securesshd : Restart SSH daemon] **************************
changed: [ubuntu-testhost]

PLAY RECAP *****************************************************************
ubuntu-testhost            : ok=3     changed=2    unreachable=0    failed=0

~/hands-on-automation/chapter07/example09> cat /etc/ssh/sshd_config
# Configured by Ansible ubuntu-testhost
ChallengeResponseAuthentication no
UsePAM yes
X11Forwarding no
PrintMotd no
AcceptEnv LANG LC_*
Subsystem       sftp    /usr/lib/openssh/sftp-server
PasswordAuthentication no
PermitRootLogin no
~/hands-on-automation/chapter07/example09>
```

As can be seen here, the template has been copied across to the target host, and the variable in the header comment has been processed and the appropriate value substituted.

This becomes incredibly powerful as our configuration becomes more complex as, no matter how large and complex the template, the role still only requires the one `template` task. Returning to our MariaDB server, suppose that we want to set a number of parameters on a per-server basis to effect tuning appropriate to the different workloads we are deploying. Perhaps we want to set the following:

- The server bind-address, defined by `bind-address`
- The maximum binary log size, defined by `max_binlog_size`
- The TCP port that MariaDB listens on, as defined by `port`

All of these parameters are defined in `/etc/mysql/mariadb.conf.d/50-server.cnf`. However, as discussed earlier, we need to also ensure the integrity of `/etc/mysql/mariadb.cnf` to ensure it includes this (and other) files, to reduce the possibility of someone overriding our configuration. Let's start building our templates—first of all, a simplified version of the `50-server.cnf` file, with some variable substitutions. The first part of this file is shown in the following code—note the `port` and `bind-address` parameters, which are now defined using Ansible variables, denoted in the usual manner with pairs of curly braces:

```
[server]
[mysqld]
user = mysql
pid-file = /var/run/mysqld/mysqld.pid
socket = /var/run/mysqld/mysqld.sock
port = {{ mariadb_port }}
basedir = /usr
datadir = /var/lib/mysql
tmpdir = /tmp
lc-messages-dir = /usr/share/mysql
skip-external-locking
bind-address = {{ mariadb_bind_address }}
```

The second part of this file looks as follows—you will observe here the presence of the `mariadb_max_binlog_size` variable, while all other parameters remain static:

```
key_buffer_size = 16M
max_allowed_packet = 16M
thread_stack = 192K
thread_cache_size = 8
myisam_recover_options = BACKUP
query_cache_limit = 1M
query_cache_size = 16M
log_error = /var/log/mysql/error.log
expire_logs_days = 10
max_binlog_size = {{ mariadb_max_binlog_size }}
```

```
character-set-server = utf8mb4
collation-server = utf8mb4_general_ci
[embedded]
[mariadb]
[mariadb-10.1]
```

Now, let's also add in a templated version of `/etc/mysql/mariadb.cnf`, as follows:

```
[client-server]
!includedir /etc/mysql/conf.d/
!includedir /etc/mysql/mariadb.conf.d/
```

This file might be short, but it serves a really important purpose. It is the first file that is read by the MariaDB service when it loads, and it references other files or directories to be included. If we did not maintain control of this file using Ansible, then anyone with sufficient privileges could log in and edit the file, possibly including entirely different configurations and bypassing our Ansible-defined configuration entirely. Whenever you deploy configuration with Ansible, it is important to consider factors such as this, as otherwise, your configuration changes might be bypassed by a well-meaning (or otherwise) administrator.

 A template doesn't have to have any Jinja2 constructs in it—if there are no variables to insert, as in our second example, the file will simply be copied as-is to the target machine.

Obviously, it would be slightly more efficient to use the copy module to send this static configuration file to the remote server, but this requires two tasks, where we can use just one with a loop to process all our templates. Such an example is shown in the following code block:

```
---
- name: Copy MariaDB configuration files to host
  template:
    src: {{ item.src }}
    dest: {{ item.dest }}
    owner: root
    group: root
    mode: 0644
  loop:
    - { src: 'templates/mariadb.cnf.j2', dest: '/etc/mysql/mariadb.cnf' }
    - { src: 'templates/50-server.cnf.j2', dest:
'/etc/mysql/mariadb.conf.d/50-server.cnf' }
  notify:
    - Restart MariaDB Server
```

Finally, we define a handler to restart MariaDB if the configuration has changed, as follows:

```
---
- name: Restart MariaDB Server
  service:
    name: mariadb
    state: restarted
```

Now, before we run this, a word on variables. In Ansible, variables can be defined at a wide number of levels. In a case such as this, where we are applying a different configuration to different hosts with differing purposes, it makes sense to define the variables at the host or hostgroup level. However, what happens if someone were to forget to put these in the inventory, or in another appropriate location? Fortunately, we can leverage the variable precedence order of Ansible to our advantage here and define default variables for our role. These are second lowest on the order of precedence, so are almost always overridden by another setting elsewhere, yet they provide a safety net, should they be missed accidentally. As our preceding templates have been written, if the variables are not defined anywhere, the configuration file will be invalid and the MariaDB server will refuse to start—a case we would definitely like to avoid.

Let's define the default values for these variables in our role now under `defaults/main.yml`, as follows:

```
---
mariadb_bind_address: "127.0.0.1"
mariadb_port: "3306"
mariadb_max_binlog_size: "100M"
```

With this complete, our role structure should look like this:

```
roles/
└── configuremariadb
    ├── defaults
    │   └── main.yml
    ├── handlers
    │   └── main.yml
    ├── tasks
    │   └── main.yml
    └── templates
        ├── 50-server.conf.j2
        └── mariadb.cnf.j2
```

Naturally, we want to override the default values, so we will define these in our inventory grouping—this is a good use case for inventory groups. All MariaDB servers that serve the same function would go in one inventory group, and then have a common set of inventory variables assigned to them, such that they all receive the same configuration. However, the use of templates in our role means that we can reuse this role in a number of situations, simply by providing differing configurations through variable definition. We will create an inventory for our test host that looks like this:

```
[dbservers]
ubuntu-testhost

[dbservers:vars]
mariadb_port=3307
mariadb_bind_address=0.0.0.0
mariadb_max_binlog_size=250M
```

With this complete, we can finally run our playbook and observe what happens. The result is shown in the following screenshot:

With this successfully run, we have shown a complete end-to-end example of how to manage configuration on an enterprise scale, all while avoiding the pitfalls of regular expression substitutions and multi-part configurations. Although these examples are simple, they should serve as the basis for any well-thought-out enterprise automation strategy where a configuration is required.

Summary

Managing configuration across an enterprise Linux estate is filled with pitfalls and the potential for configuration drift. This can be caused by people with good intentions, even in *break-fix* scenarios where changes have to be made in a hurry. However, it can also be caused by those with malicious intent, seeking to circumvent security requirements. Good use of Ansible, especially templating, enables the construction of easy-to-read, concise playbooks that make it easy to ensure configuration management is reliable, repeatable, auditable, and version-controlled—all the basic tenets we set out earlier in this book for good enterprise automation practice.

In this chapter, you gained practical experience in extending a Linux machine with new software packages. You then learned how to apply simple, static configuration changes to those packages, and the potential pitfalls associated with this. Finally, you learned best practices for managing configuration across an enterprise using Ansible. In the next chapter, we proceed to look at internal repository management with Pulp.

Questions

1. What are the different Ansible modules commonly used for making changes to configuration files?
2. How does templating work in Ansible?
3. Why must you consider configuration file structure when making changes with Ansible?
4. What are the pitfalls of using regular expressions when making file modifications?
5. How does a template behave if there are no variables in it?
6. How can you check that a configuration template you have deployed is valid before committing it to disk?
7. How can you quickly audit the configuration of 100 machines against a known template with Ansible?

Further reading

- For an in-depth understanding of Ansible, please refer to *Mastering Ansible, Third Edition*, by *James Freeman* and *Jesse Keating* (https://www.packtpub.com/gb/virtualization-and-cloud/mastering-ansible-third-edition).

Section 3: Day-to-Day Management

This section covers how the management of Linux servers in the Enterprise does not end with good build processes—it is vital that ongoing management is effective and efficient. In this section, we will explore the use of Ansible and other tools to achieve these goals.

This section comprises the following chapters:

8
Enterprise Repository Management with Pulp

So far in this book, we have covered several tasks related to the build and configuration of Linux servers for deployment in an Enterprise environment. While much of the work we have completed scales well to cover most scenarios, it must be noted that so far we have only installed packages from one of two sources—either the upstream public package repositories corresponding to each Linux distribution we are using or, in the case of our PXE booting chapter, from an ISO image we downloaded.

Needless to say, this presents several challenges, especially when it comes to creating repeatable, manageable builds of Linux. We will explore these in greater depth in the section titled *Installing Pulp for patch management*, but suffice to say, using the publicly available repositories means that two builds being performed on two different weekdays could be different! The ISO installation method presents the other end of the spectrum and always produces consistent builds regardless of when they are performed, but in this case, no security (or other) updates are received! What is required is a compromise between these two extremes, and thankfully, one exists in the form of a software package called **Pulp**.

We shall explore Pulp in this chapter, specifically covering the following:

- Installing Pulp for patch management
- Building repositories in Pulp
- Patching processes with Pulp

Technical requirements

This chapter includes examples based on the following technologies:

- Ubuntu Server 18.04 LTS
- CentOS 7.6
- Ansible 2.8

To run through these examples, you will need access to two servers or virtual machines running one of each of the operating systems listed previously and Ansible. Note that the examples provided in this chapter may be destructive in nature and if run as-is are only intended to be run in an isolated test environment.

All example code discussed in this chapter is available on GitHub at the following URL: `https://github.com/PacktPublishing/Hands-On-Enterprise-Automation-on-Linux/tree /master/chapter08`.

Installing Pulp for patch management

Before we delve into the practical aspects of installing Pulp, let's take a more in-depth look at why you would use it. Throughout this book, we have advocated building a Linux environment that is standardized and features high degrees of repeatability, audibility, and predictability. These are important not just as a foundation for automation, but also serves as good practice in the enterprise.

Let's assume that you build a server and deploy a new service to it with Ansible, as we have set out earlier in this book. So far, so good—the Ansible playbooks provide documentation on the build standard and ensure the build can be accurately repeated at a later date. There is a catch, however. Let's say that, a few months later, you return to create another server—perhaps to scale an application or for a **Disaster Recovery** (**DR**) scenario. Depending on the source for your packages, one of two things will happen:

- If you install from the public internet-facing repositories, both builds will have the latest versions of all the packages that were installed on the date they were built. This difference may be significant, and if time has been put into testing and qualifying software on a given build of Linux, you may not be able to guarantee this with different package versions. Sure, everything is up to date, and you will have all of the latest security patches and bug fixes, but every time you perform this build on a different day, you are prone to getting different package versions. This causes problems with repeatability, especially when ensuring that code that has been tested in one environment works in another.

- At the other end of the scale is the ISO build repositories that we used in `Chapter 6`, *Custom Builds with PXE Booting*. These never change (unless someone downloads a newer ISO and extracts it over the old one), and so while it produces builds that are of a completely known quantity (and hence support our repeatability goal), they never receive any security updates. This in itself may be a problem.

The compromise is, of course, to find a middle ground between these two extremes. What if it were possible to create our own repositories of packages that were a snapshot of a given point in time of a public repository? Hence, they remain static when we need them to (thus ensuring consistent builds), and yet can be updated on demand if an important security fix comes out. The Pulp project comes to our rescue here and is capable of doing exactly these things. It is also a component in some of the more complex infrastructure management solutions such as Katello, as we shall see in the next chapter.

However, for installations where a **Graphical User Interface** (**GUI**) is not a requirement, Pulp meets our needs perfectly. Let's take a look at how we might install it.

Installing Pulp

As we discussed in `Chapter 1`, *Building a Standard Operating Environment on Linux*, in this book, there will be times when even though you may have built a standardized operating environment around a given Linux distribution such as Ubuntu Server, you have to create an exception. Pulp is such a case, for although it can manage both `.rpm` and `.deb` packages (hence handling repository requirements for a wide variety of Linux distributions), it is only packaged for (and therefore is easiest to install) on CentOS, Fedora, and RHEL-based operating systems. You can still manage your Ubuntu Server estate with Pulp—you just need to install it on CentOS (or your preferred Red Hat variant).

There are several facets to the Pulp installation. For example, Pulp relies on a MongoDB installation, which may be external if desired. Similarly, it also relies on a message bus, and it is possible to use either RabbitMQ or Qpid as preferred. Most organizations will have their own standards for these things, and so it is left as an exercise to you to define the architecture best suited to your enterprise. In this chapter, we will perform a very simple installation of Pulp on a single server to demonstrate the steps involved.

Given the relative complexity of installing Pulp, it is recommended that you create an Ansible Playbook for your Pulp installation. However, in this chapter, we will complete the installation manually to demonstrate the work involved—there is no one-size-fits-all Pulp installation:

1. Before we can begin the installation, we must build a virtual (or physical) server to host our Pulp repositories. For our example, we will base this on CentOS 7.6, which is the latest supported version for Pulp at the time of writing. Also, note the following filesystem requirements:

   - `/var/lib/mongodb`: We will build our example Pulp server with MongoDB on the same host. The MongoDB database can grow to over 10 GB in size, and it is recommended to mount this path on a dedicated LVM backed filesystem so that it can be easily grown if required, and so that if it ever does fill up, it doesn't halt the rest of the system.
   - `/var/lib/pulp`: This directory is where the Pulp repositories are housed, and again it should be on a dedicated LVM backed filesystem. The size will be determined by the repositories you wish to create—for example, if you want to mirror a 20 GB upstream repository, then `/var/lib/pulp` needs to be a minimum of 20 GB in size. This filesystem also must be XFS-based—if created on `ext4`, you run the risk of running out of inodes.

2. Once these requirements are met, we must install the EPEL repository as the Pulp install will draw packages from here:

   ```
   $ sudo yum install epel-release
   ```

3. We then need to install the Pulp repository file:

   ```
   $ sudo wget -O /etc/yum.repos.d/rhel-pulp.repo
   https://repos.fedorapeople.org/repos/pulp/pulp/rhel-pulp.repo
   ```

4. Next, we set up the MongoDB server—this must be completed before we proceed with the Pulp installation. It is expected that most enterprises will have some internal standards for the database servers that they will follow—here, we will suffice with a default installation with SSL encryption:

   ```
   $ sudo yum install mongodb-server
   ```

5. Again, it is fair to say that most enterprises will have their own certificate authority, be it internal or otherwise. For our example server, we will generate a simple self-signed certificate with the following command:

```
$ sudo openssl req -x509 -nodes -newkey rsa:4096 -keyout
/etc/ssl/mongodb-cert.key -out /etc/ssl/mongodb-cert.crt -days 3650
-subj "/C=GB/CN=pulp.example.com"
```

6. We then need to concatenate the private key and certificate into one file for MongoDB to pick up:

```
$ sudo cat /etc/ssl/mongodb-cert.key /etc/ssl/mongodb-cert.crt |
sudo tee /etc/ssl/mongodb.pem > /dev/null
```

7. With this complete, we must reconfigure MongoDB to pick up the newly created certificate file and enable SSL. Edit the `/etc/mongod.conf` file and configure the following parameters (any other parameters in the file can be left at their defaults):

```
# Use ssl on configured ports
sslOnNormalPorts = true

# PEM file for ssl
sslPEMKeyFile = /etc/ssl/mongodb.pem
```

8. At this stage, we can now enable the MongoDB service to start on boot and start it:

```
$ sudo systemctl enable mongod.service
$ sudo systemctl restart mongod.service
```

9. With our Mongo database server running, we now need to install the message bus. Again, most enterprises will have corporate standards for this and it is recommended to adhere to these where they are defined. The following example is the minimum required set of steps for a functional demo—it should not be considered fully secured, but it is functional for the sake of testing and evaluating pulp. Here, we simply install the required packages and then enable and start the services:

```
$ sudo yum install qpid-cpp-server qpid-cpp-server-linearstore
$ sudo systemctl enable qpidd.service
$ sudo systemctl start qpidd.service
```

10. With our underlying infrastructure completed, we can now install Pulp itself. The initial steps are to install the base packages:

```
$ sudo yum install pulp-server python-gofer-qpid python2-qpid qpid-
tools
```

Pulp uses a plugin-based architecture to host the various repositories it is capable of serving. At the time of writing, Pulp is capable of hosting the following:

- RPM-based repositories (for example, CentOS, RHEL, and Fedora)
- DEB-based repositories (for example, Debian and Ubuntu)
- Python modules (for example, for mirroring PyPI content)
- Puppet manifests
- Docker images
- OSTree content

Unfortunately, this chapter does not allow us space to go into all of these modules in detail—however, it is safe to say that, at a high-level, Pulp operates in the same manner across all these different technologies. Whether working with Python modules, Docker images, or RPM packages, you can create a central repository that is stable and can be version controlled to ensure an up-to-date environment can be maintained without losing control of what that environment contains.

As our use case is Pulp for serving out Linux packages, we will install the RPM- and DEB-based plugins:

```
$ sudo yum install pulp-deb-plugins pulp-rpm-plugins
```

11. With Pulp installed, we must configure the core services. This is performed by editing /etc/pulp/server.conf—most of the default settings are fine for a simple demo such as ours—however, as we enabled SSL support on our MongoDB backend, we must tell the Pulp server we have done this and disable SSL verification as we are using self-signed certificates. The [database] section of the aforementioned file should look like this:

```
[database]
ssl: true
verify_ssl: false
```

If you examine this file, you will see there is a great deal of configuration that can be carried out, all of which is well documented with comments. Specifically, you can customize the following sections:

- [email]: This is off by default but if you want your Pulp server to send email reports, you would configure this here.
- [database]: We have simply turned on SSL support in this section, but if the database was on an external server or required more advanced parameters, these would be specified here.
- [messaging]: For communication between different Pulp components, the default Qpid message broker requires no further configuration here, but if you are using RabbitMQ and/or have turned on authentication/SSL support, then that will need to be configured here.
- [tasks]: Pulp can have separate message brokers for inter-component communication and its asynchronous tasks, and the broker for the latter can be configured here. As we are using the same Qpid instance for both functions, nothing further is required for this example.
- [server]: This is used to configure the server's default credentials, hostname, and such.

12. Once the Pulp server is configured, we must generate the RSA key pair and CA certificate for Pulp using the following two commands:

```
$ sudo pulp-gen-key-pair
$ sudo pulp-gen-ca-certificate
```

13. Pulp uses Apache to serve its HTTP(S) content, and so we must configure this. First of all, we initialize the backend database by running the following command (note it is run as the apache user):

```
$ sudo -u apache pulp-manage-db
```

14. If you are intending to use SSL transport with Apache, be sure to configure it to your enterprise requirements. CentOS installs a self-signed certificate for Apache SSL by default, but you may want to replace this with a certificate signed by your Enterprise CA. Also, be sure to disable the insecure SSL protocols—as a minimum, it is recommended to place the following two settings into `/etc/httpd/conf.d/ssl.conf`:

```
SSLProtocol all -SSLv2 -SSLv3

SSLCipherSuite HIGH:3DES:!aNULL:!MD5:!SEED:!IDEA
```

This, of course, is only a guide, and most enterprises will have their own security standards that should be adhered to here.

 As new vulnerabilities are discovered, these requirements may change. The preceding configuration is believed to be good practice at the time of writing, but could change at any time without notice. It is up to you to check any and all security-related settings for your environment.

15. With Apache configured, set it to start on boot and start it up:

```
$ sudo systemctl enable httpd.service
$ sudo systemctl start httpd.service
```

16. Pulp has several other backend services that are required for it to be operational. Each of these can be configured and tuned as required, but again, for the sake of our example server, it is sufficient to enable and start each in turn:

```
$ sudo systemctl enable pulp_workers.service
$ sudo systemctl start pulp_workers.service

$ sudo systemctl enable pulp_celerybeat.service
$ sudo systemctl start pulp_celerybeat.service

$ sudo systemctl enable pulp_resource_manager.service
$ sudo systemctl start pulp_resource_manager.service
```

17. Our final task is to install the administrative components of Pulp so that we can manage our server:

```
$ sudo yum install pulp-admin-client pulp-rpm-admin-extensions
pulp-deb-admin-extensions
```

18. There is one final task to complete for our server. Pulp is designed to be administered remotely, and as such, it communicates over SSL to ensure the security of all transactions. Although we have created an *all-in-one* host and throughout this chapter will perform the server admin from the same host, we need to tell the Pulp admin client that we are using self-signed certificates—otherwise, SSL validation will fail. To do this, edit `/etc/pulp/admin/admin.conf`, and in the `[server]` section, define the following parameter:

```
verify_ssl: False
```

19. Finally, we can test that our Pulp server is operational by logging in to it. Although Pulp supports multiple user accounts, and even integration with LDAP backends, a simple installation such as ours comes with one administrator account, where the username and password are both `admin`.

    If all goes well, you should see output similar to the following and be able to query to server status (note that the output has been truncated to save space):

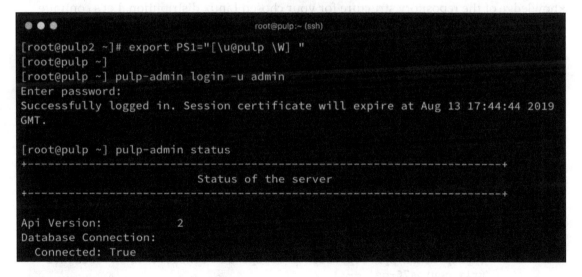

```
[root@pulp2 ~]# export PS1="[\u@pulp \W] "
[root@pulp ~]
[root@pulp ~] pulp-admin login -u admin
Enter password:
Successfully logged in. Session certificate will expire at Aug 13 17:44:44 2019
GMT.

[root@pulp ~] pulp-admin status
+------------------------------------------------------------------+
                        Status of the server
+------------------------------------------------------------------+

Api Version:            2
Database Connection:
  Connected: True
```

Now that we have a fully operational Pulp server, we shall demonstrate the process of creating repositories for managed stable updates and system builds using our newly built Pulp system.

Building repositories in Pulp

Although in this chapter we will only be using a subset of the features available in Pulp, it is intended that a viable workflow is demonstrated here that showcases why you might choose Pulp to manage Enterprise repositories, rather than rolling your own solution (for example, copying packages off an ISO as we did in Chapter 6, *Custom Builds with PXE Booting*).

The process for handling RPM-based package repositories and DEB-based ones is broadly similar.

Let's start by exploring how to create and manage RPM-based repositories.

Building RPM-based repositories in Pulp

Although installing Pulp is quite a complex process, once it is installed, the process of managing repositories is incredibly straightforward. However, it does require a little knowledge of the repository structure for your chosen Linux distribution. Let's continue with the CentOS 7 build that we have been using as an example throughout this book.

The core CentOS 7 repositories are split into two—first of all, there is the OS repository; this contains all of the files for the latest point release of CentOS 7—which, at the time of writing, is 7.6. This was last updated in November 2018 and will remain static until CentOS 7.7 is released. The updates for this release are then contained in a separate repository, and so to build a fully functional mirror for CentOS 7 in our Pulp server, we need to mirror both of these paths.

Let's start by creating a mirror of the base operating system:

1. The first step is to log into the `pulp-admin` client, as we demonstrated at the end of the previous section. Then, from there, we run the following command to create a new repository:

```
$ pulp-admin rpm repo create --repo-id='centos76-os' --relative-
url='centos76-os' --
feed=http://mirror.centos.org/centos/7/os/x86_64/
```

Let's break that command down:

- `rpm repo create`: This set of keywords tells the Pulp server to create a new RPM-based repository definition. Note that nothing is synchronized or published at this stage—this is simply creating metadata for a new repository.
- `--repo-id='centos76-os'`: This tells Pulp that the ID of our new repository is `centos76-os`—this is like a unique key and should be used to differentiate your new repository from others.
- `--relative-url='centos76-os'`: This instructs Pulp where to publish the repository—RPM-based repositories are published at `http(s)://pulp-server-address/pulp/repos/<relative-url>`.
- `--feed=http://mirror.centos.org/centos/7/os/x86_64/`: This is the upstream location from which RPM-based content will be synchronized.

2. With our repository definition created, the next step is to synchronize the packages from the upstream server. This is as simple as running this command:

```
$ pulp-admin rpm repo sync run --repo-id='centos76-os'
```

3. This kicks off an asynchronous command that runs in the background on the server—you can check the status at any time using this command:

```
$ pulp-admin rpm repo sync status --repo-id='centos76-os'
```

4. Finally, once the synchronization is completed, the repository must be published—this effectively makes the synchronized content available over the Apache web server installed as part of the Pulp installation earlier:

```
$ pulp-admin rpm repo publish run --repo-id='centos76-os'
```

Now, with this completed, you have an internal snapshot of the upstream CentOS 7.6 OS repository defined by the `--feed` parameter, which will remain constant on our Pulp server even when CentOS 7.7 is released.

Now, of course, we also need updates to ensure we get the latest security patches, bug fixes, and so on. The frequency of updates of your repositories will depend upon your patching cycle, internal security policies, and so on. Hence, we will define a second repository to house the update packages.

We will issue an almost identical set of commands to the preceding ones to create the updates repository, only this time there are two key differences:

- We are using the `/updates/` path for the feed rather than `/os/`.
- We have put a date stamp into `repo-id` and `relative-url`—you could, of course, adopt your own versioning scheme here—however, as this repository will be a snapshot of all CentOS 7 updates to August 7, 2019, using the date of the snapshot as an identifier is one sensible approach:

```
$ pulp-admin rpm repo create --repo-id='centos7-07aug19' --
relative-url='centos7-07aug19' --
feed=http://mirror.centos.org/centos/7/updates/x86_64/
$ pulp-admin rpm repo sync run --repo-id='centos7-07aug19'
$ pulp-admin rpm repo publish run --repo-id centos7-07aug19
```

With this run, we can then use the `pulp-admin` client to inspect the repositories and inspect the disk usage. At present, we can see that the Pulp filesystem has 33 GB used, though not all of this is for CentOS as there are other repositories on this test system. This level of usage will become important in a minute.

In an enterprise environment, a good practice would be to build or update a set of test CentOS 7 systems to this August 7 snapshot and perform the requisite testing on them to ensure confidence in the build. This is especially important in physical systems where kernel changes could cause issues. Once confidence has been established in this build, it becomes the baseline for all CentOS 7 systems. The great thing about this for an enterprise scenario is that all systems (provided they use the Pulp repository) will have the same versions of all packages. This, combined with good automation practices, as we have discussed throughout this book so far, brings almost Docker-like stability and platform confidence to a Linux environment.

Building on this scenario, suppose that overnight a critical security patch is released for CentOS 7. As important it is to apply this patch in a timely manner, it also is important to perform testing on it to ensure it doesn't break any existing services. As a result, we do not wish to update our `centos7-07aug19` repository mirror, as this is a known stable snapshot (in other words, we have tested it and are happy with it—it is stable within our enterprise environment).

If we were just using the upstream internet-facing repositories, then we would have no control over this and our CentOS 7 servers would blindly pick up the patch the next time an update was run. Equally, if we were manually building repository mirrors using a tool such as `reposync`, we would have one of two choices. First, we could update our existing mirror, which would cost us little disk space, but would bring the same problems as using the upstream repositories (that is, all servers pick up the new patch as soon as an update is run). Alternatively, we could create a second snapshot for testing purposes. I estimated that mirroring the CentOS 7 updates on the Pulp server required approximately 16 GB of disk space and so creating a second snapshot would require around 32 GB of disk space. As time goes on, more snapshots would require more and more disk space, which is incredibly inefficient.

This is where Pulp really shines—not only can it create and manage RPM-based repositories in an efficient manner, but it also knows not to download packages that it already has on a sync operation and not to duplicate packages on a publish—hence, it is very efficient in terms of both bandwidth and disk usage. Due to this, we can issue the following command set to create a new snapshot of the CentOS 7 updates on August 8:

```
$ pulp-admin rpm repo create --repo-id='centos7-08aug19' --relative-
url='centos7-08aug19' --
feed=http://mirror.centos.org/centos/7/updates/x86_64/
$ pulp-admin rpm repo sync run --repo-id='centos7-08aug19'
$ pulp-admin rpm repo publish run --repo-id centos7-08aug19
```

You will recognize the similarity with the commands we ran earlier in this section to create the August 7, 2019 snapshot—they are, in fact, identical except for the new repository ID (--repo-id) and URL (--relative-url), which carry the new date in to differentiate it from our earlier one. This process will run as before, as shown in the following screenshot—it appears that all packages are downloaded and at this stage, there is little clue as to what goes on behind the scenes:

```
● ● ●                              root@pulp:~ (ssh)

[root@pulp ~] pulp-admin rpm repo create --repo-id='centos7-08aug19' --relative-url='
centos7-08aug19' --feed=http://mirror.centos.org/centos/7/updates/x86_64/
Successfully created repository [centos7-08aug19]

[root@pulp ~] pulp-admin rpm repo sync run --repo-id='centos7-08aug19'
+------------------------------------------------------------------+
            Synchronizing Repository [centos7-08aug19]
+------------------------------------------------------------------+

This command may be exited via ctrl+c without affecting the request.

Downloading metadata...
[-]
... completed

Downloading repository content...
[|]
[================================================] 100%
```

However, let's now examine the disk usage:

```
● ● ●                              root@pulp:~ (ssh)

[root@pulp ~] df -h | grep pulp
/dev/mapper/vg_pulp-lv_pulp     60G    34G    27G   57% /var/lib/pulp
```

Here, we can see that the disk usage has been rounded up to 34 GB—we would likely find the usage considerably less if we used a more fine-grained measure. In this way, Pulp allows us to create snapshots almost as we require them, without consuming vast amounts of disk space, while retaining older ones for stability purposes until new ones are proved, at which point redundant snapshots can be deleted.

It is worth saying in this regard that deleting a repository from Pulp does not necessarily free up disk space. The reason for this is that the package de-duplication at the backend must be careful not to delete any packages that are still required. In our example, more than 99% of the packages from our August 7 snapshot are also in the August 8 one, and so it is important that if we delete either of these, that the other remains intact.

In Pulp, this process is called orphan recovery, and it is the very process of finding packages that no longer belong to any repository (presumably because the repository was deleted) and tidying them up.

Completing our current example, suppose that we tested our August 8 snapshot and the updated packages in it caused problems in testing. From this, we have determined that this snapshot is not suitable for production and that we will delete it, pending creation of a new snapshot when a fix becomes available:

1. First of all, we must delete the repository itself:

   ```
   $ pulp-admin rpm repo delete --repo-id='centos7-08aug19'
   ```

   This removes the repository definition and the published URL on the Apache server so that it can no longer be used.

2. To clean up any orphan packages, we can then issue the following command:

   ```
   $ pulp-admin orphan remove --all
   ```

   This command is a general cleanup that removes all orphans from across the entire Pulp server and is a good general maintenance step. However, the command can receive more fine-grained control to remove only a specific type of orphan (for example, you could clean out all orphan RPMs, but not DEB packages):

```
[root@pulp ~] pulp-admin rpm repo delete --repo-id='centos7-08aug19'
This command may be exited via ctrl+c without affecting the request.


[\]
Running...


Repository [centos7-08aug19] successfully deleted


[root@pulp ~] pulp-admin orphan remove --all
This command may be exited via ctrl+c without affecting the request.


[/]
Running...

Task Succeeded
```

3. Once this step is completed, we will see that our additional disk space used by the new snapshot has been recovered:

```
●  ●  ●                               root@pulp:~ (ssh)
[root@pulp ~] df -h | grep pulp
/dev/mapper/vg_pulp-lv_pulp        60G    33G    28G   54% /var/lib/pulp
```

In this section, so far we have stepped through all the Pulp commands and activities manually—this has been done to provide you with a good understanding of the steps required in setting up Pulp and the accompanying repositories. In regular services, best practice would dictate that these steps are performed with Ansible—however, there are no native Ansible modules to cover all of the tasks we have performed in this chapter.

For example, the `pulp_repo` module (introduced to Ansible in version 2.3) is capable of creating and deleting repositories, as we have done so far in this chapter with `pulp-admin rpm repo create`. However, it cannot perform orphan clean-up, and so this command would need to be issued using the `shell` or `command` Ansible modules. Full automation with Ansible is left as an exercise for you.

Once our repos are set up, the final step is to put them into use on our Enterprise Linux servers, and we will cover this in the next section of this chapter.

First, though, we will look at some of the nuances of managing DEB packages in Pulp in contrast to RPM-based management.

Building DEB-based repositories in Pulp

Although there are some subtle differences in the command-line structure between the RPM repository plugin for Pulp and the DEB one, the overall process is the same. As before, some prior knowledge is also required of the repository structure to create an effective mirror. In this book, we have worked with Ubuntu Server 18.04 LTS as an example, and the default repository set that is configured on this is as follows:

- `bionic`: This is the baseline repository for the release of Ubuntu Server 18.04 (codename Bionic Beaver), and as with the OS repository for CentOS 7, does not change following the release of the operating system
- `bionic-security`: These are security-specific updates for the bionic operating system built post-release
- `bionic-updates`: These are non-security updates for the bionic operating system release

There are other repositories too, such as `backports`, and in addition to
the `main` component (which we will concern ourselves with here), there is a wide array of
packages available in the `restricted`, `universe`, and `multiverse` components. Going
into greater detail about the Ubuntu repository structure is beyond the scope of this book,
but suffice to say there is a wide array of documentation available on this subject. The
following link is a good place to start reading about the different Ubuntu repositories you
may wish to mirror: `https://wiki.ubuntu.com/SecurityTeam/FAQ#Repositories_and_`
`Updates`.

For now, let's suppose we are updating a minimal build of Ubuntu Server 18.04 LTS. For
this, we are only interested in packages in the `main` component, but we do need a snapshot
of all the security fixes and updates at a given point in time, just like one we had for our
CentOS 7 build:

1. First of all, having ensured we are logged in to the `pulp-admin` client as before,
   we will create a repository in Pulp for the `main` component and the operating
   system release packages:

   ```
   $ pulp-admin deb repo create --repo-id='bionic-amd64-08aug19' --
   relative-url='bionic-amd64-08aug19' --
   feed='http://de.archive.ubuntu.com/ubuntu' --releases=bionic --
   components=main --architectures='amd64' --serve-http=true
   ```

   As you can see, the preceding command is very similar to our RPM repository
   creation command. We specify `repo-id` and `relative-url` in the same manner
   as before and specify an upstream `feed` URL. This time, though, we are
   specifying the Ubuntu `releases`, `components`, and `architectures` as
   command-line options whereas, in our CentOS 7 example, these were implicit in
   the URL we mirrored. In addition to these DEB-specific configuration parameters,
   we are now also specifying the `--serve-http` option. By default, Pulp serves all
   repository content over HTTPS only. However, owing to some limitations around
   package signing for DEB packages in Pulp, which will be discussed later in this
   chapter, we must enable the serving of repository content over plain HTTP.

    Note that, as the plural naming of the `--releases` option implies, more
   than one release may be specified here. Although this works at repository
   creation time, the sync process is, at the time of writing, broken, and so
   one separate Pulp repository must be created for each Ubuntu release we
   wish to mirror. This is expected to be fixed at a future date.

Having done this, we will create two more repositories for
the `security` and `updates` repositories:

```
$ pulp-admin deb repo create --repo-id='bionic-security-
amd64-08aug19' --relative-url='bionic-security-amd64-08aug19' --
feed='http://de.archive.ubuntu.com/ubuntu' --releases=bionic-
security --components=main --architectures='amd64' --serve-
http=true

$ pulp-admin deb repo create --repo-id='bionic-updates-
amd64-08aug19' --relative-url='bionic-updates-amd64-08aug19' --
feed='http://de.archive.ubuntu.com/ubuntu' --releases=bionic-
updates --components=main --architectures='amd64' --serve-http=true
```

2. With our repository creation completed, we can run our sync processes, just like
   we did previously:

```
$ pulp-admin deb repo sync run --repo-id='bionic-amd64-08aug19'

$ pulp-admin deb repo sync run --repo-id='bionic-security-
amd64-08aug19'

$ pulp-admin deb repo sync run --repo-id='bionic-updates-
amd64-08aug19'
```

3. Finally, we publish the repositories:

```
$ pulp-admin deb repo publish run --repo-id='bionic-amd64-08aug19'

$ pulp-admin deb repo publish run --repo-id='bionic-security-
amd64-08aug19'

$ pulp-admin deb repo publish run --repo-id='bionic-updates-
amd64-08aug19'
```

It is worth noting that Ubuntu repositories tend to be much larger than their CentOS
counterparts, especially the `updates` and `security` ones. During the sync process, the
packages are downloaded into `/var/cache/pulp` temporarily before they are archived
into the `/var/lib/pulp` directory. If `/var/cache/pulp` is on your root filesystem, there is
a significant danger of your root filesystem filling up, and as such, it may be best to create a
new volume for this purpose and mount at `/var/cache/pulp` to prevent a disk full
situation from stopping your Pulp server.

The DEB plugin for Pulp features the same package deduplication as its RPM counterpart and publishes packages over HTTPS (and optionally HTTP) in the same manner. With a few changes to the syntax of the commands, we can effectively create snapshots of upstream Linux repositories for most of the major distributions that are found in enterprise environments.

As a result of completing this section, you have learned how to create your own repository mirrors for both RPM- and DEB-based content in Pulp, which may be treated as stable and unchanging and hence provide an excellent basis for patch management in an enterprise.

In the next section of this chapter, we will look at how to deploy these repositories to two different types of Linux server.

Patching processes with Pulp

It is worth mentioning at the outset of this section that Pulp supports two main methods for the distribution of packages from the repositories created within it. The first is a kind of push-based distribution that uses something called the **Pulp Consumer**.

We will not be exploring this in this chapter for the following reasons:

- The Pulp Consumer only works with RPM-based repositories and distributions, and at the time of writing, there is no equivalent client available for Ubuntu or Debian. This means that our processes cannot be uniform across the enterprise, which, in an ideal world, they would be.
- Using the Pulp Consumer means we would have two overlapping means of automation. Distributing packages to nodes using the consumer is a task that can be performed with Ansible, and if we use Ansible for this task, then we have an approach that is common across all of our platforms. This supports the principles of automation in an enterprise context that we established earlier in this book around lowering barriers to entry, ease of use, and so on.

As such, we will build out separate Ansible-based examples for managing repositories and updates using the repositories we created in the previous section, entitled *Building repositories in Pulp*. These can be managed along with all the other Ansible playbooks and can be run through a platform such as AWX to ensure a single pane of glass is used wherever possible for all tasks.

Let's get started by looking at how to patch RPM-based systems using a combination of Ansible and Pulp.

RPM-based patching with Pulp

In the previous section of this chapter, we created two repositories for our CentOS 7 build—one for the operating system release and another to contain the updates.

The process of updating a CentOS 7 build from these repositories is, at a high level, done as follows:

1. Move aside any existing repository definitions in /etc/yum.repos.d to ensure we only load repositories from the Pulp server.
2. Deploy the appropriate configuration using Ansible.
3. Employ Ansible to pull the updates (or any required packages) from the Pulp server using the new configuration.

Before we proceed with creating the appropriate playbooks, let's take a look at what the repository definition file would look like on our CentOS 7 machine if we created it by hand. Ideally, we want it to look something like this:

```
[centos-os]
name=CentOS-os
baseurl=https://pulp.example.com/pulp/repos/centos76-os
gpgcheck=1
gpgkey=file:///etc/pki/rpm-gpg/RPM-GPG-KEY-CentOS-7
sslverify=0

[centos-updates]
name=CentOS-updates
baseurl=https://pulp.example.com/pulp/repos/centos7-07aug19
gpgcheck=1
gpgkey=file:///etc/pki/rpm-gpg/RPM-GPG-KEY-CentOS-7
sslverify=0
```

There's nothing particularly unique about this configuration—we are using the relative-url we created earlier with our repository using pulp-admin. We are using GPG checking of package integrity, along with the CentOS 7 RPM GPG key, which we know will already be installed on our CentOS 7 machine. The only tweak we've had to make to this otherwise standard configuration is to turn off SSL verification since our demo Pulp server features a self-signed certificate. Of course, if we are using an enterprise certificate authority and the CA certificates are installed on each machine, then this problem goes away.

Given the power of Ansible, we can be a bit clever about how we do this. There's no point creating and deploying static configuration files when we know that, at some point, we're going to update the repository—meaning, at the very least, that baseurl might change.

Let's start off by creating a role called `pulpconfig` to deploy the correct configuration—`tasks/main.yml` should look like this:

```
---
  - name: Create a directory to back up any existing REPO configuration
    file:
      path: /etc/yum.repos.d/originalconfig
      state: directory

  - name: Move aside any existing REPO configuration
    shell: mv /etc/yum.repos.d/*.repo /etc/yum.repos.d/originalconfig

  - name: Copy across and populate Pulp templated config
    template:
      src: templates/centos-pulp.repo.j2
      dest: /etc/yum.repos.d/centos-pulp.repo
      owner: root
      group: wheel

  - name: Clean out yum database
    shell: "yum clean all"
```

The accompanying `templates/centos-pulp.repo.j2` template should look like this:

```
[centos-os]
name=CentOS-os
baseurl=https://pulp.example.com/pulp/repos/{{ centos_os_relurl }}
gpgcheck=1
gpgkey=file:///etc/pki/rpm-gpg/RPM-GPG-KEY-CentOS-7
sslverify=0

[centos-updates]
name=CentOS-updates
baseurl=https://pulp.example.com/pulp/repos/{{ centos_updates_relurl }}
gpgcheck=1
gpgkey=file:///etc/pki/rpm-gpg/RPM-GPG-KEY-CentOS-7
sslverify=0
```

Notice the variable substitutions at the end of each of the `baseurl` lines—these allow us to keep the same template (which should be common for most purposes) but change the repository URL over time to adapt to updates.

Next, we will define a second role specifically for updating the kernel—this will be very simple for our example and `tasks/main.yml` will contain the following:

```
---
  - name: Update the kernel
```

```
yum:
  name: kernel
  state: latest
```

Finally, we will define `site.yml` at the top level of the playbook structure to pull all of this together. We could, as we discussed previously, define the variables for the relative URLs in a whole host of places, but for the sake of this example, we will put them in the `site.yml` playbook itself:

```
---
- name: Install Pulp repos and update kernel
  hosts: all
  become: yes
  vars:
    centos_os_relurl: "centos76-os"
    centos_updates_relurl: "centos7-07aug19"

  roles:
    - pulpconfig
    - updatekernel
```

Now, if we run this in the usual manner, we will see output similar to the following:

So far, so good—the `changed` statuses from the preceding play tell us that the new configuration was applied successfully.

Those with a keen eye will have observed the warning on the `Clean out yum database` tasks—Ansible detects when a raw shell command is being used that has overlapping functionality with a module and recommends that you use the module instead for reasons of repeatability and idempotency, as we discussed earlier. However, as we want to ensure all traces of any earlier `yum` databases are removed (which can present problems), I have adopted a *brute force* method here to clean up the old databases.

Now, as I'm sure you will have spotted, the great thing about this approach is that if, say, we want to test our `08aug19` repository snapshot that we created in the previous section, all we have to do is modify the `vars:` block of `site.yml` so that it looks like this:

```
vars:
  centos_os_relurl: "centos76-os"
  centos_updates_relurl: "centos7-08aug19"
```

Hence, we can reuse the same playbook, roles, and templates in a variety of scenarios simply by changing one or two variable values. In an environment such as AWX, these variables could even be overridden using the GUI, making the whole process even easier.

In this way, combining Ansible with Pulp lends itself to a really stable enterprise framework for managing and distributing (and even testing) updates. However, before we look at this process on Ubuntu, a word on rollbacks. In the previous section, we hypothesized an example where our `08aug19` snapshot failed testing and so had to be deleted. As far as CentOS 7 servers are concerned, rollbacks are not as straightforward as simply installing the earlier repository definitions and performing an update since the update will detect newer packages that have been installed and take no action.

The Pulp repository does, of course, provide a stable base to roll back to—however, rollbacks are generally quite a manual process as you must identify the transaction ID in the `yum` database that you want to roll back to and validate the actions to be performed and then roll back to it. This, of course, can be automated, provided you have a reliable way of retrieving the transaction ID.

The following screenshot shows a simple example of identifying the transaction ID for the kernel update we just automated and establishing the details of the change that was performed:

```
●  ●  ●                        james@automation-02:~ (ssh)

[james@automation-02 ~]$ sudo yum history list | head -4
Loaded plugins: fastestmirror
ID      | Login user              | Date and time      | Action(s)      | Altered
-------------------------------------------------------------------------------
    21 | James Freeman <james>   | 2019-08-12 12:16 | Install        |      1
[james@automation-02 ~]$ sudo yum history info 21
Loaded plugins: fastestmirror
Transaction ID : 21
Begin time      : Mon Aug 12 12:16:06 2019
Begin rpmdb     : 480:690551a4737caf86edb5f3fd102e34d1d29bb6e2
End time        :            12:17:08 2019 (62 seconds)
End rpmdb       : 481:4228b21b69d1b276b9de6fd9fa694963a89dbf05
User            : James Freeman <james>
Return-Code     : Success
Command Line    : -d 2 -y install kernel
Transaction performed with:
    Installed      rpm-4.11.3-35.el7.x86_64                     @anaconda
    Installed      yum-3.4.3-161.el7.centos.noarch              @anaconda
    Installed      yum-metadata-parser-1.1.4-10.el7.x86_64      @anaconda
    Installed      yum-plugin-fastestmirror-1.1.31-50.el7.noarch @anaconda
Packages Altered:
    Install kernel-3.10.0-957.27.2.el7.x86_64 @centos-updates
history info
[james@automation-02 ~]$
```

Then, we can (if we so choose) roll back the transaction using the command shown in the following screenshot:

```
● ● ●                        james@automation-02:~ (ssh)
[james@automation-02 ~]$ sudo yum history undo 21
Loaded plugins: fastestmirror
Undoing transaction 21, from Mon Aug 12 12:16:06 2019
    Install kernel-3.10.0-957.27.2.el7.x86_64 @centos-updates
Resolving Dependencies
--> Running transaction check
---> Package kernel.x86_64 0:3.10.0-957.27.2.el7 will be erased
--> Finished Dependency Resolution

Dependencies Resolved

================================================================================
 Package        Arch         Version                 Repository         Size
================================================================================
Removing:
 kernel         x86_64       3.10.0-957.27.2.el7     @centos-updates    63 M

Transaction Summary
================================================================================
Remove  1 Package

Installed size: 63 M
Is this ok [y/N]: y
Downloading packages:
Running transaction check
Running transaction test
Transaction test succeeded
Running transaction
  Erasing    : kernel-3.10.0-957.27.2.el7.x86_64                        1/1
  Verifying  : kernel-3.10.0-957.27.2.el7.x86_64                        1/1

Removed:
  kernel.x86_64 0:3.10.0-957.27.2.el7
```

Using this simple process and the playbooks offered here as a guide, it should be possible to establish a solid, stable, automated update platform for any RPM-based Linux distribution.

In the next section, we will look at the method we can use to perform the same set of tasks, except for DEB-based systems such as Ubuntu.

DEB-based patching with Pulp

At a high level, the process of managing updates on Ubuntu from our Pulp server is exactly the same as it is for managing the RPM based updates for CentOS (save for the fact that we have no option regarding the use of the Pulp Consumer and must use Ansible for the update process).

There are, however, a couple of limitations when it comes to the use of Pulp with Ubuntu's APT repository system:

- At the time of writing, there is an issue whereby the Pulp sync process does not mirror the signing keys from the upstream Ubuntu repository. This means that even though the upstream repository features `Release.gpg`, it is not mirrored on the Pulp server. Hopefully, in the future, this will be fixed, but in this chapter, we will work around this by adding implicit trust to the packages.
- HTTPS support on Ubuntu is configured not to accept updates from unverifiable (that is, self-signed) certificates by default. Although we can turn off SSL verification as we did on CentOS, Ubuntu's APT package manager then goes in search of an `InRelease` file (which should have the aforementioned GPG key embedded). As we discussed in the previous point, the Pulp DEB plugin does not support the signing of mirrored repositories, and so right now, the only workaround for this is to use unencrypted HTTP traffic. Hopefully, in a future release, these two issues will be fixed—however, at the time of writing, there appears to be no documented fix or workaround for them.

With these two limitations understood, we can define our APT sources file for the repository set we created earlier. Following on from the examples in the previous section, our `/etc/apt/sources.list` file could look like this:

```
deb [trusted=yes] http://pulp.example.com/pulp/deb/bionic-amd64-08aug19
bionic main
deb [trusted=yes]
http://pulp.example.com/pulp/deb/bionic-security-amd64-08aug19 bionic-
security main
deb [trusted=yes]
http://pulp.example.com/pulp/deb/bionic-updates-amd64-08aug19 bionic-
updates main
```

The `[trusted=yes]` string tells the APT package manager to ignore the lack of package signing. The file structure itself is incredibly simple, and so just as with our CentOS example, we can create a template file so that the relative URL can be populated using a variable:

1. First, we'll create a role called `pulpconfig` and create the following `templates/sources.list.j2` template:

```
deb [trusted=yes] http://pulp.example.com/pulp/deb/{{
ubuntu_os_relurl }} bionic main
deb [trusted=yes] http://pulp.example.com/pulp/deb/{{
ubuntu_security_relurl }} bionic-security main
deb [trusted=yes] http://pulp.example.com/pulp/deb/{{
ubuntu_updates_relurl }} bionic-updates main
```

2. Then, we will create some tasks with the role to install this template and move aside any old configuration for APT:

```
---
- name: Create a directory to back up any existing REPO
configuration
  file:
    path: /etc/apt/originalconfig
    state: directory

- name: Move existing config into backup directory
  shell: mv /etc/apt/sources.list /etc/apt/originalconfig

- name: Copy across and populate Pulp templated config
  template:
    src: templates/sources.list.j2
    dest: /etc/apt/sources.list
    owner: root
    group: root

- name: Clean out dpkg database
  shell: "apt-get clean"
```

3. Finally, we will define a role to update the kernel, but this time using APT:

```
---
- name: Update the kernel
  apt:
    name: linux-generic
    state: latest
```

4. Our `site.yml` playbook for Ubuntu systems now looks like this—save for the variable differences, it is almost identical to the CentOS 7 one, once again highlighting the value in using Ansible as an automation platform:

```
---
- name: Install Pulp repos and update kernel
  hosts: all
  become: yes
  vars:
    ubuntu_os_relurl: "bionic-amd64-08aug19"
    ubuntu_security_relurl: "bionic-security-amd64-08aug19"
    ubuntu_updates_relurl: "bionic-updates-amd64-08aug19"

  roles:
    - pulpconfig
    - updatekernel
```

5. Now, after putting this all together and running it, we should see output similar to what can be seen in the following screenshot:

```
●●●                james@automation-01: ~/hands-on-automation/chapter08/example02 (ssh)

~/hands-on-automation/chapter08/example02> ansible-playbook -i hosts site.yml

PLAY [Install Pulp repos and update kernel] ********************************

TASK [Gathering Facts] ****************************************************
ok: [ubuntu-testhost]

TASK [pulpconfig : Create a directory to back up any existing REPO configuration
] ***
changed: [ubuntu-testhost]

TASK [pulpconfig : Move existing config into backup directory] *****************
changed: [ubuntu-testhost]

TASK [pulpconfig : Copy across and populate Pulp templated config] *************
changed: [ubuntu-testhost]

TASK [pulpconfig : Clean out dpkg database] ***********************************
 [WARNING]: Consider using the apt module rather than running 'apt-get'.  If
you need to use command because apt is insufficient you can add 'warn: false'
to this command task or set 'command_warnings=False' in ansible.cfg to get rid
of this message.

changed: [ubuntu-testhost]

TASK [updatekernel : Update the kernel] ***************************************
changed: [ubuntu-testhost]

PLAY RECAP ****************************************************************
ubuntu-testhost            : ok=6    changed=5    unreachable=0    failed=0

~/hands-on-automation/chapter08/example02>
```

Putting aside the security limitations present in the current Pulp Debian support, this provides a neat space-efficient solution for managing Ubuntu updates across an enterprise infrastructure in a manner that is repeatable and lends itself well to automation. As with our earlier CentOS-based example, it would be very easy to test packages from a new snapshot by simply changing the variable definitions passed to our roles.

As with CentOS, should a new package set not be suitable for production use, Ansible makes it easy to restore the previous repository configuration. However, rolling back packages on Ubuntu (and other Debian-based distributions) is a much more manual process than we saw in the previous section. Fortunately, there is a great deal of history regarding package transactions kept in `/var/log/dpkg.log` and `/var/log/apt/history.log*`, which can be used to determine which packages were installed and/or upgraded and when. The `apt-get` command can then be used to install a specific version of a package using the `apt-get install <packagename>=<version>` syntax. There are many elegant scripted solutions to this problem on the internet, and so it is left as an exercise for you to determine the one best suited to your needs and environment.

Summary

Managing package repositories in an enterprise setting can present numerous challenges, especially when it comes to efficient storage, conservation of internet bandwidth, and ensuring build consistency. Fortunately, the Pulp software package provides an elegant solution to these challenges for most of the common Linux distributions and lends itself well to effective management in the enterprise.

In this chapter, you learned how to install Pulp to begin patching an Enterprise Linux environment. You then learned how to build repositories in Pulp for both RPM-based and DEB-based Linux distributions through hands-on examples, before gaining practical knowledge of deploying the appropriate Pulp configuration and updating packages using Ansible.

In the next chapter, we will explore how the Katello software tools complement Pulp in enterprise environment management.

Questions

1. Why would you want to create a repository with Pulp rather than just a simple mirror of files that you could download manually?
2. What are the issues around building and testing Linux patch repositories in an enterprise environment?
3. What components does Pulp need to run?
4. Specify the filesystem requirements for successfully installing Pulp.
5. How would you patch an RPM-based system from a Pulp repository you created previously?
6. Why would you use Ansible to deploy patches from a Pulp repository rather than the Pulp Consumer?
7. Does the removal of a Pulp repository free up disk space? If not, how is this performed?

Further reading

- For more in-depth details on the Pulp project and how to make use of this tool, please refer to the official documentation (https://pulpproject.org/).

Patching with Katello

9

In `Chapter 8`, *Enterprise Repository Management with Pulp*, we explored the Pulp software package and how it lends itself to automated, repeatable, controllable patching in an enterprise setting. In this chapter, we will build on this by taking a look at a product called **Katello**, which is complementary to Pulp and lends itself to not just patching but complete infrastructure management.

Katello is a GUI-driven tool that provides advanced solutions for enterprise infrastructure management, and in many ways can be considered to be the successor to the venerable Spacewalk product that many are familiar with. We will explore why you would choose Katello for this purpose and then proceed with hands-on examples of how to build a Katello server and perform patching.

The following topics will specifically be covered in this chapter:

- Introduction to Katello
- Installing a Katello server
- Patching with Katello

Technical requirements

The minimum requirements for completing the hands-on exercises in this chapter are a single CentOS 7 server with around 80 GB of disk space allocated, 2 CPU cores (virtual or physical), and 8 GB of memory. Although we will only look at a subset of the Katello features in this chapter, it should be noted that Foreman in particular (which is installed under Katello) is capable of acting as a DHCP server, DNS server, and PXE boot host and, as such, if configured incorrectly could cause issues if deployed on a production network.

For this reason, it is recommended that all exercises are performed in an isolated network suitable for testing. Where Ansible code is given, it will have been developed and tested in Ansible 2.8. For testing patching from Katello, you will need a CentOS 7 virtual machine.

All example code discussed in this book is available from GitHub at: `https://github.com/PacktPublishing/Hands-On-Enterprise-Automation-on-Linux`.

Introduction to Katello

Katello is not actually a single product in isolation, but a union of several open source infrastructure management products into one cohesive infrastructure management solution. Where Pulp is solely focused on the efficient, controllable storage of packages (and other important content for infrastructure management), Katello brings together the following:

- **Foreman**: This is an open source product designed to handle the provisioning and configuration of both physical and virtual servers. Foreman includes a rich web-based GUI, a RESTful API, and a CLI tool called **Hammer**, providing a rich and varied means of management. It also provides integration with several automation tools, originally just Puppet but more recently also Ansible.
- **Katello**: Katello is actually a plugin for Foreman and provides additional features such as the rich version control of content (more so than Pulp alone) and subscription management.
- **Candlepin**: Provides software subscription management, especially integration with environments such as the **Red Hat Subscription Management** (RHSM) model. Although it is possible to mirror Red Hat repositories in Pulp, the process is cumbersome, and you risk violating your license terms because there is no visibility on the number of systems you are managing or their relationship to your Red Hat subscriptions.
- **Pulp**: This is the very same Pulp software that we explored in the last chapter, now integrated into one fully featured project.
- **Capsule**: A proxy service for distributing content and controlling updates across a geographically diverse infrastructure while maintaining a single management console.

The use of Katello hence provides several advantages over using Pulp alone, and even if you use it just for patch management (as we will explore in this chapter, in the section entitled *Patching with Katello*), the rich web GUI, CLI, and API lend itself to integration with enterprise systems. Beyond this though, Katello (and more specifically Foreman, which underpins it) provides many other benefits such as being able to dynamically PXE boot servers and control both container and virtualization systems, and it can even act as both the DNS and DHCP servers for your network. Indeed, it is fair to say that the combination of Katello/Foreman is designed to sit at the heart of your network, although it will only perform the functions you ask of it, so those with existing DNS and DHCP infrastructures need not fear.

It is worth mentioning that Katello also features tight integration with the Puppet automation tool. The original project was sponsored by Red Hat, and before their acquisition of Ansible, Red Hat and Puppet had a strategic alliance, which led to it becoming heavily featured in the Katello project (which is available commercially as Red Hat Satellite 6). Given the Ansible acquisition, while the Puppet integration still remains in Katello, support for integration with Ansible, especially through Ansible Tower/AWX, has evolved rapidly and it is entirely up to the user which automation tool they wish to use.

At this stage, the venerable **Spacewalk** software tool deserves an honorable mention. Spacewalk is the upstream open source version of Red Hat Satellite 5 and is still being actively developed and maintained. There is a huge degree of overlap between the two systems in terms of high-level functionality; however, Katello/Satellite 6 is a complete from-the-ground-up rewrite of the platform and so there is no clear upgrade path between the two. Given that Red Hat's contribution to the Spacewalk program is likely to decrease when they end-of-life their Satellite 5 product, our focus in this book will be on Katello.

Indeed, it is fair to say that Katello deserves a book of its own, so rich is its feature set. Our goal in this chapter is simply to raise awareness of the Katello platform and to demonstrate how it lends itself to patching in an enterprise environment. Many of the additional features, such as the PXE booting of servers, require an understanding of the concepts we have already covered in this book, and hence it is hoped that, should you decide upon Katello or Satellite 6 as a platform for managing your infrastructure, then you will be able to build on the foundation that this book provides and explore additional resources to take you further.

Let's get started by taking a practical look in the next section at how to install a simple standalone Katello server so that we can explore this more fully.

Installing a Katello server

This is a hands-on book, so without further ado, let's get started and set up our very own Katello server. Alongside the advantages of Katello already discussed, another is the packaging of the product. When we set up our Pulp server, there were many individual components where we had to make decisions (for example, RabbitMQ versus Qpid) and then additional setup to perform (for example, SSL transport for MongoDB). Katello has even more *moving parts* than Pulp (if Pulp is considered as just a component of the Katello platform), and hence installing it by hand would be a vast and complex task.

Thankfully, Katello provides an installation system that can get you up and running with just a few commands, which we will explore in the next section of this chapter.

Preparing to install Katello

Katello, as with Pulp, only installs (at the time of writing) on Enterprise Linux 7 variants—so here, again, we will use the latest stable release of CentOS 7. The requirements for Katello change from time to time as the product grows, and it is always worth reviewing the installation documentation for yourself before proceeding. At the time of writing, version 3.12 is the latest stable release, and the installation documentation can be found here: https://theforeman.org/plugins/katello/3.12/installation/index.html. Now, let's follow these steps:

1. As before, our biggest concern is ensuring we have sufficient disk space allocated, and just as for a standalone Pulp installation, we must ensure that we have enough disk space allocated in /var/lib/pulp and /var/lib/mongodb for all of the Linux distributions we may wish to mirror. Again, as with Pulp, they should be separate from the root volume to ensure that if one fills up, the entire server does not die.

2. With the filesystem set up, our first step is to install the required repositories so that all required packages for installation can be downloaded—this requires setting up several external repositories that provide packages not included by default with CentOS 7. The following commands set up the repositories for Katello, Foreman, Puppet 6, and the EPEL repository before actually installing the Foreman release package tree:

```
$ yum -y localinstall
https://fedorapeople.org/groups/katello/releases/yum/3.12/katello/e
l7/x86_64/katello-repos-latest.rpm
$ yum -y localinstall
https://yum.theforeman.org/releases/1.22/el7/x86_64/foreman-release
```

```
.rpm
$ yum -y localinstall
https://yum.puppet.com/puppet6-release-el-7.noarch.rpm
$ yum -y localinstall
https://dl.fedoraproject.org/pub/epel/epel-release-latest-7.noarch.
rpm
$ yum -y install foreman-release-scl
```

3. From here, it is recommended to bring the base system fully up to date:

   ```
   $ yum -y update
   ```

4. The final step before the actual installation is to install the Katello package and its dependencies:

   ```
   $ yum -y install katello
   ```

5. From here on, all installation tasks are performed with the `foreman-installer` command—there are a huge plethora of options that can be specified and, with most of them, if you need to change your decision, you can run the installer again with the different flags and it will perform the changes without any data loss. To see all possible options, run the following command:

   ```
   $ foreman-installer --scenario katello --help
   ```

6. To build our demo server, the defaults will mostly suffice—however, if you explore the options, you will see that many will need to be specified in an enterprise setting. For example, SSL certificates can be specified at install time (rather than relying on self-signed ones that will be generated otherwise), default secrets for underlying transports are set, and so on. It is highly recommended that you review the output of the preceding command for yourself when installing in a production setting. For now, we will issue the following installation command to initiate the installation:

   ```
   $ foreman-installer --scenario katello --foreman-initial-admin-
   password=password --foreman-initial-location='London' --foreman-
   initial-organization='HandsOn'
   ```

This is probably the simplest possible installation case for a Katello server, and it perfectly serves our examples in this book. However, in a Production environment, I highly recommend that you explore the more advanced installation features to ensure that the server will meet your requirements, especially where security and availability are concerned. This is left as an exercise for you to explore.

Note that, in this scenario, the installer checks several prerequisites, including that the forward and reverse DNS lookups for the Katello server name resolve correctly and that the machine has 8 GB of RAM available. The installer will refuse to proceed if these prerequisites are not met.

7. The Katello installation should run to completion provided all prerequisites have been met, and once completed, you should be presented with a screen similar to the one shown in the following screenshot, detailing the login details, as well as other pertinent information such as how to set up a proxy server for another network if required:

```
● ● ●                        root@katello:~ (ssh)
[root@katello ~]# foreman-installer --scenario katello --foreman-initial-admin-p
assword=password --foreman-initial-location='London' --foreman-initial-organizat
ion='HandsOn'
Preparing installation Done
  Success!
  * Katello is running at https://katello.example.com
      Initial credentials are admin / password
  * To install an additional Foreman proxy on separate machine continue by runni
ng:

      foreman-proxy-certs-generate --foreman-proxy-fqdn "$FOREMAN_PROXY" --certs
-tar "/root/$FOREMAN_PROXY-certs.tar"
  The full log is at /var/log/foreman-installer/katello.log
[root@katello ~]# █
```

8. The only task not completed by the installer is setting up the local firewall on the CentOS 7 machine. Luckily, there is a FirewallD service definition included with Katello that covers all of the services likely to be required—this derives its named from the commercial Red Hat Satellite 6 product and can be enabled by running the following commands as root:

```
$ firewall-cmd --permanent --zone=public --add-service=RH-
Satellite-6
$ firewall-cmd --reload
```

9. With those steps completed, it will be possible to load the web interface of Katello and log in with the details shown:

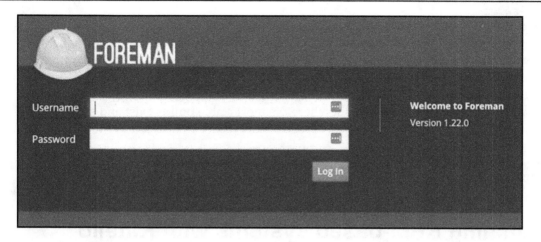

Technically speaking, Katello is a module that sits on top of Foreman and provides important features that we will look at later in this chapter—for example, a web UI for the Pulp repository management system that is also installed behind the scenes. Hence, the Foreman branding of the code stands out, and you will find the name comes up frequently. Once logged in, you should be presented with the default dashboard page, and we can start to configure some repositories for patching purposes, which we will commence in the next section.

Patching with Katello

As Katello is built around technologies we have already explored, such as Pulp, it carries with it the same limitations we have already seen regarding DEB packages. For instance, although repositories of DEB packages can be built up easily in Katello, and even the appropriate GPG public keys imported, the resulting published repositories do not feature an `InRelease` or `Release.gpg` file and so must be implicitly trusted by all hosts that use these. Similarly, although there is a complete subscription management framework available for RPM-based hosts consisting of the `subscription-manager` tool and the Pulp Consumer agent, again, no such equivalent exists for DEB hosts and so these must be configured manually.

Although it would be entirely possible to configure RPM-based hosts to use the built-in technologies, DEB-based ones would have to be configured with Ansible, just as for Pulp, and given the importance of commonality across environments in an enterprise, configuring all servers in the same manner rather than using two contrasting solutions for two different host types is advised.

One of the advantages that Katello brings over Pulp, other than the web user interface, is the concept of lifecycle environments. This feature acknowledges that most businesses will have separate technology environments for differing purposes. For example, your enterprise may well have a `Development` environment for developing new software and testing bleeding edge packages, then a `Testing` environment for testing releases, and finally, a `Production` environment where the most stable builds exist and services for customers and clients are run.

Let's now explore some hands-on examples of building up repositories in Katello for patching purposes.

Patching RPM-based systems with Katello

Let's consider the use of Katello to build repositories for our CentOS 7 system across multiple lifecycle environments. As Katello supports the key-based validation of RPMs, our first task is to install the GPG public key for the RPMs. A copy of this is freely downloadable from the CentOS project and can be found on most CentOS 7 systems in `/etc/pki/rpm-gpg/RPM-GPG-KEY-CentOS-7`:

1. To add this public key to Katello, navigate to **Content | Content Credentials** from the menu bar. Then, click **Create Content Credential**:

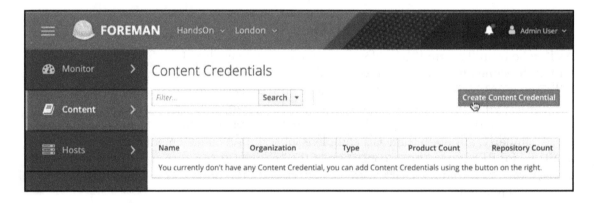

2. Give the key a suitable name and either upload the key file or copy and paste the contents of it into the textbox on the screen. Click **Save** when done:

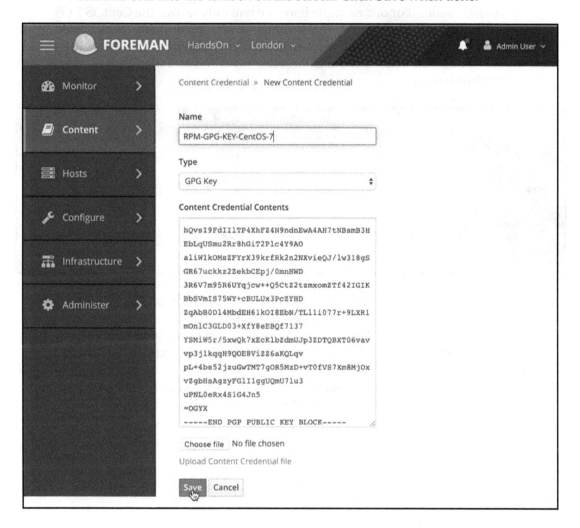

3. Next, we will create a product—in Katello, a product is a logical grouping of repositories, and this is incredibly useful for creating manageable scalable configurations. For our example here, we will only mirror the CentOS 7 OS repository, but when you start mirroring the updates and any other related repositories, it would make sense to group these together under a single product. Navigate to **Content | Products** from the menu bar, and then click on the **Create Product** button:

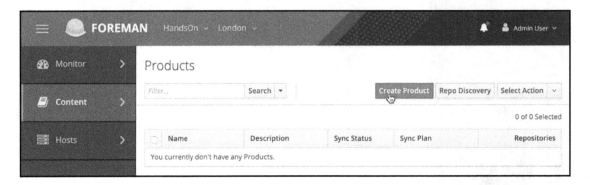

4. Now, define the high-level product definition—for a simple CentOS 7 repository mirror, we simply need to create **Name** and **Label** and associate the GPG key we uploaded previously. The various SSL options are for upstream repositories that feature two-way SSL validation. Note also that all products can be synced according to a **Sync Plan** (essentially a schedule)—however, for this example, we will simply perform a manual sync. The screen should look something like the following screenshot when completed:

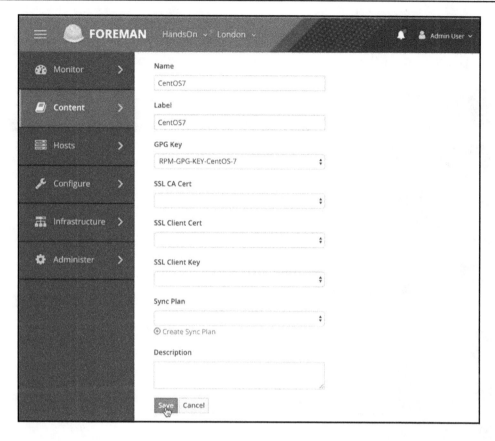

5. With the high-level product definition completed, we can now create our CentOS
   7 repository under it by clicking on the **New Repository** button:

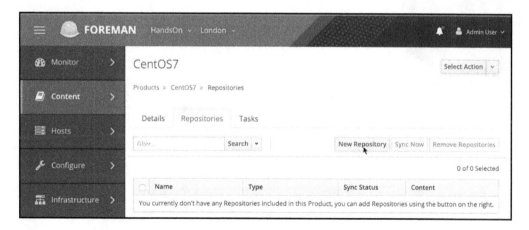

6. Complete the repository details on the screen provided. Set the **Type** field as yum and enter the URL of the upstream repository in the appropriate field (this is the same as the --feed parameter when using Pulp from the command line):

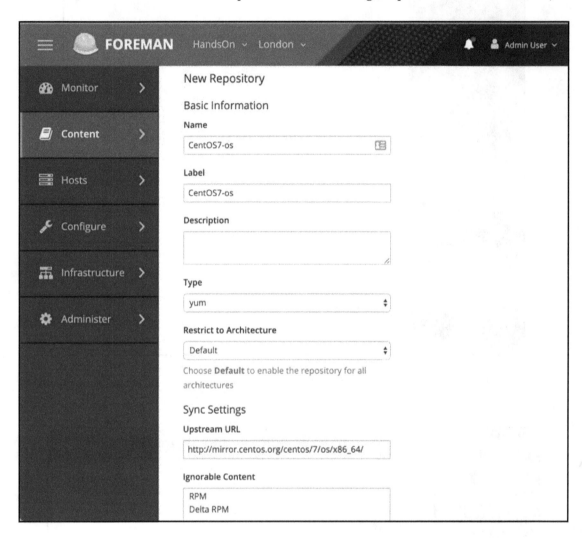

7. Scrolling down the same screen, ensure that **Publish via HTTP** is ticked and associate the GPG uploaded previously, as shown in the following screenshot:

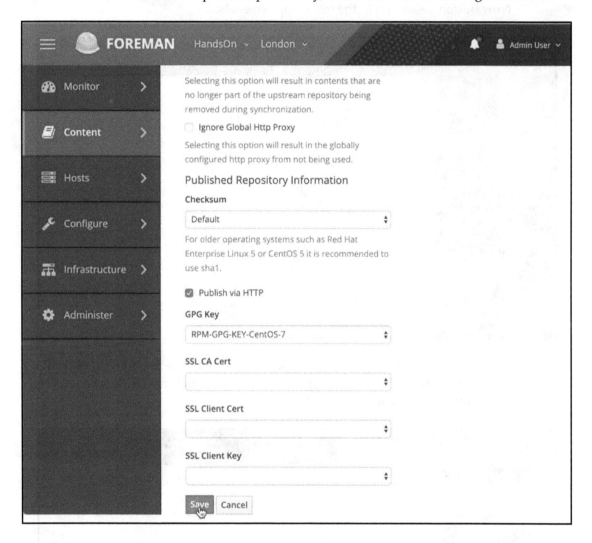

8. For our example, we'll immediately kick off a sync of this repository by putting a tick against it in the table of repositories, and then clicking on the **Sync Now** button, as shown in the following screenshot:

9. The synchronization begins in the background immediately—you can always check on its progress (and kick off further manual synchronizations) by navigating to the **Content | Sync Status** page:

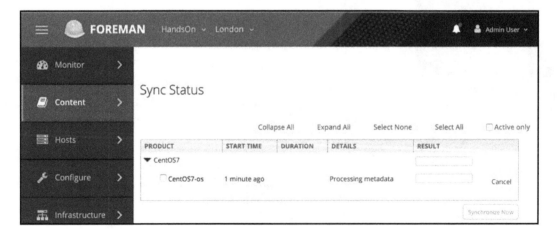

10. While the sync process completes, let's go and create some lifecycle environments.

 Note that while you can have discrete products and separate repositories within them, lifecycle environments are global and apply to everything. In an enterprise context, this makes sense, as you would most likely still have a Development, Test, and Production environment regardless of which underlying technologies you use.

From the menu bar, navigate to **Content** | **Lifecycle Environments Paths**, and then click the **Create Environment Path** button:

11. Create an initial environment called Development by following the instructions onscreen. You should be presented with a screen such as the one shown in the following screenshot:

12. Now, we'll add `Testing` and `Production` environments so that our example enterprise has a logical flow through these three environments. Click the **Add New Environment** button, and then add each in turn, ensuring they have the correct **Prior Environment** set to maintain the correct sequence. The following screenshot shows an example of creating the `Production` environment as the next step from the `Testing` one:

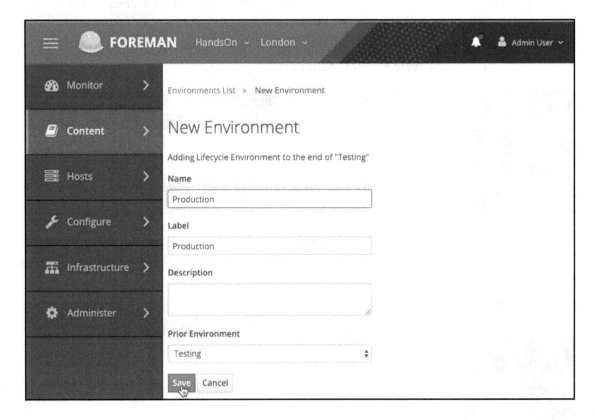

13. The final configuration should look like the following example screenshot:

Once our sync process has completed and we have created our environments, we can proceed to the final part of our RPM repository setup—Content Views. In Katello, a content view is a user-defined amalgamation of the various content forms that can be ingested, version-controlled, and distributed to a given environment. This is best explained through a practical example.

When we used Pulp alone, we created a repository called `centos7-07aug19`. When we wanted to test out an update released a day later, we then created a second repository called `centos7-08aug19`. Although this works, and we demonstrated how Pulp deduplicates packages and saves on disk space while neatly publishing apparently separate repositories, you can quickly see how this mechanism for content management could become unwieldy, especially at enterprise scale, with numerous environments and some months (or years) worth of snapshots to manage.

This is where `Content Views` come to the rescue. Although we have mirrored the CentOS 7 OS repository here, suppose we had mirrored the updates one. With `Content Views`, we don't need to create a new product or repository to test out updates. Instead, the workflow is, at a high level, as follows:

1. Create a product and a corresponding repository and perform sync (for example, on August 7, 2019).
2. Create a content view containing the repository created in the previous step.
3. Publish the content view on August 7, 2019—this creates a version-numbered snapshot of this repository on this date (for example, version `1.0`).

4. Promote the content view to the `Development` environment. Perform testing, and when validated, promote it to testing. Repeat the cycle to reach `Production`. This can all happen asynchronously to the next steps.

5. On August 8, perform another sync of the repository created in *step 1* (if you have an overnight sync happening automatically through `Sync Plan`, this will already be done for you on the morning of the 8th).

6. Publish the content view on August 8, 2019, following the sync. This creates a +1 version of the repository for this date (for example, version 2.0).

7. Now, at this stage, you have snapshots of the CentOS 7 channel on both August 7 and 8. However, all servers will still receive updates from the August 7 channel.

8. Promote the `Development` environment to version 2.0. The machines in the `Development` environment now receive (with no additional configuration required on them) the repository snapshot of August 8.

9. The `Testing` and `Production` environments, which were not promoted to this version, still receive packages from the August 7 snapshot.

In this way, Katello makes managing numerous versions (snapshots) of repositories easy across differing environments, with the added bonus that the repository configuration on each host always remains the same, removing the need to push new repository information through Ansible as we did with Pulp.

Let's step through an example of the preceding process in our demo Katello environment:

1. First of all, create a new content view for the preceding process.
2. Navigate to **Content** | **Content Views** and click on the **Create New View** button:

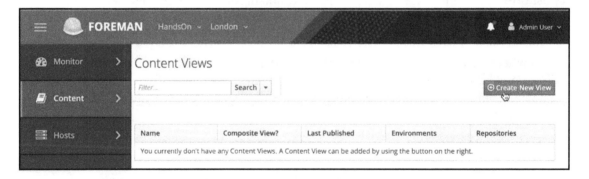

3. For our purposes, the new content view only requires a **Name** and a **Label**, such as those shown in the following screenshot:

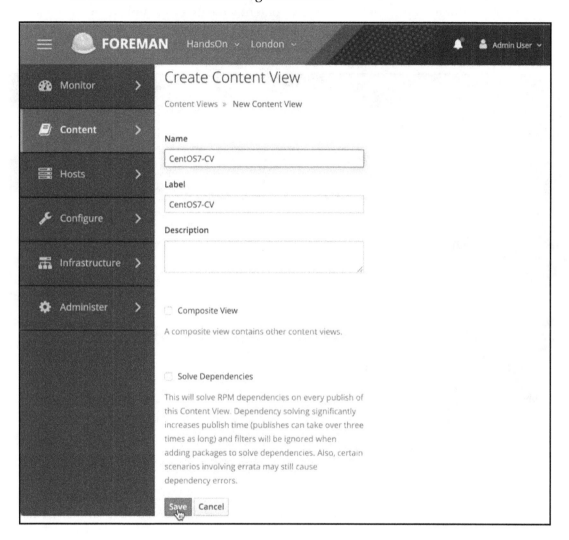

4. Once you have clicked on the **Save** button, navigate to the **Yum Content** tab within the new content view, and ensure the **Add** sub-tab is selected. Tick the repositories you want to add to the content view (in our simple demo, we only have one CentOS 7 repository, so select that), and click on the **Add Repositories** button:

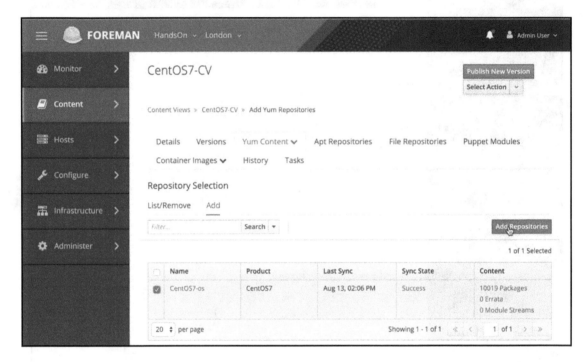

5. Now, navigate back to the **Versions** tab and click the **Publish New Version** button. This creates the hypothetical August 7 version we discussed earlier. Note that `Publish` and `Promote` operations take an enormous amount of disk I/O and will be very slow, especially on slow mechanically-backed storage arrays. Although there are no published requirements for I/O performance for either Katello or Red Hat Satellite 6, they perform best on flashbacked storage, or if this is not available, fast mechanical storage that is not shared with other devices. The following screenshot shows the **Publish New Version** button being clicked for the **CentOS7-CV** content view:

6. The `Publish` operation is asynchronous and you can see it complete on this screen, although if you navigate away, it will still complete. You can see that it is automatically numbered `Version 1.0`—this numbering is, at the time of writing, automatic and you cannot choose your own version numbering. You can, however, add notes to each published version, which can be incredibly useful to track which version is which and why they were created. This is highly recommended. The following screenshot shows the promotion in progress on our **Version 1.0** environment:

7. Once the `Publish` operation is completed, the **Promote** button (shown grayed out in the preceding screenshot) will become active. You will note that this version is automatically published to the `Library` environment—the latest version of any content view is always automatically promoted to this environment.

8. To simulate the August 8 snapshot we discussed earlier, let's perform a second publish of this content view. This will produce a `Version 2.0` environment, which can then be promoted to the `Development` environment by clicking on the **Promote** button and selecting the required environment. The following screenshot shows our two versions, with `Version 1.0` available to only the `Production` environment and `Version 2.0` available to the `Development` environment (and the built-in `Library` one). Note that as we have not promoted the `Testing` environment to either version and that no packages are available to machines in the `Testing` environment. You must promote it to all environments that require packages—the following screenshot shows the two versions we have published and which environments are associated with which versions:

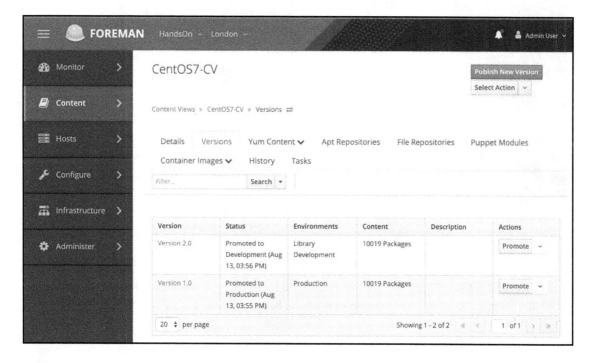

9. In the following screenshot, the promotion process is shown for reference—this is how you would promote the `Production` environment to `Version 2.0`:

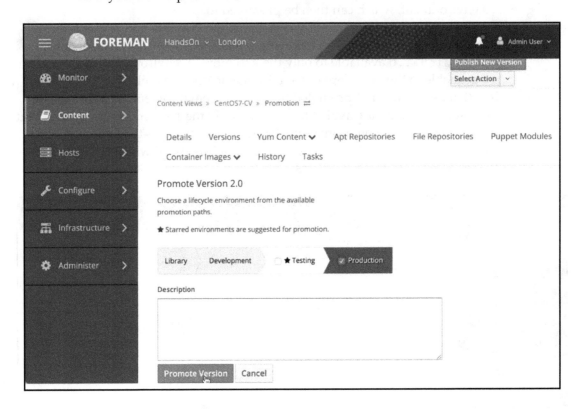

The one remaining piece of the puzzle here is to configure the clients to receive packages from the Katello server. Here, we will perform a simple manual integration, as this method is common to both DEB- and RPM-based packages and hence supports a common approach across the enterprise. The process for distributing RPM packages from Katello using the `subscription-manager` tool and the Katello agent is well documented and is left as an exercise for you.

The official Katello documentation for Activation Keys is a good place to start: `https://theforeman.org/plugins/katello/3.12/user_guide/activation_keys/index.html`

To make use of the content we have published in this example, machines in the Development environment would have a repository file with content such as this:

```
[centos-os]
name=CentOS-os
baseurl=http://katello.example.com/pulp/repos/HandsOn/Development/CentOS7-C
V/custom/CentOS7/CentOS7-os/
gpgcheck=1
gpgkey=file:///etc/pki/rpm-gpg/RPM-GPG-KEY-CentOS-7
```

Your base URL will surely vary—at the very least, your Katello hostname will be different. RPM-based repositories published and promoted in Katello are generally available at the following path:

```
http://KATELLOHOSTNAME/pulp/repos/ORGNAME/LIFECYCLENAME/CONTENTVIEWNAME/cus
tom/PRODUCT/REPO
```

Here, we have the following:

- KATELLOHOSTNAME: The hostname of your Katello server (or nearest Capsule/Proxy if you are using them)
- ORGNAME: The name of the Katello organization in which your Content View lives—we defined ours as HandsOn during the installation process
- LIFECYCLENAME: The name of the Lifecycle Environment, for example, Development
- CONTENTVIEWNAME: The name you gave your Content View
- PRODUCT: The name you gave your Product
- REPO: The name you gave to your repository within the Product

This makes the URLs entirely predictable and easy to deploy to target machines using Ansible, just as we did in the previous chapter regarding Pulp. Note that accessing the repositories over HTTPS from Katello requires the installation of SSL certificates for trust validation, which is beyond the scope of this chapter—instead, we will simply make use of plain HTTP.

As the lifecycle environment name remains constant, no matter whether we sync, publish, or promote an environment, the repository URL, as shown previously, remains constant and hence we never have to perform client configuration work even when a new package repository snapshot is published. This is a significant advantage over Pulp, where we would have to push a new configuration using Ansible every time a new version is created.

Once the repository configuration has been built as shown previously, you can patch your systems in the normal manner. This can be done as follows:

- Manually, using a command such as `yum update` on each machine
- Centrally, using an Ansible playbook
- From the Katello user interface, if the `katello-agent` package is installed on your target machines

Given the varied nature of the tools available, we won't go into any greater depth in this chapter but will instead leave this as an exercise for you. Experience has shown that central deployment using Ansible is the most robust method, but you are welcome to experiment and find the path that best suits you.

That concludes our brief tour of RPM-based patching with Katello, though it is hoped that it has shown you enough to give you a taste of how it might prove valuable in your enterprise. In the next section, we will look at the process of patching DEB-based systems with Katello.

Patching DEB-based systems with Katello

The patching of DEB-based systems such as Ubuntu through Katello is broadly similar to the RPM-based process, save for a few changes in the GUI, and the limitations around package signing discussed earlier in this chapter, in the section entitled *Patching with Katello*. Let's briefly walk through an example now for Ubuntu Server 18.04:

1. First, create a new product for our Ubuntu package repositories:

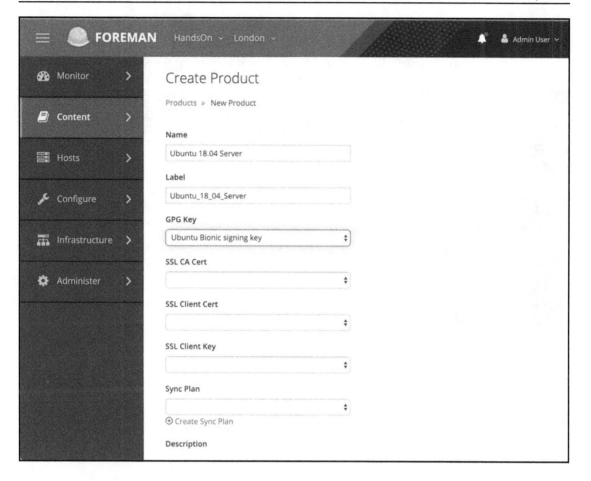

It is important to state here that importing the Ubuntu signing public key makes no impact on the published repository and so can be specified or ignored as you prefer. The resulting repository will not have a signed `Release` file and so must be treated as implicitly trusted.

2. Once the product is saved, create a new repository within it to contain the packages—the package mirror creation requires the same parameters we used on the command line with Pulp, as shown in the following screenshot:

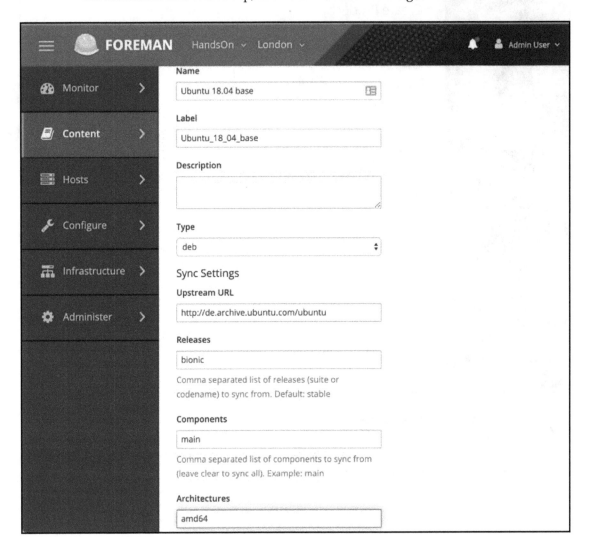

Sync the newly created repository as before, and ensure this has completed successfully before proceeding to the content view creation.

3. Once it has, create a separate content view for our Ubuntu content—the following screenshot shows the content view creation in progress:

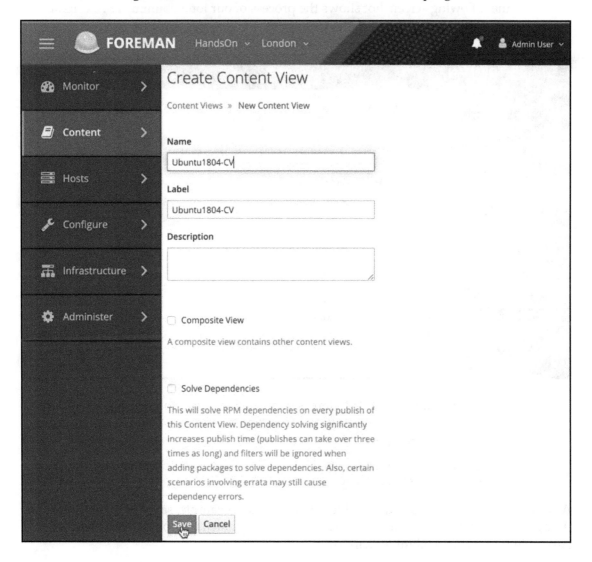

4. This time, navigate to the **Apt Repositories** tab and select the appropriate Ubuntu repositories—again, in our simple example here, we only have one, and the following screenshot shows the process of our lone `Ubuntu 18.04 base` repository being added to the **Ubuntu1804-CV** content view:

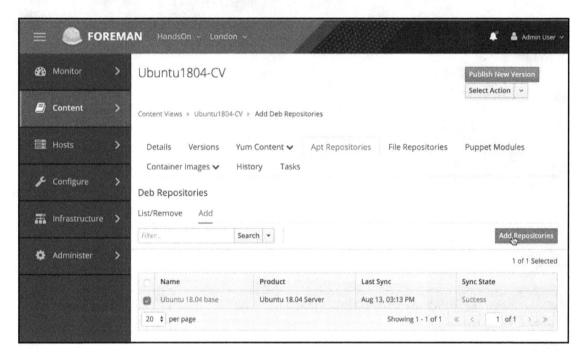

5. From here, our new content view is published and promoted just as we did for the RPM-based one. The resulting repository is accessible again at a predictable URL, this time being of the following pattern:

```
http://KATELLOHOSTNAME/pulp/deb/ORGNAME/LIFECYCLENAME/CONTENTVIEWNA
ME/custom/PRODUCT/REPO
```

As can be seen, this is almost identical to the RPM-based example, save for the initial path. An appropriate entry for `/etc/apt/sources.list` to match the content view we just created in this example might look like this:

```
deb [trusted=yes]
http://katello.example.com/pulp/deb/HandsOn/Development/Ubuntu1804-CV/custo
m/Ubuntu_18_04_Server/Ubuntu_18_04_base/ bionic main
```

As before, this URL remains constant regardless of when we might sync, publish, or promote this content view and so it need only be deployed once to target systems to ensure they can receive packages from the Katello server. Again, you can perform this patching manually through the `apt update` and `apt upgrade` commands on the end systems, or centrally through Ansible.

 Note that there is no `katello-agent` package for Debian/Ubuntu-based systems at the time of writing.

In this chapter, we have barely scratched the surface of all that Katello can do, yet this example alone demonstrates how effective a tool it is for enterprise patch management. It is highly recommended that you explore this further to establish whether it meets your wider infrastructure needs.

It must be stressed that, in this chapter, we have really only scratched the surface of what Katello can do—however, it is hoped that the work we have done so far gives you enough to make an informed decision on whether to proceed with this incredibly powerful and versatile platform as part of your Linux architecture.

Summary

Katello is actually an amalgamation of several incredibly powerful open source infrastructure management tools, including Pulp, which we have already explored. It is incredibly adept at patch management in an infrastructure setting, offering numerous advantages over a standalone Pulp installation and can handle most build and maintenance tasks from a single pane of glass—more than we have had space to cover!

In this chapter, you gained an understanding of what the Katello project actually is and the components that it is comprised of. You then learned how to perform a standalone installation of Katello for patching purposes and then how to build out repositories suitable for patching both RPM- and DEB-based Linux distributions and the basics of integrating these two operating systems with Katello content views.

In the next chapter, we will explore how Ansible can be effectively employed in an enterprise for user management.

Questions

1. Why would you want to use Katello over a product such as Pulp?
2. What is a Product in Katello terms?
3. What is a content view in Katello?
4. Can Foreman (which underpins Katello) assist with the PXE booting of bare-metal servers?
5. How would you use lifecycle environments in Katello?
6. What is the difference between the `Publish` and `Promote` operations on a content view?
7. When would you want to perform a `Promote` operation on a previously published content view?

Further reading

For a greater understanding of Katello, please refer to the official Red Hat Satellite 6 documentation as this is the commercial version of Katello and all of the documentation is usually written for this platform—however, the features and menu structure are almost identical (`https://access.redhat.com/documentation/en-us/red_hat_satellite/`).

10
Managing Users on Linux

No Linux server is complete without a method for users to access it. Whether administrators or end users, and whether using local or centralized credentials, Linux servers need a mechanism for users (and even tools such as Ansible!) to access them.

User management is, like all good server configuration and maintenance activities, an ongoing job. Credentials need rotating on a regular basis, to ensure the security and integrity of systems. Employees come and go, meaning access details must be updated accordingly. Indeed, access management can, in a busy organization, be a full-time job in itself!

In this chapter, we will explore, through hands-on examples, how to automate your user and access management through Ansible, in a way that is consistent with our **Standard Operating Environment (SOE)** model.

The following topics will be covered in this chapter:

- Performing user account management tasks
- Centralizing user account management with **Lightweight Directory Access Protocol (LDAP)**
- Enforcing and auditing configuration

Technical requirements

This chapter includes examples, based on the following technologies:

- Ubuntu Server 18.04 LTS
- CentOS 7.6
- Ansible 2.8

To run through these examples, you will need access to two servers or virtual machines running one each of the operating systems just listed, and also, Ansible. Note that the examples given in this chapter may be destructive in nature (for example, they add and remove user accounts, and make changes to server configuration) and, if run as is, are only intended to be run in an isolated test environment.

Once you are satisfied that you have a safe environment in which to operate, let's get started on looking at the installation of new software packages with Ansible.

All example code discussed in this chapter is available from GitHub, at the following URL: `https://github.com/PacktPublishing/Hands-On-Enterprise-Automation-on-Linux/tree/master/chapter10`.

Performing user account management tasks

At the most fundamental level, every Linux server in your environment will require some degree of access for users. In an enterprise setting where there could be hundreds, if not thousands, of servers, a centralized user management system such as LDAP or Active Directory would be an ideal solution as, taking the examples of a user leaving or changing their password, they can do this in one place, and it is applied across all servers. We will explore this aspect of Enterprise Linux management and automation in the next section, *Centralizing user account management with LDAP*.

For now, though, let us concern ourselves with local account management—that is, accounts that are created on each and every Linux server where access is required. Even when a centralized solution such as LDAP is present, local accounts are still a requirement—if for no other purpose than to serve as an emergency access solution, should the directory service fail.

 Note that, as with all Ansible examples in this book, they can be run equally well on 1, 100, or even 1,000 servers. In fact, the use of Ansible reduces the need for a centralized user management system, as user account changes can be pushed out across the entire estate of servers with ease. However, there are good reasons not to rely solely on this—for example, one server being down for maintenance during an Ansible playbook run means it will not receive the account changes being made. In the worst-case scenario, this server could then pose a security risk once it is brought back into service.

Starting in the next section, we will explore the ways in which Ansible can assist with your local account management.

Adding and modifying users with Ansible

Whether you are configuring a brand new server for the first time after it has been built or making changes when a new employee joins the company, adding user accounts to a server is a commonly required task. Thankfully, Ansible has a module called `user`, which is designed to perform user account management tasks, and we shall proceed to use exactly this.

Throughout our previous examples, we have been very careful to highlight the differences between platforms such as Ubuntu and CentOS, and user account management requires a little consideration here too.

Take, for example, the following shell command (which we will later automate in Ansible):

```
$ useradd -c "John Doe" -s /bin/bash johndoe
```

This command could be run on either CentOS 7 or Ubuntu Server 18.04, and would yield the same results, namely:

- The user account `johndoe` would be added with the next free **user identification number** (**UID**) for users.
- The account comment would be set to `John Doe`.
- The shell would be set to `/bin/bash`.

Indeed, you could run this command on just about any Linux system, and it would work. The differences start, however, when you consider groups, especially built-in ones. For example, if you wanted this account to be able to use sudo for root access (that is, `johndoe` is a system administrator), you would want to put this account into the `wheel` group on CentOS 7. On Ubuntu Server, however, there is no wheel group, and attempting to put the user into such a group would result in an error. Instead, on Ubuntu, this user would go into the `sudo` group.

It is subtle differences like this that could trip you up when it comes to automated user account management across different Linux distributions—however, as long as you remain mindful of such things, you can easily create Ansible playbooks or roles, to manage your Linux users with ease.

Let's build on this example, to instead create the `johndoe` user in an Ansible role, such that access for them can be rolled out on all Linux servers. The code for `roles/addusers/tasks/main.yml` to perform the same function as the shell of the preceding command should look something like the following:

```
---
- name: Add required users to Linux servers
  user:
    name: johndoe
    comment: John Doe
    shell: /bin/bash
```

If we run this role in the usual way, we can see that the user account gets created on the first run, and that no action is taken if we run the playbook a second time. This is denoted in the following screenshot, which shows the preceding role being run twice—the `changed` and `ok` statuses show when a user account is added, and when no action is taken because it already exists respectively:

```
● ● ●                james@automation-01: ~/hands-on-automation/chapter10/example01 (ssh)
~/hands-on-automation/chapter10/example01> ansible-playbook -i hosts site.yml

PLAY [Manage user accounts] ************************************************************

TASK [Gathering Facts] ****************************************************************
ok: [ubuntu-testhost]

TASK [addusers : Add required users to Linux servers] **********************************
changed: [ubuntu-testhost]

PLAY RECAP ****************************************************************************
ubuntu-testhost              : ok=2    changed=1    unreachable=0    failed=0

~/hands-on-automation/chapter10/example01> ansible-playbook -i hosts site.yml

PLAY [Manage user accounts] ************************************************************

TASK [Gathering Facts] ****************************************************************
ok: [ubuntu-testhost]

TASK [addusers : Add required users to Linux servers] **********************************
ok: [ubuntu-testhost]

PLAY RECAP ****************************************************************************
ubuntu-testhost              : ok=2    changed=0    unreachable=0    failed=0
```

So far, so good—however, this example is rather skeletal in nature—our user has no password set, no group membership, and no authorized SSH keys. We demonstrated previously that we can run an Ansible role containing the user module more than once and changes will only be made if required, and we can leverage this to our advantage. Let's now expand our example role, to add these things.

Before we get into our next example, we will demonstrate how to generate a password hash, using Ansible. Here, we will choose the word `secure123`. The `user` module of Ansible is capable of setting and modifying user account passwords, but it does not (for very good reasons) allow you to specify the password in plaintext. Instead, you must create a password hash, to send to the machine being configured. In `Chapter 6`, *Custom Builds with PXE Booting*, we looked at a way to do this with a small amount of Python code, and you are welcome to reuse this method here. However, you can also make use of Ansible's vast array of filters, to generate a password hash from a string. Run the following command from the shell:

```
$ ansible localhost -i localhost, -m debug -a "msg={{ 'secure123' |
password_hash('sha512') }}"
```

Running this produces a password hash that you can copy and paste into your role, as shown in the following screenshot:

This is very useful in itself—however, let's bear something in mind: no password hash is completely secure. Remember that once, MD5 hashes were considered secure, but are now not. Ideally, you should not be storing the hash in plaintext either, and should regenerate it on every system as it contains a unique salt. Luckily, we can use the `password_hash` filter in a role directly to achieve this.

In the following example, we demonstrate how to store the password string in a variable, and then, how to use the `password_hash` filter to generate the hash for the remote system. In a real-world use case, you would replace the plaintext variable file with an Ansible vault file so that at no point is either the original password or hash stored unencrypted.

1. First of all, let's create `roles/addusers/vars/main.yml`, and store John Doe's password in a variable, as follows:

   ```
   ---
   johndoepw: secure123
   ```

2. Next, let's create an SSH key pair for this user, in the directory `roles/addusers/files/`, by running the following command in that directory:

   ```
   $ ssh-keygen -b 2048 -t rsa -f ./johndoe_id_rsa -q -N ''
   ```

   Of course, it is likely in an enterprise setting that the user would generate their own key pair and provide an administrator with the public key for distribution to the systems they will use—however, for our example here, it is easier to demonstrate with a newly generated key pair.

3. Finally, let's say that `johndoe` is going to administer Ubuntu systems, and so, should be in the `sudo` group. Our resulting role should now look like this:

   ```
   ---
   - name: Add required users to Linux servers
     user:
       name: johndoe
       comment: John Doe
       shell: /bin/bash
       groups: sudo
       append: yes
       password: "{{ johndoepw | password_hash('sha512') }}"

   - name: Add user's SSH public key
     authorized_key:
       user: johndoe
       state: present
       key: "{{ lookup('file', 'files/johndoe_id_rsa.pub') }}"
   ```

4. Running the code yields `changed` results, as we would expect, and the following screenshot shows the successful addition of the user and their corresponding SSH public key:

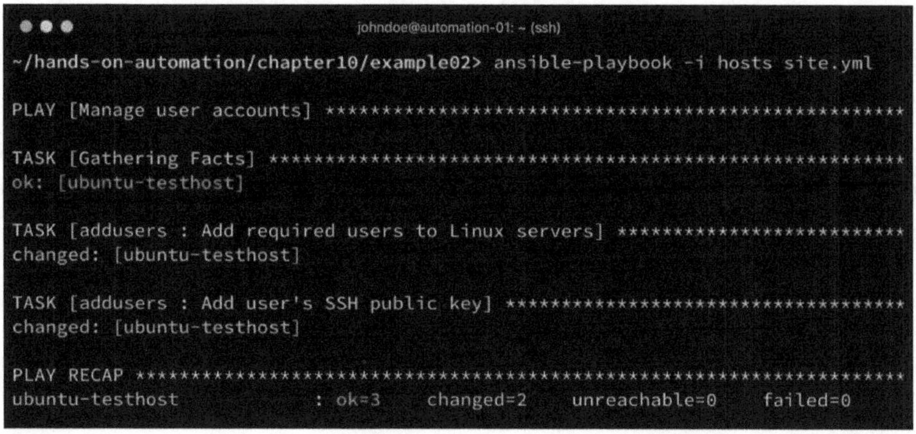

Note that we have successfully modified the `johndoe` account here, as we created it earlier in this section—however, we could also have run this most recent role before the account creation, and the end result would have been the same. That is the beauty of Ansible—you don't need to write different code for modifications and additions. There are many other modifications possible with the `user` module, and it should serve most of your needs.

Returning briefly to the `vars/main.yml` file we created earlier, we left this in plaintext for simplicity in this example. However, we can very easily encrypt our existing file, using the following command:

```
$ ansible-vault encrypt main.yml
```

The following screenshot shows this encryption process in action:

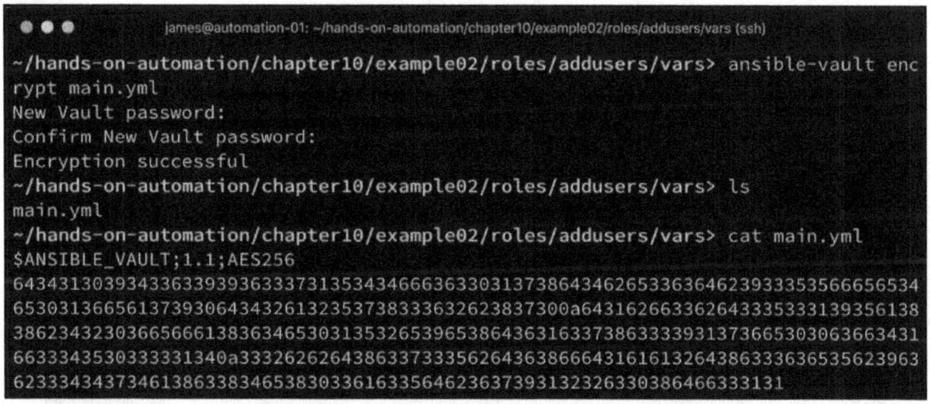

The data is now encrypted at rest! We can still run the playbook without decrypting it—simply add the `--ask-vault-pass` parameter to the `ansible-playbook` command, and enter your chosen vault password when prompted.

Before concluding this section, it is worth noting that we can also leverage `loops`, to create multiple accounts at once. The following example creates two new users with differing group membership, and with distinct username and matching comments on their accounts. Expanding this example to address initial passwords and/or SSH keys is left as an exercise for you, but you should have enough information to build upon to achieve this. The code can be seen below:

```
---
- name: Add required users to Linux servers
  user:
    name: "{{ item.name }}"
    comment: "{{ item.comment }}"
    shell: /bin/bash
    groups: "{{ item.groups }}"
    append: yes
    state: present
  loop:
    - { name: 'johndoe', comment: 'John Doe', groups: 'sudo'}
    - { name: 'janedoe', comment: 'Jane Doe', groups: 'docker'}
```

Noting that we created `johndoe` earlier in this chapter, we can see that if we run this role, the `janedoe` user is the only account created as they did not already exist—the following screenshot shows exactly this. `janedoe` shows a `changed` status, informing us that a change was made—in this case, the account was created. The `ok` status against the `johndoe` user account tells us that no action was performed, as can be seen in the following screenshot:

In this way, user accounts can be created and managed at scale, across a wide number of Linux servers. As we can see in the preceding screenshot, in the usual Ansible manner, only the required changes are made, with existing accounts left unchanged. While adding accounts is straightforward, we must also consider that employees also leave enterprises from time to time, and so, account cleanup is also required in this instance.

We will explore the ways in which Ansible can assist with removing user accounts and tidying up after them, in the next section.

Removing users with Ansible

Although we have shown that it is easy to add and modify user accounts with Ansible, we must consider removal as a separate case. The reason for this is simple—Ansible assumes that, if we use the `user` module in conjunction with a `loop` to add both `johndoe` and `janedoe`, it will add them if they do not exist; otherwise, it will modify them. If, of course, they match the state described by the role or playbook, then it will do nothing at all.

However, Ansible assumes nothing about the state prior to it being run. Thus, if we delete `johndoe` from the loop described previously and run the playbook again, this account is not removed. As a direct result of this, we must handle account removal separately.

The following code will remove this user account:

```
---
- name: Add required users to Linux servers
  user:
    name: johndoe
    state: absent
```

Now, if we run this command, the output should look something like the following screenshot:

Running this role is the equivalent of using the `userdel` command in the shell—the user account is removed, along with all group memberships. However, the `home` directory is left intact. This is normally the safest route, as users might have stored important code or other data in their `home` directory, and often, it is best for someone to sanity-check that the directory is safe to remove, before it is actually removed. If you are sure that you want to remove the directory (which is best practice, for both security reasons and to free up disk space), then add the following code to the role we just created:

```
- name: Clean up user home directory
  file:
    path: /home/johndoe
    state: absent
```

This performs a recursive delete of the `path` specified, so use this with care!

With these practical examples and a little additional detail from the documentation, you should be in a good position to automate your local account tasks with Ansible. In the next section, we will explore the use of centralized user account management with LDAP.

Centralizing user account management with LDAP

Although Ansible performs a fine job when it comes to managing user accounts across an estate of servers, the best practice in an enterprise is to make use of a centralized directory system. A centralized directory is able to perform a number of tasks that Ansible can not—for example, enforcing password security criteria, such as length and character types, password expiry, and account lockout when too many incorrect passwords are tried. As such, it is highly recommended that such a system be used in the enterprise.

Indeed, many enterprises already have such a system in place, two common ones being FreeIPA and Microsoft **Active Directory** (**AD**). In the following sections, we will explore the integration of these two systems with your Linux servers.

Microsoft AD

As this is a book on Linux automation, an in-depth discussion of Microsoft AD and its setup and configuration is well beyond its scope. Suffice to say that in the context of Linux, AD is best suited to centralized user account management, although, of course, its capabilities are far greater than this. Most organizations that need an AD server will already have one set up, and so, our concern is not with this aspect, but with getting our Linux servers to authenticate against it.

On most modern Linux distributions, the `realmd` tool is used to join the Linux server in question to AD. Next, we consider a hypothetical example of joining a CentOS 7 server to AD—however, every organization, their AD setup, organizational units, and so on will be different, and so, there is no one-size-fits-all solution here.

 As you will no doubt be aware by now, performing this process on Ubuntu will be very similar, except that you will use the `apt` module in place of `yum`, and the package names could differ. Once `realmd` and its required packages are installed, the process is identical.

It is hoped, though, that the following code given provides you with a good basis on which to develop your own Ansible role to join AD.

1. Before beginning the process of joining the directory, it is vital that the Linux server is using the correct DNS servers that contain the appropriate **Service (SRV)** records for the domain. Often, these DNS servers will be the AD servers themselves, but that again will vary from organization to organization.

2. The `realmd` tool must be installed, along with a number of supporting packages. Let's create a role called `realmd`, using our familiar `roles` directory structure. The `roles/realmd/tasks/main.yml` should begin with the following code, to install the required packages:

```
---
- name: Install realmd packages
  yum:
    name: "{{ item }}"
    state: present
  loop:
    - realmd
    - oddjob
    - oddjob-mkhomedir
    - sssd
    - samba-common
    - samba-common-tools
    - adcli
```

```
     - krb5-workstation
     - openldap-clients
     - policycoreutils-python
```

Some of these packages offer supporting functions—for example, `openldap-clients` is not directly required, but can be very useful in debugging directory issues.

3. Once our prerequisite packages are installed, our next task is to join the Active Directory itself. Here, we are assuming the presence of `roles/realmd/vars/main.yml` with the `realm_join_password`, `realm_join_user`, and `realm_domain` variables set. As this file might well contain a password with sufficient privileges to join the AD domain, it is recommended that this variables file be encrypted with `ansible-vault`. Run the following code:

```
- name: Join the domain
    shell: echo '{{ realm_join_password }}' | realm join --user={{
realm_join_user }} {{ realm_domain }}
    register: command_result
    ignore_errors: True
    notify:
      - Restart sssd
```

The use of the `shell` module to perform the `realm join` requires special consideration, as running this task twice will not yield the normal clean behavior of Ansible. Indeed, performing a second `realm join` when the server is already a domain member results in an error. As a result, we set `ignore_errors: True`, and `register` the result of the command so that we can later evaluate if it ran successfully. We also notify a handler that we will define later, to restart the `sssd` service. The aforementioned `vars` file should look something like this:

```
---
realm_join_password: securepassword
realm_join_user: administrator@example.com
realm_domain: example.com
```

Be sure to substitute the variable values with ones appropriate to your own environment.

4. We immediately follow this task with a check, to see if the `realm join` was successful. If it was successful, we should either get a return code of 0 or an error, informing us that the server is `Already joined to this domain`. If we don't get these expected results, then we will fail the entire play to ensure that the issue can be rectified, as follows:

```
- name: Fail the play when the realm join fails
    fail:
      msg="Realm join failed with this error: {{
command_result.stderr }}"
      when: "'Already joined to this domain' not in
command_result.stderr and command_result.rc != 0"
```

5. Finally, we create the handler, to restart `sssd` in `roles/realmd/handlers/main.yml`, as follows:

```
---
- name: Restart sssd
  service:
    name: sssd
    state: restarted
    enabled: yes
```

These steps are all sufficient to perform the basic addition of a Linux server to an AD domain. Although the example is given for CentOS 7, the process should be broadly similar for operating systems like Ubuntu, as long as you take account of the different package manager and package names.

There are, of course, a vast number of enhancements that can be made to the preceding procedure, most of which will be performed with the `realm` command. Sadly, at the time of writing, there is no `realm` module for Ansible, so, all `realm` commands must be issued with the `shell` module—though this still enables automated rollouts of AD membership to Linux servers using Ansible.

Possible enhancements for you to consider to the preceding process (all of which can easily be automated by extending the example playbook we have previously suggested) are as follows:

- Specify the **organizational unit** (**OU**) that the Linux server is to go into when the join is complete. Without specifying this, it will go into the default `Computers` OU. You can change this, by specifying something like `--computer-ou=OU=Linux,OU=Servers,OU=example,DC=example,DC=com` within your `realm join` command. Be sure the OU has been created first, and adjust the preceding parameter to match your environment.

- By default, all valid domain user accounts will be able to log in to the Linux server. This may not be desirable and, if not, you will need to first of all deny all access, using the command `realm deny --all`. Then, to say you wish to allow all users in the `LinuxAdmins` AD group, you would then issue the following command: `realm permit -g LinuxAdmins`.

- It is unlikely you will have a group in your AD called `wheel` or `sudo`, and as a result, AD users may find themselves unable to execute privileged commands. This can be rectified by adding the appropriate users or groups into `/etc/sudoers` or, better still, a unique file under `/etc/sudoers.d` that Ansible can manage. For example, creating `/etc/sudoers.d/LinuxAdmins` with the following content would enable all members of the `LinuxAdmins` AD group to perform sudo commands without re-entering their passwords:

```
%LinuxAdmins ALL=(ALL) NOPASSWD: ALL
```

All of these tasks are left as an exercise for you, though it is expected that the information given in this chapter is sufficient for you to build up your own playbook suited to your AD infrastructure.

In the next section, we will look at the use of the FreeIPA directory service that is native to Linux, and how to integrate this into your environment with Ansible.

FreeIPA

FreeIPA is a freely available open source directory service that is simple to install and manage. It runs on Linux and runs primarily on CentOS or **Red Hat Enterprise Linux (RHEL)**, though client support is readily available on Ubuntu and other Linux platforms. Integration with Windows AD is even possible, though is in no way required.

If you are building a purely Linux environment, it makes sense to look at FreeIPA, as opposed to putting in a proprietary solution such as Microsoft AD.

FreeIPA and Microsoft AD are by no means the only two options on the market for directory services, and a number of cloud-based alternatives are now available, including JumpCloud, AWS Directory Service, and many others. Always make your own independent decisions regarding the best option for you as the field is fast evolving, especially when it comes to cloud-based directory services.

As with the previous section on Microsoft AD, the design and deployment of a FreeIPA infrastructure are beyond the scope of this book. Directory services are core services on your network—imagine if you only built a single directory server, and then had to shut it down for maintenance. Even a simple reboot would leave users unable to log in to all machines joined to it for the duration the services were down. For these reasons, it is vitally important that you design your directory service infrastructure to take account of redundancy and disaster recovery. It is also important that you have well-secured local accounts in case your directory infrastructure does fail, as discussed earlier in this chapter, in the section entitled *Performing user account management tasks*.

Once you have designed a suitably redundant infrastructure for your FreeIPA installation, there are a series of playbooks and roles available on GitHub, created by the FreeIPA team, to install your server and clients, and you can explore these further here: `https://github.com/freeipa/ansible-freeipa`

This book leaves the task of installing your FreeIPA infrastructure to you—however, let's take a look at the use of the freely available FreeIPA roles, to install clients on your infrastructure. After all, this is one of the key benefits of open source software—the sharing of knowledge, information, and code.

1. First of all, we clone the `ansible-freeipa` repository to our local machine, and change into the directory to make use of it, as follows:

```
$ cd ~
$ git clone https://github.com/freeipa/ansible-freeipa
$ cd ansible-freeipa
```

2. Next, create symbolic links to `roles` and `modules` we just cloned into our local Ansible environment, as follows:

```
$ ln -s ~/ansible-freeipa/roles/ ~/.ansible/
$ mkdir ~/.ansible/plugins
$ ln -s ~/ansible-freeipa/plugins/modules ~/.ansible/plugins/
$ ln -s ~/ansible-freeipa/plugins/module_utils/ ~/.ansible/plugins/
```

3. Once that is done, we must create a simple inventory file that includes appropriate variables, to define the FreeIPA realm and domain, and also, the password of the `admin` user (which is required to join a new server to the IPA realm). The following example is shown, but be sure to customize it to your requirements:

```
[ipaclients]
centos-testhost

[ipaclients:vars]
```

```
ipaadmin_password=password
ipaserver_domain=example.com
ipaserver_realm=EXAMPLE.COM
```

4. With the appropriate variables set and the inventory compiled, we can then run the playbooks provided, with the code downloaded from GitHub. An example of this FreeIPA client installation playbook running is shown, as follows:

```
james@automation-01: ~/hands-on-automation/chapter10/example07 (ssh)

~/hands-on-automation/chapter10/example07> ansible-playbook -i hosts ~/ansible-f
reeipa/playbooks/install-client.yml

PLAY [Playbook to configure IPA clients with username/password] ****************

TASK [Gathering Facts] *********************************************************
ok: [centos-testhost]

TASK [ipaclient : Import variables specific to distribution] *******************
ok: [centos-testhost] => (item=/home/james/ansible-freeipa/roles/ipaclient/vars/
CentOS-7.yml)

TASK [ipaclient : Install IPA client] ******************************************
included: /home/james/ansible-freeipa/roles/ipaclient/tasks/install.yml for cent
os-testhost

TASK [ipaclient : Install - Ensure that IPA client packages are installed] *****
changed: [centos-testhost]

TASK [ipaclient : Install - Set ipaclient_servers] *****************************
skipping: [centos-testhost]

TASK [ipaclient : Install - Set ipaclient_servers from cluster inventory] ******
skipping: [centos-testhost]
```

The preceding output shown is truncated but shows the FreeIPA client installation in process. As usual for examples in this book, we have kept it simple, but this could just as easily be run against 100, or even 1,000, servers.

As these playbooks and roles are provided by the official FreeIPA project, they are a trustworthy source for installing both servers and clients, and although it is highly recommended to test and review any code you download, these should serve well for building up your FreeIPA-based infrastructure.

In the next section, we will take a look at the ways in which Ansible can help with enforcing and auditing user accounts and configuration.

Enforcing and auditing configuration

When it comes to user account management, security is important. As we discussed in the section entitled *Centralizing user account management with LDAP*, Ansible is not designed specifically for enforcement or auditing— however, it can help us greatly. Let's consider a few of the security risks around user management that Ansible can help to mitigate, starting with the sudoers file.

Managing sudoers with Ansible

The /etc/sudoers file is one of the most sensitive on most Linux systems, as it defines which user accounts can run commands as the superuser. Needless to say, this file being compromised or modified in an unauthorized way could pose a huge security risk to not just the Linux server in question, but to the network at large.

Thankfully, Ansible templates can help us to manage this file effectively. Like other modern Linux configurations, the sudoers configuration is broken up into several files, to make it more manageable. The files are, typically, as follows:

- /etc/sudoers: This is the master file, and references all other files that might be considered.
- /etc/sudoers.d/*: These files are normally included by a reference in the /etc/sudoers file.

As we discussed in the chapter entitled *Configuration Management with Ansible*, someone could potentially edit /etc/sudoers and tell it to include a completely different path in addition to, or instead of, /etc/sudoers.d/*, meaning that it is vital we deploy this file through a template. This ensures we maintain control of which files provide sudo configuration.

We will not repeat our discussion on templates and their deployment with Ansible, as the techniques discussed in Chapter 7, *Configuration Management with Ansible* apply equally well here. However, we will add an important caveat. If you break the sudo configuration by deploying a file with (for example) a syntax error in it, you risk locking all users out of privileged access. This would mean the only way to fix the problem would be to log in to the server using the root account, and if this is disabled (as it is by default on Ubuntu, and is recommended in many environments), then your path to recovery becomes quite tricky.

As with so many scenarios, prevention is better than cure, and the template module we used earlier has a trick up its sleeve, to help us out here. When you edit the sudoers file using visudo on a Linux system, the file you have created is checked automatically before it is written to disk. If there is an error, you are warned and given the option to rectify it. Ansible can make use of this utility through the addition of the validate parameter to the template module. Thus, a very simple role, to deploy a new version of the sudoers file with Ansible, might look like this:

```
---
- name: Copy a new sudoers file on if visudo validation is passed
  template:
    src: templates/sudoers.j2
    dest: /etc/sudoers
    validate: /usr/sbin/visudo -cf %s
```

In the preceding example, the template module passes the name of the file specified by dest to the command in the validate parameter—this is the significance of the %s. If the validation is passed, the new file is written into place. If the validation fails, then the new file is not written and the old one remains. In addition, when validation fails, the task results in a failed status, thus ending the play and alerting the user to rectify the condition.

This isn't the only task that the validate parameter can be used to complete—it can be used to check the results of any template operation, provided you can define a shell command that will perform a suitable check on the template operation. This might be as simple as using grep to check for a line in a file, or a check to see that a service restarts.

In the next section, we will take a look at how Ansible can assist with enforcing and auditing user accounts across a large number of servers.

Auditing user accounts with Ansible

Say your enterprise has 1,000 Linux servers, all using directory services for authentication, as we have discussed so far. Now, suppose an errant user, wishing to bypass this privilege management, manages to create a local account called `john` on a single server. This might happen when privileges are temporarily granted for a change request but then revoked—unscrupulous individuals can easily create their own access methods, to bypass the security provided by your directory service.

How would you find this had happened? Although Ansible is not technically a tool for auditing, it has the benefit of being able to run a command (or set of commands) on 1,000 servers at once and returning the results to you for processing.

As all your server builds should be to a given standard (see `Chapter 1`, *Building a Standard Operating Environment on Linux*), then you should know which accounts are supposed to be on each Linux server. It is possible that there will be some variance—for example, if you install the PostgreSQL database server, this normally creates a local user account called `postgres`. However, these cases are well understood, and can quickly and easily be filtered out.

We don't even need to write a complete playbook for Ansible to help us out here—once you have an inventory file with your Linux server (or servers) in, you can run what is called an ad hoc command. This is simply a single-line command that can run any single Ansible module with a set of arguments—much like a playbook with just one task in it.

Thus, to obtain a list of all user accounts on all my servers, I could run the following command:

```
$ ansible -i hosts -m shell -a 'cat /etc/passwd' all
```

That's all there is to it—Ansible will faithfully connect to all servers in the inventory file specified by the `-i` parameter, and dump the `/etc/passwd` file contents to the screen. You could pipe this output to a file for further processing and analysis, rather than having to log on to each box. Although Ansible is not actually doing any analysis, it makes for a very powerful and easy tool to perform the data gathering for the purposes of auditing, and, as is the beauty of Ansible, no agent is required on the remote machines.

The following screenshot shows an example of Ansible obtaining the local user accounts from one of our test systems, using a simple `grep` command to filter out two commonly present accounts. Naturally, you can expand this example as you wish, to improve the data processing and hence make your task easier:

```
● ● ●                james@automation-01: ~/hands-on-automation/chapter10/example08 (ssh)
~/hands-on-automation/chapter10/example08> ansible -i hosts -m shell -a "cat /et
c/passwd | grep -Ev 'root|daemon'" all
ubuntu-testhost | CHANGED | rc=0 >>
bin:x:2:2:bin:/bin:/usr/sbin/nologin
sys:x:3:3:sys:/dev:/usr/sbin/nologin
sync:x:4:65534:sync:/bin:/bin/sync
games:x:5:60:games:/usr/games:/usr/sbin/nologin
man:x:6:12:man:/var/cache/man:/usr/sbin/nologin
lp:x:7:7:lp:/var/spool/lpd:/usr/sbin/nologin
mail:x:8:8:mail:/var/mail:/usr/sbin/nologin
news:x:9:9:news:/var/spool/news:/usr/sbin/nologin
uucp:x:10:10:uucp:/var/spool/uucp:/usr/sbin/nologin
proxy:x:13:13:proxy:/bin:/usr/sbin/nologin
www-data:x:33:33:www-data:/var/www:/usr/sbin/nologin
backup:x:34:34:backup:/var/backups:/usr/sbin/nologin
list:x:38:38:Mailing List Manager:/var/list:/usr/sbin/nologin
irc:x:39:39:ircd:/var/run/ircd:/usr/sbin/nologin
gnats:x:41:41:Gnats Bug-Reporting System (admin):/var/lib/gnats:/usr/sbin/nologi
n
nobody:x:65534:65534:nobody:/nonexistent:/usr/sbin/nologin
systemd-network:x:100:102:systemd Network Management,,,:/run/systemd/netif:/usr/
sbin/nologin
systemd-resolve:x:101:103:systemd Resolver,,,:/run/systemd/resolve:/usr/sbin/nol
ogin
syslog:x:102:106::/home/syslog:/usr/sbin/nologin
```

In this manner, you can make good use of Ansible, to gather useful information from a large number of systems for further processing—as the results are returned directly to the Terminal, it is easy to pipe them to a file and then process them with your favorite tools (for example, AWK) to establish whether there are any systems queried that violate enterprise policies. While this example has been performed with the local user account list, it could just as effectively be performed on any given text file on the remote systems.

This, as you can see, is a very simple example, but it is a fundamental building block, on top of which you can build other playbooks. Here are some ideas for you to explore further by yourself:

- Change the ad hoc command we ran previously, and run it as a playbook instead.

- Schedule the preceding playbook to run on a regular basis in AWX.
- Modify the playbook to check for certain key user accounts.

Your ability to audit users doesn't stop there, though—although centralized logging should (and probably will) be part of your infrastructure, you can also interrogate log files with Ansible. Using the ad hoc command structure previously shown, you could run the following command against a group of Ubuntu servers:

```
$ ansible -i hosts -m shell -a 'grep "authentication failure | cat"
/var/log/auth.log' all
```

On CentOS, these log messages would appear in `/var/log/secure` instead, so you would alter the path accordingly for these systems.

> The `grep` command returns code 1 if the string you specify is not found, and Ansible, in turn, interprets this as a failure, reporting the task as failed. As a result, we pipe the output of `grep` into the `cat` command, which always returns zero, and hence, the task does not fail, even if the string we are searching for is not found.

As I'm sure you have realized by now, these commands would be far better run as a playbook, with some detection for the operating system and the appropriate paths used in each case—however, the goal of this section is not to provide you with an exhaustive set of solutions, but rather, to inspire you to go and build your own code based on these examples, to help you audit your infrastructure with Ansible.

The fact that Ansible can perform such a wide variety of commands, and that it has agentless access across your infrastructure, means that it can be an effective solution in your toolbox, both for configuring your Linux servers and for maintaining the integrity of the configuration, and, even, auditing them.

Summary

User account and access management is an integral part of any Enterprise Linux environment, and Ansible can be a key component in both configuring this and rolling it out across a wide number of servers. Indeed, in the case of FreeIPA, there are already freely available Ansible roles and playbooks that can set up not only the Linux clients, but even your server architecture as well. Thus, automation of all key components within your Linux infrastructure can be achieved.

In this chapter, you learned how to effectively manage user accounts with Ansible across a large number of Linux servers. You then learned how to integrate logins with common directory servers such as FreeIPA and Microsoft AD using Ansible, and finally, you learned how Ansible can be used to enforce configuration and audit its state.

In the next chapter, we will explore the use of Ansible in database management.

Questions

1. What are the benefits of local user accounts, even when a directory service is employed?
2. Which module is used to create and manipulate user accounts in Ansible?
3. How would you generate an encrypted password hash, using just Ansible?
4. Which package is used to integrate Linux servers with AD?
5. How can you use Ansible to audit configuration from a group of servers?
6. What is the purpose of validating the sudoers file when deploying it from a template?
7. What additional benefits does a directory service bring that Ansible could not provide, even though it can deploy user accounts across all your servers?
8. How would you make the choice between FreeIPA and AD?

Further reading

- For an in-depth understanding of Ansible, please refer to *Mastering Ansible, Third Edition—James Freeman* and *Jesse Keating* (https://www.packtpub.com/gb/virtualization-and-cloud/mastering-ansible-third-edition).
- To explore the setup and use of AD in greater depth, readers may refer to *Mastering Active Directory, Second Edition—Dishan Francis* (https://www.packtpub.com/cloud-networking/mastering-active-directory-second-edition).

11
Database Management

No application stack is complete without data, and this is commonly stored in a database. There is a myriad of databases to choose from when your platform is Linux, and the whole topic of database management and administration often warrants entire books by itself—in fact, normally one book per database technology. In spite of the vastness of this topic, a little knowledge of Ansible can assist greatly when it comes to database administration.

Indeed, whether you are installing a new database server, or performing maintenance or administration tasks on an existing one, our original principles discussed in Chapter 1, *Building a Standard Operating Environment on Linux* still apply. Indeed, why would you go to all the trouble of standardizing your Linux environment and ensuring all changes are automated, only to insist on manual management of the database tier? This could easily result in a lack of standardization, auditability, and even traceability (for example, who made which changes, and when?). Ansible can perform database operations and configuration via modules. It is perhaps not a replacement for some of the more advanced database management tools available on the market, but if these can be driven through the command line, it can execute these on your behalf, as well as taking care of many tasks itself. Ultimately, you want all changes to be documented (or self-documented) and auditable, and Ansible (combined with Ansible Tower, or AWX) can help you achieve this. This chapter explores methods that will help you with this.

The following topics will be covered in this chapter:

- Installing databases with Ansible
- Importing and exporting data
- Performing routine maintenance

Technical requirements

This chapter includes examples, based on the following technologies:

- Ubuntu Server 18.04 LTS
- CentOS 7.6
- Ansible 2.8

To run through these examples, you will need access to two servers or virtual machines running one each of the operating systems just listed, and also, Ansible. Note that the examples given in this chapter may be destructive in nature (for example, they add and remove databases and tables, and change database configuration) and, if run as is, are only intended to be run in an isolated test environment. Once you are satisfied that you have a safe environment in which to operate, let's get started on looking at the installation of new software packages with Ansible. All example code discussed in this chapter is available from GitHub, at the following URL: `https://github.com/PacktPublishing/Hands-On-Enterprise-Automation-on-Linux/tree/master/chapter11`.

Installing databases with Ansible

In `Chapter 7`, *Configuration Management with Ansible*, we explored a few examples of package installation and used MariaDB server in some of our examples. Of course, MariaDB is only one of a myriad of databases available on Linux, and there are too many to cover in detail here. Nonetheless, Ansible can help you install just about any database server on Linux, and in this chapter, we will proceed through a series of examples that will provide you with the tools and techniques to install your own database server, no matter what it is.

Let's get started in the next section, by building on our example of installing MariaDB.

Installing MariaDB server with Ansible

Although earlier in the book, we installed the native `mariadb-server` package that ships with CentOS 7, most enterprises that need a MariaDB server would choose to standardize on a specific release directly from MariaDB. This is often more up to date than the version shipped with a given Linux release, and hence provides newer features and, sometimes, performance improvements. In addition, standardizing on a release directly from MariaDB ensures consistency of your platform, a principle we have kept to throughout this book.

Let's take a simple example—suppose you are running your infrastructure on **Red Hat Enterprise Linux** (**RHEL**) 7. This ships with MariaDB version 5.5.64. Now, suppose you want to standardize your infrastructure on the newly released RHEL 8—if you are relying on the packages supplied by Red Hat, this suddenly moves you to version 10.3.11 of MariaDB, meaning not only an upgrade to your Linux infrastructure but also to your databases, too.

Instead, it would be better to standardize upfront on a release directly from MariaDB itself. At the time of writing, the latest stable release of MariaDB is 10.4—but let us suppose that you have standardized on the 10.3 release, as it is known, and tested successfully in your environment.

The installation process is quite straightforward and is well documented on the MariaDB website—see `https://mariadb.com/kb/en/library/yum/` for CentOS- and Red Hat-specific examples. However, this details the manual installation process, and we wish to automate this with Ansible. Let's now build this into a real, working Ansible example.

 In this example, we will follow the instructions from MariaDB, which includes downloading the packages from their repository. Although for simplicity we will follow this example through, you could mirror the MariaDB package repositories into Pulp or Katello, as detailed in `Chapter 8`, *Enterprise Repository Management with Pulp* and `Chapter 9`, *Patching with Katello*.

1. First of all, we can see from the installation documentation that we need to create a `.repo` file, to tell `yum` where to download the packages from. We can use a template to provide this, such that the MariaDB version can be defined by a variable and thus changed in the future when migration to version 10.4 (or indeed, any other future version) is deemed necessary.

   Thus, our template file, defined in `roles/installmariadb/templates/mariadb.repo.j2`, would look like this:

   ```
   [mariadb]
   name = MariaDB
   baseurl = http://yum.mariadb.org/{{ mariadb_version }}/centos7-amd64
   gpgkey=https://yum.mariadb.org/RPM-GPG-KEY-MariaDB
   gpgcheck=1
   ```

2. Once we have created this, we should also create a default for this variable, to prevent any issues or errors if it is not specified when the role is run—this will be defined in `roles/installmariadb/defaults/main.yml`. Ordinarily, this variable would be provided in the inventory file for a given server or group of servers, or by one of the many other supported methods in Ansible, but the `defaults` file provides a catch-all, in case it gets overlooked. Run the following code:

```
---
mariadb_version: "10.3"
```

3. With this defined, we can now begin to build up the tasks in our role in `roles/installmariadb/tasks/main.yml`, as follows:

```
---
- name: Populate MariaDB yum template on target host
  template:
    src: templates/mariadb.repo.j2
    dest: /etc/yum.repos.d/mariadb.repo
    owner: root
    group: root
    mode: '0644'
```

This will ensure that the correct repository file is written to the server, and if it is ever incorrectly modified, restored to its original, desired state.

 On CentOS or RHEL, you could also use the `yum_repository` Ansible module to perform this task—however, this has the disadvantage of being unable to modify an existing repository definition, and so, in a scenario where we might wish to change the repository version in future, we are better off using a template.

4. Next, we should clean out the `yum` cache—this is especially important when upgrading MariaDB to a new version, as package names will be the same, and cached information could cause issues with the installation. At present, cleaning the `yum` cache is achieved using the `shell` module, to run the `yum clean all` command. However, as this is a shell command, it will always run, and this could be considered inefficient—especially as this command being run would result in any future package operations needing to update the yum cache again, even if we didn't modify the MariaDB repository definition. Thus, we want to run it only when the `template` module task results in a changed state.

To do this, we must first add this line to our `template` task, to store the results of the task:

```
register: mariadbtemplate
```

5. Now, when we define our shell command, we can tell Ansible to only run it if the `template` task resulted in a `changed` state, as follows:

```
- name: Clean out yum cache only if template was changed
  shell: "yum clean all"
  when: mariadbtemplate.changed
```

6. With our cache appropriately cleared out, we can then install the required MariaDB packages—the list used in the task shown in the following code block is taken from the MariaDB documentation referenced earlier in this section, but you should tailor it to your exact requirements:

```
- name: Install MariaDB packages
  yum:
    name:
      - MariaDB-server
      - galera
      - MariaDB-client
      - MariaDB-shared
      - MariaDB-backup
      - MariaDB-common
    state: latest
```

The use of `state: latest` ensures that we always install the latest packages from the repository file created by our `template` task. Thus, this role can be used equally for initial installation and upgrade to the latest version. However, if you do not want this behavior, change this statement to `state: present`—this simply ensures that the packages listed are installed on our target host. If they are, it does not update them to the latest version—it simply returns an `ok` status and proceeds to the next task, even if updates are available.

7. With the packages installed, we must ensure that the server service is then started at boot time. We would probably also want to start it now so that we can perform any initial configuration work on it. Thus, we will add a final task to our `installmariadb` role that looks like this:

```
- name: Ensure mariadb-server service starts on boot and is started
  now
  service:
    name: mariadb
    state: started
    enabled: yes
```

8. Also, we know that CentOS 7 has a firewall enabled by default—as such, we must change the firewall rules to ensure that our newly installed MariaDB server can be accessed. The task to perform this would look something like this:

```
- name: Open firewall port for MariaDB server
  firewalld:
    service: mysql
    permanent: yes
    state: enabled
    immediate: yes
```

9. Let's now run this role and see it in action—the output should look something like this:

```
● ● ●            james@automation-01: ~/hands-on-automation/chapter11/example01 (ssh)

~/hands-on-automation/chapter11/example01> ansible-playbook -i hosts site.yml

PLAY [Install MariaDB] *********************************************************

TASK [Gathering Facts] *********************************************************
ok: [centos-testhost]

TASK [installmariadb : Populate MariaDB yum template on target host] ***********
changed: [centos-testhost]

TASK [installmariadb : Clean out yum cache only if template was changed] *******
 [WARNING]: Consider using the yum module rather than running 'yum'.  If you
need to use command because yum is insufficient you can add 'warn: false' to
this command task or set 'command_warnings=False' in ansible.cfg to get rid of
this message.

changed: [centos-testhost]

TASK [installmariadb : Install MariaDB packages] *******************************
changed: [centos-testhost]
```

The output has been truncated to conserve space, but clearly shows the installation in progress. Note that the warning can safely be ignored—the Ansible engine has detected our `yum clean all` command and is helpfully advising us to use the `yum` module—however, the `yum` module in this instance does not provide the function we need, and hence, we used the `shell` module instead.

With the database installed and running, we have the following three high-level tasks to perform next:

- Update the MariaDB configuration.
- Secure the MariaDB installation.
- Load initial data (or schemas) into the database.

Of these tasks, we explored, in detail, methods to use the Ansible `template` module effectively to manage the MariaDB configuration in Chapter 7, *Configuration Management with Ansible* (see the *Making scalable dynamic configuration changes* section). As such, we will not go into detail on this here—however, check the configuration file structure for your chosen version of MariaDB, as it might differ from that shown in the aforementioned chapter.

If you have installed MariaDB RPMs on a platform such as CentOS, you can find out where the configuration files live, by running the command `rpm -qc MariaDB-server` in a root shell.

Thus, assuming that you have the installation and configuration of the database server in hand, let us proceed to secure it. This, at a bare minimum, will entail changing the `root` password, though good practice states that you should also remove remote root access, the `test` database, and the anonymous user accounts that come with a default MariaDB installation.

MariaDB comes with a command-line utility called `mysql_secure_installation`, to perform exactly these tasks—however, it is an interactive tool and does not lend itself to automation with Ansible. Luckily, Ansible provides modules for interacting with the database that can assist us in performing exactly these tasks.

To separate out these tasks from the installation, we'll create a new role called securemariadb. Before we can define the tasks, we must define a variable to contain the root password for the MariaDB installation. Note that normally, you would provide this in a more secure manner—perhaps through an Ansible Vault file, or using some of the advanced features in AWX or Ansible Tower. For simplicity, in this example, we will define a variables file in the role (in roles/securemariadb/vars/main.yml), as follows:

```
---
mariadb_root_password: "securepw"
```

Now, let's build up the tasks for the role. Ansible includes a few native modules for use in database management, and we can make use of these here, to make the required changes to our MariaDB database.

 Note, however, that some modules have certain Python requirements, and in the case of our example system—MariaDB on CentOS 7—we must install the MySQL-python package.

Knowing this, the first step in building up our role is to install the prerequisite Python package, as follows:

```
---
- name: Install the MariaDB Python module required by Ansible
  yum:
    name: MySQL-python
    state: latest
```

Our most immediate task, once this is installed, is to set the password on the local root account, and prevent anyone from logging in without authentication. Run the following code:

```
- name: Set the local root password
  mysql_user:
    user: root
    password: "{{ mariadb_root_password }}"
    host: "localhost"
```

So far, this is a textbook example of how to use the mysql_user module—however, there is a twist in our usage from here. The preceding example takes advantage of the fact that no root password is set—it is implicitly manipulating the database as root, by virtue of the fact that we will put become: yes in our site.yml file, and thus, the playbook will be run as root. At the time that this task is run, the root user has no password, and so, the above task will run satisfactorily.

The answer to this is to add the `login_user` and `login_password` parameters to the module for all future tasks, to ensure that we have authenticated successfully with the database to perform the required tasks.

> This role will only run successfully once as it is written—on the second run, a password will be set for the root MariaDB user, and the preceding task will fail. However, if we specify a `login_password` for the above task, and the password is blank (as in the initial run), the task will also fail. There are a number of ways around this, such as setting the old password in another variable or, indeed, committing to only running this role once. You could also specify `ignore_errors:  yes` under this task so that, if the root password is already set, we simply carry on to the next tasks, which should run successfully.

With this condition understood, we now add another task to the role, to remove the remote root accounts, as follows:

```
- name: Delete root MariaDB user for remote logins
  mysql_user:
    user: root
    host: "{{ ansible_fqdn }}"
    state: absent
    login_user: root
    login_password: "{{ mariadb_root_password }}"
```

Again, this code is quite self-explanatory—however, note here too that running this task a second time will also yield an error, this time because on the second run, these privileges will not exist because we deleted them on the first run. Thus, this is almost certainly a role to run once only—or where careful consideration must be applied to the code and the error handling logic.

We now add a task to delete the anonymous user accounts, as follows:

```
- name: Delete anonymous MariaDB user
  mysql_user:
    user: ""
    host: "{{ item }}"
    state: absent
    login_user: root
    login_password: "{{ mariadb_root_password }}"
  loop:
    - "{{ ansible_fqdn }}"
    - localhost
```

You will see the use of a `loop` here—this is used to remove both the local and remote privileges within a single task. Finally, we remove the `test` database, which is redundant in most enterprise scenarios, by running the following code:

```
- name: Delete the test database
  mysql_db:
    db: test
    state: absent
    login_user: root
    login_password: "{{ mariadb_root_password }}"
```

With the role fully complete, we can run it in the usual manner, and secure our newly installed database. The output should look something like this:

```
● ● ●                james@automation-01: ~/hands-on-automation/chapter11/example02 (ssh)
~/hands-on-automation/chapter11/example02> ansible-playbook -i hosts site.yml

PLAY [Secure MariaDB] ************************************************************

TASK [Gathering Facts] **********************************************************
ok: [centos-testhost]

TASK [securemariadb : Install the MariaDB Python module required by Ansible] ***
changed: [centos-testhost]

TASK [securemariadb : Set the local root password] *****************************
changed: [centos-testhost]

TASK [securemariadb : Delete root MariaDB user for remote logins] **************
changed: [centos-testhost]

TASK [securemariadb : Delete anonymous MariaDB user for remote logins] *********
changed: [centos-testhost] => (item=automation-02)
changed: [centos-testhost] => (item=localhost)

TASK [securemariadb : Delete the test database] ********************************
changed: [centos-testhost]
```

With these two roles and some input from `Chapter 7`, *Configuration Management with Ansible*, we have successfully installed, configured, and secured a MariaDB database on CentOS. This is, obviously, a very specific example—however, if you were to perform this on Ubuntu, the process would be very similar. The differences would be the following:

- The `apt` module would be used in place of the `yum` module in all tasks.
- Package names would have to be changed for Ubuntu.
- Defining the repository source would be performed under `/etc/apt` rather than `/etc/yum.repos.d`, with the file format adjusted accordingly.
- Configuration paths may be different for MariaDB on Ubuntu.
- Ubuntu normally uses `ufw` instead of `firewalld`—by default, you might find that `ufw` is disabled, so, this step could be skipped.

With these changes taken into account, the preceding process can be very quickly adapted for Ubuntu (or, indeed, any other platform, provided the appropriate changes are made). Once the packages are installed and configured, as the modules such as `mysql_user` and `mysql_db` are cross-platform, they will work equally well on all supported platforms.

So far in this book, we have focused very heavily on MariaDB—this is not because of any inherent bias toward this database, nor indeed should it be inferred as any recommendation. It has simply been chosen as a relevant example and built upon throughout the text. Before we proceed to look at the process of loading data or schemes into a newly installed database, we will take a brief look in the next section at how to apply the processes we have learned so far to another popular Linux database—PostgreSQL.

Installing PostgreSQL Server with Ansible

In this section, we will demonstrate how the principles and high-level processes we have looked at so far for MariaDB on CentOS can be applied to another platform. Taking a high-level view, these processes can be applied to almost any database and Linux platform, with the proper attention to detail. Here, we will install PostgreSQL Server onto Ubuntu Server, and then secure it by setting the root password—essentially, analogous to the process we have performed in the preceding section.

Let us get started by creating a role called `installpostgres`. In this role we will again define a template for the package downloads from the official PostgreSQL sources, this time—of course—tailoring it to the fact that we're using Ubuntu Server, and not CentOS. The following code shows the template file—note that this is specific for Ubuntu Server 18.04 LTS—codename `bionic`:

```
deb http://apt.postgresql.org/pub/repos/apt/ bionic-pgdg main
```

As before, once our package sources are defined, we can proceed to create the tasks that will install the database. In the case of Ubuntu, we must add the package-signing key manually to the `apt` keyring, in addition to copying the preceding template into place. Thus, our tasks within the role begin, as follows:

```
---
- name: Populate PostgreSQL apt template on target host
  template:
    src: templates/pgdg.list.j2
    dest: /etc/apt/sources.list.d/pgdg.list
    owner: root
    group: root
    mode: '0644'
```

We could also use `apt_repository` here, but, for consistency with the previous MariaDB example, we are using template. Both will achieve the same end result.

When the `template` package is in place, we must then add the package-signing key to `apt`'s keyring, as follows:

```
- name: Add key for PostgreSQL packages
  apt_key:
    url: https://www.postgresql.org/media/keys/ACCC4CF8.asc
    state: present
```

The `postgresql-11` and other supporting packages are then installed (as per the documentation at `https://www.postgresql.org/download/linux/ubuntu/`), as follows:

```
- name: Install PostgreSQL 11 packages
  apt:
    name:
      - postgresql-11
      - postgresql-client-11
    state: latest
    update_cache: yes
```

As our default Ubuntu Server install is not running a firewall, the final task in this playbook is to start the service, and ensure it starts at boot time, as follows:

```
- name: Ensure PostgreSQL service is installed and started at boot time
  service:
    name: postgresql
    state: started
    enabled: yes
```

Running this should yield output similar to the following:

```
james@automation-01: ~/hands-on-automation/chapter11/example03 (ssh)

~/hands-on-automation/chapter11/example03> ansible-playbook -i hosts site.yml

PLAY [Install PostgreSQL] ***************************************************

TASK [Gathering Facts] *****************************************************
ok: [ubuntu-testhost]

TASK [installpostgres : Populate PostgreSQL yum template on target host] *******
changed: [ubuntu-testhost]

TASK [installpostgres : Add key for PostgreSQL packages] ***********************
changed: [ubuntu-testhost]

TASK [installpostgres : Install PostgreSQL 11 packages] ***********************
changed: [ubuntu-testhost]

TASK [installpostgres : Ensure PostgreSQL service is installed and started at bo
ot time] ***
ok: [ubuntu-testhost]

PLAY RECAP ****************************************************************
ubuntu-testhost             : ok=5    changed=3    unreachable=0    failed=0
```

By default, *out-of-the-box* installation of PostgreSQL is much more secure than MariaDB. Without additional configuration, no remote logins are allowed at all, and although no password is set for the superuser account, it can only be accessed on the local machine from the postgres user account. Similarly, there is no test database to drop.

Thus, although the high-level process is the same, you must be aware of the nuances of both the database server you are using and the underlying operating system.

By way of example and to complete this section, let's create a database called `production`, and an associated user called `produser` who will be given access to it. Although technically, this overlaps with the next section on loading initial data, it is provided here to be analogous to the preceding section on MariaDB, and to demonstrate how to use the native Ansible modules for PostgreSQL.

1. Let's create a role called `setuppostgres`, and start by defining a task to install the Ubuntu package necessary to support the Ansible PostgreSQL modules, as follows:

```
---
- name: Install PostgreSQL Ansible support packages
  apt:
    name: python-psycopg2
    state: latest
```

2. After this, we add a task to create the database (this is a very simple example—you will want to tailor it to your exact requirements), as follows:

```
- name: Create production database
  postgresql_db:
    name: production
    state: present
  become_user: postgres
```

3. Notice how we leverage the local `postgres` account on the target machine for database superuser access with the `become_user` statement. Next, we'll add the user, and give them privileges on this database, as follows:

```
- name: Add produser account to database
  postgresql_user:
    db: production
    name: produser
    password: securepw
    priv: ALL
    state: present
  become_user: postgres
```

As usual, you would not just specify the password in plaintext like this—this has been done here for simplicity. As usual, substitute appropriate data for variables, and if those variables are sensitive, either encrypt them at rest using Ansible Vault or prompt the user for them when the playbook is run.

4. Now, to get PostgreSQL to listen for remote connections for this user, we need to perform two more actions. We need to add a line to `pg_hba.conf`, to tell PostgreSQL to allow the user we just created to access this database from the appropriate network—the following example is shown, but be sure to tailor it to your network and requirements:

```
- name: Grant produser access to the production database over the
  local network
    postgresql_pg_hba:
      dest: /etc/postgresql/11/main/pg_hba.conf
      contype: host
      users: produser
      source: 192.168.81.0/24
      databases: production
      method: md5
```

5. We must also change the `listen_addresses` parameter in the `postgresql.conf` file, which defaults to local connections only. The exact location of this file will vary depending on your operating system and version of PostgreSQL—the following example shown is suitable for our install of PostgreSQL 11 on Ubuntu Server 18.04:

```
- name: Ensure PostgreSQL is listening for remote connections
    lineinfile:
      dest: /etc/postgresql/11/main/postgresql.conf
      regexp: '^listen_addresses ='
      line: listen_addresses = '*'
    notify: Restart PostgreSQL
```

6. Observant readers will have noticed the use of handlers here too—the `postgresql` service must be restarted to pick up any changes to this file. However, this should only be performed when the file is changed, and hence we make use of handlers. Our `handlers/main.yml` file will look like this:

```
---
- name: Restart PostgreSQL
    service:
      name: postgresql
      state: restarted
```

7. With our playbook assembled, we can now run it, and the output should look something like the following screenshot:

```
● ● ●                    james@automation-01: ~/hands-on-automation/chapter11/example04 (ssh)
~/hands-on-automation/chapter11/example04> ansible-playbook -i hosts site.yml

PLAY [Install PostgreSQL] ***********************************************************

TASK [Gathering Facts] **************************************************************
ok: [ubuntu-testhost]

TASK [setuppostgres : Install PostgreSQL Ansible support packages] **************
 [WARNING]: Could not find aptitude. Using apt-get instead

changed: [ubuntu-testhost]

TASK [setuppostgres : Create production database] ******************************
changed: [ubuntu-testhost]

TASK [setuppostgres : Add produser account to database] ************************
changed: [ubuntu-testhost]

TASK [setuppostgres : Grant produser access to the production database over the
local network] ***
changed: [ubuntu-testhost]

TASK [setuppostgres : Ensure PostgreSQL is listening for remote connections] ***
changed: [ubuntu-testhost]

RUNNING HANDLER [setuppostgres : Restart PostgreSQL] ***************************
changed: [ubuntu-testhost]
```

Although this example is not strictly the same as the replication of the `mysql_secure_installation` tool in the previous section, it does show how to use native Ansible modules to configure and secure a PostgreSQL database and shows how Ansible can powerfully assist you in setting up and securing new database servers. These principles can be applied to just about any database server that is compatible with Linux, though the modules available for each database will vary. A full list of modules can be found here: https://docs.ansible.com/ansible/latest/modules/list_of_database_modules.html

Now that we have looked at the process of installing a database server, in the next section, we will build on our installation work, to load initial data and schemas.

Importing and exporting data

No database is complete simply by installing the software and configuring it—often, there is a very important intermediate stage, which involves loading an initial dataset. This might be a backup from a previous database, a sanitized dataset for testing purposes, or, simply, a schema into which application data can be loaded.

Although Ansible has modules for a limited set of database functions, the functionality here is not as complete as that for other automation tasks. The most complete support offered for a database by Ansible is for PostgreSQL—with lesser support for some other databases. Through some clever use of the `shell` module, any manual task that you can perform on the command line can be replicated into an Ansible task. It is up to you to apply logic to the tasks to handle errors or conditions where, for example, a database already exists, and we shall see an example of this in the next section.

In the next section, we will look at how you could use Ansible to automate the task of loading a sample database into a MariaDB database.

Automating MariaDB data loading with Ansible

MariaDB is a good choice for this chapter because it offers a middle-of-the-road view when it comes to database management with Ansible. There is some native module support in Ansible, but this is not complete for all tasks you might want to execute. As a result, we will develop the following example, which automates the loading of a sample set of data, using just the `shell` Ansible modules. We will then develop this to show how it would be completed with the `mysql_db` module, to provide you with a direct comparison between the two automation techniques.

 Note that the following examples performed using the `shell` module could be adapted for almost any database you can manage from the command line, and so it is hoped these will provide you with a valuable reference for automating your database management tasks.

In terms of example databases, we will work with the publicly available **Employees** sample database, as this is available to everyone reading this book. You can, of course, choose your own set of data to work with—however, it is, as ever, hoped that this following practical example will teach you the skills you need to load data into your newly installed database with Ansible:

1. To start with, let's create a role called `loadmariadb`. Into the `roles` directory structure, create a directory called `files/`, and clone the `employees` sample database. This is publicly available on GitHub, and, at the time of writing, could be cloned using the following command:

```
$ git clone https://github.com/datacharmer/test_db.git
```

2. From here, we create a `tasks/` directory within the role and write the code for our role tasks themselves. To start with, we need to copy the database files across to our database server, by running the following code:

```
---
- name: Copy sample database to server
  copy:
    src: "{{ item }}"
    dest: /tmp/
  loop:
    - files/test_db/employees.sql
    - files/test_db/load_departments.dump
    - files/test_db/load_employees.dump
    - files/test_db/load_dept_emp.dump
    - files/test_db/load_dept_manager.dump
    - files/test_db/load_titles.dump
    - files/test_db/load_salaries1.dump
    - files/test_db/load_salaries2.dump
    - files/test_db/load_salaries3.dump
    - files/test_db/show_elapsed.sql
```

3. Once the data files are copied to the server, it is simply a matter of loading them into the database. However, as there is no module for this task, we must revert to a shell command to handle this, as shown in the following code block:

```
- name: Load sample data into database
  shell: "mysql -u root --password={{ mariadb_root_password }} <
/tmp/employees.sql"
  args:
    chdir: /tmp
```

4. The role tasks are simplicity themselves—however, before we can run the playbook, we need to set the `mariadb_root_password` variable, ideally in a vault, but for simplicity in this book, we will put it in a plaintext `vars` file in the role. The file `vars/main.yml` should look like this:

```
---

mariadb_root_password: "securepw"
```

As you will have spotted, this playbook assumes that you already installed and configured MariaDB in a previous role—the password used in the preceding code block is that set in the previous section when we installed MariaDB and secured it using Ansible.

5. Running the playbook should yield results like this:

```
● ● ●            james@automation-01: ~/hands-on-automation/chapter11/example05 (ssh)
~/hands-on-automation/chapter11/example05> ansible-playbook -i hosts site.yml

PLAY [Load MariaDB data] ***************************************************

TASK [Gathering Facts] *****************************************************
ok: [centos-testhost]

TASK [loadmariadb : Copy sample database to server] ************************
changed: [centos-testhost] => (item=files/test_db/employees.sql)
changed: [centos-testhost] => (item=files/test_db/load_departments.dump)
changed: [centos-testhost] => (item=files/test_db/load_employees.dump)
changed: [centos-testhost] => (item=files/test_db/load_dept_emp.dump)
changed: [centos-testhost] => (item=files/test_db/load_dept_manager.dump)
changed: [centos-testhost] => (item=files/test_db/load_titles.dump)
changed: [centos-testhost] => (item=files/test_db/load_salaries1.dump)
changed: [centos-testhost] => (item=files/test_db/load_salaries2.dump)
changed: [centos-testhost] => (item=files/test_db/load_salaries3.dump)
changed: [centos-testhost] => (item=files/test_db/show_elapsed.sql)

TASK [loadmariadb : Load sample data into database] ************************
changed: [centos-testhost]

PLAY RECAP *****************************************************************
centos-testhost            : ok=3    changed=2    unreachable=0    failed=0    s
kipped=0    rescued=0    ignored=0
```

Here, we have not only loaded a sample schema, but also sample data, into our database. In your enterprise, you could choose to perform either of these tasks in isolation, as required.

You will probably have spotted that this playbook is extremely dangerous. As we discussed previously, the issue with using the `shell` module in Ansible playbooks is that the results of the task will vary as the shell command is always run, whether it needs running or not. Thus, if you ran this playbook against a server with an existing database called `employees`, it would overwrite all the data in it with the sample data! Contrast this with the `copy` module, which only copies the files if they do not already exist on the receiving end.

Given the lack of native database modules at the time of writing, we need to devise a more intelligent way of running this command. Here, we can make use of some of the clever error handling built into Ansible.

The `shell` module assumes that the command it is running has run successfully if it returns exit code zero. This results in the task returning the `changed` status we saw in this playbook run. However, if the exit code is not zero, the `shell` module will instead return a status of `failed`.

We can take advantage of this knowledge, and couple it with a useful MariaDB command that will return a zero exit code if the database we query exists, and non-zero if it doesn't. See the following screenshot for an example:

```
james@automation-02:~ (ssh)
[james@automation-02 ~]$ mysqlshow -u root --password=securepw employees
Database: employees
+-----------------------+
|        Tables         |
+-----------------------+
| current_dept_emp      |
| departments           |
| dept_emp              |
| dept_emp_latest_date  |
| dept_manager          |
| employees             |
| salaries              |
| titles                |
+-----------------------+
[james@automation-02 ~]$ echo $?
0
[james@automation-02 ~]$ mysqladmin -u root --password=securepw drop employees
Dropping the database is potentially a very bad thing to do.
Any data stored in the database will be destroyed.

Do you really want to drop the 'employees' database [y/N] y
Database "employees" dropped
[james@automation-02 ~]$ mysqlshow -u root --password=securepw employees
mysqlshow: Unknown database 'employees'
[james@automation-02 ~]$ echo $?
1
```

We can make use of this command by running it before our task that loads the data. We can ignore any errors from the command, and instead register them in a variable. We use this to conditionally run the data load, loading it only if an error occurred (this is the instance where the database does not exist, and so it is safe to load the data).

The copy task remains the same, but the tail end of the tasks now looks like this:

```
- name: Check to see if the database exists
  shell: "mysqlshow -u root --password={{ mariadb_root_password }}
employees"
  ignore_errors: true
  register: dbexists

- name: Load sample data into database
  shell: "mysql -u root --password={{ mariadb_root_password }} <
/tmp/employees.sql"
  args:
    chdir: /tmp
  when: dbexists.rc != 0
```

Now, we will only load the data if the database doesn't exist. This code has been kept simple for the sake of providing an example, and it is left to you to enhance it—for example, by putting the filenames and database name into a variable so that the role becomes reusable in a variety of circumstances (which, after all, is one of the goals of writing a role).

If we now run this code, we can see that it operates as desired—on the first run, the data is loaded, as the following screenshot shows:

```
james@automation-01: ~/hands-on-automation/chapter11/example06 (ssh)
~/hands-on-automation/chapter11/example06> ansible-playbook -i hosts site.yml

PLAY [Load MariaDB data] ********************************************************

TASK [Gathering Facts] *********************************************************
ok: [centos-testhost]

TASK [loadmariadb : Copy sample database to server] ****************************
changed: [centos-testhost] => (item=files/test_db/employees.sql)
changed: [centos-testhost] => (item=files/test_db/load_departments.dump)
changed: [centos-testhost] => (item=files/test_db/load_employees.dump)
changed: [centos-testhost] => (item=files/test_db/load_dept_emp.dump)
changed: [centos-testhost] => (item=files/test_db/load_dept_manager.dump)
changed: [centos-testhost] => (item=files/test_db/load_titles.dump)
changed: [centos-testhost] => (item=files/test_db/load_salaries1.dump)
changed: [centos-testhost] => (item=files/test_db/load_salaries2.dump)
changed: [centos-testhost] => (item=files/test_db/load_salaries3.dump)
changed: [centos-testhost] => (item=files/test_db/show_elapsed.sql)

TASK [loadmariadb : Check to see if the database exists] ***********************
fatal: [centos-testhost]: FAILED! => {"changed": true, "cmd": "mysqlshow -u root
 --password=securepw employees", "delta": "0:00:00.009714", "end": "2019-09-19 1
6:04:53.643027", "msg": "non-zero return code", "rc": 1, "start": "2019-09-19 16
:04:53.633313", "stderr": "mysqlshow: Unknown database 'employees'", "stderr_lin
es": ["mysqlshow: Unknown database 'employees'"], "stdout": "", "stdout_lines":
[]}
...ignoring

TASK [loadmariadb : Load sample data into database] ****************************
changed: [centos-testhost]

PLAY RECAP *********************************************************************
centos-testhost            : ok=4    changed=3    unreachable=0    failed=0    s
```

However, on the second run, it is not—the following screenshot shows the playbook being run a second time, and the data load task being skipped because the database exists:

```
● ● ●                james@automation-01: ~/hands-on-automation/chapter11/example06 (ssh)


~/hands-on-automation/chapter11/example06> ansible-playbook -i hosts site.yml

PLAY [Load MariaDB data] ***********************************************************

TASK [Gathering Facts] *************************************************************
ok: [centos-testhost]

TASK [loadmariadb : Copy sample database to server] ********************************
ok: [centos-testhost] => (item=files/test_db/employees.sql)
ok: [centos-testhost] => (item=files/test_db/load_departments.dump)
ok: [centos-testhost] => (item=files/test_db/load_employees.dump)
ok: [centos-testhost] => (item=files/test_db/load_dept_emp.dump)
ok: [centos-testhost] => (item=files/test_db/load_dept_manager.dump)
ok: [centos-testhost] => (item=files/test_db/load_titles.dump)
ok: [centos-testhost] => (item=files/test_db/load_salaries1.dump)
ok: [centos-testhost] => (item=files/test_db/load_salaries2.dump)
ok: [centos-testhost] => (item=files/test_db/load_salaries3.dump)
ok: [centos-testhost] => (item=files/test_db/show_elapsed.sql)

TASK [loadmariadb : Check to see if the database exists] **************************
changed: [centos-testhost]

TASK [loadmariadb : Load sample data into database] ******************************
skipping: [centos-testhost]

PLAY RECAP ***********************************************************************
centos-testhost            : ok=3    changed=1    unreachable=0    failed=0    s
kipped=1    rescued=0    ignored=0
```

Although these examples are specific to MariaDB, the high-level process performed here should work with just about any database. The key element is to use the `shell` module to load the data and/or schema but to do so in a way that reduces the right of a valid database getting overwritten, in the event that the playbook gets run twice. You should extend this logic to any other task you perform—your ultimate goal should be that if your playbook is run unintentionally, then no damage is done to the existing database.

Having completed this example, it is worth noting that Ansible does provide a module called `mysql_db`, which can natively handle tasks such as dumping and importing database data. Let's now develop an example that makes use of the native `mysql_db` module:

1. If we were to develop a role to perform exactly the same task as shown previously, but using this native module, we would first of all check to see if the database exists as before, registering the result to a variable, like this:

```
---
- name: Check to see if the database exists
  shell: "mysqlshow -u root --password={{ mariadb_root_password }}
employees"
  ignore_errors: true
  register: dbexists
```

2. We then create a `block` in our tasks file, as there is no point running any of the tasks after this step if the database exists. The `block` uses the `when` clause we used before, to determine whether the tasks inside it should run or not, as follows:

```
- name: Import new database only if it doesn't already exist
  block:

  when: dbexists.rc != 0
```

3. Inside the `block`, we copy over all the SQL files to import just as we did before, like this:

```
- name: Copy sample database to server
  copy:
    src: "{{ item }}"
    dest: /tmp/
  loop:
    - files/test_db/employees.sql
    - files/test_db/load_departments.dump
    - files/test_db/load_employees.dump
    - files/test_db/load_dept_emp.dump
```

```
- files/test_db/load_dept_manager.dump
- files/test_db/load_titles.dump
- files/test_db/load_salaries1.dump
- files/test_db/load_salaries2.dump
- files/test_db/load_salaries3.dump
- files/test_db/show_elapsed.sql
```

4. Now, an important difference emerges between using the `shell` module, and `mysql_db`. When using the `shell` module, we used the `chdir` argument to change the working directory to `/tmp`, which is where all our SQL files were copied to. The `mysql_db` module has no `chdir` (or equivalent) argument, and so will fail when it comes to try to load the `*.dump` files that are sourced via `employees.sql`. To work around this, we use the Ansible `replace` module, to add the full path to these files into the appropriate lines in `employees.sql`, as follows:

```
- name: Add full paths to employees.sql as mysql_db won't know
  where to load them from otherwise
  replace:
    path: /tmp/employees.sql
    regexp: '^source (.*)$'
    replace: 'source /tmp/\1'
```

5. Finally, we use the `mysql_db` module to load in the data (this is analogous to the shell command we performed in our earlier example), as follows:

```
- name: Load sample data into database
  mysql_db:
    name: all
    state: import
    target: /tmp/employees.sql
    login_user: root
    login_password: "{{ mariadb_root_password }}"
```

6. When we run this code, it achieves the same end result as our previous role that used the `shell` module, as the following screenshot shows:

```
• • •                    james@automation-01: ~/hands-on-automation/chapter11/example06a

~/hands-on-automation/chapter11/example06a> ansible-playbook -i hosts site.yml

PLAY [Load MariaDB data] ******************************************************

TASK [Gathering Facts] ********************************************************
ok: [centos-testhost]

TASK [loadmariadb : Check to see if the database exists] **********************
fatal: [centos-testhost]: FAILED! => {"changed": true, "cmd": "mysqlshow -u root
--password=securepw employees", "delta": "0:00:00.010516", "end": "2019-12-18 1
1:32:05.042517", "msg": "non-zero return code", "rc": 1, "start": "2019-12-18 11
:32:05.032001", "stderr": "mysqlshow: Unknown database 'employees'", "stderr_lin
es": ["mysqlshow: Unknown database 'employees'"], "stdout": "", "stdout_lines":
[]}
...ignoring

TASK [loadmariadb : Copy sample database to server] ***************************
changed: [centos-testhost] => (item=files/test_db/employees.sql)
changed: [centos-testhost] => (item=files/test_db/load_departments.dump)
changed: [centos-testhost] => (item=files/test_db/load_employees.dump)
changed: [centos-testhost] => (item=files/test_db/load_dept_emp.dump)
changed: [centos-testhost] => (item=files/test_db/load_dept_manager.dump)
changed: [centos-testhost] => (item=files/test_db/load_titles.dump)
changed: [centos-testhost] => (item=files/test_db/load_salaries1.dump)
changed: [centos-testhost] => (item=files/test_db/load_salaries2.dump)
changed: [centos-testhost] => (item=files/test_db/load_salaries3.dump)
changed: [centos-testhost] => (item=files/test_db/show_elapsed.sql)

TASK [loadmariadb : Add full paths to employees.sql as mysql_db won't know where
 to load them from otherwise] ***
changed: [centos-testhost]

TASK [loadmariadb : Load sample data into database] ***************************
changed: [centos-testhost]

PLAY RECAP ********************************************************************
centos-testhost            : ok=5    changed=4    unreachable=0    failed=0    s
kipped=0    rescued=0    ignored=1
```

This process works equally well for backing up databases, too. If you were to use the `shell` module, you could use the `mysqldump` command to back up a database, and then copy the backed-up data to your Ansible host (or indeed, another) for archiving. A simple piece of example code to achieve this might be constructed as follows:

1. As we want the backup filename to be dynamic and include useful information such as the current date and hostname on which the backup is being performed, we use the `set_fact` module, along with some internal Ansible variables, to define a filename for the backup data, as follows:

```
---
- name: Define a variable for the backup file name
  set_fact:
    db_filename: "/tmp/{{ inventory_hostname }}-backup-{{
ansible_date_time.date }}.sql"
```

2. We then use the `shell` module to run `mysqldump`, with the appropriate parameters for creating a backup—going into depth on these is beyond the scope of this book, but the following example creates a backup of all databases on your server, without locking the tables during the backup:

```
- name: Back up the database
  shell: "mysqldump -u root --password={{ mariadb_root_password }}
--all-databases --single-transaction --lock-tables=false --quick >
{{ db_filename }}"
```

3. The `fetch` module is then used to retrieve the data for archiving—fetch works just like the `copy` module that we used earlier in this section, except that it copies data in the reverse direction (that is, from the inventory host to the Ansible server). Run the following code:

```
- name: Copy the backed up data for archival
  fetch:
    src: "{{ db_filename }}"
    dest: "/backup"
```

4. Running this in the usual manner results in a complete backup of the database, with the resulting file being copied to our Ansible server, as the following screenshot shows:

```
james@automation-01: ~/hands-on-automation/chapter11/example06b

~/hands-on-automation/chapter11/example06b> ansible-playbook -i hosts site.yml

PLAY [Backup MariaDB data] ***********************************************

TASK [Gathering Facts] ***************************************************
ok: [centos-testhost]

TASK [backupmariadb : Define a variable for the backup file name] ************
ok: [centos-testhost]

TASK [backupmariadb : Back up the database] *********************************
changed: [centos-testhost]

TASK [backupmariadb : Copy the backed up data for archival] *******************
changed: [centos-testhost]

PLAY RECAP ***************************************************************
centos-testhost            : ok=4    changed=2    unreachable=0    failed=0    s
kipped=0     rescued=0     ignored=0
```

This example could also be achieved using the `mysql_db` module, just as we did before—the `set_fact` and `fetch` tasks remain exactly the same, while the `shell` task is replaced with the following code:

```
- name: Back up the database
  mysql_db:
    state: dump
    name: all
    target: "{{ db_filename }}"
    login_user: root
    login_password: "{{ mariadb_root_password }}"
```

Thus, Ansible can assist you both with loading data into your databases and backing it up. As we have discussed previously, it is generally better to use the native Ansible modules (such as `mysql_db`) where they are available, but, provided you apply the correct logic to it, the `shell` module can assist you, if native modules don't exist or provide the functionality you need.

Now that we have considered the process of creating databases and loading data into them, we will proceed in the next section to demonstrate how to build on this work, to perform routine database maintenance with Ansible.

Performing routine maintenance

Loading schemas and/or data is not the only task you would perform with Ansible on a database. Sometimes, manual intervention is required in a database. For example, PostgreSQL requires VACUUM operations from time to time, to free up unused space in the database. MariaDB has a maintenance tool called `mysqlcheck` that can be used to verify the integrity of tables and perform optimization. Each platform will have its own specific tools for maintenance operations, and it is up to you to establish the best practices for database maintenance on your chosen platform. Furthermore, sometimes it is necessary to make simple changes to a database. For example, it might be necessary to delete (or update) a row from a table, to clear an error situation that has occurred in an application.

Of course, all these activities could be performed manually—however, this (as always) brings about the risk of losing track of what happened, who ran a task, and how they ran it (for example, which options were provided). If we move this example into the world of Ansible and AWX, suddenly we have a complete audit trail of activities, and we know exactly what was run and how it was run. Furthermore, if special options are required for a task, these will be stored within the playbooks, and thus the *self-documentation* that Ansible provides is available here too.

As our examples thus far have been very MariaDB-centric, let's take a look at how you might run a full vacuum on a table in PostgreSQL, with Ansible.

Routine maintenance on PostgreSQL with Ansible

PostgreSQL is something of a special case on Ansible, as it has more native modules to support database activities than most other databases. Let's consider an example case: performing a vacuum on the `sales.creditcard` table in the publicly available AdventureWorks sample database (available here: `https://github.com/lorint/AdventureWorks-for-Postgres`).

Vacuuming is a PostgreSQL-specific maintenance process and one that you might want to consider running on a regular basis, especially if your tables have a lot of deletes or modifications. Although a full discussion of this is beyond the scope of this book, it is important to consider that tables that are subject to these activities can become bloated in size and queries can become slow over time, and vacuuming is a way to release unused space and speed up queries again.

Now, to perform a vacuum on this table by hand, you would log in to the `psql` client utility with appropriate credentials, and then run the following commands to connect to the database and perform the task:

```
postgres=# \c AdventureWorks
AdventureWorks=# vacuum full sales.creditcard;
```

In a real enterprise, this would be a task that encompasses many more tables, and even databases, but here, we will once again keep the example simple, to demonstrate the principles involved. Scaling this up is then left as a task for you to perform. Let's automate this, first of all using the `shell` module in Ansible. This is a useful example, as this technique will work with most major databases—simply, you must establish the command needed for your particular maintenance operation, and then run it.

A simple role to perform this task would look like this:

```
---
- name: Perform a VACUUM on the sales.credit_card table
  shell: psql -c "VACUUM FULL sales.creditcard" AdventureWorks
  become: yes
  become_user: postgres
```

Note—as before—very simple use of the `shell` module with the appropriate command, except that, this time, we are using the `become_user` parameter to switch to the `postgres` user account, which has superuser rights on the database on the host to which we connect. Let's see what happens when we run this, as follows:

```
james@automation-01: ~/hands-on-automation/chapter11/example07 (ssh)
~/hands-on-automation/chapter11/example07> ansible-playbook -i hosts site.yml

PLAY [Maintain PostgreSQL database] ********************************************

TASK [Gathering Facts] *********************************************************
ok: [ubuntu-testhost]

TASK [maintainpostgres : Perform a VACUUM on the sales.credit_card table] ******
changed: [ubuntu-testhost]

PLAY RECAP *********************************************************************
ubuntu-testhost            : ok=2    changed=1    unreachable=0    failed=0    s
kipped=0    rescued=0    ignored=0
```

Naturally, this could be scaled to just about any other database—for example, you could use the `mysql` client tool on a MariaDB database, or even run the `mysqlcheck` tool, as discussed earlier. The limit really is on what you can script for the `shell` module to run, and because Ansible runs the command over SSH on the database server itself, you don't need to worry about opening up your database for access across the network—it can remain tightly locked down.

In addition to using the `shell` module, Ansible offers us the option to actually run queries directly from a module called `postgresql_query`. This is unique, though such support could be added for any other database if someone was willing to write the module and submit it.

Unfortunately for Ansible versions prior to 2.9, it was not possible to extend our VACUUM example to this as the `postgresql_query` module runs transactions inside a block, and it is not possible to run a VACUUM inside a transaction block. If you are running version 2.9 or later, you can now run a VACUUM using example code, as shown here:

```
---
- name: Perform a VACUUM on the sales.credit_card table
  postgresql_query:
    db: AdventureWorks
    query: VACUUM sales.creditcard
    autocommit: yes
  become_user: postgres
  become: yes
```

By way of another simple example, we could also use the `postgresql_query` module to directly manipulate the database.

Suppose that a bug in the application using this database has occurred, and an operator must manually insert a credit card number into the database. The SQL code to perform this might look something like this:

```
INSERT INTO sales.creditcard ( creditcardid, cardtype, cardnumber,
expmonth, expyear ) VALUES ( 0, 'Visa', '0000000000000000', '11', '2019' );
```

We could achieve the same end result in Ansible, using a role that looks like the following:

```
---
- name: Manually insert data into the creditcard table
  postgresql_query:
    db: AdventureWorks
    query: INSERT INTO sales.creditcard ( creditcardid, cardtype,
cardnumber, expmonth, expyear ) VALUES ( 0, 'Visa', '0000000000000000',
'11', '2019' );
  become_user: postgres
  become: yes
```

Naturally, you would use variables for the data values, and sensitive data like this should always be stored in a vault (or, perhaps, entered by hand when the role is run).

 AWX has a feature called **Surveys**, which presents the user with a series of predefined questions to answer before a playbook is run. The answers to these questions are stored in Ansible variables— thus, a role such as the preceding one could be parameterized, and run from AWX with all the values entered into a Survey, negating the need for a vault and concerns over sensitive customer data being stored in Ansible.

As you can see here, when we run this role, we actually get a changed status when the INSERT operation is successful—very useful for monitoring such tasks and ensuring they have run as desired. The following screenshot shows this role being run, and the changed status, denoting the successful insertion of data into the sales.creditcard table:

```
● ● ●          james@automation-01: ~/hands-on-automation/chapter11/example08 (ssh)
~/hands-on-automation/chapter11/example08> ansible-playbook -i hosts site.yml

PLAY [Maintain PostgreSQL database] ********************************************

TASK [Gathering Facts] *********************************************************
ok: [ubuntu-testhost]

TASK [maintainpostgres : Manually insert data into the creditcard table] *******
changed: [ubuntu-testhost]

PLAY RECAP *********************************************************************
ubuntu-testhost            : ok=2    changed=1    unreachable=0    failed=0    s
kipped=0    rescued=0    ignored=0
```

The world really is your oyster when it comes to database management with Ansible, and, regardless of the task required, it is desirable that all database tasks be handled in a standardized, repeatable, and auditable manner, just like the rest of your Enterprise Linux estate. It is hoped that this chapter has gone some way in showing you how to achieve this.

Summary

Databases are a core part of the application stack in most enterprises, and there is a multitude of databases available on the Linux platform. Although many databases have their own management tools, Ansible is well suited to assist with a wide array of database management tasks, from the installation of database services and loading of initial data or schemas (or even restoring from backups) to handling day-to-day maintenance tasks. Combining Ansible's error handling and secure automation, there is virtually no limit to the types of database management tasks you can perform with Ansible.

In this chapter, you learned how to use Ansible to install database servers in a consistent and repeatable manner. You then learned how to import initial data and schemas, and how to extend this to automate backup tasks. Finally, you gained hands-on knowledge of some routine database maintenance tasks with Ansible.

In the next chapter, we will look at how Ansible can assist with the task of routine maintenance on your Linux servers.

Questions

1. Why is it prudent to install and manage your database platform with Ansible?
2. What are the best practices for database configuration file management with Ansible?
3. How can Ansible help you keep your database secure on the network?
4. When would you use the `shell` module instead of a native database module in Ansible?
5. Why would you want to perform routine maintenance with Ansible?
6. How would you perform a PostgreSQL database backup with Ansible?
7. Which module would you use to manipulate the users on a MariaDB database?
8. How is PostgreSQL support unique in Ansible at the present time?

Further reading

- For an in-depth understanding of Ansible, please refer to *Mastering Ansible, Third Edition—James Freeman* and *Jesse Keating* (`https://www.packtpub.com/gb/virtualization-and-cloud/mastering-ansible-third-edition`).
- To learn more about the specifics relating to PostgreSQL database management, readers may refer to *Learning PostgreSQL 11, Third Edition—Andrey Volkov, Salahadin Juba* (`https://www.packtpub.com/gb/big-data-and-business-intelligence/learning-postgresql-11-third-edition`).
- Similarly, to learn more about MariaDB database management, readers can refer to *MariaDB Essentials—Federico Razzoli, Emilien Kenler* (`https://www.packtpub.com/gb/application-development/mariadb-essentials`).
- For a full list of available Ansible modules, readers should refer to `https://docs.ansible.com/ansible/latest/modules/list_of_database_modules.html`.

12
Performing Routine Maintenance with Ansible

As you have worked through this book, you will have completed many steps to define and build a Linux environment for your enterprise that supports automation. However, Ansible's assistance with your environment does not end here. Even an environment that has been built and is in active use requires maintenance and intervention from time to time. Historically, these interventions would have been performed manually by system administrators, using shell commands or scripts.

As we have discussed many times throughout this book, tasks that are run by hand present a number of challenges for the enterprise—not least that they may not be well documented, and hence there is a steep learning curve for new members of staff. In addition, our old friends auditability and repeatability come into play—how can you be sure of who did what, and when, if everyone is logging on to the shell of your Linux machines and performing tasks by hand?

In this chapter, we explore the ways in which Ansible can assist the enterprise with the day-to-day management of the Linux estate and, especially, in performing routine maintenance tasks. Ansible is extremely powerful, and your possibilities for routine maintenance are not limited to the examples in this chapter—rather, they are intended to get you started, and show by example the kinds of tasks you may be able to automate.

Specifically, we will cover the following topics in this chapter:

- Tidying up disk space
- Monitoring for configuration drift
- Managing processes with Ansible
- Rolling updates with Ansible

Technical requirements

This chapter includes examples, based on the following technologies:

- Ubuntu Server 18.04 LTS
- CentOS 7.6
- Ansible 2.8

To run through these examples, you will need access to two servers or virtual machines running one each of the operating systems just listed, and also Ansible. Note that the examples given in this chapter may be destructive in nature (for example, they delete files, and make changes to server configuration), and if run as is, are only intended to be run in an isolated test environment.

Once you are satisfied that you have a safe environment in which to operate, let's get started with routine system maintenance, with Ansible.

All example code discussed in this chapter is available from GitHub, at the following URL: `https://github.com/PacktPublishing/Hands-On-Enterprise-Automation-on-Linux/tree/master/chapter12`.

Tidying up disk space

One of the most routine and mundane (and yet, vitally important) tasks that a system administrator has to complete on a routine basis is clearing out disk space. Although ideally, systems should be well behaved—for example, log files should be rotated, and temporary files cleaned up—those with experience in the industry will know that this is not always the case. The author of this book has worked in environments where clearing out a given directory was considered a routine task—hence, a prime candidate for automation.

Of course, you would not just randomly delete files from a filesystem. Any task like this should be performed in a precise manner. Let's proceed with a practical example—as this is hypothetical, let's create some test files to work with. Suppose our fictional application creates a data file every day, and never prunes its `data` directory. To synthesize this, we might create some data files, as follows:

```
$ sudo mkdir -p /var/lib/appdata
$ for i in $(seq 1 20); do DATE=$(date -d "-$i days" +%y%m%d%H%M); sudo
touch -t $DATE /var/lib/appdata/$DATE; done
```

The preceding commands create a directory called /var/lib/appdata, and then create one (empty) file for each day, for the last 20 days. We could, of course, create files with data in, but it makes no difference to this example—we don't actually want to fill the disk up!

Now, let's suppose that our disk is getting full and that we want to prune this directory, keeping only the last 5 days' worth. If we were to do this by hand, we might use the venerable find command, to list the files meeting our criteria, and remove anything older. This might look something like this:

```
$ sudo find /var/lib/appdata -mtime +5 -exec rm -f '{}' \;
```

That is an easy enough command to run, and you might be surprised to learn how common it is to see commands like that in enterprise run-books for Linux servers. Let's improve on this, with Ansible. We know that if we implement this in Ansible, the following will be the case:

- The Ansible engine will return an appropriate status—ok, changed, or failed, depending on the actions taken. The find command shown in the preceding code block will return the same output and exit code, whether it deletes any files or not.
- The Ansible code we write will be self-documenting—for example, it will begin with an appropriate name—perhaps Prune /var/lib/appdata.
- The Ansible code can be run from AWX or Ansible Tower, ensuring that this routine task can be delegated to the appropriate team, using the built-in role-based access controls.
- In addition, the task can be given a user-friendly name in AWX, meaning operators don't need any specialist knowledge to jump in and start being effective in assisting with Linux environment management.
- AWX and Ansible Tower will faithfully log the output from the task run, to ensure it is possible to audit these cleanup jobs in the future.

Of course, none of these Ansible benefits is new to us by now—we have frequently referred to them throughout the book. Nonetheless, it is my wish to impress upon you the benefits of effective automation in the enterprise. Let's start by defining a role to perform exactly this function—prune a directory of files over 5 days old with Ansible:

1. We start by making use of the Ansible `find` module, which enables us to build up a list of filesystem objects (such as files or directories), just as the `find` shell command does. We will `register` the output in an Ansible variable to make use of it later on, as follows:

```
- name: Find all files older than {{ max_age }} in {{ target_dir }}
  find:
    paths: "{{ target_dir }}"
    age: "{{ max_age }}"
    recurse: yes
  register: prune_list
```

The code fragment shown here should be fairly self-explanatory—note, however, that we have made use of variables for the `path` and `age` parameters; this is with good reason. Roles are all about reuse of code, and if we define these parameters using variables, we can reuse this role to prune other directories (for example, for different applications), without needing to change the role code itself. You will also observe that we can use the variables in the `name` of the task—very useful and powerful when returning to audit Ansible runs in the future.

2. The `find` module will build up a list of files we need to delete—however, given our goal of auditing, it might be useful for us to print these filenames in the Ansible output, to ensure we can come back later and find out exactly what was deleted. Note that we could print more data than just the path—perhaps also capturing size and timestamp information could be useful? All of this is available in the `prune_list` variable we captured earlier, and it is left as an exercise for you to explore this. (Hint: Replace `msg: "{{ item.path }}"` with `msg: "{{ item }}"`, to see all the information captured by the `find` task.) Run the following code:

```
- name: Print file list for auditing purposes
  debug:
    msg: "{{ item.path }}"
  loop:
    "{{ prune_list.files }}"
  loop_control:
    label: "{{ item.path }}"
```

Here, we are simply using an Ansible loop to iterate over the data generated by the `find` module—specifically, extracting the `path` dictionary item from the `files` dictionary within our variable. The `loop_control` option prevents Ansible from printing the entire dictionary structure above each `debug` message, instead, just using the `path` to each file as the `label`.

3. Finally, we use the `file` module to remove the files, again looping over `prune_list`, just as we did previously, as follows:

```
- name: Prune {{ target_dir }}
  file:
    path: "{{ item.path }}"
    state: absent
  loop:
    "{{ prune_list.files }}"
  loop_control:
    label: "{{ item.path }}"
```

4. With the role complete, we must define the variables for our play—in this example, I am defining them in the `site.yml` playbook that references our new role, as follows:

```
---
- name: Prune Directory
  hosts: all
  become: yes
  vars:
    max_age: "5d"
    target_dir: "/var/lib/appdata"

  roles:
    - pruneappdata
```

Running this code with the test files generated earlier in this section will result in an output that looks something like this:

```
• • •                    james@automation-01: ~/hands-on-automation/chapter12/example01 (ssh)

~/hands-on-automation/chapter12/example01> ansible-playbook -i hosts site.yml

PLAY [Prune Directory] ****************************************************************

TASK [Gathering Facts] ****************************************************************
ok: [ubuntu-testhost]

TASK [pruneappdata : Find all files older than 5d in /var/lib/appdata] *********
ok: [ubuntu-testhost]

TASK [pruneappdata : Print file list for auditing purposes] ********************
ok: [ubuntu-testhost] => (item=/var/lib/appdata/1909201147) => {
    "msg": "/var/lib/appdata/1909201147"
}
ok: [ubuntu-testhost] => (item=/var/lib/appdata/1909211147) => {
    "msg": "/var/lib/appdata/1909211147"
}

TASK [pruneappdata : Prune /var/lib/appdata] **********************************
changed: [ubuntu-testhost] => (item=/var/lib/appdata/1909201147)
changed: [ubuntu-testhost] => (item=/var/lib/appdata/1909211147)

PLAY RECAP ****************************************************************************
ubuntu-testhost            : ok=4    changed=1    unreachable=0    failed=0    s
kipped=0    rescued=0    ignored=0
```

The test file set has been reduced for the preceding screenshot, to ensure it fits on the screen—however, you can clearly see the output, and which files were deleted.

While good housekeeping is an essential part of server maintenance, sometimes it is only desirable to take action (such as pruning a directory) if it is absolutely necessary. What if we decided that this role should only run when there is 10% or less disk space remaining on the filesystem containing /var/lib/appdata?

The following process demonstrates how Ansible can be used to perform conditional housekeeping, operating only when the disk is more than 90% full:

1. We start by modifying our existing role—first of all, we add a new task to the role, to get the disk usage as a percentage from our `target` directory, as follows:

```
---
- name: Obtain free disk space for {{ target_dir }}
  shell: df -h "{{ target_dir }}" | tail -n 1 | awk {'print $5 '} |
sed 's/%//g'
  register: dfresult
  changed_when: false
```

Although there are Ansible facts that contain disk usage information, we use the `df` command here because it can query our directory directly—we must somehow trace this back to the mount point on which it lives if we are to successfully use Ansible facts. We also make use of `changed_when: false`, as this shell task will always show a changed result otherwise, which can be confusing in the output—this is a read-only query, so nothing should have changed!

2. With this data gathered and registered in the `dfresult` variable, we then wrap our existing code in a block. A block in Ansible is simply a way of wrapping a set of tasks together—thus, rather than having to put a `when` condition on each of our three tasks from our earlier example, we simply put the conditional on the block instead. The block would begin something like this:

```
- name: Run file pruning only if disk usage is greater than 90
percent
  block:

  - name: Find all files older than {{ max_age }} in {{ target_dir
}}
    find:
```

Note how the previous set of tasks is now indented by two spaces. This ensures that Ansible understands it is part of the block. Indent all the existing tasks, and conclude the block with the following code:

```
      loop_control:
        label: "{{ item.path }}"
    when: dfresult.stdout|int > 90
```

Here, we are using the standard output captured in the `dfresult` variable, casting it to an integer, and then, checking to see if it is 90% or more. Thus, we only run the pruning tasks if the filesystem is more than 90% full. This is, of course, just one conditional—you could gather any data that you require to make any of your tasks run, in a variety of other cases. Running this new role on my test server, which has much less than 90% disk utilization, shows the pruning tasks being skipped altogether now, as can be seen in the following screenshot:

```
● ● ●                james@automation-01: ~/hands-on-automation/chapter12/example02 (ssh)
~/hands-on-automation/chapter12/example02> ansible-playbook -i hosts site.yml

PLAY [Prune Directory] ****************************************************

TASK [Gathering Facts] ****************************************************
ok: [ubuntu-testhost]

TASK [pruneappdata : Obtain free disk space for /var/lib/appdata] *************
ok: [ubuntu-testhost]

TASK [pruneappdata : Find all files older than 5d in /var/lib/appdata] ********
skipping: [ubuntu-testhost]

TASK [pruneappdata : Print file list for auditing purposes] ******************
skipping: [ubuntu-testhost]

TASK [pruneappdata : Prune /var/lib/appdata] *********************************
skipping: [ubuntu-testhost]

PLAY RECAP ***************************************************************
ubuntu-testhost            : ok=2    changed=0    unreachable=0    failed=0    s
kipped=3    rescued=0    ignored=0
```

In this way, it is easy for us to perform routine disk housekeeping tasks across a large enterprise estate, and—as is ever the case with Ansible—the sky is the limit for what you can do. Hopefully, the examples from this section will give you some ideas on how to get started. In the next section, we will look at how Ansible can be used to effectively monitor for configuration drift, across your Linux estate.

Monitoring for configuration drift

In `Chapter 7`, *Configuration Management with Ansible*, we have explored the ways that Ansible can be used both to deploy configuration at an enterprise scale and to enforce it. Let us now build on this, with something else—monitoring for configuration drift.

As we discussed in Chapter 1, *Building a Standard Operating Environment on Linux*, manual changes are the enemy of automation. Beyond this, they are also a security risk. Let us work with a specific example here, to demonstrate. As was suggested previously in this book, it would be advisable to manage the **Secure Shell** (**SSH**) server configuration with Ansible. SSH is the standard protocol for managing Linux servers and can be used not only for management but also for file transfer. In short, it is one of the key mechanisms through which people will access your servers, and hence it is vital that it is secure.

It is also common, however, for a variety of people to have root access to Linux servers. Whether developers are deploying code, or system administrators are performing routine (or break-fix) work, it is considered perfectly normal for many people to have root access to a server. This is fine if everyone is *well behaved*, and actively supports the principles of automation in your enterprise. However, what happens if someone makes unauthorized changes?

Through the SSH configuration, they might enable remote root logins. They might turn on password-based authentication when you have disabled this in favor of key-based authentication. Many times, these kinds of changes are made to support laziness—it is easier to copy files around as a root user, for example.

Whatever the intention and root cause, someone manually making these changes to a Linux server you deployed previously is a problem. How do you go about detecting them, though? Certainly, you don't have time to log in to every server and check the files by hand. Ansible, however, can help.

In Chapter 7, *Configuration Management with Ansible*, we proposed a simple Ansible example that deployed the SSH server configuration from a template and restarted the SSH service if the configuration was changed using a handler.

We can actually repurpose this code for our configuration drift checks. Without even making any code changes, we can run the playbook with Ansible in *check* mode. Check mode makes no changes to the systems on which it is working—rather, it tries its best to predict any changes that might occur. The reliability of these predictions depends very much on the modules used in the role. For example, the template module can reliably predict changes because it knows whether the file that would be written is different from the file that is in place. Conversely, the shell module can never know the difference between a change and an ok result because it is such a general-purpose module (though it can detect failures with a reasonable degree of accuracy). Thus, I advocate strongly the use of changed_when when this module is used.

Let's see what happens if we rerun the `securesshd` role from before, this time in check mode. The result can be seen in the following screenshot:

```
● ● ●          james@automation-01: ~/hands-on-automation/chapter12/example03 (ssh)
~/hands-on-automation/chapter12/example03> ansible-playbook -C -i hosts site.yml


PLAY [Secure SSH configuration] ************************************************

TASK [Gathering Facts] *********************************************************
ok: [ubuntu-testhost]

TASK [securesshd : Copy SSHd configuration to target host] *********************
changed: [ubuntu-testhost]

RUNNING HANDLER [securesshd : Restart SSH daemon] ******************************
changed: [ubuntu-testhost]

PLAY RECAP *********************************************************************
ubuntu-testhost            : ok=3    changed=2    unreachable=0    failed=0    s
kipped=0    rescued=0    ignored=0
```

Here, we can see that someone has indeed changed the SSH server configuration—if it matched the template we were providing, the output would look like this instead:

```
● ● ●          james@automation-01: ~/hands-on-automation/chapter12/example03 (ssh)
~/hands-on-automation/chapter12/example03> ansible-playbook -C -i hosts site.yml


PLAY [Secure SSH configuration] ************************************************

TASK [Gathering Facts] *********************************************************
ok: [ubuntu-testhost]

TASK [securesshd : Copy SSHd configuration to target host] *********************
ok: [ubuntu-testhost]

PLAY RECAP *********************************************************************
ubuntu-testhost            : ok=2    changed=0    unreachable=0    failed=0    s
kipped=0    rescued=0    ignored=0
```

So far, so good—you could run this against a hundred, or even a thousand, servers, and you would know that any `changed` results came from servers where the SSH server configuration no longer matches the template. You could even run the playbook again to rectify the situation, only this time not in check mode (that is, without the -C flag on the command line).

In an environment such as AWX or Ansible Tower, jobs (that is to say, running playbooks) are categorized into two different states—success and failure. Success is categorized as any playbook that runs to completion, producing only `changed` or `ok` results. Failure, however, comes about from one or more `failed` or `unreachable` states being returned from the playbook run.

Thus, we could enhance our playbook by getting it to issue a `failed` state if the configuration file is different from the templated version. The bulk of the role remains exactly the same, but, on our template task, we add the following clauses:

```
register: template_result
failed_when: (template_result.changed and ansible_check_mode == True) or
template_result.failed
```

These have the following effect on the operation of this task:

- The result of the task is registered in the `template_result` variable.
- We change the failure condition of this task to the following:
    - The template task result was changed, and we are running it in check mode.
    - Or, the template task failed for some other reason—this is a catch-all case, to ensure we still report other failure cases correctly (for example, access denied to a file).

You will observe the use of both logical `and` and `or` operators in the `failed_when` clause—a powerful way to expand on the operation of Ansible. Now, when we run the playbook in check mode and the file has changed, we see the following result:

```
james@automation-01: ~/hands-on-automation/chapter12/example04 (ssh)
~/hands-on-automation/chapter12/example04> ansible-playbook -C -i hosts site.yml


PLAY [Secure SSH configuration] *********************************************

TASK [Gathering Facts] ******************************************************
ok: [ubuntu-testhost]

TASK [securesshd : Copy SSHd configuration to target host] ******************
fatal: [ubuntu-testhost]: FAILED! => {"changed": true, "failed_when_result": tru
e}

PLAY RECAP ******************************************************************
ubuntu-testhost            : ok=1    changed=0    unreachable=0    failed=1    s
kipped=0    rescued=0    ignored=0
```

Now, we can very clearly see that there is an issue on our host, and it will be reported as a failure in AWX and Ansible Tower too.

Of course, this works very well for plain text files. What about binary files, though? Ansible is, of course, not a complete replacement for a file integrity monitoring tool such as **Advanced Intrusion Detection Environment (AIDE)** or the venerable **Tripwire**—however, it can help with the use of binary files too. In fact, the process is very simple. Let's suppose you want to ensure the integrity of /bin/bash—this is the shell that everyone uses by default on most systems, so the integrity of this file is incredibly important. If you have space to store a copy of the original binary on your Ansible server, then you can use the copy module to copy it across to the target hosts. The copy module makes use of checksumming to determine whether a file needs to be copied, and so, you can be sure that, if the copy module results in a changed result, then the target file differs from your original version, and integrity is compromised. The role code for this would look very similar to our template example here:

```
---
- name: Copy bash binary to target host
  copy:
    src: files/bash
    dest: /bin/bash
    owner: root
    group: root
    mode: 0755
  register: copy_result
  failed_when: (copy_result.changed and ansible_check_mode == True) or
copy_result.failed
```

Of course, storing original binaries on your Ansible server is inefficient, and also, means you have to keep them up to date, in line with your server patching schedule, which is not desirable when you have a large number of files to check. Fortunately, the Ansible stat module can generate checksums, as well as returning lots of other useful data about files, and so, we could very easily write a playbook to check that our binary for Bash has not been tampered with, by running the following code:

```
---
- name: Get sha256 sum of /bin/bash
  stat:
    path: /bin/bash
    checksum_algorithm: sha256
    get_checksum: yes
  register: binstat

- name: Verify checksum of /bin/bash
  fail:
```

```
        msg: "Integrity failure - /bin/bash may have been compromised!"
    when: binstat.stat.checksum !=
  'da85596376bf384c14525c50ca010e9ab96952cb811b4abe188c9ef1b75bff9a'
```

This is a very simple example and could be enhanced significantly by ensuring the file path and name, and checksum, are variables rather than static values. It could also be made to loop over a dictionary of files and their respective checksums—these tasks are left as an exercise for you, and this is entirely possible, using techniques we have covered throughout this book. Now, if we run this playbook (whether in check mode or not), we will see a failed result if the integrity of Bash has not been maintained, and `ok` otherwise, as follows:

```
● ● ●              james@automation-01: ~/hands-on-automation/chapter12/example06 (ssh)

~/hands-on-automation/chapter12/example06> ansible-playbook -i hosts site.yml

PLAY [Check the integrity of core system files] ********************************

TASK [Gathering Facts] *********************************************************
ok: [ubuntu-testhost]

TASK [checkbash : Get sha256 sum of /bin/bash] *********************************
ok: [ubuntu-testhost]

TASK [checkbash : Verify checksum of /bin/bash] ********************************
fatal: [ubuntu-testhost]: FAILED! => {"changed": false, "msg": "Integrity failur
e - /bin/bash may have been compromised!"}

PLAY RECAP *********************************************************************
ubuntu-testhost            : ok=2    changed=0    unreachable=0    failed=1    s
kipped=0    rescued=0    ignored=0
```

Checksumming can be used to verify the integrity of configuration files too, so, this example role serves as a good basis for any file integrity checking you might wish to undertake.

We have now completed our exploration of file and integrity monitoring with Ansible, and hence, the ability check for configuration drift. In the next section of this chapter, we'll take a look at how Ansible can be used to manage processes across an Enterprise Linux estate.

Understanding process management with Ansible

Sooner or later, you will end up with the need to manage, and possibly even kill, processes on one or more Linux servers within your enterprise. Obviously, this is not an ideal scenario, and in day-to-day operations, most services should be managed using the Ansible `service` module, many examples of which we have seen in this book.

What if, however, you need to actually kill a service that has hung? Obviously, a system administrator could SSH into the errant server and issue commands such as the following:

```
$ ps -ef | grep <processname> | grep -v grep | awk '{print $2}'
$ kill <PID1> <PID2>
```

If the process refuses stubbornly to terminate, then the following may become necessary:

```
$ kill -9 <PID1> <PID2>
```

While this is a fairly standard practice, in which most system administrators will be well versed (and indeed, may have their own favorite tools to handle, such as `pkill`), it suffers the same problem as most manual interventions on a server—how can you keep track of what happened, and which processes were affected? If numeric **process IDs** (**PIDs**) were used, then even with access to the command history, it is still impossible to tell which process historically held that numeric PID.

What we propose here is an unconventional use of Ansible—yet one that, if run through a tool such as AWX or Ansible Tower, would enable us to track all operations that were performed, along with details of who ran them and, if we put the process name in a parameter, what the target was too. This could be useful if, in the future, it becomes necessary to analyze the history of a problem, whereupon it would be easy to check which servers were acted upon, and which processes were targeted, along with precise timestamps.

Let's build up a role to perform exactly this set of tasks. This chapter was originally written against Ansible 2.8, which did not feature a module for process management, and so, the following example uses native shell commands to handle this case:

1. We start by running the process listing we proposed earlier in this section, but this time, registering the list of PIDs into an Ansible variable, as follows:

```
---
- name: Get PID's of running processes matching {{ procname }}
  shell: "ps -ef | grep -w {{ procname }} | grep -v grep | grep -v
ansible | awk '{print $2\",\"$8}'"
  register: process_ids
```

Most people familiar with shell scripting should be able to understand this line—we are filtering the system process table for whole-word matches for the Ansible variable `procname`, and removing any extraneous process names that might come up and confuse the output, such as `grep` and `ansible`. Finally, we use `awk` to process the output into a comma-separated list, containing the PID, in the first column, and the process name itself in the second.

2. Now, we must start to take action on this output. We now loop over the `process_ids` variable populated previously, issuing a `kill` command against the first column in the output (that is, the numeric PID), as follows:

```
- name: Attempt to kill processes nicely
  shell: "kill {{ item.split(',')[0] }}"
  loop:
    "{{ process_ids.stdout_lines }}"
  loop_control:
    label: "{{ item }}"
```

You will observe the use of Jinja2 filtering here—we can use the built-in `split` function to split the data we created in the previous code block, taking only the first column of output (the numeric PID). However, we use the `loop_control` label to set the task label containing both the PID and process name, which could be very useful in an auditing or debugging scenario.

3. Any experienced system administrator will know that it is not sufficient to just issue a `kill` command to a process—some processes must be forcefully killed as they are hung. Not all processes exit immediately, so we will use the Ansible `wait_for` module to check for the PID in the `/proc` directory—when it becomes `absent`, then we know the process has exited. Run the following code:

```
- name: Wait for processes to exit
  wait_for:
    path: "/proc/{{ item.split(',')[0] }}"
    timeout: 5
    state: absent
  loop:
    "{{ process_ids.stdout_lines }}"
  ignore_errors: yes
  register: exit_results
```

We have set the timeout here to 5 seconds—however, you should set it as appropriate in your environment. Once again, we register the output to a variable—we need to know which processes failed to exit, and hence, try killing them more forcefully. Note that we set `ignore_errors` here, as the `wait_for` module produces an error if the desired state (that is, `/proc/PID` becomes `absent`) does not occur within the `timeout` specified. This should not be an error in our role, simply a prompt for further processing.

4. We now loop over the results of the `wait_for` task —only this time, we use the Jinja2 `selectattr` function, to select only dictionary items that have `failed` asserted; we don't want to forcefully terminate non-existent PIDs. Run the following code:

```
- name: Forcefully kill stuck processes
  shell: "kill -9 {{ item.item.split(',')[0] }}"
  loop:
    "{{ exit_results.results | selectattr('failed') | list }}"
  loop_control:
    label: "{{ item.item }}"
```

Now, we attempt to kill the stuck processes with the -9 flag—normally, sufficient to kill most hung processes. Note again the use of Jinaj2 filtering and the tidy labeling of the loop, to ensure we can use the output of this role for auditing and debugging.

5. Now, we run the playbook, specifying a value for `procname`—there is no default process to be killed, and I would not suggest that setting a default value for this variable is safe. Thus, in the following screenshot, I am setting it using the `-e` flag when I invoke the `ansible-playbook` command:

```
● ● ●          james@automation-01: ~/hands-on-automation/chapter12/example07 (ssh)
~/hands-on-automation/chapter12/example07> ansible-playbook -i hosts site.yml -e
 procname=mysqld

PLAY [Kill processes in a controlled manner] *********************************

TASK [Gathering Facts] *******************************************************
ok: [ubuntu-testhost]

TASK [killproc : Get PID's of running processes matching mysqld] *************
changed: [ubuntu-testhost]

TASK [killproc : Attempt to kill processes nicely] ***************************
changed: [ubuntu-testhost] => (item=15165,/usr/sbin/mysqld)

TASK [killproc : Wait for processes to exit] *********************************
ok: [ubuntu-testhost] => (item=15165,/usr/sbin/mysqld)

TASK [killproc : Forcefully kill stuck processes] ****************************

PLAY RECAP *******************************************************************
ubuntu-testhost            : ok=4    changed=2    unreachable=0    failed=0    s
kipped=1    rescued=0    ignored=0
```

From the preceding screenshot, we can clearly see the playbook killing the `mysqld` process, and the output of the playbook is tidy and concise, yet contains enough information for debugging, should the need occur.

As an addendum, if you are using Ansible 2.8 or later, there is now a native Ansible module called `pids` that will return a nice, clean list of PIDs for a given process name, if it is running. Adapting our role for this new functionality, we can, first of all, remove the shell command and replace it with the `pids` module, which is much easier to read, like this:

```
---
- name: Get PID's of running processes matching {{ procname }}
  pids:
    name: "{{ procname }}"
  register: process_ids
```

From this point on, the role is almost identical to before, except that, rather than the comma-separated list we generated from our shell command, we have a simple list that just contains the PIDs for each running process that matches the procname variable in name. Thus, we no longer need to use the split Jinja2 filter on our variables when executing commands on them. Run the following code:

```
- name: Attempt to kill processes nicely
  shell: "kill {{ item }}"
  loop:
    "{{ process_ids.pids }}"
  loop_control:
    label: "{{ item }}"

- name: Wait for processes to exit
  wait_for:
    path: "/proc/{{ item }}"
    timeout: 5
    state: absent
  loop:
    "{{ process_ids.pids }}"
  ignore_errors: yes
  register: exit_results

- name: Forcefully kill stuck processes
  shell: "kill -9 {{ item.item }}"
  loop:
    "{{ exit_results.results | selectattr('failed') | list }}"
  loop_control:
    label: "{{ item.item }}"
```

This block of code performs the same functions as before, only now, it is a little more readable, as we've reduced the number of Jinja2 filters required, and we have removed one shell command, in favor of the `pids` module. These techniques, combined with the `service` module discussed earlier, should give you a sound basis to meet all of your process control needs with Ansible.

In the next and final section of this chapter, we'll take a look at how to use Ansible when you have multiple nodes in a cluster, and you don't want to take them all out of service at once.

Rolling updates with Ansible

No chapter on routine maintenance would be complete without a look at rolling updates. So far in this book, we have kept our examples simple with one or two hosts, and have worked on the basis that all examples can be scaled up to manage hundreds, if not thousands, of servers using the same roles and playbooks.

This, by and large, holds true—however, there are certain special cases where perhaps we need to look a little deeper at the operation of Ansible. Let's build up a hypothetical example, where we have four web application servers behind a load balancer. A new release of the web application code needs to be deployed, and the deployment process requires multiple steps (thus, multiple Ansible tasks). In our simple example, the deployment process will be as follows:

1. Deploy the web application code to the server.
2. Restart the web server service, to pick up the new code.

 In a production environment, you would almost certainly want to take further steps to ensure the integrity of your web service—for example, if it is behind a load balancer, you would take it out of service during the code deployment, and ensure it is not returned to service until it is validated as working properly. It is not anticipated that everyone reading this book will have access to such an environment, and so, the example has been kept simple, to ensure everyone can try it out.

We could easily write a simple Ansible role to perform this task—an example is shown, as follows:

```
---
- name: Deploy new code
  template:
    src: templates/web.html.j2
    dest: /var/www/html/web.html

- name: Restart web server
  service:
    name: nginx
    state: restarted
```

This code performs our two steps in turn, exactly as we desire. However, let's have a look at what happens when we run this role in a playbook. The result is shown in the following screenshot:

```
● ● ●                    james@automation-01: ~/hands-on-automation/chapter12/example08 (ssh)

~/hands-on-automation/chapter12/example08> ansible-playbook -i hosts site.yml

PLAY [Deploy web server code] ********************************************************

TASK [Gathering Facts] ********************************************************
ok: [cluster4]
ok: [cluster3]
ok: [cluster2]
ok: [cluster1]

TASK [deployweb : Deploy new code] ********************************************************
changed: [cluster4]
changed: [cluster2]
changed: [cluster3]
changed: [cluster1]

TASK [deployweb : Restart web server] ********************************************************
changed: [cluster4]
changed: [cluster1]
changed: [cluster2]
changed: [cluster3]

PLAY RECAP ********************************************************
cluster1                   : ok=3    changed=2    unreachable=0    failed=0    s
kipped=0    rescued=0    ignored=0
```

Notice how Ansible performed the tasks. First of all, the new code was deployed on all four servers. Only then, were they restarted. This may not be desirable, for a number of reasons. For example, the servers may be in an inconsistent state after the first task, and you would not want all four servers to be in an inconsistent state at once, as anyone using the web application would experience errors. Also, if the playbook goes wrong for some reason and produces a failed state, it will faithfully fail on all four servers, thus breaking the entire web application for everyone, and causing a service outage.

To prevent these kinds of issues from occurring, we can use the `serial` keyword, to ask Ansible to only perform the update on a given number of servers at a time. For example, if we insert the line `serial: 2` into the `site.yml` playbook calling this role, suddenly the behavior becomes rather different, as the following screenshot shows:

```
● ● ●              james@automation-01: ~/hands-on-automation/chapter12/example09 (ssh)
~/hands-on-automation/chapter12/example09> ansible-playbook -i hosts site.yml

PLAY [Deploy web server code] ********************************************************

TASK [Gathering Facts] ***************************************************************
ok: [cluster2]
ok: [cluster1]

TASK [deployweb : Deploy new code] ***************************************************
changed: [cluster2]
changed: [cluster1]

TASK [deployweb : Restart web server] ************************************************
changed: [cluster2]
changed: [cluster1]

PLAY [Deploy web server code] ********************************************************

TASK [Gathering Facts] ***************************************************************
ok: [cluster4]
ok: [cluster3]

TASK [deployweb : Deploy new code] ***************************************************
changed: [cluster4]
changed: [cluster3]
```

The preceding output is truncated to save space but clearly shows that the playbook is now being run on only two servers at a time—thus, during the initial phase of the run, only `cluster1` and `cluster2` are inconsistent, while `cluster3` and `cluster4` remain consistent and untouched. Only when all tasks are completed on the first two servers are the next two processed.

Failure handling is also important, and a danger of automation is that you could break an entire environment very easily if an issue exists in the code or playbook. For example, if our `Deploy new code` task fails for all servers, running the playbook on two servers at a time will not help. Ansible will still faithfully do what it is asked—in this case, break all four servers.

In this instance, it is a good idea to add to the playbook the `max_fail_percentage` parameter too. For example, if we set this to `50`, then Ansible will stop processing hosts as soon as 50% of its inventory has failed, as shown in the following screenshot:

```
● ● ●                  james@automation-01: ~/hands-on-automation/chapter12/example10 (ssh)
~/hands-on-automation/chapter12/example10> ansible-playbook -i hosts site.yml

PLAY [Deploy web server code] *********************************************************

TASK [Gathering Facts] ****************************************************************
ok: [cluster2]
ok: [cluster1]

TASK [deployweb : Deploy new code] ****************************************************
fatal: [cluster1]: FAILED! => {"changed": true, "checksum": "cb6fb9883d95a1878e7
71a7a4934bccc0057a84c", "dest": "/var/www/html/web.html", "failed_when_result":
true, "gid": 0, "group": "root", "md5sum": "fbf4ff61a186520a32c254b227cad4b1", "
mode": "0644", "owner": "root", "size": 138, "src": "/home/james/.ansible/tmp/an
sible-tmp-1569585205.18-27799675831076/source", "state": "file", "uid": 0}
fatal: [cluster2]: FAILED! => {"changed": true, "checksum": "31d254e3fc98f978343
dbd6d7843ed0727e898ef", "dest": "/var/www/html/web.html", "failed_when_result":
true, "gid": 0, "group": "root", "md5sum": "f72f24be17d76bd1fdf3b0eeb067ba55", "
mode": "0644", "owner": "root", "size": 138, "src": "/home/james/.ansible/tmp/an
sible-tmp-1569585205.21-189436425724816/source", "state": "file", "uid": 0}

NO MORE HOSTS LEFT ********************************************************************

NO MORE HOSTS LEFT ********************************************************************

PLAY RECAP ***************************************************************************
cluster1                   : ok=1     changed=0    unreachable=0    failed=1    s
kipped=0     rescued=0    ignored=0
cluster2                   : ok=1     changed=0    unreachable=0    failed=1    s
```

As we can see here, even though our inventory has not been changed, Ansible has stopped after processing cluster1 and cluster2—because they failed, it is not performing any tasks on cluster3 and cluster4; thus, at least two hosts remain in service with good code, allowing users to continue using the web application, in spite of the failure.

It is important to make use of these Ansible features when working with large, load-balanced environments, to ensure that failures do not propagate to an entire estate of servers. That concludes our look at the use of Ansible in routine server maintenance—as ever, the possibilities are endless, but it is hoped that once again, this chapter has given you some inspiration and examples upon which to build.

Summary

Ansible is a very powerful tool, but not just for deployment and configuration management. Although these are core strengths it possesses, it is also of powerful assistance when it comes to day-to-day management tasks. As ever, when coupled with an enterprise management tool such as AWX or Ansible Tower, it becomes incredibly important in the management of your Linux estate, especially for auditing and debugging purposes.

In this chapter, you learned how to tidy up disk space using Ansible, and how to make this conditional. You then learned how Ansible can help monitor configuration drift, and even alert to possible tampering with binary files. You learned how to manage processes on remote servers using Ansible, and finally, how to perform rolling updates in a graceful and managed fashion, across a load-balanced pool of servers.

In the next chapter, we take a look at securing your Linux servers in a standardized fashion, with CIS Benchmarks.

Questions

1. Why might you make use of the output from the df command rather than an Ansible fact when examining disk space?
2. Which Ansible module is used to locate files based on given criteria, such as age?
3. Why is it important to monitor for configuration drift?
4. What are two ways in which you can monitor a text-based configuration file for changes in Ansible?
5. How would you manage a systemd service on a remote server using Ansible?
6. What is the name of the built-in filtering within Ansible that can help process string output (for example, to split a comma-separated list)?
7. How would you split a comma-separated list in an Ansible variable?
8. When operating in a load-balanced environment, why would you not want all tasks performed on all the servers in one go?
9. Which Ansible feature can prevent you from rolling out a failed task to all servers?

Further reading

- For an in-depth understanding of Ansible, please refer to *Mastering Ansible, Third Edition—James Freeman* and *Jesse Keating* (`https://www.packtpub.com/gb/virtualization-and-cloud/mastering-ansible-third-edition`)

Section 4: Securing Your Linux Servers

4

In this section, we go hands-on with security benchmarks and cover practical examples of how to apply, enforce, and audit them in the Enterprise.

This section comprises the following chapters:

- Chapter 13, *Using CIS Benchmarks*
- Chapter 14, *CIS Hardening with Ansible*
- Chapter 15, *Auditing Security Policy with OpenSCAP*
- Chapter 16, *Tips and Tricks*

13
Using CIS Benchmarks

When implementing Linux in the Enterprise, security is paramount. There is no one step that can be taken to achieve the nirvana of a truly *secure* environment—rather, the approach is an amalgamation of disparate steps that come together to build an environment that is as safe and secure as it can be. Indeed, this statement brings us to another important point—security is a moving target. As just one example, SSLv2 was considered to be secure and was used to secure websites across the internet for many years. Then came the DROWN attack in 2016, which rendered it insecure. Thus, a server secured for internet traffic (perhaps a frontend web server) in 2015 would have, at the time, been considered secure. However, in 2017, it would have been considered highly vulnerable.

Linux itself has always been considered a secure operating system, though its high and increasing levels of adoption has seen attacks on the rise. Throughout this book, we have advocated, at a high level, good security practices in the design of your Linux estate, for example, not installing unnecessary services on your base operating system image. Nonetheless, there is much more we can do to make our Linux environment more secure and, in this chapter, we will explore the ways in which standards have been developed to ensure the security of Linux environments. Specifically, we will consider the use of the CIS Benchmarks, along with some practical examples of how to apply them.

Specifically, the following topics will be covered in this chapter:

- Understanding CIS Benchmarks
- Applying security policy wisely
- Scripted deployment of server hardening

Technical requirements

This chapter includes examples based on the following technologies:

- CentOS 7.6
- Ansible 2.8

To run through these examples, you will need access to two servers or virtual machines running the operating system listed previously, along with Ansible. Note that the examples given in this chapter may be destructive in nature (for example, they delete files and make changes to server configuration) and, if run as shown, are only intended to be run in an isolated test environment.

Once you are satisfied that you have a safe environment to operate in, let's get started with routine system maintenance with Ansible.

All example code discussed in this chapter is available from GitHub at the following URL: `https://github.com/PacktPublishing/Hands-On-Enterprise-Automation-on-Linux/tree/master/chapter13`.

Understanding CIS Benchmarks

Before we delve into what a CIS Benchmark actually consists of, let's take a look at why they exist and, conceptually, what they are.

What is a CIS Benchmark?

Securing servers, regardless of their operating system, is a big task. It requires being constantly up to date with new attack vectors and vulnerabilities as they are discovered (see the mention of the DROWN attack and SSLv2 in the introduction to this chapter). Some things are well-known and considered *normal*. For example, on Linux, it is generally frowned upon to ever log in as root—instead, it is almost universally recognized that each individual user should have their own user account and should perform all commands requiring elevated permissions using the `sudo` command. Thus, some Linux distributions such as Ubuntu come with remote root access disabled by default. Others, such as CentOS, do not. Even between these two key distributions commonly found in the enterprise, you know that, for one, you need to actively turn off remote root SSH access and, for the other, you just need to check that it is turned off.

Of course, defining a security policy goes far deeper than whether root access is allowed over SSH. Over the years, individuals build up a wealth of knowledge about what works and, perhaps by learning the hard way, what doesn't. However, the security of your environment should not be defined by how experienced your system administrators are. Rather, there should be some defined standard for how to best secure a server to prevent most of the common attacks, and also to ensure that a suitable level of information is logged in the case that an audit is ever required to find the root cause of an event.

This is where the concept of the CIS Benchmark comes in. Many people are familiar with the concept of a benchmark as a performance test (that is, speed). However, whether your server is secure or not is something that can be tested by looking for certain criteria, and thus the CIS Benchmark exists. Quoting directly from the **Community for Internet Security** (**CIS** for short) website:

> *"CIS Benchmarks are developed through a unique consensus-based process comprised of cybersecurity professionals and subject matter experts around the world."*

Thus, these benchmarks can be considered an amalgamation of best practices from industry professionals. Further, they are regularly updated and so can be used by engineers and administrators to keep abreast of best practices when it comes to securing a server.

It should, of course, be noted that there are other security standards out there that go to even greater depths than the CIS Benchmark, for example, FedRAMP and NSA security requirements. It would be impossible to go into detail of all the different profiles available within this book, and so we will focus on the CIS Benchmark, which is freely available (in exchange for some personal information) and is also well regarded.

 That this book focuses on the CIS Benchmarks should not be taken as an implicit statement that you should implement these on your server estate in order for it to be secure. It is the duty of each and every reader to ensure they understand their own security requirements and to implement the correct ones accordingly. In this chapter, we work through the use of CIS Benchmarks as a worked example of server hardening to a given standard.

Also of note is that the CIS Benchmarks are divided by technology. For example, there is a CIS Benchmark for both Red Hat Enterprise Linux 7 and Ubuntu Server, which you can apply to your Enterprise Linux estate. However, these focus on securing the base operating system, and if you install an application layer on top of it, then you must apply the appropriate security policy for that as well.

There are CIS Benchmarks for more than 140 technologies, including common Linux services such as nginx, Apache, and PostgreSQL. Thus, if you are building an internet-facing web server, it would make sense to apply both the operating system benchmark and then the appropriate one for the chosen web server.

If you have a bespoke application layer, or indeed are simply using a technology not listed on the CIS website, do not despair—secure the underlying operating system using the appropriate benchmark and then apply security practices in the best way you can. Often, there is good advice on the internet, but figuring this out is beyond the scope of this book.

A full list of the technologies for which there are CIS Benchmarks can be found here: `https://www.cisecurity.org/cis-benchmarks/`.

Once you have obtained the security benchmark for your chosen operating system, it is time to consider the application of it. Before we get this far, though, in the next section of this chapter, we will explore in greater detail the contents of a CIS Benchmark for the Linux operating system.

Exploring CIS Benchmarks in detail

Let's take a practical example to explore CIS Benchmarks in greater detail by looking at the one for RHEL 7. At the time of writing, this is on release version 2.2.0 and consists of 386 pages! Thus, immediately we can see that implementing this benchmark is unlikely to be a trivial activity.

As you explore the document, you will find that the section of most interest to us—the *Recommendations* section—is divided into subsections. Each of these focuses on a specific area of security within the operating system. At the time of writing, *section 1* is all about the initial setup of the operating system; parameters and configuration likely to be applied at build time. *Section 2* is all about securing common services that might be installed by default on a RHEL 7 server. *Section 3* deals with network configuration, while *section 4* goes into detail on your logging and audit logging setup to ensure you are capturing the requisite amount of data during daily use. This is to ensure you can audit your servers and find out what happened if you are unfortunate enough to suffer a breach or an outage. *Section 5* considers access to your server and authentication (this is where you will find SSH server security mentioned—in fact, you will see that our example of disabling remote root logins is benchmark 5.2.8 in version 2.2.0 of the document). Finally, *section 6* is entitled *System Maintenance* and is intended to be run not once, but regularly, to ensure the integrity of the system.

Of course, we have discussed previously in this book that it is possible for anyone with root privileges to change core system configuration, and thus it is recommended that all of the benchmarks be run (or at least checked) on a regular basis to ensure compliance with the original policy.

We will explore this across the next two chapters of this book; however, for now, let's return to furthering our understanding of the CIS Benchmark itself. As you look into each recommendation, you will notice that each has a level associated with it and is either *Scored* or *Not Scored* (this is stated in the title of each benchmark).

Each of these benchmarks are intended to contribute to a final report or scoring of a system as part of a compliance check—and recommendations that are scored quite literally contribute to the final score. Thus, if your system meets the check, then the final score is increased—however, if it is not met, the final score is decreased. Those marked as *Not Scored* have no bearing on the final score at all. In other words, you are not marked down for failing to implement them.

This, of course, does not mean they are any less important to consider. By way of example, let's consider benchmark 3.7 of the version 2.2.0 RHEL 7 benchmark, which is entitled *Ensure wireless interfaces are disabled*. The rationale between each benchmark is given in the details of the benchmark, and this one states the following:

> *"If wireless is not to be used, wireless devices can be disabled to reduce the potential attack surface."*

This is a logical approach—we know that if your device has a wireless interface, it should be disabled unless it is in use. In addition, wireless security protocols have been historically broken, just as SSLv2 was, and thus, in the long term, wireless network communication might not be considered to be truly secure. Nonetheless, on a corporate laptop running RHEL 7, you cannot guarantee that it will be connected to a wired network connection. Wireless networking might be the only option and, in this instance, you would need to leave it turned on.

Of course, the CIS Benchmark cannot make this decision for you—only you can know whether your system needs to have its wireless network adapters enabled (if present), and so it is reasonable that this is a non-scorable item.

By contrast, our old friend benchmark 5.2.8 (disabling remote root SSH access) is scored as there should be no rational reason for enabling this in an enterprise environment. Thus, we would expect our system to be scored down if this benchmark could not be met.

Each benchmark has details on how to test for the presence of the condition or configuration mentioned, along with the details on how to apply the desired configuration.

In addition to these details, you will also note that each benchmark has a level associated with it that can be either 1 or 2. In each case, for RHEL 7, you will see that these levels are applied to two different scenarios—the use of RHEL 7 as a server and as a workstation. Again, this makes sense when we delve into the meaning of these levels.

Level 1 is intended to be a sensible security baseline for you to apply to your environment to reduce the attack surface. It is not intended to have an extensive impact on the day-to-day business usage of your Linux environment, and so level 1 benchmarks are the less intrusive ones to implement.

By contrast, level 2 benchmarks are offered to provide a much more rigorous level of security, and are highly likely to have an impact on the day-to-day usage of your environment.

If we look again at benchmark 3.7, we will see that it is categorized as level 1 for servers and level 2 for workstations. This makes sense—a server is unlikely to have a wireless network adapter, and even less likely to be using it, even if present, thus disabling it has little or no impact on the day-to-day usage of the server. However, a RHEL 7 laptop would become a lot less portable if benchmark 3.7 was implemented on it, and so the level 2 categorization warns us of this. Imagine having a laptop and not being able to use it on a wireless network—this is a concept that, to many, is unfeasible in this day and age!

Benchmark 5.2.8 is considered level 1 for both server and workstation because it is already considered good practice not to use the root account for day-to-day operations—thus, disabling access to it over SSH should not have any impact on a day-to-day basis.

In an ideal world, you should read and understand all benchmarks before you apply them in case they have an impact on your way of doing things—for example, I still come across systems that make use of the root account over SSH for scripted operations, and while my first task is normally to rectify this, if I were to blindly apply the CIS Benchmark to these systems, I would break an otherwise working setup.

However, accepting that anyone who manages an Enterprise Linux environment is incredibly busy, you could be forgiven for thinking that you could just apply the scored level 1 benchmarks to your systems. Indeed, this would give you a reasonable security baseline while incurring a relatively low risk—yet there is no substitute for being thorough. In the next section of this chapter, we will look in greater detail at how to wisely select benchmarks without causing issues in your environment!

Applying security policy wisely

As we had begun to explore in the previous section, each CIS Benchmark has a level and scoring associated with it. The level is of particular concern to us as, while we wish to secure our systems as effectively as possible, we would not wish to break any running systems. For this reason, it is highly advisable to apply the benchmarks in an isolated test environment and test your applications before deploying them to a production environment. Indeed, if the application of a benchmark breaks a given system, the following process should be executed in the enterprise to resolve it:

1. Establish which benchmark caused the issue.
2. Determine which internal systems were affected by the benchmark.
3. Decide whether the internal systems can be changed to work with the benchmarks (for example, use an unprivileged account over SSH rather than root).
4. Implement the changes to the internal systems and apply the benchmark universally or (only if there is a good reason to) make an exception for that benchmark and record it.

 The CIS Benchmarks could even break your Ansible automation—the simplest example being that you are using the root account to perform your automation tasks over, and you disable this as part of your CIS Benchmark deployment. In this instance, you would find Ansible locked out of all of your systems and, in the worst case, you would have to manually modify each server to reinstate Ansible access.

Although we can't go through the benchmarks one by one in this chapter, in the following subsections, we will explore some of the relevant examples to look out for. It is hoped this will give you enough information to review the benchmark for your chosen version of Linux, and then make informed decisions on what security policies are in the best interests of your environment.

We will continue with our example of using the RHEL 7 benchmark version 2.2.0. However, most of what we describe here will be applicable to other Linux platforms too. Configuration file paths and even log file paths might vary, but these will be detailed in the relevant CIS Benchmark for your operating system, so be sure to download the benchmark that is most relevant to you.

Now that we have considered the overall principles of security policy application, we will dive into some specific examples, starting with the SELinux policy in the next section.

Applying the SELinux security policy

Section 1.6.1 of the RHEL 7 benchmark concerns the implementation of SELinux and consists of checks to ensure SELinux is in enforcing mode rather than disabled at some level. You will note that these checks are all level 2 benchmarks, meaning they could break existing systems.

Enabling and applying SELinux is a very good idea on operating systems that support it, yet even at the time of writing there are many Linux applications that do not work with it and whose installation instructions state that SELinux must be disabled for the application to function. This, of course, is not ideal and instead you should create an SELinux policy that allows your application stack to work without the need to disable it.

Not all enterprises will have the skill set of time to allow this to be completed, though, and so some careful consideration needs to be given to this set of benchmarks—in short, it should be applied if at all possible, but exceptions may be required.

If you are working with Ubuntu, the same logic should be applied to AppArmor, which is enabled by default on Ubuntu Server.

In the next section of this chapter, we will take a look at how the CIS Benchmarks affect the way filesystems are mounted on Linux.

Mounting of filesystems

All filesystems in Linux must be mounted before they can be used—this is quite simply the mapping of block devices such as a partition on a disk to a path. To most users, this is transparent and happens at boot time, but to those responsible for configuring systems, it needs some attention. For example, the `/tmp` filesystem is usually writable to all users, and so it is desirable to not let people execute files from this directory as they could put any arbitrary binary in there to be run by themselves or someone else. Thus, this filesystem is often mounted with the `noexec` flag to achieve exactly this.

Changing mount options for partitions (and indeed partition structure) can be problematic on machines that have already been deployed. In addition, many cloud platforms feature a flat filesystem structure and, as such, the preceding example of `/tmp` may not be achievable as it cannot be mounted separately from the `root` partition. As a result, I recommend that you factor this part of the CIS Benchmark into your server (or image) build process and create exclusions for public cloud platforms where required.

The benchmarks in *section 1.1* of the CIS Benchmark (entitled *Filesystem Configuration*) concern exactly these kinds of details and, again, these will need to be tailored to your environment. For example, benchmark 1.1.1.8 recommends disabling the ability to mount FAT filesystems, and *section 1.1.5* recommends disabling binary execution on /tmp, as discussed previously. These are both scored benchmarks and, at the time of writing, there should be little need to use or mount FAT volumes or execute files from /tmp. However, in some legacy environments, this could still be required and so this should be applied with some care.

Similarly, there are many recommendations around having separate filesystems for important paths such as /tmp and /var, and also special mount options. All of these will work in a large number of cases but, again, it would be too bold to state that this will work for everyone, especially in preexisting environments, and so these should be applied but with an understanding of the environmental requirements.

Having looked at the implications of the CIS Benchmarks on how filesystems are mounted, we will proceed to look at the recommendations around intrusion detection using file checksumming.

Installing Advanced Intrusion Detection Environment (AIDE)

Benchmark 1.3.1 concerns the installation of **Advanced Intrusion Detection Environment (AIDE)**—a modern replacement for the venerable **Tripwire** utility that can scan the filesystem and checksum all the files, thus providing a reliable way of detecting modifications to the filesystem.

On the face of it, installing and using AIDE is a very good idea—however, if you have an environment with 100 machines in it and you update all of them, you will get 100 reports, each containing details of a large number of file changes. There are other solutions to this problem, including the open source OSSEC project (https://www.ossec.net/), but this is not checked for as part of the CIS Benchmark and so it is left for you to decide what the right solution is for your enterprise.

This, of course, is not to say that AIDE should not be used—far from it. Rather, it is to say that, if you choose to use AIDE, make sure you have processes in place to process and understand the reports, and to ensure that you can distinguish false positives (for example, a change in the checksum of a binary due to a package update) from genuinely malicious and unexpected modifications (for example, /bin/ls changes even though no package update has been performed).

Having looked at whether AIDE is a viable tool to install on your Linux infrastructure, we will proceed to look at how the CIS Benchmarks impact the default configuration of services at boot time.

Understanding CIS Service benchmarks

Section 2.2 of the benchmark details a number of scored level 1 benchmarks around services that are to be disabled. Again, the rationale behind this is that the attack surface should be minimized, and so, for example, httpd should not be running unless a server is intended to be a web server.

While logical in itself, a review of this section turns up a large number of services that could be vital for your environment, including squid, httpd, and snmpd. For all of these benchmarks, they should only be applied if it makes sense to do so. You would not turn off Apache on a web server, and neither would you disable squid on a proxy server.

However, good guidance is given with regard to these benchmarks about when they should be applied and, in the case of snmpd, there is even guidance on securing the service if your environment relies on this for monitoring purposes.

X Windows

Benchmark 2.2.2 goes as far as ensuring that the X Windows server is actually uninstalled from your systems. Most servers are headless and it would be possible to do this—however, you would not do this for a workstation or for a system that performs remote desktop functions.

Be sure to apply this benchmark to your servers, but only when you know it is safe to apply it.

Allowing hosts by network

Benchmarks 3.4.2 and 3.4.3 ensure that /etc/hosts.allow and /etc/hosts.deny are configured—this means that, for all services that process these two files, only connections from networks that are allowed are actually processed.

This is generally a good idea—however, many organizations have good firewalls and some actually have policies of not allowing local firewalls on their servers because it complicates the process of debugging. If a connection is denied, the more firewalls you have, the more you have to check to find out where it was denied.

Thus, it is recommended you apply these two benchmarks in accordance with your corporate security policy.

Local firewalls

The same applies for the benchmarks in *section 3.6* that concern the installation and configuration of iptables. Although this local firewall increases your level of server security, it is in contrast to many corporate security policies of having fewer, more centralized, firewalls rather than many localized ones. Apply these benchmarks in accordance with corporate policy.

Overall guidance on scoring

You will note that many of the benchmarks I have advised you to exercise caution over applying are actually scored. This brings us to a wider point regarding scoring—the aim of applying CIS Benchmarks is not to achieve a 100% score. Rather, it is to achieve the highest possible score that is right for your environment and enables your enterprise to function correctly.

Scoring should instead be used to establish your own baseline—once you have worked through all benchmarks in the manner discussed in this chapter, you will know which are right for your enterprise and, hence, what your target score is.

Through a process of auditing the results of repeated applications of the benchmark, repeated scoring exercises can be performed to track overall environment compliance and drift over time. For example, if repeated audits show an ever-decreasing score, then you know you have a problem with regards to compliance, for the root cause must be established—whether that is users making unauthorized changes to systems, or even rolling out new servers that have not been correctly secured.

Either way, your CIS Benchmark score will become a useful tool in monitoring the compliance of your Linux estate with your security policy. In the next section of this chapter, we will explore scripted approaches to CIS Benchmark application and compliance.

Scripted deployment of server hardening

We have spent some time exploring the CIS Benchmarks and how they are intended to be worked with. Now, let us turn our attention to more practical matters—how to audit them and how to implement them. In this book, we have focused on Ansible as our chosen tool for automating such tasks, and indeed Ansible is an excellent solution for this purpose. With that said, of course, you will have noticed that the examples in the CIS Benchmark document itself are often shell commands or, in some cases, are simply statements regarding configuration lines that should exist (or not exist) in a given file.

In order to clearly explain the auditing and implementation of the CIS Benchmark on a Linux system, I have split the examples into two. In this part of this chapter, we will develop traditional shell scripts for checking for CIS Benchmark compliance, and then for implementing the recommendations if required. This will look very similar to the CIS Benchmark document itself and thus will help with generating an understanding of how to implement them. Then, in the next chapter, we will develop these shell script-based examples into Ansible roles so that we can use our favorite automation tool to manage our CIS Benchmark compliance.

Let's work through some examples to demonstrate how to develop such scripts, starting with our root login over SSH example.

Ensuring SSH root login is disabled

CIS recommendation 5.2.8 in version 2.2.0 of the RHEL 7 benchmark is that we should disable remote root logins. We have visited this example already in other guises, and here we will look specifically at the recommendations in the CIS Benchmark document to help us understand how this should be implemented.

The document states that, to audit for this requirement (and thus score this item), the following test result should be observed:

```
# grep "^PermitRootLogin" /etc/ssh/sshd_config
PermitRootLogin no
```

Note that the command is intended for a human being to interpret the output of it—this command will return the `PermitRootLogin` line from this file, regardless of whether it is enabled or disabled. The text shows the desired output, but assumes that the person running the test will read the output and check whether it is enabled or not—workable on a small scale, but not viable for automation purposes. The remediation suggested is to edit `/etc/ssh/sshd_config` to set the following parameter:

```
PermitRootLogin no
```

So far, so good—the CIS Benchmark document is quite descriptive, and even gives us a head start with our coding. However, as stated previously, these snippets don't really help us to either check or implement this recommendation in an automated manner.

Suppose we want to audit for this condition using a shell script. In this instance, we would want to run the `grep` command mentioned in the benchmark document, but use a more precise pattern to ensure we only match the `PermitRootLogin` line when it is set to `no`. We would then check for the desired output and `echo` a suitable message to the console, depending on the result of the check. This script might look like this (noting that there are multiple ways to achieve the same end result in shell scripting!):

```
#!/bin/sh
#
# This file implements CIS Red Hat Enterprise Linux 7 Benchmark
# Recommendation 5.2.8 from version 2.2.0
echo -n "Ensure root logins are disabled on SSH... "
OUTPUT=$(grep "^PermitRootLogin no" /etc/ssh/sshd_config)
if [ "x$OUTPUT" == "x" ]; then
  echo FAILED!
else
  echo OK
fi
```

The script is fairly straightforward for anyone familiar with shell scripts, but in brief, here are the steps:

1. We put some useful documentation in the comments at the top of the file so that we know which recommendation we are testing for. Note that recommendation numbers might change between document versions and so it is important to record both.
2. We `echo` a line of informative text about the test we are running.
3. Then, the suggested audit command from the CIS Benchmark is run, only this time we are checking for the presence of the `PermitRootLogin no` line. The output is captured in an `OUTPUT` variable.

4. If the contents of OUTPUT are blank, then we know the line we are checking for does not exist in the file and the test is assumed to have failed. We can safely assume this because root logins are enabled by default in the OpenSSH server, and so if this line is absent from the configuration file, then provided there were no issues with our grep pattern, root logins are enabled. We echo this to the Terminal so that the user knows to take action.

5. The only condition under which the OUTPUT variable should contain text is when the grep command finds the desired pattern. If this condition is achieved, then we echo a different message for the user so that they know that this test has passed and no further action is required.

Let's see this script in action, along with an attempt to fix the problem by hand:

```
● ● ●                james@automation-02: ~/hands-on-automation/chapter13/example01 (ssh)

~/hands-on-automation/chapter13/example01> ./cis_v2.2.0_recommendation_5.2.8.sh
Ensure root logins are disabled on SSH... FAILED!
~/hands-on-automation/chapter13/example01> cat /etc/ssh/sshd_config
# Configured by Ansible ubuntu-testhost
ChallengeResponseAuthentication no
UsePAM yes
X11Forwarding no
PrintMotd no
AcceptEnv LANG LC_*
Subsystem       sftp    /usr/lib/openssh/sftp-server
PasswordAuthentication yes
~/hands-on-automation/chapter13/example01> echo "PermitRootLogin no" | sudo tee
-a /etc/ssh/sshd_config 1>/dev/null
~/hands-on-automation/chapter13/example01> ./cis_v2.2.0_recommendation_5.2.8.sh
Ensure root logins are disabled on SSH... OK
~/hands-on-automation/chapter13/example01>
```

Here, we can see a prime example of the manual process, which many system administrators and engineers will be familiar with when managing their estates. We ran the check script defined previously and it yielded the response FAILED!. Thus, our first step was to take a look at the config file to see why the test failed. There were one of two possibilities that would have caused this result—either the line containing PermitRootLogin was not present at all, or it was commented out. In this case, the former proved to be true.

If the line had been present, but commented out, we could have used `sed` (or another inline editing tool) to uncomment the line and set the parameter to `no`. However, as the line was not present, we needed to append the line to the file, which we have done in the previous screenshot using the `tee -a` command. Note that this was needed in conjunction with `sudo` because only `root` can write to this file. We then run the test a second time and it passes. Of course, you will note that it would have been entirely possible to simply open this file with `vim` (or your favorite editor) and correct the issue manually; however, the previous example could lend itself to a scripted solution.

As shown from the preceding example, this is an incredibly slow and manual process. This would be bad enough to perform on a single server (for example, the template image), but imagine scaling this up across an entire estate of Linux servers, and then to all the recommendations in the CIS Benchmark document. The task would be a full-time (and very tedious) job for someone.

It's better to automate the process and you will note that, in the CIS Benchmark document, there is not only a test case for auditing the recommendation on a server, but also a recommended alteration. In most cases, this is simply a statement of the line(s) that should be present in the given configuration file(s). In this case, we want to assert the following:

```
PermitRootLogin no
```

If we were to try and remedy this issue by developing our shell script further, we would need to perform the following steps when the test results are in a `FAILED!` state (on an `OK` result, no further action is necessary):

1. As we have failed to match the desired pattern in the file, we know that the line is either present, but has the wrong setting, or is not present at all (either absent or commented out). We can ignore the difference between the last two possibilities as it will do no harm to leave the commented out line in place and add the correct line in. Thus, our first task is to test for the presence of the `PermitRootLogin` line, regardless of its setting:

    ```
    OPTPRESENT=$(grep -e "^PermitRootLogin.*" /etc/ssh/sshd_config)
    if [ "x$OPTPRESENT" == "x" ]; then
    ...
    else
    ...
    fi
    ```

2. In the previous screenshot, we are looking for any line in the configuration file that begins with `PermitRootLogin`. If we get nothing back (our positive test case), then we know we must add the line to the file by adding the following directly under the `if` statement:

```
echo "Configuration not present - attempting to add"
echo "PermitRootLogin no" | sudo tee -a /etc/ssh/sshd_config
1>/dev/null
```

3. So far, so good. However, if our `grep` command did return some output, we know the line is present and the value is incorrect, and so we can use a tool such as `sed` to modify the line in place:

```
echo "Configuration present - attempting to modify"
sudo sed -i 's/^PermitRootLogin.*/PermitRootLogin no/g'
/etc/ssh/sshd_config
```

4. When we have modified the file (regardless of the route taken), we know we must restart `sshd` for the changes to be picked up. Thus, under the closing `fi` statement of the inner `if` construct, we add the following:

```
sudo systemctl restart sshd
```

5. When we run this with an SSH configuration where this setting is not present, we see the following behavior—note that a second run of the script shows that the modifications were successful:

```
james@automation-02: ~/hands-on-automation/chapter13/example02 (ssh)
~/hands-on-automation/chapter13/example02> ./cis_v2.2.0_recommendation_5.2.8.sh
Ensure root logins are disabled on SSH... FAILED!
Configuration not present - attempting to add
~/hands-on-automation/chapter13/example02> ./cis_v2.2.0_recommendation_5.2.8.sh
Ensure root logins are disabled on SSH... OK
~/hands-on-automation/chapter13/example02>
```

6. Similarly, if we run it and the line is present and not correct according to the CIS Benchmark, we see the following:

```
●  ●  ●                james@automation-02: ~/hands-on-automation/chapter13/example02 (ssh)

~/hands-on-automation/chapter13/example02> ./cis_v2.2.0_recommendation_5.2.8.sh
Ensure root logins are disabled on SSH... FAILED!
Configuration present - attempting to modify
~/hands-on-automation/chapter13/example02> ./cis_v2.2.0_recommendation_5.2.8.sh
Ensure root logins are disabled on SSH... OK
~/hands-on-automation/chapter13/example02>
```

This is excellent—we have just used shell scripts to automate one of the recommendations in the CIS Benchmark document. However, you will note that the shell script we developed contains a lot of repetition and would not be easy to pick up by someone else.

Further, this recommendation is one of the more simple ones—there is only one line to modify in one file in this case. What if the recommendation is more in depth? Let's take a look at that in the next section.

Ensuring packet redirect sending is disabled

Recommendation 3.1.2 of the version 2.2.0 RHEL benchmark is somewhat more detailed—this is a scored level 1 benchmark that ensures that your servers do not send routing information to other hosts. Unless they have been configured as a router, there should be no good reason for them to do this.

From the documentation itself, we can see that the recommended audit commands (and results) are as follows:

```
$ sysctl net.ipv4.conf.all.send_redirects
net.ipv4.conf.all.send_redirects = 0
$ sysctl net.ipv4.conf.default.send_redirects
net.ipv4.conf.default.send_redirects = 0
$ grep "net\.ipv4\.conf\.all\.send_redirects" /etc/sysctl.conf
/etc/sysctl.d/*
net.ipv4.conf.all.send_redirects = 0
$ grep "net\.ipv4\.conf\.default\.send_redirects" /etc/sysctl.conf
/etc/sysctl.d/*
net.ipv4.conf.default.send_redirects= 0
```

The commands to be run begin with the $ character, while the desired results are shown on the following line. We can already see that developing this into a shell script is going to take some work—we need to validate the output of the two `sysctl` commands, and then also check the configuration files to ensure that the parameters will persist across reboots and kernel parameter reloads.

We can check for the current kernel parameter setting quite easily using some shell code such as this:

```
echo -n "Ensure net.ipv4.conf.all.send_redirects = 0... "
OUTPUT=$(sysctl net.ipv4.conf.all.send_redirects | grep
"net.ipv4.conf.all.send_redirects = 0" 2> /dev/null)
if [ "x$OUTPUT" == "x" ]; then
    echo FAILED!
  else
    echo OK
fi
```

You will note that the code structure is almost identical to that which we used to check the `PermitRootLogin` parameter for SSH—hence, although the code to automate our auditing process is getting easier, it is also getting highly repetitious and inefficient. A similar block of code would then be used to check the value of the `net.ipv4.conf.default.send_redirects` parameter.

We can also check the persistent configuration of these parameters, again, by building the audit commands from the CIS Benchmark document into a conditional structure similar to what we did previously:

```
echo -n "Ensure net.ipv4.conf.all.send_redirects = 0 in persistent
configuration..."
OUTPUT=$(grep -e "^net\.ipv4\.conf\.all\.send_redirects = 0"
/etc/sysctl.conf /etc/sysctl.d/*)
if [ "x$OUTPUT" == "x" ]; then
    echo FAILED!
  else
    echo OK
fi
```

Once again, we would replicate this block for the `net.ipv4.conf.default.send_redirects` parameter. Thus, once again, we have successfully built up a script to audit this benchmark—running it on our system looks something like this:

```
james@automation-02: ~/hands-on-automation/chapter13/example03 (ssh)

~/hands-on-automation/chapter13/example03> ./cis_v2.2.0_recommendation_3.1.2.sh
Ensure net.ipv4.conf.all.send_redirects = 0... FAILED!
Ensure net.ipv4.conf.default.send_redirects = 0... FAILED!
Ensure net.ipv4.conf.all.send_redirects = 0 in persistent configuration...FAILED
!
Ensure net.ipv4.conf.default.send_redirects = 0 in persistent configuration...FA
ILED!
~/hands-on-automation/chapter13/example03>
```

That's 35 lines of shell script (albeit with a few comments at the top of the file), much of it repetitious, and all just to know that we have completely failed to meet this requirement! Once again, if we are to expand this example to resolve the issues, we need to expand our script.

Setting the active kernel parameters is quite easy—we just need to add a series of commands such as the following into the `FAILED!` branch of our first two `if` constructs:

```
echo "Attempting to modify active kernel parameters"
sudo sysctl -w net.ipv4.conf.all.send_redirects=0
sudo sysctl -w net.ipv4.route.flush=1
```

We could add something similar for `net.ipv4.conf.default.send_redirects` in the appropriate place.

For our persistent parameters, however, things are a bit more tricky—we need to deal with the two possible configuration file scenarios as with the `PermitRootLogin` example, but now we have a configuration that is built up of a series of files and we must choose which file to modify if the parameter isn't present.

Thus, once again, we must build up a block of code to handle these two differing scenarios:

```
OPTPRESENT=$(grep -e "^net\.ipv4\.conf\.all\.send_redirects"
/etc/sysctl.conf /etc/sysctl.d/*)
    if [ "x$OPTPRESENT" == "x" ] ; then
      echo "Line not present - attempting to append configuration"
      echo "net.ipv4.conf.all.send_redirects = 0" | sudo tee -a
/etc/sysctl.conf 1>/dev/null
    else
      echo "Line present - attempting to modify"
      sudo sed -i -r
's/^net\.ipv4\.conf\.all\.send_redirects.*/net.ipv4.conf.all.send_redirects
= 0/g' /etc/sysctl.conf /etc/sysctl.d/*
    fi
```

That's a pretty ugly and difficult-to-read piece of code. What it does is as follows:

1. It runs a second `grep` against the known configuration files to see whether the parameter is in there, regardless of its value.
2. If the parameter is not set, then we choose to append it to `/etc/sysctl.conf`.
3. If the parameter is set, we instead use `sed` to modify the parameter, forcing it to our desired value of `0`.

Now when we run this script as before, we get the following:

```
● ● ●              james@automation-02: ~/hands-on-automation/chapter13/example04 (ssh)
~/hands-on-automation/chapter13/example04> ./cis_v2.2.0_recommendation_3.1.2.sh
Ensure net.ipv4.conf.all.send_redirects = 0... FAILED!
Attempting to modify active kernel parameters
net.ipv4.conf.all.send_redirects = 0
net.ipv4.route.flush = 1
Ensure net.ipv4.conf.default.send_redirects = 0... FAILED!
Attempting to modify active kernel parameters
net.ipv4.conf.default.send_redirects = 0
net.ipv4.route.flush = 1
Ensure net.ipv4.conf.all.send_redirects = 0 in persistent configuration...FAILED
!
Line not present - attempting to append configuration
Ensure net.ipv4.conf.default.send_redirects = 0 in persistent configuration...FA
ILED!
Line not present - attempting to append configuration
~/hands-on-automation/chapter13/example04> ./cis_v2.2.0_recommendation_3.1.2.sh
Ensure net.ipv4.conf.all.send_redirects = 0... OK
Ensure net.ipv4.conf.default.send_redirects = 0... OK
Ensure net.ipv4.conf.all.send_redirects = 0 in persistent configuration...OK
Ensure net.ipv4.conf.default.send_redirects = 0 in persistent configuration...OK
~/hands-on-automation/chapter13/example04>
```

As we can see, this works nicely; however, we are now up to 57 lines of shell code and much of it starting to get quite unreadable. All of this is for setting just two kernel parameters, and although we have now built up a fairly solid code base for taking the CIS Benchmarks (along with their recommended audit and remediation steps), it is not scaling at all well.

Further, these scripts are all being run locally in the preceding example—what if we wanted to run them from a central place? In the next section, we will take a look at exactly that.

Running CIS Benchmark scripts from a remote location

The challenge with shell scripting is that, while it is easy to run on the machine where the scripts exist, it is a little more difficult to do on a remote machine.

The scripts we developed previously are designed to be run from an unprivileged account—thus, we have used `sudo` on the steps that specifically require root access to be run. This is fine when you have passwordless sudo access set up, but when a password is required for elevated access using `sudo`, this further complicates the task of running the scripts remotely.

Of course, the entire script could be run as root and, depending on your use case and security requirements, this may or may not be desirable. Let's take a look at the task of running our send redirect example on a remote system called `centos-testhost`. To achieve this, we need to do the following:

1. SSH into the remote system and authenticate—this could be with a password or SSH keys that were set up previously.
2. Invoke the shell required to run the script we have developed—in our examples, this is `/bin/bash`.
3. We add the `-s` flag to the `bash` command—this causes the shell to read its command from the standard input (that is, the commands can be piped to it).
4. Finally, we pipe our script across to `bash`.

There is one further caveat to this approach—in our script, we have boldly assumed that the commands we rely on (such as `sysctl`) exist within one of the directories defined in the PATH variable. It could be argued that this is flawed—however, it can also make script development easier, especially when building up scripts that might be used in a cross-platform environment.

For example, although we have been exclusively working with the RHEL 7 CIS Benchmark in this chapter, it is fair to assume that Ubuntu Server would also want to have SSH root logins disabled, and not send packet redirect information unless it is explicitly configured as a router. Hence, we might reasonably expect the scripts we have developed so far to work on both systems and save us some development effort.

However, on RHEL 7 (and CentOS 7), the `sysctl` command is found in `/usr/sbin/sysctl`, whereas on Ubuntu it is in `/sbin/sysctl`. This difference in itself could be handled by defining the path to `sysctl` in a variable at the top of the script, and then calling it via this—however, even so, it would mean modifying many scripts related to CIS hardening, like so:

```
# RHEL 7 systems
SYSCTL=/usr/sbin/sysctl
$SYSCTL -w net.ipv4.conf.all.send_redirects=0

# Ubuntu systems
```

```
SYSCTL=/sbin/sysctl
$SYSCTL -w net.ipv4.conf.all.send_redirects=0
```

In short, this is better than our original approach, but still highly manual and messy. Returning to the task of running our existing script remotely, putting all our requirements together, we might run it using the following command:

```
$ ssh centos-testhost 'PATH=$PATH:/usr/sbin /bin/bash -s' <
cis_v2.2.0_recommendation_3.1.2.sh
```

The preceding command assumes we are running the script as the current user on the local system—we could explicitly set the user by adding it before the hostname:

```
$ ssh james@centos-testhost 'PATH=$PATH:/usr/sbin /bin/bash -s' <
cis_v2.2.0_recommendation_3.1.2.sh
```

Running this against our remote system (including a second run to ensure the modifications took place effectively) will look something like this:

```
● ● ●          james@automation-01: ~/hands-on-automation/chapter13/example04 (ssh)
~/hands-on-automation/chapter13/example04> ssh centos-testhost 'PATH=$PATH:/usr/
sbin /bin/bash -s' < cis_v2.2.0_recommendation_3.1.2.sh
Ensure net.ipv4.conf.all.send_redirects = 0... FAILED!
Attempting to modify active kernel parameters
net.ipv4.conf.all.send_redirects = 0
net.ipv4.route.flush = 1
Ensure net.ipv4.conf.default.send_redirects = 0... FAILED!
Attempting to modify active kernel parameters
net.ipv4.conf.default.send_redirects = 0
net.ipv4.route.flush = 1
Ensure net.ipv4.conf.all.send_redirects = 0 in persistent configuration...FAILED
!
Line not present - attempting to append configuration
Ensure net.ipv4.conf.default.send_redirects = 0 in persistent configuration...FA
ILED!
Line not present - attempting to append configuration
~/hands-on-automation/chapter13/example04> ssh centos-testhost 'PATH=$PATH:/usr/
sbin /bin/bash -s' < cis_v2.2.0_recommendation_3.1.2.sh
Ensure net.ipv4.conf.all.send_redirects = 0... OK
Ensure net.ipv4.conf.default.send_redirects = 0... OK
Ensure net.ipv4.conf.all.send_redirects = 0 in persistent configuration...OK
Ensure net.ipv4.conf.default.send_redirects = 0 in persistent configuration...OK
~/hands-on-automation/chapter13/example04>
```

We can see that this has been effective against our remote system and that no modification to our original script was required. All of this, while very effective, is somewhat inefficient and cumbersome, especially when compared to our experience with Ansible. In fact, it is fair to say that these examples demonstrate the value that Ansible brings to automating fundamental system administration tasks. To develop this, in the next chapter, we will look at how to build upon our foundation in CIS Benchmarks by developing Ansible playbooks to carry out the tasks required.

Summary

In today's highly connected world, system security is paramount, and while Linux has long been regarded as a secure operating system, there is much that can be done to enhance its security. CIS Benchmarks provided one such standardized approach by bringing together a consensus on security best practices from across the technology industry. CIS Benchmarks, however, are extensive and, if applied by hand, would take many hours for an engineer to implement on a single system. Thus, automating their deployment is of vital importance.

In this chapter, you have learned about CIS Benchmarks, what they are for, and the benefits they bring. You then learned about the balance between security and application support, and how to make informed decisions when applying a server hardening policy. You also learned how to make use of shell scripts to apply some example security policies on a Linux server.

In the next chapter, we will develop this concept further by demonstrating effective methods for automating the deployment of CIS Benchmark recommendations using Ansible.

Questions

1. Why are CIS Benchmarks relevant to securing Linux servers?
2. If you secure Ubuntu Server with the appropriate benchmark and then install nginx on that server, does that also need hardening?
3. What is the difference between a level 1 and a level 2 benchmark?
4. Why are some benchmarks scored and others not?
5. How can you check using a shell script that a given audit requirement has been met?

6. State three possible issues relating to automated modification of configuration files using a shell script.
7. Why do shell scripts not scale well for the automated rollout of CIS Benchmarks?
8. How can you run a CIS Benchmark shell script on a remote server using SSH?
9. Why would you want to make use of a variable to specify the path to a binary used to implement a CIS recommendation?
10. Why might you use sudo for individual commands within a script rather than needing the whole script to run as root?

Further reading

- To review common questions about the CIS Benchmarks, please refer to `https://www.cisecurity.org/cis-benchmarks/cis-benchmarks-faq/`.
- A full list of CIS Benchmarks is available at `https://www.cisecurity.org/cis-benchmarks/`.
- For a greater understanding of Linux shell scripting, please refer to *Mastering Linux Shell Scripting, Second Edition, Andrew Mallett* and *Mokhtar Ebrahim* (`https://www.packtpub.com/gb/virtualization-and-cloud/mastering-linux-shell-scripting-second-edition`).
- To understand more about SELinux and how to create your own policies, please refer to *SELinux System Administration, Second Edition, Sven Vermeulen* (`https://www.packtpub.com/gb/networking-and-servers/selinux-system-administration-second-edition`).

CIS Hardening with Ansible

14

In `Chapter 13`, *Using CIS Benchmarks*, we explored in detail the concept of CIS Benchmarks, how they benefit Linux security in the enterprise, and how to apply them. We examined in some detail an example of the CIS hardening benchmarks, that being the one for Red Hat Enterprise Linux (and CentOS) 7. Although we concluded that the benchmark document provided a great deal of detail regarding the validation checks, and even how to implement the benchmarks, we also saw that the whole process was incredibly manual. Further, with almost 400 pages of detail to a single operating system benchmark, we established that the potential workload for an engineer to implement this on just one server would be huge.

In this chapter, we will once again bring Ansible into consideration. We have already established that Ansible lends itself extremely well to automation at enterprise scale, and implementation of the CIS Benchmarks is no exception. As we proceed through this chapter, we will learn how to rewrite the CIS Benchmarks in Ansible, and then how to apply them at enterprise scale and even maintain oversight of the ongoing compliance of your Linux servers against these benchmarks going forward. In doing this, we will develop a highly scalable, repeatable approach to implementing security benchmarks in the enterprise in a manner that is manageable, repeatable, reliable, and secure – all the hallmarks of effective automation in the enterprise.

The following topics will be covered in this chapter:

- Writing Ansible security policies
- Application of enterprise-wide policies with Ansible
- Testing security policies with Ansible

Technical requirements

This chapter includes examples based on the following technologies:

- CentOS 7.6
- Ansible 2.8

To run through these examples, you will need access to a server or virtual machine running the operating system listed previously, alongside Ansible. Note that the examples given in this chapter may be destructive in nature (for example, they delete files and make changes to server configuration) and if run as shown are only intended to be run in an isolated test environment.

Once you are satisfied that you have a safe environment to operate in, we can get started with routine system maintenance with Ansible.

All example code discussed in this chapter is available on GitHub at the following URL: `https://github.com/PacktPublishing/Hands-On-Enterprise-Automation-on-Linux/tree/master/chapter14`.

Writing Ansible security policies

In `Chapter 13`, *Using CIS Benchmarks*, we explored the CIS Benchmark for Red Hat Enterprise Linux 7 (version 2.2.0) and looked in detail at the document and implementation techniques. Although throughout this book we have focused on two of the more common operating systems found in the enterprise – Ubuntu Server LTS and RHEL/CentOS 7 – in the previous chapter, we chose to focus on the CIS Benchmark for RHEL 7 alone. This was purely for simplicity, as many of the good security practices that apply to RHEL 7 will also apply to Ubuntu Server LTS. For example, neither system should have root SSH logins enabled, and neither should have packet redirect sending enabled unless it is core to their role.

In this chapter, we will continue to develop our RHEL 7-based example. Please know that most of the techniques employed in this chapter for automating the implementation of this benchmark with Ansible will apply equally well to Ubuntu Server LTS, and so it is hoped that the knowledge you gain from this chapter will serve you well when it comes to implementing security benchmarks on Ubuntu, or any other Linux server to which they may apply.

Let's get straight into some practical, hands-on examples of developing CIS Benchmark implementations, only this time we will use Ansible rather than shell scripts based on the example code in the CIS Benchmark document.

Let's start by considering our old friend, the remote root login.

Ensuring remote root login is disabled

In the previous chapter, we devised the following shell script to test for the condition described in CIS Benchmark recommendation 5.2.8 (RHEL 7, benchmark version 2.2.0), and then implemented it if the condition was not met. It is included here so that it can be contrasted against the Ansible solution we are about to create:

```
#!/bin/bash
#
# This file implements CIS Red Hat Enterprise Linux 7 Benchmark
# Recommendation 5.2.8 from version 2.2.0
echo -n "Ensure root logins are disabled on SSH... "
OUTPUT=$(grep -e "^PermitRootLogin no" /etc/ssh/sshd_config)
if [ "x$OUTPUT" == "x" ]; then
  echo FAILED!
  OPTPRESENT=$(grep -e "^PermitRootLogin.*" /etc/ssh/sshd_config)
  if [ "x$OPTPRESENT" == "x" ]; then
    echo "Configuration not present - attempting to add"
    echo "PermitRootLogin no" | sudo tee -a /etc/ssh/sshd_config
1>/dev/null
  else
    echo "Configuration present - attempting to modify"
    sudo sed -i 's/^PermitRootLogin.*/PermitRootLogin no/g'
/etc/ssh/sshd_config
  fi
  sudo systemctl restart sshd
else
  echo OK
fi
```

This shell script is for just one of the numerous benchmarks, and although it does work, it is quite fragile and does not scale across multiple systems. Further, the script is not at all easy to read, and so imagine the scale of the script that would be required if all the CIS Benchmark recommendations were implemented!

Let's consider how we might rewrite this functionality in an Ansible role instead. First of all, we know we are testing for a specific line of configuration in a single file. If it is not present, then we know that the configuration (implicit or otherwise) is to allow remote root logins. In this instance, we carry out two actions: first of all, we modify the configuration file to insert the correct line (or modify the existing line if it exists but has the wrong value configured). Then, we restart the SSH daemon if the configuration file was changed.

Our experience with Ansible has shown us that the `lineinfile` module can handle nearly all of the work-related to both checking the configuration file and modifying it if the requisite line isn't correctly configured. We have also learned that the `service` module can easily restart the SSH daemon, and that this module would be run from a `handler` rather than in the main task flow to ensure that the daemon is not restarted unless the configuration is actually modified.

Thus, we might define a role containing a single task that looks like this in a role called `rhel7cis_recommendation528`:

```
---
- name: 5.2.8 Ensure SSH root login is disabled (Scored - L1S L1W)
  lineinfile:
    state: present
    dest: /etc/ssh/sshd_config
    regexp: '^PermitRootLogin'
    line: 'PermitRootLogin no'
  notify: Restart sshd
```

Notice how we have given the task a meaningful name – taken, in fact, directly from the CIS Benchmark document itself. Thus, we know exactly which benchmark this is, what it is for, and whether or not it is scored. We have also inserted the level information into the title as again this would save us from cross-referencing the original CIS Benchmark document later on.

Alongside our role tasks, we also want to create a handler to restart the SSH daemon if we modify the configuration file (it will not pick up the changes without this) – an example of suitable code for this handler is as follows:

```
---
- name: Restart sshd
  service:
    name: sshd
    state: restarted
```

We can already see that this playbook is much easier to read than our original shell script – there is none of the code duplication we found when we implemented this benchmark in a shell script, and the `lineinfile` module is so powerful that it wraps all of our various checks up into one single Ansible task.

Running the role should yield output similar to that shown in the following screenshot on a system that has remote root logins enabled:

```
• • •          james@automation-01: ~/hands-on-automation/chapter14/example01 (ssh)
~/hands-on-automation/chapter14/example01> ansible-playbook -i hosts site.yml

PLAY [Test and implement CIS benchmark 5.2.8] **********************************

TASK [Gathering Facts] *********************************************************
ok: [centos-testhost]

TASK [rhel7cis_recommendation528 : 5.2.8 Ensure SSH root login is disabled (Scor
ed - L1S L1W)] ***
changed: [centos-testhost]

RUNNING HANDLER [rhel7cis_recommendation528 : Restart sshd] ********************
changed: [centos-testhost]

PLAY RECAP *********************************************************************
centos-testhost            : ok=3    changed=2    unreachable=0    failed=0    s
kipped=0    rescued=0    ignored=0
```

By contrast, if the recommendation is already implemented, then the output will look like
that shown in the following screenshot:

```
• • •          james@automation-01: ~/hands-on-automation/chapter14/example01 (ssh)
~/hands-on-automation/chapter14/example01> ansible-playbook -i hosts site.yml

PLAY [Test and implement CIS benchmark 5.2.8] **********************************

TASK [Gathering Facts] *********************************************************
ok: [centos-testhost]

TASK [rhel7cis_recommendation528 : 5.2.8 Ensure SSH root login is disabled (Scor
ed - L1S L1W)] ***
ok: [centos-testhost]

PLAY RECAP *********************************************************************
centos-testhost            : ok=2    changed=0    unreachable=0    failed=0    s
kipped=0    rescued=0    ignored=0
```

As you can see, if the condition is met, the lineinfile module makes no changes
(resulting in the ok status seen in the preceding screenshot), and the handler does not run
at all.

This in itself is extremely powerful, and a huge improvement over our shell script in terms
of both manageability and coding effort. Nonetheless, the RHEL 7 CIS Benchmark contains
almost 400 recommendations, and you would not want to have to create and include 400
roles in a playbook run as this would detract from the otherwise manageable nature of our
Ansible automation.

In the next section of this chapter, we will look at expanding our current playbook by adding another recommendation from *section 5* of the CIS Benchmark, thus building up our playbook code in a scalable, manageable fashion.

Building up security policies in Ansible

If we were to proceed precisely as we did in the previous section, then when it comes to *section 5.2.9* of the RHEL 7 CIS Benchmark version 2.2.0 (Ensure SSH `PermitEmptyPasswords` is disabled), we would create a new role called `rhel7cis_recommendation529` and put the relevant tasks and handlers inside it.

I'm sure that you will be able to see that this does not scale well – the creation of a new role means we need to specify it in our top-level playbook, which would look something like the following:

```
---
- name: Test and implement CIS benchmark
  hosts: all
  become: yes

  roles:
    - rhel7cis_recommendation528
    - rhel7cis_recommendation529
```

Having one role per line, with almost 400 roles to include, would quickly become tedious and detract from the highly manageable nature of our Ansible code.

Exactly how you divide up your Ansible tasks into roles is up to you, and you should utilize the method that you find most manageable. As a suggestion, though, looking at the table of contents for our example CIS Benchmark, we can see that the recommendations are divided into six sections. Those in *section 5* relate specifically to *Access, Authentication, and Authorization*, and thus it is entirely logical that we might want to group all of these together into one role, perhaps called `rhel7cis_section5`.

With this decision made regarding playbook structure, we can now proceed to build both the checks for recommendations 5.2.8 and 5.2.9 into the same role. They can share the same handler too, as both relate to SSH daemon configuration. Thus, our new role's tasks could look like the following:

```
---
- name: 5.2.8 Ensure SSH root login is disabled (Scored - L1S L1W)
  lineinfile:
    state: present
    dest: /etc/ssh/sshd_config
```

```
      regexp: '^PermitRootLogin'
      line: 'PermitRootLogin no'
    notify: Restart sshd

  - name: 5.2.9 Ensure SSH PermitEmptyPasswords is disabled (Scored - L1S
  L1W)
    lineinfile:
      state: present
      dest: /etc/ssh/sshd_config
      regexp: '^PermitEmptyPasswords'
      line: 'PermitEmptyPasswords no'
    notify: Restart sshd
```

The resulting code is still highly readable and is broken down into manageable chunks, but is now not so granular that it would be difficult to maintain the top-level playbook.

Our handler code remains the same as before, and now when we run the role on a system that does not meet either of these recommendations, the output should look something like the following screenshot:

```
james@automation-01: ~/hands-on-automation/chapter14/example02 (ssh)
~/hands-on-automation/chapter14/example02> ansible-playbook -i hosts site.yml

PLAY [Test and implement CIS benchmarks - section 5] ****************************

TASK [Gathering Facts] *********************************************************
ok: [centos-testhost]

TASK [rhel7cis_section5 : 5.2.8 Ensure SSH root login is disabled (Scored - L1S
L1W)] ***
changed: [centos-testhost]

TASK [rhel7cis_section5 : 5.2.9 Ensure SSH PermitEmptyPasswords is disabled (Sco
red - L1S L1W)] ***
changed: [centos-testhost]

RUNNING HANDLER [rhel7cis_section5 : Restart sshd] *****************************
changed: [centos-testhost]

PLAY RECAP *********************************************************************
centos-testhost            : ok=4    changed=3    unreachable=0    failed=0    s
kipped=0    rescued=0    ignored=0
```

This is very clean and tidy, and hopefully you can see how this could scale well when it comes to implementing all of the nearly 400 recommendations from the CIS Benchmark if you chose to do so. However, it also raises an important consideration: in an ideal world, all of the CIS recommendations would be applied to every machine, yet in reality, this is not always possible. In the *Applying security policy wisely* section of Chapter 13, *Using CIS Benchmarks*, we discussed a variety of recommendations that you would apply caution to implementing. In addition, as much as it is desirable to never perform a remote login with the root account over SSH, I have come across systems where this is actually required to support some kind of legacy system until it can be updated.

In short, there will always be a requirement for exceptions in the process of policy enforcement. The important thing is to handle this in a graceful manner. Say you have 100 Linux machines to apply our newly written mini security policy to, but that two require remote root logins to be enabled.

In this instance, we have two choices:

- Maintain a separate set of playbooks for the two servers where the exceptions are required
- Find a way to selectively run the tasks in our role without having to modify it

Of these choices, the second is clearly the better of them as it supports us in maintaining one single playbook. But how do we achieve this?

Ansible offers us two tools to approach this problem. The first is the when clause that we have already considered several times in this book. So far, we have only looked at this clause to evaluate a condition programatically (for example, to run a disk cleanup on the condition that free space on the disk falls below a certain value). In this instance, we employ a much simpler implementation – simply evaluating whether a Boolean value is true or not.

Suppose that we add the following code below our task to implement recommendation 5.2.8:

```
when:
  - recommendation_528|default(true)|bool
```

These two lines evaluate a variable called `recommendation_528` and applies two Jinja2 filters to ensure it is processed correctly, even when the variable is undefined:

- The `default` filter sets the variable to `true` by default as Ansible will fail the play with an error if any variable it encounters is undefined. This removes the need for us to define these variables up-front – our role simply defaults them to `true` unless we set them otherwise.
- The second filter casts them to a `bool` type to ensure a reliable evaluation of the condition.

> Remember that `true` can be both a string and a Boolean value, depending on how you interpret it. Using the `|bool` filter ensures that Ansible evaluates it in the Boolean context.

Similarly, for the second task, we would add the following immediately below the `notify` clause:

```
when:
  - recommendation_529|default(true)|bool
```

Now, if we run the playbook without doing anything else to it against a system that is not compliant, it behaves exactly as it did before, as shown in the following screenshot:

```
● ● ●                    james@automation-01: ~/hands-on-automation/chapter14/example03 (ssh)
~/hands-on-automation/chapter14/example03> ansible-playbook -i hosts site.yml

PLAY [Test and implement CIS benchmarks - section 5] ***************************

TASK [Gathering Facts] *********************************************************
ok: [centos-testhost]

TASK [rhel7cis_section5 : 5.2.8 Ensure SSH root login is disabled (Scored - L1S
L1W)] ***
changed: [centos-testhost]

TASK [rhel7cis_section5 : 5.2.9 Ensure SSH PermitEmptyPasswords is disabled (Sco
red - L1S L1W)] ***
changed: [centos-testhost]

RUNNING HANDLER [rhel7cis_section5 : Restart sshd] *****************************
changed: [centos-testhost]

PLAY RECAP *********************************************************************
centos-testhost            : ok=4    changed=3    unreachable=0    failed=0    s
kipped=0    rescued=0    ignored=0
```

The magic now happens when we want to run it against a system where we wish to skip one or both of these recommendations. Imagine that our host, `legacy-testhost`, is a legacy system where remote root logins are still a requirement. To use this role on this particular system, we know that we must set `recommendation_528` to `false`. This can be performed at a variety of levels, and the inventory is probably the most sensible place to define it as it prevents someone from accidentally running the playbook in the future without defining this and hence breaking our legacy code by denying remote root logins. We can create a new inventory for this system that might look something like this:

```
[legacyservers]
legacy-testhost

[legacyservers:vars]
recommendation_528=false
```

Having set the variable for the recommendation we want to skip to `false`, we can then run our role against this new inventory, and the results should look something like those shown in the following screenshot:

This was exactly what we desired – recommendation 5.2.8 was skipped on our legacy system, and all we had to do was define a variable in the inventory – the role code from all our other servers was reused.

Using the when clause with a simple Boolean variable works well for simple decisions like this, but what about when you have multiple criteria to evaluate? Although the when clause can evaluate both logical and and or constructs, this could become somewhat difficult to manage as complexity increases.

Ansible tags are the second tool that will help us here, and these are a special feature that is designed specifically to allow you to run only desired portions of a role or playbook, rather than having to run the whole thing from start to finish. Suppose that we add the following tags below our task for implementing recommendation 5.2.8:

```
tags:
  - notlegacy
  - allservers
```

Below the task for recommendation 5.2.9, we might add the following:

```
tags:
  - allservers
```

The behavior of these tags is best explained by example, and as this is a hands-on book, we will do exactly that. The first thing to note is that adding tags to a playbook (or role within a playbook) does absolutely nothing unless you specify which tags to run, or to skip. Thus, if we run our playbook in its current form, it behaves exactly as it always has, in spite of the addition of the tags, as the following screenshot shows:

The magic comes when we specify which tags are to be run. Let's repeat the previous command, but this time add `--skip-tags=notlegacy`. The switch does exactly what it implies – all tasks with the `notlegacy` tag are ignored. The following screenshot shows the output from such a run of this playbook:

```
james@automation-01: ~/hands-on-automation/chapter14/example04 (ssh)

~/hands-on-automation/chapter14/example04> ansible-playbook -i hosts site.yml --
skip-tags=notlegacy

PLAY [Test and implement CIS benchmarks - section 5] ***************************

TASK [Gathering Facts] ********************************************************
ok: [centos-testhost]

TASK [rhel7cis_section5 : 5.2.9 Ensure SSH PermitEmptyPasswords is disabled (Sco
red - L1S L1W)] ***
changed: [centos-testhost]

RUNNING HANDLER [rhel7cis_section5 : Restart sshd] ****************************
changed: [centos-testhost]

PLAY RECAP ********************************************************************
centos-testhost            : ok=3    changed=2    unreachable=0    failed=0    s
kipped=0    rescued=0    ignored=0
```

Here, we see a marked difference from the use of the `when` clause – where previously we observed that our task for recommendation 5.2.8 was evaluated but subsequently skipped, it does not even appear in the preceding playbook output – in short, the entire task has been treated as if it didn't exist.

If we had run the playbook with the `--tags=allservers` option, we would have observed both tasks running, as both were tagged with this value.

This becomes incredibly useful not only for our example here, but when considering the wider benchmark document. For example, we have already discussed that all recommendations are either level 1 or level 2. Equally, we know that some are scored, and some not.

Knowing that level 1 benchmarks are less likely to disrupt the day-to-day running of a Linux server, we could implement all recommendations in a playbook with the level as one of the tags for each, and then if we were to run the playbook with `--tag=level1`, then only the level 1 recommendations would be implemented. Working with this example, the tags for our task for recommendation 5.2.8 might be as follows:

```
tags:
    - notlegacy
    - allservers
    - level1
    - scored
```

When you are building up your roles and playbooks to implement security benchmarks, regardless of the operating system or security standard, it is recommended that you make use of the when clause and tags to the best of your advantage. Remember – when automating at enterprise scale, the last thing you want is lots of fragmented pieces of code to manage, all of which are similar but do slightly different things. The more you can standardize, the more manageable your enterprise will be, and appropriate use of these features will serve you well in ensuring you can maintain a single Ansible code base, and yet tailor its actions at runtime to handle the exceptions in your server estate.

Since we have been considering appropriate playbook and role structure for our security benchmark, we have deliberately kept our examples simple in this section. In the next section, we will revisit some of the more complex examples we highlighted in Chapter 13, *Using CIS Benchmarks*, and demonstrate how Ansible makes them far easier to code and understand.

Implementing more complex security benchmarks in Ansible

One of the examples we considered in detail in Chapter 13, *Using CIS Benchmarks*, was recommendation 3.1.2, which is concerned with packet redirect sending being disabled. This is considered important on any machine that is not supposed to be acting as a router (though it should not be implemented on a router as it would stop the router from functioning correctly).

On the face of it, this recommendation looks quite straightforward – we simply need to set these two kernel parameters, as follows:

```
net.ipv4.conf.all.send_redirects = 0
net.ipv4.conf.default.send_redirects = 0
```

In spite of this apparent simplicity, we ended up developing almost 60 lines of shell script to implement this check because we had to check both the currently active kernel parameters and persistent configuration file values, and then perform the appropriate changes if the values were not set as desired.

Here, once again, Ansible comes to our rescue. The sysctl module within Ansible wraps up many of the tests and configuration work that we constructed into our shell script. Further, we can use a loop so that the same task code can we run twice – once against each of the aforementioned kernel parameters.

When developing a role for this, we could define a single task that looks something like this:

```
---
- name: 3.1.2 Ensure packet redirect sending is disabled (Scored - L1S L1W)
  sysctl:
    name: "{{ item.paramname }}"
    value: "{{ item.paramvalue }}"
    reload: yes
    ignoreerrors: yes
    sysctl_set: yes
    state: present
  loop:
    - { paramname: net.ipv4.conf.all.send_redirects, paramvalue: 0 }
    - { paramname: net.ipv4.conf.default.send_redirects, paramvalue: 0 }
  notify:
    - Flush IPv4 routes
```

The recommendation also says that if we implement these changes, we should also flush out the IPv4 routes on the system. This is also achieved through a sysctl parameter, and so we simply use the sysctl module again, only this time in a handler:

```
- name: Flush IPv4 routes
  sysctl:
    name: net.ipv4.route.flush
    value: "1"
    sysctl_set: yes
```

Running this against a test system might yield output similar to that shown in the following screenshot:

```
● ● ●            james@automation-01: ~/hands-on-automation/chapter14/example05 (ssh)
~/hands-on-automation/chapter14/example05> ansible-playbook -i hosts site.yml

PLAY [Test and implement CIS benchmarks - section 3] ****************************

TASK [Gathering Facts] *********************************************************
ok: [centos-testhost]

TASK [rhel7cis_section3 : 3.1.2 Ensure packet redirect sending is disabled (Scor
ed - L1S L1W)] ***
changed: [centos-testhost] => (item={u'paramvalue': 0, u'paramname': u'net.ipv4.
conf.all.send_redirects'})
ok: [centos-testhost] => (item={u'paramvalue': 0, u'paramname': u'net.ipv4.conf.
default.send_redirects'})

RUNNING HANDLER [rhel7cis_section3 : Flush IPv4 routes] *************************
changed: [centos-testhost]

PLAY RECAP *********************************************************************
centos-testhost            : ok=3    changed=2    unreachable=0    failed=0    s
kipped=0    rescued=0    ignored=0
```

As we can see from the preceding screenshot, this code has run successfully and applied the setting recommended by the benchmark, and as a direct result of the change, the handler has fired and flushed the IPv4 routes. The overall result of this is that what took 57 lines of fairly unreadable shell script can now be achieved in 14 lines of far more readable YAML.

So far, we have built up a clear picture of how Ansible can make the design and implementation of CIS recommendations straightforward, especially when compared to alternatives such as shell scripting. We have noted that native Ansible modules such as `sysctl` and `lineinfile` can gracefully wrap up a multitude of steps that would have have been performed by a shell script. However, there are times when you, as the playbook author, must make some important decisions for your playbooks, and we will look at this in more detail in the following section.

Making appropriate decisions in your playbook design

As you build up your roles and playbooks to implement security baselines, you will discover that some of your implementation will be cut and dried (for example, you will almost certainly know whether you want root SSH logins to be possible or not), whereas there will be decisions to be made for other aspects. Time synchronization is one such example, and in this section, we will explore this in more detail to demonstrate the kinds of decisions you can expect to make when designing your roles, as well as how to address them in a constructive manner.

If you review *section 2.2.1* of the RHEL 7 CIS Benchmark (version 2.2.0), you will see that it is entirely concerned with time synchronization. Indeed, this is an important function in just about every Enterprise Linux infrastructure, and discrepancies between the clocks on servers can cause issues such as with certificate validity and Kerberos tickets.

Although it is almost universally agreed that time synchronization is vitally important, there is less agreement on the way to achieve it. For example, there are two main time synchronization services available for most mainstream Linux distributions:

- `chrony`
- `ntpd`

Although `chrony` is now the standard on RHEL 7, this does not mean that the venerable `ntpd` service will no longer work – in fact, some enterprises still choose to implement this because they have extensive experience with it.

It is entirely possible to get Ansible to detect which of these two services a given Linux server is using – at a high level, we could get Ansible to do the following:

1. Query the RPM package database to see whether `ntpd`, `chrony`, or both are installed.
2. If one or both are installed, detect which one is active:

    a. If neither are active, this needs rectifying as we have established the need for time synchronization.

    b. If both are active, the services will clash and one should be disabled.

As I'm sure you will see, there comes a point in the preceding process where an intervention is required – if neither service is started, we need to choose one to start. If both are active, we need to disable one. This is where Ansible's ability to help ends – it cannot decide for your particular enterprise which of these two perfectly valid services is best for your use case.

Thus, it is important to make a decision up-front about which time synchronization service you are using. With this decision made, playbooks can then be specifically coded to perform the appropriate checks and equally perform the appropriate remediation steps as required. In addition, we know from our discussion in Chapter 1, *Building a Standard Operating Environment on Linux*, that automation at enterprise scale is supported by commonality and standards – so we know from these principles that we should choose a standard time synchronization service and stick with it except where there is a good business reason to raise an exception.

To progress this example, let's look at recommendation 2.2.1.1. This states that we should ensure that a time synchronization service is in use – though it is agnostic about which one. If we have made our decision up-front about which service is relevant, our playbook development is easy. Suppose we have chosen chrony (the default for RHEL 7); our role for this recommendation might be as follows:

```
---
- name: 2.2.1.1 Ensure time synchronization is in use (Not Scored - L1S
L1W)
  yum:
    name: chrony
    state: present

- name: 2.2.1.1 Ensure time synchronization is in use (Not Scored - L1S
L1W)
  service:
    name: chronyd
    state: started
```

This simple code ensures that we both check for and satisfy recommendation 2.2.1.1 without the need for any logic to detect which time service is in use. Of course, we could choose to be more thorough and check that ntpd is not started, but this is left as an exercise to you.

Naturally, we cannot fit all the Ansible code that's required for the roughly 400 recommendations in this CIS Benchmark into this book – that would deserve an entire book to itself! In addition, this example is just for one benchmark – if your enterprise introduces a new operating system such as RHEL 8, you can be sure there will be a separate CIS Benchmark for this operating system that will need to be implemented. However, it is hoped that the development of these examples from the RHEL 7 CIS Benchmark is sufficient for you to design and build your own policy. Thus, in the next section of this chapter, we will look at techniques for making this task manageable at enterprise scale.

Application of enterprise-wide policies with Ansible

Although we have seen the significant benefits that Ansible can bring to CIS Benchmark implementation, I'm sure it is apparent at this stage that development and maintenance of these policies could turn into a full-time job, especially when coupled with the need to run them against the infrastructure and manage the results of each run.

Fortunately, the spirit of open source development brings a solution to this dilemma. Imagine if someone had already spent a great deal of time and effort developing a high-quality set of Ansible roles for implementing CIS Benchmarks, and that this was available as open source code so that you could audit it, ensure it was fit for your environment, and tailor it easily if required. Further, imagine that they had put a great deal of time and effort into tagging each task, and adding appropriate variable structure to allow you to easily specify your choices such as which time synchronization service your enterprise uses.

Thankfully, this work has already been completed by MindPoint Group, and their code has been made freely available on GitHub at `https://github.com/MindPointGroup/RHEL7-CIS`.

 At the time of writing, the latest CIS Benchmark available for EL7 systems is version 2.2.0, whereas the aforementioned playbooks are written against version 2.1.1 of the benchmark. It is up to you to ensure you are aware of the benchmark version you are implementing, as well as any possible security implications if you implement a slightly older version.

In addition to this, just as users of Ubuntu may choose paid support or to use the free open source operating system, and EL7 users may choose between Red Hat Enterprise Linux 7 or CentOS 7, MindPoint Group also offers a commercially supported version of their Ansible hardening code, available via `https://www.lockdownenterprise.com/`. Thus, they offer support for both ends of the spectrum, respecting that some enterprises will absolutely require an enterprise support contract, while others will prefer to use freely available open source software.

Let's explore how we might use the open source code against our CentOS 7 server:

1. First of all, we need to clone the GitHub repository:

   ```
   $ cd roles
   $ git clone https://github.com/MindPointGroup/RHEL7-CIS.git
   $ cd ..
   ```

2. Once this is complete, we can then proceed to use the code exactly as we would use any other role. Where appropriate, we should set variables, which can be set either in the inventory or in the main playbook (more on this in a second).

   Thus, the purest and simplest possible implementation of the MindPoint Group CIS Benchmark in Ansible once the role has been cloned from GitHub is a playbook that looks like this:

   ```
   ---
   - name: Implement EL7 CIS benchmark
     hosts: all
     become: yes

     roles:
       - RHEL7-CIS
   ```

3. With these steps complete, you can literally begin implementing the EL7 benchmark and its near 400 recommendations on your Linux servers in a matter of minutes – the playbook is run in the normal manner, and will produce many pages of output as all the checks are performed and recommendations implemented (if/when required). The following screenshot shows the playbook being run and the initial page of output:

```
● ● ●              james@automation-01: ~/hands-on-automation/chapter14/example07 (ssh)
~/hands-on-automation/chapter14/example07> ansible-playbook -i hosts site.yml

PLAY [Implement EL7 CIS benchmark] ********************************************

TASK [Gathering Facts] ********************************************************
ok: [centos-testhost]

TASK [RHEL7-CIS : Check OS version and family] ********************************
skipping: [centos-testhost]

TASK [RHEL7-CIS : Check ansible version] **************************************
skipping: [centos-testhost]

TASK [RHEL7-CIS : PRELIM | List users accounts] *******************************
ok: [centos-testhost]

TASK [RHEL7-CIS : PRELIM | Gather accounts with empty password fields] *********
ok: [centos-testhost]

TASK [RHEL7-CIS : PRELIM | Gather UID 0 accounts other than root] **************
ok: [centos-testhost]

TASK [RHEL7-CIS : PRELIM | Section 4.1 | Configure System Accounting (auditd)] *
**
ok: [centos-testhost]
```

Now, a word on variables. As we established in the previous section (*Writing Ansible security policies*), there will be occasions where you need to vary your playbook run. The variables and tags are all documented in the README.md file that accompanies the GitHub repository we cloned earlier, and for purposes of illustration, let's consider a few examples.

First off, suppose we only want to implement the level 1 recommendations (those that are less risky to day-to-day operations). This can be achieved by running the playbook and using the level1 tag:

```
$ ansible-playbook -i hosts site.yml --tags=level1
```

Alternatively, you might be running the hardening playbooks against a set of servers that act as routers. In this instance, we would need to set the `rhel7cis_is_router` variable to `false` to ensure that kernel parameters that disable router functionality are not set.

This could be done on the command line as follows:

```
$ ansible-playbook -i hosts site.yml -e rhel7cis_is_router=true
```

However, this is very manual, and it would be far too easy for someone to accidentally run the playbook without setting this variable, suddenly disabling the router.

It would be far better to set this variable at the inventory level, thus ensuring that it is always set correctly whenever the playbook is run. Thus, we might create an inventory such as this:

```
[routers]
router-testhost

[routers:vars]
rhel7cis_is_router=true
```

With this inventory in place, running the playbook against the routers is performed using a command such as the following:

```
$ ansible-playbook -i routers site.yml
```

As long as this inventory file is used, there is no danger of someone forgetting to set the `rhel7cis_is_router` variable to `true`.

Of course, this discussion does not mean that you must download and use these playbooks – it is still entirely possible to develop and maintain your own playbooks to your own requirements. Indeed, there may be situations in which this strategy is actually preferable.

What is important is that you choose the strategy that is best for your enterprise. When selecting your strategy for implementing security policy at scale, you should take the following into account:

- Whether you want to own your own code (with all the advantages and disadvantages that brings)
- Whether you want to be responsible for the maintenance of your code base going forward
- That you should standardize on one code base as far as possible to ensure your code structure remains maintainable
- Whether you need third-party support on implementing these benchmarks or whether you are happy that you have the skills and resources in-house

Once you have made your evaluation, you will be well placed to define your path forward with creating Ansible playbooks to implement your chosen security standards. It is intended that the information provided to you in this chapter so far will be sufficient to support you in whichever path you choose. Although we have focused on EL7 (Red Hat Enterprise Linux 7 and CentOS 7) in this chapter, everything we have discussed will scale well to other operating systems for which there exist security benchmarks (for example, Ubuntu Server 18.04). In fact, if you run through the processes we have discussed within this chapter using the CIS Benchmark for Ubuntu Server 18.04, you will find a great deal of similarity can be achieved.

So far, we have dealt almost exclusively with the implementation of CIS Benchmarks. This chapter would not be complete, however, without providing a method to check levels of enforcement without the need to make changes. After all, auditing is an important part of most enterprise policies, especially where security is concerned, yet changes must be made under an authorized change request window.

Testing security policies with Ansible

As we have discussed so far, it is important to ensure that not only can you implement security policies in an efficient and repeatable manner, but that it should also be possible to audit them. There are a variety of tools available for this task, both closed source and open source. Before we consider any other tools, though, it is worthwhile looking at how Ansible itself can assist with this task.

Let's return to one of our original examples, where we were implementing two of the recommendations from *section 5* of the CIS Benchmark.

Previously, we ran this with the following command:

```
$ ansible-playbook -i hosts site.yml
```

This ran through the two checks, implementing the changes if the system was not already compliant with the security recommendations. However, Ansible also has a mode of operation called check mode. In this mode, Ansible does not make any changes to the remote system(s) – rather, it tries to predict all changes that might be made to the systems instead.

Not all modules are compatible with check mode, and so some care is advised when using this mode. For example, Ansible cannot possibly know the output of running a particular shell command using the `shell` module, as there are so many possible permutations of commands. Also, running shell commands might be destructive or cause a change to the system, and so any tasks that use the `shell` module are skipped during a check run.

However, many of the core modules we have already used, such as `yum`, `lineinfile`, and `sysctl`, do support check mode and so can be used quite effectively in this mode.

Thus, if we run our example playbook again, only this time in check mode, we would see an output similar to what's shown in the following screenshot:

```
● ● ●              james@automation-01: ~/hands-on-automation/chapter14/example08 (ssh)

~/hands-on-automation/chapter14/example08> ansible-playbook -C -i hosts site.yml


PLAY [Test and implement CIS benchmarks - section 5] ****************************

TASK [Gathering Facts] *********************************************************
ok: [centos-testhost]

TASK [rhel7cis_section5 : 5.2.8 Ensure SSH root login is disabled (Scored - L1S
L1W)] ***
changed: [centos-testhost]

TASK [rhel7cis_section5 : 5.2.9 Ensure SSH PermitEmptyPasswords is disabled (Sco
red - L1S L1W)] ***
changed: [centos-testhost]

RUNNING HANDLER [rhel7cis_section5 : Restart sshd] *****************************
changed: [centos-testhost]

PLAY RECAP *********************************************************************
centos-testhost            : ok=4    changed=3    unreachable=0    failed=0    s
kipped=0    rescued=0    ignored=0
```

You will notice that this looks exactly like any other playbook run – there are, in fact, no clues at all that it is running in check mode, other than the -C flag on the command line invoking this run. However, if you examine the target system, you will see that no changes were made.

The preceding output is very useful, though, for auditing processes – it demonstrates to us that the target system does not meet the recommendations for either *section 5.2.8* or *5.2.9* of the benchmark – if these were met, then the result should have been `ok`. Equally, we know that the handler only fires in the event that changes are required on the remote system, and again this tells us that the system is not compliant in some way.

It is accepted that some interpretation of the output is going to be required – however, by exercising good design practices in your roles when you write them (especially when putting the benchmark section number and title into the task names), then you can very quickly start to interpret the output and see which systems are not compliant, and further, which recommendations specifically they fail on.

Further, the variable structure we put in place to determine which tasks are run and when still applies in check mode, so if we run this playbook on the legacy hosts that need remote root logins enabled (but this time in check mode), we can see that this task is skipped, ensuring that we don't get false positives during an audit. The following screenshot shows this being run:

```
james@automation-01: ~/hands-on-automation/chapter14/example08 (ssh)

~/hands-on-automation/chapter14/example08> ansible-playbook -C -i legacyhosts si
te.yml

PLAY [Test and implement CIS benchmarks - section 5] ***************************

TASK [Gathering Facts] ********************************************************
ok: [legacy-testhost]

TASK [rhel7cis_section5 : 5.2.8 Ensure SSH root login is disabled (Scored - L1S
L1W)] ***
skipping: [legacy-testhost]

TASK [rhel7cis_section5 : 5.2.9 Ensure SSH PermitEmptyPasswords is disabled (Sco
red - L1S L1W)] ***
changed: [legacy-testhost]

RUNNING HANDLER [rhel7cis_section5 : Restart sshd] ****************************
changed: [legacy-testhost]

PLAY RECAP ********************************************************************
legacy-testhost            : ok=3    changed=2    unreachable=0    failed=0    s
kipped=1    rescued=0    ignored=0
```

In this manner (coupled with good playbook design), Ansible code can be reused not just for implementation purposes, but for auditing purposes too.

It is hoped that this chapter has given you sufficient knowledge to proceed with confidence when it comes to implementing security hardening on your Linux servers at enterprise scale, and even auditing them as part of an ongoing process.

Summary

Ansible is an incredibly powerful tool that lends itself well to the implementation and auditing of security benchmarks such as the CIS security benchmark. We have demonstrated through practical example how it can reduce a shell script of nearly 60 lines down to less than 20, and how the same code can be easily reused in a variety of scenarios, and even be used to audit security policies across the enterprise.

In this chapter, you learned how to write Ansible playbooks to apply server hardening benchmarks such as CIS. You then gained hands-on knowledge of applying server hardening policies across the enterprise using Ansible, and how to make use of publicly available open source roles to assist you in this. Finally, you learned about how Ansible supports testing and auditing of successful policy application.

In the next chapter, we will look at an open source tool called **OpenSCAP** that can be used to perform effective auditing of security policies across the enterprise.

Questions

1. How do Ansible modules such as `lineinfile` make security benchmark implementation code more efficient than shell scripting?
2. How can Ansible tasks be made conditional for a specific server or group of servers?
3. What are good practices for naming your tasks when writing Ansible tasks to implement the CIS Benchmark?
4. How might you modify a playbook so that you can easily get the CIS level 1 benchmarks to run without any of the level 2 ones being evaluated?
5. What is the difference between the `--tags` and `--skip-tags` options when running an Ansible playbook?
6. Why would you want to make use of publicly available open source code for your CIS Benchmark implementation?
7. What does the `-C` flag do to a playbook run when used with the `ansible-playbook` command?
8. Does the `shell` module support check mode?

Further reading

- To review common questions about the CIS Benchmarks, please refer to `https:/` `/www.cisecurity.org/cis-benchmarks/cis-benchmarks-faq/`.
- A full list of CIS Benchmarks is available at `https://www.cisecurity.org/cis-` `benchmarks/`.
- For an in-depth understanding of Ansible, please refer to *Mastering Ansible, Third Edition* by *James Freeman* and *Jesse Keating* (`https://www.packtpub.com/gb/` `virtualization-and-cloud/mastering-ansible-third-edition`).

15
Auditing Security Policy with OpenSCAP

Throughout the two chapters that preceded this one, we established the value of applying a security policy such as the CIS Benchmark to your Enterprise Linux infrastructure. We have discussed a variety of methods for both applying it and ensuring it remains enforced; the latter point is especially important in an infrastructure where a wide array of people have superuser access to your Linux servers. Although we have established ways that both shell scripting and Ansible can assist with auditing the compliance of your infrastructure with your chosen security policy, we have also established that neither of these are particularly suited to providing readable and actionable reports of a large infrastructure. For example, it is entirely reasonable that an infrastructure security team might want a readable report showing the compliance of the infrastructure with the security policy, and neither shell scripting nor Ansible immediately lend themselves to this task.

Although there are a wide variety of infrastructure scanning tools available on the market, most of these are commercial and the focus of this book is on open source solutions that are accessible to any enterprise, regardless of their budget. Hence, in this chapter, we will consider the freely available OpenSCAP tool. **SCAP** stands for **Security Content Automation Protocol**, and it is a standardized solution for checking a Linux infrastructure for compliance against a given security policy (in our case, CIS). OpenSCAP is hence an open source implementation of SCAP that has been widely adopted by Enterprise Linux vendors including Red Hat. We will hence explore the process for setting up your own OpenSCAP infrastructure for compliance scanning and reporting. This, in turn, will enable all teams with a vested interest in infrastructure security to get oversight of the levels of compliance.

Specifically, we will cover the following topics in this chapter:

- Installing your OpenSCAP server
- Evaluating and selecting policies
- Scanning the enterprise with OpenSCAP
- Interpreting results

Technical requirements

This chapter includes examples based on the following technologies:

- Ubuntu Server 18.04 LTS
- CentOS 7.6
- Ansible 2.8

To run through these examples, you will need access to two servers or virtual machines running one each of the operating systems listed previously and Ansible.

All example code discussed in this book is available from GitHub at: `https://github.com/PacktPublishing/Hands-On-Enterprise-Automation-on-Linux`.

Installing your OpenSCAP server

When it comes to scanning your infrastructure, we have a few decisions to make, as the OpenSCAP project provides a few tools that have overlapping functions. The reason for this is that they are targeted at different audiences—some are purely command line-driven and so lend themselves extremely well to scheduled, scripted tasks such as a monthly compliance report. At the time of writing, there are a total of five OpenSCAP tools available, and we will look at each of these in more detail in the following sections to enable you to make an educated decision as to which tool (or tools) are right for your enterprise.

In the following subsection, we will start by looking at the most fundamental tool, OpenSCAP Base.

Running OpenSCAP Base

The OpenSCAP Base tool provides the very fundamentals required to scan a single Linux machine and report on its compliance against a given policy. It actually consists of two components and so is a requirement for some of the other tools we will look at in the following subsections.

The first component of this tool is a command-line utility called `oscap`. This tool can be run on the local machine using an appropriate security policy and profile to produce a report of compliance. The report is generated in HTML and so although the process of report creation is very much manual, the final report is very easy to read and so is well suited for sending to a security or compliance team for audit or evaluation.

The second component of OpenSCAP Base includes a library that is used as a building block for other OpenSCAP services such as SCAP Workbench and the OpenSCAP Daemon—we will cover these in greater detail later in this section.

In this book, we will only make use of the library when we use other OpenSCAP tools. We will see these tools in action later in this chapter in the section entitled *Scanning the enterprise with OpenSCAP*. For now, though, we will concern ourselves with the installation of OpenSCAP Base.

Installing OpenSCAP Base by hand on a single machine is incredibly easy—it already comes pre-packaged for the two key Linux distributions we have explored in this book—Ubuntu Server and CentOS (and hence, by extension, Red Hat Enterprise Linux). To install it on CentOS 7 or RHEL 7, you would simply run the following command:

```
$ sudo yum -y install openscap-scanner
```

Similarly, on Ubuntu Server 18.04 LTS, you would run this:

```
$ sudo apt -y install libopenscap8
```

It is important to remember that these packages include both the `oscap` command-line tool and the library as stated earlier in this section. Hence, even if you never intend to run OpenSCAP using the `oscap` CLI tool, the libraries that these packages contain could still be required for your given use case (for example, performing remote scans using SCAP Workbench).

As a result, it is important to consider deploying these packages using Ansible, and it may even be desirable to include them in your standard build image so that you know that you can remotely scan any given Linux server for compliance without needing to perform any prerequisite steps. We will look at how to run scans with the `oscap` tool in a subsequent section, entitled *Scanning the enterprise with OpenSCAP*—however, for now, it is sufficient to understand what this package is and why it might be required.

In the next section, we will look at installing the OpenSCAP Daemon, another part of the OpenSCAP toolset.

Installing the OpenSCAP Daemon

Security auditing is not a one-time task—given administrator-level (that is, root) access in a Linux environment, someone could make a Linux server non-compliant at any given time, either deliberately or through a well-meaning change. Hence, the results of a security scan really only guarantee that the server being scanned was compliant (or not) at the time of the scan itself.

Hence, regular scanning of the environment is extremely important. There is a myriad of ways to achieve this, and you could even run the `oscap` command-line tool using a scheduler such as `cron` or via a scheduled Ansible playbook in AWX or Ansible Tower. However, the OpenSCAP Daemon is a native tool provided as part of the suite of OpenSCAP tools. Its purpose is to run in the background and perform scheduled scans against a given target or set of targets. This might be the local machine running the daemon, or it might be a set of remote machines, all accessed over SSH.

The process of installation is again extremely simple—if you were to do this manually, you would, on an EL7 system (for example, RHEL7 or CentOS 7), run the following:

```
$ sudo yum -y install openscap-daemon
```

On Ubuntu systems, the package name is identical, so you would run the following to install it:

```
$ sudo apt -y install openscap-daemon
```

Although you could set up every machine in your Linux environment with this daemon and configure a job for each to scan itself regularly, this is prone to abuse as it would be easy for someone with root access to disable or otherwise tamper with the scan. As a result, we recommend that you consider setting up a centralized scanning architecture, with one central secure server performing remote scans across your network.

It is upon such a server that you would install the OpenSCAP Daemon and, once completed, you can use the `oscapd-cli` utility to configure your regular scans. We will take a more detailed look at this later in this chapter, in the section entitled *Scanning the enterprise with OpenSCAP*.

Although both of the tools we have considered so far are extremely powerful and can perform all of your auditing needs, they are entirely command-line-based and so might not be suited to users who are not comfortable in a shell environment or who are responsible for auditing scan results but not necessarily running them. This requirement is fulfilled by another tool in the OpenSCAP armory—**SCAP Workbench**. We shall look at installing this in the next section.

Running SCAP Workbench

SCAP Workbench is a graphical user interface to the SCAP toolset that is designed to provide users with an easy, intuitive way of performing common scanning tasks. Hence, it is well suited to less technical users or those who are more comfortable in a graphical environment.

One thing of consideration is that SCAP Workbench is a graphical tool, and in many environments, Linux servers are run headless and without the graphical X environment installed. Hence, if you install it on an ordinary Linux server without a graphical environment, you will see an error such as the one shown in the following screenshot:

Thankfully there are several ways to run SCAP Workbench. First of all, it is worth noting that it is a true cross-platform application, with downloads available for Windows, macOS, and most common Linux platforms, and as a result, the easiest path for most users will be to run it in their native operating system.

If, for consistency, you wish to run SCAP Workbench on Linux, you would either need to set up a remote X11 session or set up a dedicated scanning host that includes the graphical desktop environment. There is no right or wrong approach here—it really is up to you to decide which path suits your environment and working patterns best.

If you choose to run from Linux, the installation of SCAP Workbench is no more difficult than for any of the other OpenSCAP tools we have considered:

1. To install it on RHEL7/CentOS 7, you would run the following:

```
$ sudo yum -y install scap-workbench
```

On Ubuntu Server, you would run this:

```
$ sudo apt -y install scap-workbench
```

2. Once this is complete, you can then open SCAP Workbench using the appropriate method for your chosen operating system. If you are running it on a Linux server using a remote X session, it is as simple as running this command:

```
$ scap-workbench &
```

We will explore how to set up and run a scan from this graphical environment later in this chapter, in the section entitled *Scanning the enterprise with OpenSCAP*. Before we complete this part of this chapter, though, we will discuss two of the other tools on offer from the OpenSCAP project—SCAPTimony and the Anaconda Addon.

Considering other OpenSCAP tools

So far in this chapter, we have considered a variety of OpenSCAP tools for scanning and auditing your infrastructure. There are, however, two further tools available to you that we have not yet considered, though neither are truly interactive tools in the way that the ones we have considered so far are, and so they are not within the scope of this book. Nonetheless, they deserve a mention as you may choose to integrate them into your environment in the future.

One of these tools is called **SCAPTimony**. Rather than being an end user application such as SCAP Workbench or `oscap`, this is a middleware, Ruby-on-Rails engine that is designed for you to integrate into your own Rails-based application. The benefit that SCAPTimony brings is that it provides both a database and storage platform for your SCAP scan results. Hence, if you do decide to write your own Rails application to handle your OpenSCAP scanning, this can be written to provide centralized reporting on OpenSCAP scans. It also enables your Rails application to manipulate and aggregate the data gathered and so is an incredibly powerful tool in managing your scan data.

Although developing a Rails application to make use of SCAPTimony is beyond the scope of this book, it is worth considering that the Katello project (and hence Red Hat Satellite 6) already makes use of SCAPTimony and so would form a good basis for you to make use of this tool without the need to create your own application.

The final tool available at the time of writing is the OSCAP Anaconda Addon. For those who are not familiar, Anaconda is the installation environment used by Linux distributions such as CentOS and Red Hat Enterprise Linux. Although this add-on cannot help us with our Ubuntu-based servers, it does provide a way to build Red Hat-based servers that are compliant from the point of installation.

As we have already considered ways to apply security policy using Ansible (see Chapter 14, *CIS Hardening with Ansible*) and have heavily advocated the use of standard images for your Linux environment, which we created in Chapter 5, *Using Ansible to Build Virtual Machine Templates for Deployment*, and Chapter 6, *Custom Builds with PXE Booting*, we will not be exploring this add-on as it duplicates functionality we have already provided cross-platform solutions for elsewhere.

By now, you should hopefully have a good feel for the OpenSCAP tools, and which might be the best fit for your environment. Before we can proceed with our first scan, however, we need an OpenSCAP security policy to utilize. In the next section, we will look at where to download these policies and how to select the right one for your environment.

Evaluating and selecting policies

OpenSCAP and its related tools are by themselves engines—they cannot actually help you to audit your environment without a security policy against which to scan. As we explored in Chapter 13, *Using CIS Benchmarks*, there are numerous security standards for Linux, and in this book, we have considered in depth the CIS Benchmarks. Sadly, this standard is not currently available for audit through OpenSCAP, though many other security policies are that would be well suited to securing your infrastructure. Also, as OpenSCAP and its policies are entirely open source, there is nothing to stop you from creating your own policy for whatever requirements you have.

There are plenty of security standards available for you to freely download and audit your infrastructure against, and in the next section, we will look at the primary one that you will most likely wish to consider—SCAP Security Guide.

Installing SCAP Security Guide

Some of the most comprehensive, ready-made security policies can be found as part of the **SCAP Security Guide** (**SSG**) project, and you will often find reference to the `ssg` acronym in the directory and sometimes even package names. These policies, just like the CIS Benchmark we explored previously, cover many facets of Linux security and offer remediation steps. Hence, OpenSCAP can be used not just for auditing, but also for enforcing a security policy. However, it must be stated that given its nature, it is my opinion that Ansible is best suited for this task, and it is notable that, in recent upstream releases of SCAP Security Guide, Ansible playbooks are now being provided alongside the XML formatted SCAP policies themselves.

OpenSCAP policies, like any security definition, will evolve and change over time as new vulnerabilities and attacks are discovered. Hence, when considering which version of SSG you wish to work with, you will need to take into account how up to date the copy you are using is and whether this meets your needs. It might seem obvious to state that you should always use the latest version, but there are exceptions as we shall see shortly.

This decision requires careful consideration, and it is not as obvious as it might at first seem to state, *just go and download the latest copy*. Although the versions that are included with most major Linux distributions tend to lag behind the versions available from the SSG project's GitHub page (see `https://github.com/ComplianceAsCode/content/releases`), in some cases (especially on Red Hat Enterprise Linux), they have been tested and are known to work on the Linux distribution they are provided with.

On other distributions, however, your mileage may vary. For example, at the time of writing, the latest publicly available version of the SSG policies is 0.1.47, while the version included with Ubuntu Server 18.04.3 is 0.1.31. This version of SSG does not even support Ubuntu 18.04, and if you attempt to run a scan against Ubuntu Server 18.04 using the Ubuntu 16.04 policy, all of the scan results will be `notapplicable`. All scans validate the host on which they are run and ensure it matches the one they were intended to be run against, and so if they detect a mismatch, they will report `notapplicable` rather than applying the tests.

 There is also a bug in the `libopenscap8` package on Ubuntu 18.04, which results in errors regarding the `/usr/share/openscap/cpe/openscap-cpe-dict.xml` file as missing. It is hoped that, in due course, the Ubuntu OpenSCAP packages are updated and fixed so that they can be used reliably.

Users of Red Hat Enterprise Linux will need to find that Red Hat will only support users with their OpenSCAP scanning if they are using the SSG policies that ship with RHEL, and so in this scenario, it is even more important to make use of the vendor-provided policy files.

As with any open source environment, the beauty is that the choice is up to you—if you wish to evaluate the newer policies available, then you are free to do so, and for Ubuntu 18.04, you must do this or the scans will not work! However, if you wish to take advantage of a commercially-supported environment, then that is available too, especially if you use RHEL.

To install the vendor-provided SSG packages on CentOS 7 or RHEL 7, you would run this command:

```
$ sudo yum -y install scap-security-guide
```

This package contains the SSG policies for all operating systems and applications that Red Hat directly supports (bearing in mind that CentOS is based on RHEL). Hence, you will only find policies for RHEL 6 and 7, CentOS 6 and 7, the **Java Runtime Environment (JRE)**, and Firefox when you install this package. At the time of writing, this installs version 0.1.43 of the SSG.

On Ubuntu Server, SSG is split across multiple packages but offers cross-platform support. To install the complete set of SSG packages on Ubuntu Server 18.04, you would run the following:

```
$ sudo apt -y install ssg-base ssg-debderived ssg-debian ssg-nondebian ssg-
applications
```

These packages provide policies for the following systems:

ssg-base	SSG Base content and documentation files
ssg-debderived	SSG policies for Debian-derived operating systems such as Ubuntu Server
ssg-debian	SSG policies for Debian operating systems
ssg-nondebian	SSG policies for other Linux operating systems such as RHEL and SuSE Enterprise Linux
ssg-applications	SSG policies for securing applications such as the **Java Runtime Environment (JRE)**, Firefox, and Webmin

Hence, it is fair to say that, at the time of writing, although Ubuntu Server ships a much older package version (0.1.13), it offers support for a wider range of platforms.

The choice of which SSG you wish to install is up to you, or if you are feeling bold, you may even choose to write your own! The most important thing is that you make an informed choice and retain support from your operating system vendor if that is a requirement for you. Before we proceed to explore other policies you might also download, it is worth looking in greater detail at two of the security policy file formats you may come across when you are searching for and implementing your OpenSCAP auditing architecture. We shall proceed with this in the next section.

Understanding the purpose of XCCDF and OVAL policies

When you download policies, you will often find that you see the terms **Open Vulnerability and Assessment Language** (**OVAL**) and **eXtensible Configuration Checklist Description Format** (**XCCDF**). Some security policies you will come across are only available in OVAL format. Hence, we must take a moment to consider these different file types.

First of all, it is important to state that they are not interchangeable—instead, they should be thought of as hierarchical in nature. At the lower level in the hierarchy is the OVAL file, which in essence describes all of the system-level checks that the OpenSCAP scanning engine should perform. This might, for example, consist of checking whether a given package is newer than a given version as a known vulnerability might exist in the older one. Or it might be a check to ensure that an important system file such as /etc/passwd is owned by root.

These checks are all incredibly valuable when it comes to auditing a system's compliance against your security policy, but they might not be very readable for managers or security teams. They would be more interested in a high-level security policy, such as *Verify Permissions on Important Files and Directories*. Indeed, this check would almost certainly encompass the check on the ownership of /etc/passwd, along with a whole set of other vital system files such as /etc/group and /etc/shadow.

This is where the XCCDF format becomes relevant—this can be thought of as the next level in the hierarchy as it provides a set of human-readable security policies (along with valuable documentation and references) that would be useful to an audience such as a manager or information security team. These describe the state of a system in reference to the checks performed by the OVAL definition. The XCCDF files do not contain any check definitions for the scanning engine (for example, oscap)—instead, they reference the checks that have been written in the OVAL file and hence can be thought of as sitting on top of the OVAL files in the hierarchy.

Therefore, an OVAL file can be used for auditing purposes in isolation, but an XCCDF file cannot be used unless its corresponding OVAL file is present.

XCCDF files also contain a selection of scanning profiles that tell the scanning engine what your policy looks like, and hence what it should scan for. This will almost certainly mean only scanning for a subset of the checks that are present in the OVAL file.

The profiles available can easily be listed using the graphical SCAP Workbench tool or on the command line by using the oscap info command. An example of this command run against SSG for CentOS 7 is shown in the following screenshot:

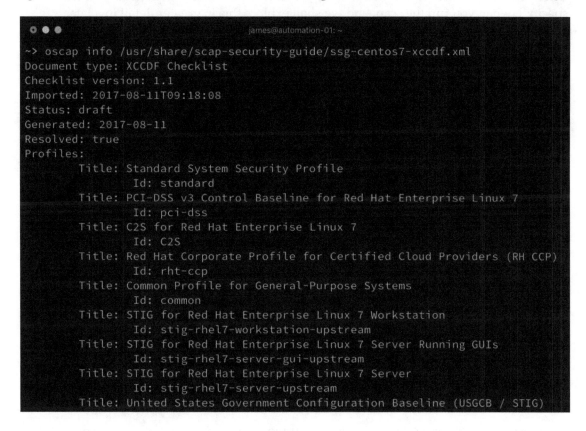

```
~> oscap info /usr/share/scap-security-guide/ssg-centos7-xccdf.xml
Document type: XCCDF Checklist
Checklist version: 1.1
Imported: 2017-08-11T09:18:08
Status: draft
Generated: 2017-08-11
Resolved: true
Profiles:
        Title: Standard System Security Profile
              Id: standard
        Title: PCI-DSS v3 Control Baseline for Red Hat Enterprise Linux 7
              Id: pci-dss
        Title: C2S for Red Hat Enterprise Linux 7
              Id: C2S
        Title: Red Hat Corporate Profile for Certified Cloud Providers (RH CCP)
              Id: rht-ccp
        Title: Common Profile for General-Purpose Systems
              Id: common
        Title: STIG for Red Hat Enterprise Linux 7 Workstation
              Id: stig-rhel7-workstation-upstream
        Title: STIG for Red Hat Enterprise Linux 7 Server Running GUIs
              Id: stig-rhel7-server-gui-upstream
        Title: STIG for Red Hat Enterprise Linux 7 Server
              Id: stig-rhel7-server-upstream
        Title: United States Government Configuration Baseline (USGCB / STIG)
```

Although the output has been truncated in the interests of space, you can clearly see the wide array of security profiles available for CentOS 7. You will notice in the screenshot that (for example) there are different profiles for CentOS 7 servers that run graphical user interfaces and for those that don't. This is because additional security measures are required on a graphical system to ensure that the X Windows subsystem is properly secured. There is a profile suitable for **Payment Card Industry** (**PCI**) environments and at the top, the most basic profile, which should be the minimum viable security policy suitable for just about any CentOS 7 server.

Once you know which profile you wish to use from your XCCDF policy file, you will specify it when you run the scan, and we shall explore this in greater detail in a later section, entitled *Scanning the enterprise with OpenSCAP*.

Before we conclude this section, it is important to state that OVAL files do not have profiles, and if you run an OVAL scan, you will automatically run all tests defined in the OVAL file on your system regardless of its purpose. This may be problematic because, taking the CentOS 7 SSG OVAL file as an example, this contains tests for the security of the X Windows graphical subsystem. These tests will fail on a system that does not have a GUI installed, and so might present false positives in your scan results.

> It is important to note that SCAP Workbench only supports scanning with XCCDF policies, and so if you are using a profile that only includes an OVAL file, you will need to use a different scanning tool.

Now that we understand more about the file formats of the various security policies you might download, let's take a look at some of the other security profiles you may wish to download.

Installing other OpenSCAP policies

It is highly possible that the SSG security policies will form the core of your auditing framework with OpenSCAP—however, given the open source nature of OpenSCAP, it is entirely possible for anyone, including you, to write a policy file.

The most likely policies you would wish to supplement your SSG ones with are ones that can check the patch level of your servers. Given the frequent nature at which patches are released for Linux operating systems, integrating such policies with SSG would create a headache for the maintainers, and so they are generally kept separate.

For example, on your CentOS 7 server, you can download the following security policy (note that it is available in OVAL format only):

```
$ wget
https://www.redhat.com/security/data/oval/com.redhat.rhsa-RHEL7.xml.bz2
$ bunzip2 com.redhat.rhsa-RHEL7.xml.bz2
```

This contains checks for all CentOS 7 (and RHEL 7) package vulnerabilities that have been found to date and checks the installed versions to ensure that they are newer than the versions where known vulnerabilities existed. Hence, this can very easily generate a report that can show you whether you need to patch your CentOS 7 or RHEL 7 systems urgently.

A similar list is available from Canonical for Ubuntu Server 18.04, which can be downloaded as follows:

```
$ wget
https://people.canonical.com/~ubuntu-security/oval/com.ubuntu.bionic.cve.ov
al.xml.bz2
$ bunzip2 com.ubuntu.bionic.cve.oval.xml.bz2
```

Once again, this contains a list of all packages vulnerabilities that have been found on Ubuntu Server 18.04 and again checks to ensure that the package versions installed on your system are newer than the vulnerable versions. For both of these security policies, all checks are run every time as they are in OVAL format—however, tests only report a failure if a package is installed and is older than the version containing the fix for the given vulnerability. Hence, you should not receive any false positives resulting from running these scans.

Unlike the SSG policies, these policies are updated regularly—at the time of writing, the Ubuntu package vulnerability scanning profile we downloaded using the preceding commands was only one hour old! As a result, part of your auditing process must involve downloading the latest package vulnerability OVAL policies and scanning against these—possibly a good job for Ansible (though this is left as an exercise for you).

By now, you should have a good understanding of the types of policies you can download, the formats you may come across them in, and what their intended purposes are. Hence, in the next section, we will proceed to demonstrate how they can be used to scan your Linux hosts and audit your compliance against your chosen security policies.

Scanning the enterprise with OpenSCAP

So far in this chapter, we have covered the various tools available from the OpenSCAP project and the security policies you might wish to employ to scan your Enterprise Linux environment. Now that we have completed that groundwork, it's time to take a look at how to make use of these to actually scan your infrastructure. As we have discussed, there are three key tools that you might use to scan your infrastructure. We will start off this process by exploring the `oscap` command-line tool in the next section.

Scanning the Linux infrastructure with OSCAP

As we discussed earlier in this chapter, the `oscap` tool is a command-line utility designed for scanning the local machine that it is installed on. The security policies that you wish to audit the host against must also be on the filesystem of the host that it runs on. If you have completed the steps in the section entitled *Evaluating and selecting policies*, then you should already have everything you need.

With that said, if using the `oscap` tool to scan your infrastructure is going to be your way forward, you may wish to consider Ansible as a tool to both install it and gather the results when the scan is complete.

Before we come to this, let's look at how we might scan a single host:

1. Assuming that we are working on our Ubuntu 18.04 server and that we have unpacked the latest upstream SSG into our current working directory so that we have the required Ubuntu 18.04 support, we would use the `oscap info` command to query the XCCDF policy file to see which policies are available to us:

```
$ oscap info scap-security-guide-0.1.47/ssg-ubuntu1804-ds.xml
```

The output of the `info` command will yield something like that shown in the following screenshot:

```
●  ●  ●                          james@automation-01: ~
Stream: scap_org.open-scap_datastream_from_xccdf_ssg-ubuntu1804-xccdf-1.2.xml
Generated: (null)
Version: 1.3
Checklists:
        Ref-Id: scap_org.open-scap_cref_ssg-ubuntu1804-xccdf-1.2.xml
                Status: draft
                Generated: 2019-11-05
                Resolved: true
                Profiles:
                        Title: Profile for ANSSI DAT-NT28 Average (Intermediate)
Level
                              Id: xccdf_org.ssgproject.content_profile_anssi_np
_nt28_average
                        Title: Profile for ANSSI DAT-NT28 High (Enforced) Level
                              Id: xccdf_org.ssgproject.content_profile_anssi_np
_nt28_high
                        Title: Profile for ANSSI DAT-NT28 Minimal Level
                              Id: xccdf_org.ssgproject.content_profile_anssi_np
_nt28_minimal
                        Title: Profile for ANSSI DAT-NT28 Restrictive Level
                              Id: xccdf_org.ssgproject.content_profile_anssi_np
_nt28_restrictive
                        Title: Standard System Security Profile for Ubuntu 18.04
                              Id: xccdf_org.ssgproject.content_profile_standard
                Referenced check files:
```

2. From here, we will choose the profile (or profiles—after all, you could always run more than one scan) that you wish to audit against. In our case, we are running a *general-purpose* server, so we will choose the profile with `Id`: `xccdf_org.ssgproject.content_profile_standard`.

3. To run this scan, and save the output in a human-readable HTML report, you would then run a command such as the following:

```
$ sudo oscap xccdf eval --profile
xccdf_org.ssgproject.content_profile_standard --report
/var/www/html/report.html ./scap-security-guide-0.1.47/ssg-
ubuntu1804-ds.xml
```

We must run this command using sudo, as it requires access to some core system files that would not otherwise be accessible. The scan runs and produces a nice human-readable output on the screen, an example of which is shown in the following screenshot:

```
~> sudo oscap xccdf eval --profile xccdf_org.ssgproject.content_profile_standard
--report /var/www/html/report.html ./scap-security-guide-0.1.47/ssg-ubuntu1804-ds
.xml
Title    Ensure the audit Subsystem is Installed
Rule     xccdf_org.ssgproject.content_rule_package_audit_installed
Result   fail

Title    Enable auditd Service
Rule     xccdf_org.ssgproject.content_rule_service_auditd_enabled
Result   fail

Title    Ensure rsyslog is Installed
Rule     xccdf_org.ssgproject.content_rule_package_rsyslog_installed
Result   pass

Title    Enable rsyslog Service
Rule     xccdf_org.ssgproject.content_rule_service_rsyslog_enabled
Result   pass

Title    Ensure Log Files Are Owned By Appropriate Group
Rule     xccdf_org.ssgproject.content_rule_rsyslog_files_groupownership
Result   fail

Title    Ensure Log Files Are Owned By Appropriate User
Rule     xccdf_org.ssgproject.content_rule_rsyslog_files_ownership
```

As you can see, the XCCDF policy produces a highly readable output, with a clear pass/fail result for each test. Hence, even within these first few lines of the output, you can see that our test system is not compliant in several areas.

Furthermore, the oscap command has also generated a nice HTML report that we have put into the web root of this server. Of course, you wouldn't do this in a production environment—the last thing you'd want to do is publicize any security issues with your server! However, you could send this report to your IT Security team, and if you were running OSCAP using an Ansible playbook, Ansible could copy the report from the remote server to a known place where the reports can be collated.

A portion of this HTML report is shown in the following screenshot—you can see how readable it is. Further, even at a quick glance, someone non-technical can see that this system fails compliance tests and needs remedial steps:

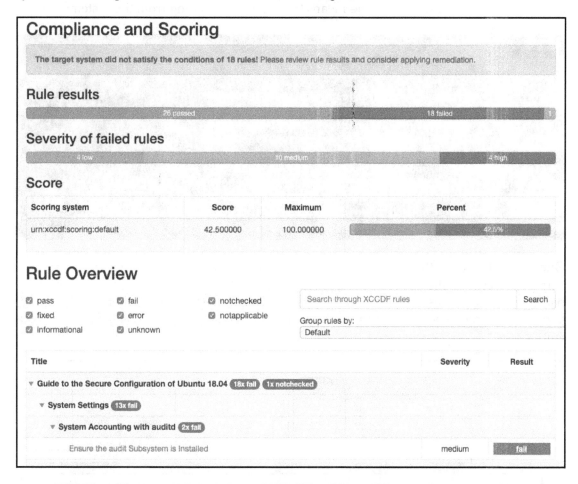

Suddenly, it becomes apparent how powerful this tool is, and why you would wish to use it to scan your infrastructure! In addition to this report, we can also check the patch status of our test system using the `com.ubuntu.bionic.cve.oval.xml` policy that we downloaded in the section entitled *Installing other OpenSCAP policies*. As we discussed, OVAL policies do not produce reports that are as readable as XCCDF reports, but nonetheless they are still incredibly valuable. To scan our Ubuntu system to see whether it is missing any critical security patches, you would run this:

```
$ sudo oscap oval eval --report /var/www/html/report-patching.html
com.ubuntu.bionic.cve.oval.xml
```

As shown in the following screenshot, the output is not as readable as the XCCDF output and needs a little more interpretation. In short, the `false` result means that the machine being scanned does not fail the compliance test, and so infers that the requisite patch has already been applied, whereas `true` means that a patch is missing from the system:

```
james@automation-01: ~
~> sudo oscap oval eval --report /var/www/html/report-patching.html com.ubuntu.bi
onic.cve.oval.xml
Definition oval:com.ubuntu.bionic:def:201999590000000: false
Definition oval:com.ubuntu.bionic:def:201999560000000: false
Definition oval:com.ubuntu.bionic:def:201999480000000: false
Definition oval:com.ubuntu.bionic:def:201999470000000: false
Definition oval:com.ubuntu.bionic:def:201999420000000: false
Definition oval:com.ubuntu.bionic:def:201999370000000: false
Definition oval:com.ubuntu.bionic:def:201999360000000: false
Definition oval:com.ubuntu.bionic:def:201999280000000: false
Definition oval:com.ubuntu.bionic:def:201999240000000: false
Definition oval:com.ubuntu.bionic:def:201999230000000: true
```

Once again, however, the HTML report comes to our rescue—to start with, it has a summary section at the top, which shows that our system has a total of 432 detected package vulnerabilities, but also 8,468 test passes. Hence, we urgently need to apply patches to fix known security vulnerabilities, as we understood by the policy file we ran the audit against:

OVAL Results Generator Information				
Schema Version	Product Name	Product Version	Date	Time
5.11.1	cpe:/a:open-scap:oscap	1.2.15	2019-11-13	11:56:42
#X	#✓	#Error	#Unknown	#Other
432	8468	0	0	1

OVAL Definition Generator Information				
Schema Version	Product Name	Product Version	Date	Time
5.11.1	Canonical CVE OVAL Generator	1.1	2019-11-13	11:32:01
#Definitions	#Tests	#Objects	#States	#Variables
8901 Total 0 1 0 0 8900	3665	1508	2332	796

System Information	
Host Name	automation-01
Operating System	Linux
Operating System Version	#75-Ubuntu SMP Tue Oct 1 05:24:09 UTC 2019
Architecture	x86_64

Of course, it is highly important to download an updated copy of this policy regularly to ensure that it is up to date. If you drill down into the report, you will see that, for each check, there is a cross-reference CVE vulnerability report so you can find out which vulnerabilities your system exhibits:

OVAL System Characteristics Generator Information					
Schema Version	Product Name		Product Version	Date	Time
5.11.1	cpe:/a:open-scap:oscap		1.1	2019-11-13	11:56:42

OVAL Definition Results

☐ ☒ | ☐ ✓ | ☐ Error | ☐ Unknown | ☐ Other

ID	Result	Class	Reference ID	Title
oval:com.ubuntu.bionic:def:201999230000000	true	vulnerability	[CVE-2019-9923]	CVE-2019-9923 on Ubuntu 18.04 LTS (bionic) - low.
oval:com.ubuntu.bionic:def:201997060000000	true	vulnerability	[CVE-2019-9706]	CVE-2019-9706 on Ubuntu 18.04 LTS (bionic) - low.
oval:com.ubuntu.bionic:def:201997050000000	true	vulnerability	[CVE-2019-9705]	CVE-2019-9705 on Ubuntu 18.04 LTS (bionic) - low.
oval:com.ubuntu.bionic:def:201997040000000	true	vulnerability	[CVE-2019-9704]	CVE-2019-9704 on Ubuntu 18.04 LTS (bionic) - low.
oval:com.ubuntu.bionic:def:201996190000000	true	vulnerability	[CVE-2019-9619]	CVE-2019-9619 on Ubuntu 18.04 LTS (bionic) - low.
oval:com.ubuntu.bionic:def:201995150000000	true	vulnerability	[CVE-2019-9515]	CVE-2019-9515 on Ubuntu 18.04 LTS (bionic) - medium.
oval:com.ubuntu.bionic:def:201995140000000	true	vulnerability	[CVE-2019-9514]	CVE-2019-9514 on Ubuntu 18.04 LTS (bionic) - medium.
oval:com.ubuntu.bionic:def:201995130000000	true	vulnerability	[CVE-2019-9513]	CVE-2019-9513 on Ubuntu 18.04 LTS (bionic) - medium.
oval:com.ubuntu.bionic:def:201995120000000	true	vulnerability	[CVE-2019-9512]	CVE-2019-9512 on Ubuntu 18.04 LTS (bionic) - medium.

Just through these few examples, I'm sure you can see how valuable these reports are and how they could be easily reviewed by an IT Security team without any specific Linux command-line knowledge.

The process for running OSCAP-based scans on CentOS or RHEL is broadly similar:

1. Assuming that you are using the SSG policy packaged by your operating system vendor and included with the OS, you would query the XCCDF profiles so that you know which to run against:

   ```
   $ oscap info /usr/share/xml/scap/ssg/content/ssg-centos7-xccdf.xml
   ```

2. You can then run an XCCDF-based scan in exactly the same way as we did on Ubuntu—here, we are choosing the standard profile to scan our system with:

   ```
   $ sudo oscap xccdf eval --fetch-remote-resources --report
   /var/www/html/report.html --profile standard
   /usr/share/xml/scap/ssg/content/ssg-centos7-xccdf.xml
   ```

You will observe the presence of the `--fetch-remote-resources` flag here too—this is used because the CentOS 7 policy requires some additional content that it downloads directly from Red Hat so that it is always working with the most up-to-date copy. The scan runs in much the same way as before, producing the same human-readable report. One thing you will see as the scan runs is that many of the tests return `notapplicable`—unfortunately, the CentOS 7 security policy is very much a work in progress and the version included with CentOS 7 at the time of writing does not include complete support for this operating system. This demonstrates how pedantic OpenSCAP policies can be—most CentOS 7 security requirements will apply equally to RHEL 7 and vice versa, yet the policies are coded to work very specifically with certain operating systems. The following screenshot shows the scan in progress and the aforementioned `notapplicable` test results:

```
james@automation-02:~
[james@automation-02 ~]$ sudo oscap xccdf eval --fetch-remote-resources --report
/var/www/html/report.html --profile standard /usr/share/xml/scap/ssg/content/ssg-
centos7-xccdf.xml
Downloading: https://www.redhat.com/security/data/oval/com.redhat.rhsa-RHEL7.xml.
bz2 ... ok
Title     Disable At Service (atd)
Rule      service_atd_disabled
Result    notapplicable

Title     Disable Odd Job Daemon (oddjobd)
Rule      service_oddjobd_disabled
Result    notapplicable

Title     Disable Apache Qpid (qpidd)
Rule      service_qpidd_disabled
Result    notapplicable

Title     Disable Automatic Bug Reporting Tool (abrtd)
Rule      service_abrtd_disabled
Result    notapplicable
```

In spite of this, the audit still reveals some valuable insights—for example, as we can see from the following screenshot of the HTML report, we have accidentally allowed accounts with empty passwords to log in:

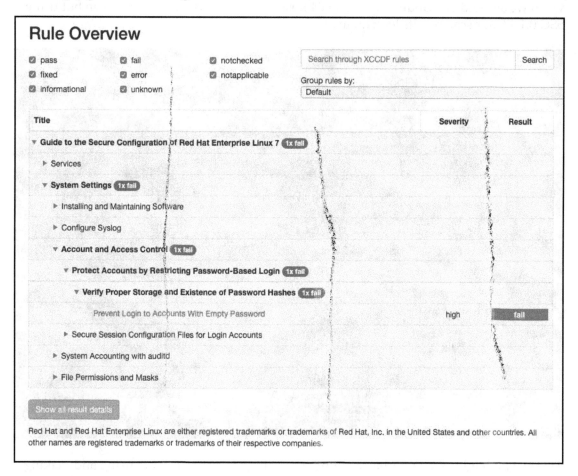

If you are running CentOS 7 specifically, you will not receive vendor support from Red Hat, and so it is worth trying the upstream SSG policy as the support for operating systems such as CentOS and Ubuntu is improving all the time (as we saw earlier in this section when we audited our Ubuntu Server 18.04 host). Rerunning the exact same scan but using SSG 0.1.47, our scan results look quite different:

```
● ● ●                        james@automation-02:~
/var/www/html/report.html --profile standard scap-security-guide-0.1.47/ssg-cento
s7-ds.xml
Downloading: https://www.redhat.com/security/data/oval/com.redhat.rhsa-RHEL7.xml
... ok
Title    Prevent Login to Accounts With Empty Password
Rule     xccdf_org.ssgproject.content_rule_no_empty_passwords
Result   fail

Title    Ensure that Root's Path Does Not Include World or Group-Writable Director
ies
Rule     xccdf_org.ssgproject.content_rule_accounts_root_path_dirs_no_write
W: probe_environmentvariable58: Entity has no value!
Result   pass

Title    Record Events that Modify the System's Mandatory Access Controls
Rule     xccdf_org.ssgproject.content_rule_audit_rules_mac_modification
Result   fail

Title    Ensure auditd Collects Information on Exporting to Media (successful)
Rule     xccdf_org.ssgproject.content_rule_audit_rules_media_export
Result   fail

Title    Record Events that Modify the System's Network Environment
Rule     xccdf_org.ssgproject.content_rule_audit_rules_networkconfig_modification
Result   fail
```

This just highlights the importance of understanding the policy you are using and making sure that you download the right version for your situation. If you are using RHEL 7, you would be advised to make use of the packages supplied by Red Hat, whereas with CentOS 7 and Ubuntu Server 18.04, you would be better off trying the latest version from the upstream GitHub repository. Indeed, the following screenshot shows the results of the exact same scan on our CentOS 7 test system using the version 0.1.47 SSG, and we can see that this time, we have run a total of 958 tests and have a much clearer understanding of the security of our server:

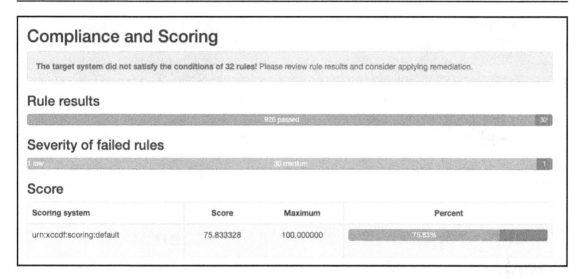

On CentOS 7, you can also run the OVAL scan for package vulnerabilities in the same manner that we did with Ubuntu Server, but using the `com.redhat.rhsa-RHEL7.xml` file that we downloaded previously. Just as we did on Ubuntu Server, we would run this scan with this command:

```
$ sudo oscap oval eval --report /var/www/html/report-patching.html
com.redhat.rhsa-RHEL7.xml
```

The report is interpreted in exactly the same way as on Ubuntu, and if we refer directly to the HTML report, we can see that this system is fully patched against known package vulnerabilities at this time:

OVAL Results Generator Information				
Schema Version	Product Name	Product Version	Date	Time
5.10	cpe:/a:open-scap:oscap	1.2.17	2019-11-12	18:51:48
#X	#✓	#Error	#Unknown	#Other
0	906	0	0	0

OVAL Definition Generator Information				
Schema Version	Product Name	Product Version	Date	Time
5.10	Red Hat OVAL Patch Definition Merger	3	2019-11-04	15:49:59
#Definitions	#Tests	#Objects	#States	#Variables
906 Total 0 0 0 906 0	12502	2365	2830	0

This wraps up our look at the `oscap` command-line tool, but by now you should have all of the information you need to run your own scans regularly. Automating this process is left as an exercise for you, but here are some tips on what I would consider a good Ansible solution:

- Use the `yum` or `apt` modules to install the required OpenSCAP packages on the server before performing any other tasks.

- Use the `get_url` module to download SSG and/or the package vulnerability OVAL definition file to ensure you have the most up-to-date copy (except on RHEL 7, where you would use the version supplied by Red Hat). Use the `unarchive` module to unzip the file you downloaded.
- Run the OSCAP scan using the `shell` module.
- Use the `fetch` module to grab a copy of the HTML report(s) for distribution and analysis.

In the next section, we will look at running scheduled regular scans using the OpenSCAP Daemon.

Running regular scans with the OpenSCAP Daemon

As you have now understood the basis of scanning with the `oscap` command-line tool, it will be easy to set up regular scanning with the OpenSCAP Daemon as the techniques involved are the same. Assuming that you have already installed the daemon, as we discussed earlier, it is fairly easy to create automated scans, although, at the time of writing, the OpenSCAP Daemon does not run on Ubuntu Server 18.04. This is a result of a missing CPE file, which, to date, has not been rectified, and although this did not impact our use of the `oscap` command-line tool (though those of who are eagle-eyed will have noticed an error relating to this file at the end of the scan), it does prevent the OpenSCAP Daemon from starting.

As a result, the examples in this section will be based on CentOS 7 only—however, the procedure would be broadly similar on Ubuntu Server 18.04 when the OpenSCAP packages are fixed. In fact, this issue, which was first reported in October 2017 according to the `ComplianceAsCode` GitHub project, seems to be relatively long-standing and so is an excellent reason to make use of Ansible in conjunction with the `oscap` tool for your scanning needs.

When this Ubuntu related issue is fixed, you will be able to schedule scans for both CentOS and Ubuntu hosts from one central scanning host using the process outlined in this chapter. Note that the SSG files for all of your hosts (be they CentOS, RHEL, or Ubuntu) must live on the same host as the OpenSCAP Daemon – they are copied across to each host to be scanned whenever a scan is run by the OpenSCAP Daemon, and so do not need to be deployed on every host.

Nonetheless, if you want to set up a scheduled scan using the OpenSCAP Daemon, the easiest way to do this is by using the `oscapd-cli` tool in interactive mode:

1. This is achieved by invoking `oscapd-cli` with the following parameters:

    ```
    $ sudo oscapd-cli task-create -i
    ```

2. This launches a text-based guided configuration that you can easily complete—the following screenshot shows an example of how I set up the daemon to run a daily scan on my CentOS 7 test system:

```
root@automation-02:~

[root@automation-02 ~]# oscapd-cli task-create -i
Creating new task in interactive mode
Title: Daily security audit
Target (empty for localhost):
Found the following SCAP Security Guide content:
        1:   /usr/share/xml/scap/ssg/content/ssg-centos6-ds.xml
        2:   /usr/share/xml/scap/ssg/content/ssg-centos7-ds.xml
        3:   /usr/share/xml/scap/ssg/content/ssg-firefox-ds.xml
        4:   /usr/share/xml/scap/ssg/content/ssg-jre-ds.xml
        5:   /usr/share/xml/scap/ssg/content/ssg-rhel6-ds.xml
        6:   /usr/share/xml/scap/ssg/content/ssg-rhel7-ds.xml
Choose SSG content by number (empty for custom content): 2
Tailoring file (absolute path, empty for no tailoring):
Found the following possible profiles:
        1:   PCI-DSS v3.2.1 Control Baseline for Red Hat Enterprise Linux 7 (id='x
ccdf_org.ssgproject.content_profile_pci-dss')
        2:   (default) (id='')
        3:   Standard System Security Profile for Red Hat Enterprise Linux 7 (id='
xccdf_org.ssgproject.content_profile_standard')
Choose profile by number (empty for (default) profile): 3
Online remediation (1, y or Y for yes, else no): no
Schedule:
 - not before (YYYY-MM-DD HH:MM in UTC, empty for NOW): 2019-11-13 13:48
 - repeat after (hours or @daily, @weekly, @monthly, empty or 0 for no repeat): @
daily
Task created with ID '1'. It is currently set as disabled. You can enable it with
`oscapd-cli task 1 enable`.
[root@automation-02 ~]# oscapd-cli task 1 enable
```

Most of the steps in that interactive setup should be self-explanatory—however, you will note a step that asks about `Online remediation`. The OpenSCAP profiles include the capability to automatically rectify any compliance issues they find as they go through the scan. It is up to you whether you wish to enable this or not, as this will depend on whether you feel happy with an automated process making changes to your systems, even for security purposes. You may want to separate your audit tasks from your policy enforcement tasks, in which case you would use Ansible for the remediation steps.

If you do enable remediation, be sure that you have tested this in an isolated environment first to ensure that the remediation steps do not break any of your existing applications. This testing must be performed not only when your application code changes, but also when new versions of SSG are downloaded as each new version might contain new remediation steps. This is the same as the guidance we explored in Chapter 13, *Using CIS Benchmarks*, only now applied to OpenSCAP SSG.

3. Once you have enabled the scan, you will find that, at the scheduled time, it deposits the scan results in /var/lib/oscapd/results. Under this, you will find a numbered subdirectory that corresponds to the task ID you were given when you created the task (1, in the preceding screenshot), and then under another numbered directory, which is the scan number. Hence, the results for the first scan for task ID 1 will be found in /var/lib/oscapd/results/1/1.

4. When you examine the contents of this directory, you will notice that the results are only stored in an XML file, which, while suited for further processing, is not very readable. Fortunately, the oscap tool that we looked at previously can easily convert scan results into human-readable HTML—for this result, we would run the following command:

```
$ sudo oscap xccdf generate report --output /var/www/html/report-
oscapd.html /var/lib/oscapd/results/1/1/results.xml
```

Once this command has run, you can view the HTML report in your web browser just as we did earlier in this chapter. Of course, if you aren't running a web server on this machine, you can simply copy the HTML report to a host that has one (or even open it locally on your computer).

The beauty of setting up the OpenSCAP Daemon is that, unlike the oscap tool, it can scan remote hosts as well as the local one. This scanning is performed over SSH, and you must ensure that you have set up passwordless SSH access from the server running the OpenSCAP Daemon to the remote host. If you are using an unprivileged account to log in, you should also ensure that the account has sudo access, again without requiring a password. This should be quite easy for any experienced system administrator to set up.

On CentOS 7, the default SELinux policy prevented the remote scan from running on my test system. I had to disable SELinux temporarily for the remote scan to run. Obviously, this is not an ideal solution—if you encounter this issue, it would be better to build an SELinux policy that enables the remote scan to run.

Once you have set up the remote access, configuring the OpenSCAP Daemon through the interactive task creation process is no more complex than for the local machine—the only difference this time around is that you need to specify the remote connection in this format:

```
ssh+sudo://<username>@<hostname>
```

If you are logging in directly as `root` (not recommended), you can leave out the `+sudo` part of the preceding string. Hence, to set up add another remote scan from my test server, I ran through the commands shown in the following screenshot:

```
● ● ●                          root@automation-02:~
[root@automation-02 ~]# oscapd-cli task-create -i
Creating new task in interactive mode
Title: Scan Remote Host using SSH
Target (empty for localhost): ssh+sudo://audit@centos-testhost2
Found the following SCAP Security Guide content:
        1:  /usr/share/xml/scap/ssg/content/ssg-centos6-ds.xml
        2:  /usr/share/xml/scap/ssg/content/ssg-centos7-ds.xml
        3:  /usr/share/xml/scap/ssg/content/ssg-firefox-ds.xml
        4:  /usr/share/xml/scap/ssg/content/ssg-jre-ds.xml
        5:  /usr/share/xml/scap/ssg/content/ssg-rhel6-ds.xml
        6:  /usr/share/xml/scap/ssg/content/ssg-rhel7-ds.xml
Choose SSG content by number (empty for custom content): 2
Tailoring file (absolute path, empty for no tailoring):
Found the following possible profiles:
        1:  PCI-DSS v3.2.1 Control Baseline for Red Hat Enterprise Linux 7 (id='x
ccdf_org.ssgproject.content_profile_pci-dss')
        2:  (default) (id='')
        3:  Standard System Security Profile for Red Hat Enterprise Linux 7 (id='
xccdf_org.ssgproject.content_profile_standard')
Choose profile by number (empty for (default) profile): 3
Online remediation (1, y or Y for yes, else no): no
Schedule:
 - not before (YYYY-MM-DD HH:MM in UTC, empty for NOW): 2019-11-13 13:59
 - repeat after (hours or @daily, @weekly, @monthly, empty or 0 for no repeat): @
daily
Task created with ID '2'. It is currently set as disabled. You can enable it with
 `oscapd-cli task 2 enable`.
[root@automation-02 ~]# oscapd-cli task 2 enable
```

As you can see, this creates task number 2 for this purpose. The advantage of this setup is that, once you have set up the SSH and sudo access, you can have one designated host that is responsible for scanning your entire estate of Linux servers. Also, the hosts being scanned only need the OpenSCAP libraries present—they do not need the OpenSCAP Daemon or the security policy files—these are automatically transferred to the hosts as part of the remote scanning process.

The results of the scheduled scan are stored in XML format in the `/var/lib/oscapd/results` directory exactly as before and can be analyzed or converted into HTML as required.

The OpenSCAP Daemon is almost certainly your quickest and easiest route to scanning your infrastructure, and the fact that it collects and stores all of the results locally as well as uses security policies stored on its own filesystem means it is fairly resistant to tampering. For automated, ongoing SCAP-based scanning of your environment, the OpenSCAP Daemon is almost certainly your best choice, and you could always create a `cron` job to automatically convert the XML results into HTML and put them into your web server root directory so that they can be viewed.

Last but not least, in the next section, we will look at the SCAP Workbench tool and see how that can help you with your security auditing.

Scanning with SCAP Workbench

The SCAP Workbench tool is an interactive, GUI-based tool for running SCAP scans. It has almost the same capabilities as the `oscap` command-line tool, except that it can scan both remote hosts over SSH (similarly to the OpenSCAP Daemon). The high-level process for using SCAP Workbench is the same as for `oscap`—you select your policy file from the policy you downloaded, select the profile from within it, and then run the scan.

This time, however, the results are displayed in the GUI and are easily interpretable without the need to generate an HTML report and load it in a browser. The following screenshot shows the equivalent of running the following on the command line with `oscap`:

```
$ sudo oscap xccdf eval --profile
xccdf_org.ssgproject.content_profile_standard ./scap-security-
guide-0.1.47/ssg-ubuntu1804-ds.xml
```

It is important to state that no report file is generated by the scan, but you can generate either an HTML- or XML-based one by clicking on the **Save Results** button at the bottom of the screen:

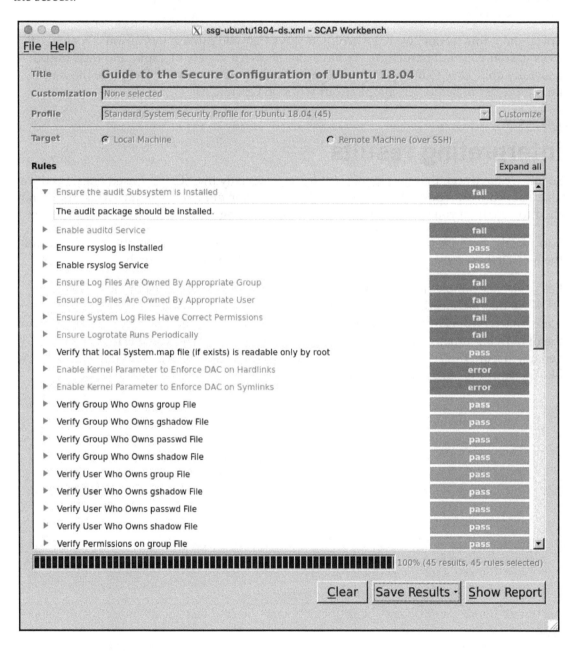

As you can clearly see, if you need to run an interactive and immediate scan of a system, SCAP Workbench is the easiest way to do it. The only limitation is that it can only process XCCDF files, so the OVAL files used to establish whether you have package vulnerabilities cannot be used here.

Throughout this section, we have explored ways that you can use the various OpenSCAP tools to scan your infrastructure. We have also shown a variety of scans, and their output is generally quite easy to interpret. However, in the next section, we will explore these in a little more depth before we complete our work on OpenSCAP.

Interpreting results

So far, we have seen that the OpenSCAP scans, especially the XCCDF-based ones, produce nice, easy-to-read reports that you can easily take action on. However, if the reports are not clear to you, then you would not know what needs fixing to rectify the lack of compliance.

Fortunately, both the OVAL policies we used earlier to check for vulnerable packages and the XCCDF-based reports contain enough information for you to do both things.

Let's take an example from our earlier scan of our CentOS 7 server using the SSG version 0.1.47. In this, we failed, among other things, a check called `Disable ntpdate Service (ntpdate)`. Suppose that this result was not obvious to you, and you were unsure what the underlying problem was or why it was an issue. Fortunately, in the HTML report generated from this scan, you can click on the check title. A screen should pop up that looks like the one in the following screenshot:

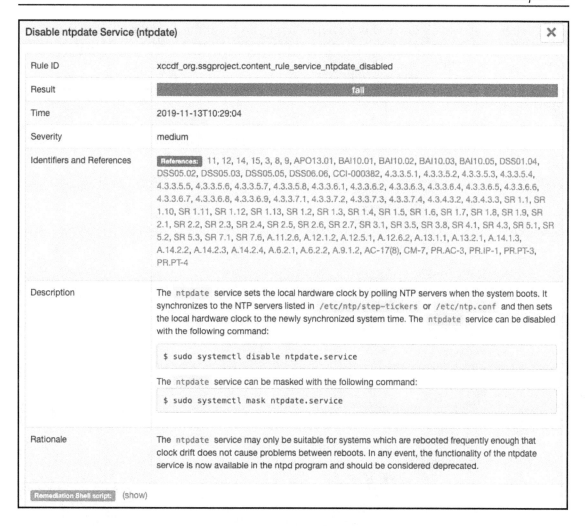

Disable ntpdate Service (ntpdate)	✕
Rule ID	xccdf_org.ssgproject.content_rule_service_ntpdate_disabled
Result	fail
Time	2019-11-13T10:29:04
Severity	medium
Identifiers and References	**References:** 11, 12, 14, 15, 3, 8, 9, APO13.01, BAI10.01, BAI10.02, BAI10.03, BAI10.05, DSS01.04, DSS05.02, DSS05.03, DSS05.05, DSS06.06, CCI-000382, 4.3.3.5.1, 4.3.3.5.2, 4.3.3.5.3, 4.3.3.5.4, 4.3.3.5.5, 4.3.3.5.6, 4.3.3.5.7, 4.3.3.5.8, 4.3.3.6.1, 4.3.3.6.2, 4.3.3.6.3, 4.3.3.6.4, 4.3.3.6.5, 4.3.3.6.6, 4.3.3.6.7, 4.3.3.6.8, 4.3.3.6.9, 4.3.3.7.1, 4.3.3.7.2, 4.3.3.7.3, 4.3.3.7.4, 4.3.4.3.2, 4.3.4.3.3, SR 1.1, SR 1.10, SR 1.11, SR 1.12, SR 1.13, SR 1.2, SR 1.3, SR 1.4, SR 1.5, SR 1.6, SR 1.7, SR 1.8, SR 1.9, SR 2.1, SR 2.2, SR 2.3, SR 2.4, SR 2.5, SR 2.6, SR 2.7, SR 3.1, SR 3.5, SR 3.8, SR 4.1, SR 4.3, SR 5.1, SR 5.2, SR 5.3, SR 7.1, SR 7.6, A.11.2.6, A.12.1.2, A.12.5.1, A.12.6.2, A.13.1.1, A.13.2.1, A.14.1.3, A.14.2.2, A.14.2.3, A.14.2.4, A.6.2.1, A.6.2.2, A.9.1.2, AC-17(8), CM-7, PR.AC-3, PR.IP-1, PR.PT-3, PR.PT-4

Description	The `ntpdate` service sets the local hardware clock by polling NTP servers when the system boots. It synchronizes to the NTP servers listed in `/etc/ntp/step-tickers` or `/etc/ntp.conf` and then sets the local hardware clock to the newly synchronized system time. The `ntpdate` service can be disabled with the following command:
	
	`$ sudo systemctl disable ntpdate.service`
	
	The `ntpdate` service can be masked with the following command:
	
	`$ sudo systemctl mask ntpdate.service`

Rationale	The `ntpdate` service may only be suitable for systems which are rebooted frequently enough that clock drift does not cause problems between reboots. In any event, the functionality of the ntpdate service is now available in the ntpd program and should be considered deprecated.
Remediation Shell script: (show)	

Here, you can see all the detail you could ever need—from the details of the scan through to the references and identifiers from the various security standards that make this recommendation, and even the manual commands that could be used to rectify the issue so that the system becomes compliant for the next scan.

Even better, if you scroll down this screen, you will find that many of the latest versions of the SSG (version 0.1.47 included) actually include a great deal of Ansible code that can be applied to remedy this situation, as shown in the following screenshot:

```
Remediation Ansible snippet:   (show)

Complexity:                                                            low

Disruption:                                                           low

Strategy:                                                             disable


 - name: Unit Service Exists - ntpdate.service
   command: systemctl list-unit-files ntpdate.service
   register: service_file_exists
   changed_when: false
   ignore_errors: true
   when: ansible_virtualization_role != "guest" or ansible_virtualization_type != "docker"
   tags:
     - service_ntpdate_disabled
     - medium_severity
     - disable_strategy
     - low_complexity
     - low_disruption
     - no_reboot_needed
     - NIST-800-53-AC-17(8)
     - NIST-800-53-CM-7

 - name: Disable service ntpdate
   systemd:
     name: ntpdate.service
     enabled: 'no'
     state: stopped
     masked: 'yes'
   when:
     - '"ntpdate.service" in service_file_exists.stdout_lines[1]'
     - ansible_virtualization_role != "guest" or ansible_virtualization_type != "docker"
   tags:
     - service_ntpdate_disabled
     - medium_severity
     - disable_strategy
     - low_complexity
     - low_disruption
     - no_reboot_needed
     - NIST-800-53-AC-17(8)
```

Hence, through a little exploration, you really can use these scan results not only to find out why your infrastructure is not compliant but to also produce the exact set of fixes you require.

OpenSCAP can also remediate (that is, fix) problems that it finds while scanning to help you to both audit and maintain compliance. However, we have not explored this here because it is vital that you understand the scans and what they will do before attempting automatic remediation. Hence, this is left as an exercise for you—however, you will see that in both the OpenSCAP Daemon and SCAP Workbench, there is a simple option you can enable that will not just perform the scan but attempt remediation.

While we have established how powerful and user-friendly the XCCDF profiles are, we have seen that reports generated by OVAL profiles are a little less readable. Fortunately, if you refer to the following screenshot, you will notice that the CVE numbers for the identified vulnerabilities are, in fact, hyperlinks:

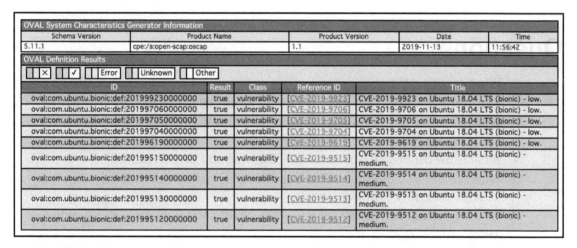

Clicking on these will take you to the operating system vendor's website, directly to a page that details the vulnerability, the affected package(s), and when the fix was implemented. As a result, you can find out exactly which packages you need to update to remedy the situation.

That concludes our look at auditing your Linux environment with OpenSCAP—it is hoped that you have found this useful and that you will be able to apply this to your environment for the benefit of your security and auditing processes.

Summary

Keeping an eye on the security compliance of your Linux infrastructure is ever more important, and given the large number of security recommendations, coupled with the large number of Linux servers that might exist in a modern enterprise, it is clear that a tool that can audit for compliance is needed. OpenSCAP provides exactly such a framework and with a little care and attention (and application of the right security profiles) can easily audit your entire Linux estate and provide you with valuable, easy to read and interpret reports of your compliance levels.

In this chapter, you gained hands-on experience of installing OpenSCAP tools for server audit and understood the available policies and how to make effective use of them in OpenSCAP. You then learned how to audit your Linux servers with the various OpenSCAP tools, and finally explored how to interpret the scan reports to take appropriate action.

In the next and final chapter of this book, we will look at some tips and tricks to make your automation tasks easier.

Questions

1. What does SCAP stand for?
2. Why are SCAP policies a valuable tool in auditing your Linux infrastructure?
3. Which OpenSCAP tool would you use to centrally perform scanning of several Linux hosts regularly?
4. What is the difference between an XCCDF file and an OVAL file?
5. When would you use the vendor-supplied SSG policies, even if they are older than the currently available ones?
6. Why might the scan results for a CentOS 7 host show `notapplicable` when using a RHEL 7 policy file?
7. Can you generate an HTML report from the XML results generated by the OpenSCAP Daemon?
8. What are the requirements for a remote SSH scan to be performed by SCAP Workbench or the OpenSCAP Daemon?

Further reading

- *Learn Ansible* by *Russ McKendrick*: `https://www.packtpub.com/gb/virtualization-and-cloud/learn-ansible`
- OpenSCAP website: `https://www.open-scap.org/`

16
Tips and Tricks

It is hoped that, by now, this book has given you a sense of how you can automate your Enterprise Linux environment and the requirements for standardization that enable tasks to be performed efficiently at large scale. However, we have kept the example code very simple throughout this book and for good reason—it is not fair to assume that every reader will have a network with hundreds or even thousands of Linux machines to test these examples against.

Hence, this concluding chapter of this book is written to provide you with some important tips and tricks that will help you to better understand how to scale the examples in this book up to enterprise scale and how to do this in a manner that will not simply move you management headaches from one part of your infrastructure to another. Automation of your Linux environment should not in itself become a headache that you need to solve, and it is important to take several factors into account early on to prevent this. This chapter explores some of the most important facets of Ansible automation you should consider to ensure your automation journey is as smooth as possible.

The following topics will be covered in this chapter:

- Version control for your scripts
- Inventories – maintaining a single source of truth
- Handling one-off tasks

Technical requirements

This chapter includes examples based on the following technologies:

- Ubuntu Server 18.04 LTS
- CentOS 7.6
- Ansible 2.8

To run through these examples, you will need access to two servers or virtual machines running one each of the operating systems listed previously and Ansible.

All example code discussed in this book is available from GitHub at: `https://github.com/PacktPublishing/Hands-On-Enterprise-Automation-on-Linux`.

Version control for your scripts

Throughout this book, we have focused heavily on creating standardized ways of doing things, whether that be how you build your Linux operating system images for deployment, how you manage configuration files and databases, or even how you patch your infrastructure. This was done for many good reasons, all of which we discussed in `Chapter 1`, *Building a Standard Operating Environment on Linux*, including minimizing your staff training requirements and ensuring you get consistent results from your automation tasks.

What is also vital to consider is ensuring your Ansible playbooks themselves (and indeed, any other scripts you might rely on) are standardized and uniform across your enterprise. Imagine if everyone just had Ansible installed on their laptop or management station, along with a set of playbooks for management tasks. How quickly would things get out of hand if one person decided a tweak was needed to a playbook and didn't distribute it to everyone else? Equally, how would you know what was run previously if the previous version of a playbook did not exist—after all, Ansible code is supposed to be self-documenting, but this value is lost if the previous versions are deleted.

In short, just as we proposed building standardized Linux images in `Chapter 5`, *Using Ansible to Build Virtual Machine Templates for Deployment*, and `Chapter 6`, *Custom Builds with PXE Booting*, so too should your Ansible playbooks be standardized across your enterprise.

The best way to achieve this will be to use version control for this purpose. Most enterprises will already have a version control system already in place. This might take the form of a corporate account on `https://github.com/`, an internal deployment of what was previously known as Microsoft Team Foundation Server (now Azure DevOps Server), or one of the many open source self-hosted Git options such as GitLab or Gitea. You may even be on a system that is not Git-based such as Subversion or Mercurial—the choice is not really important (although if you can make use of Git, Subversion, or Mercurial, this is to your advantage as we shall see in a minute).

Whatever your version control platform, it is important that you not only make effective use of it for storing and maintaining a history of your Ansible playbooks; it is also vital that you use your chosen tool effectively in the context of your enterprise. Take for example Git (whichever system you choose to manage your repository). If your users modify the same file at the same time, how do you handle that? Who's changes will take precedence? There are good practices around the use of Git in the context of teams and enterprises, and it is highly advisable that individuals make use of branches when they are working on code, then use a pull request to merge their changes back into the source tree.

Effective use of Git in an enterprise setting is a large topic that could take up an entire chapter on its own—if you are not familiar with this, then I advise you refer to the resources in the *Further reading* section of this chapter for guidance on how to make the best use of your version control system.

 For the remainder of this section, we will assume the version control system you are using is Git as this will make the examples easier to read. If you are using another system such as Subversion or Mercurial, replace the Git-specific commands to check out code, commit updates, and so on with your own.

Once you have decided upon your version control system, it is time to put it into day-to-day usage. To ensure this happens, you must consider how you are going to integrate Ansible with your version control system, and we will take a look at exactly that in the next section.

Integrating Ansible with Git

Before we proceed any further, we must point out that the title of this section is an oxymoron as Ansible itself does not integrate with Git. Specifically, Ansible playbooks and roles are stored in Git, to be checked out locally on the host that will execute them. It does have modules such as `git` and `git_config`, which allow you to write playbooks that deploy code from a Git repository, but the `ansible-playbook` command does not support running a playbook from anything other than the local filesystem.

We will make use of the publicly available `ansible-examples` repository on `github.com` for these next few examples as they are publicly available to you for testing. Hypothetically speaking, suppose that you wanted to run the playbook for installing WordPress on RHEL 7 in your enterprise from this repository. Your process to perform this would (assuming you have already defined your Ansible inventory) look something like the following example:

```
$ git clone https://github.com/ansible/ansible-examples.git
$ cd ansible-examples/wordpress-nginx_rhel7/
$ ansible-playbook site.yml
```

The preceding three commands ensure that you clone the very latest playbook from this Git repository, and the output will look a little something like the following screenshot (the deprecation warning shows that this playbook needs updating for more recent versions of Ansible):

Once checked out, the playbooks can always be updated to the latest version from the Git server (assuming there are no local changes that need to be committed):

```
$ git pull
```

Following a successful update of the local working copy of your playbooks, the latest version of the playbook can be run. This is a fairly painless process, and requiring engineers or admins to run the `git pull` command before running a playbook is not too arduous a task.

Sadly, though, this process does not really help to enforce good practices in the enterprise. It would be very easy for someone to forget to run the `git pull` command before running a playbook. Equally, there is nothing to stop administrators and engineers amassing their own playbooks and failing to share them. This is definitely a step forward, but it is by no means the full solution.

A far more robust option is to enforce the use of a tool such as AWX or Ansible Tower. These, as we saw in `Chapter 3`, *Streamlining Infrastructure Management with AWX*, enable the enforcement of good processes by ensuring that playbook runs can only be executed against playbooks pulled down from a version control system. If administrators are not given access to the filesystem of the AWX server, then it will not be possible to run arbitrary playbooks that they have knocked up themselves and they must instead pull them in from a version control source.

In *Creating a project in AWX* section of `Chapter 3`, *Streamlining Infrastructure Management with AWX*, we looked at creating a project that would actually make use of the `ansible-examples` repository we looked at earlier. This, of course, begs the question, how do you organize your playbooks within a version control system effectively? We will look at precisely this in the next section.

Organizing your version control repositories effectively

It is all very well stating that Ansible playbooks should be cloned from a version control system and cloned to the systems from which they are to be run (be that from the command line or AWX), but how do you actually organize these effectively so that you can find your code when you need it?

A clue comes to us from the user interface of the AWX tool, which refers to each version control repository you might reference as `Project`. As you build up your automation processes and solution, you could end up with many playbooks, possibly into the hundreds, depending on the size of your enterprise.

You can, of course, store all of these within the same repository. The `ansible-examples` repository is a good (albeit smaller) example of this—it contains a variety of playbooks for different purposes, each within its own directory. There are even Windows-specific playbooks that live under a Windows subdirectory. The directory structure is relatively easy to navigate for you to find playbook that you want, but you will note that all of the code contained within it are examples for people to learn Ansible with.

If you worked for an online retailer, for example, it would not be logical to put the playbooks for building the standardized Linux images into the same repository as the ones for deploying your stock control system. This would be counter-intuitive and would lead to confusion, especially when people are looking for a particular playbook.

Naturally, the decision comes down to you at the end of the day—only you can decide on the structure that will suit your enterprise best. However, the division of repositories by project is a good starting point for anyone looking for a sound starting point to build on.

There will always be gray areas too – for example, in `Chapter 12`, *Performing Routine Maintenance with Ansible*, we advocated building Ansible playbooks for performing frequent housekeeping tasks such as cleaning up disk space. Now, suppose you have a playbook that cleans up a directory structure, but that it is specific to the stock control system we mentioned earlier— does that go in the stock control repository or the general maintenance repository?

Again, the choice is yours—but the stock control cleanup playbook will not run properly (and might even be dangerous) on systems that do not run the stock control system, so I would advocate making it a sub-directory within the stock control repository.

So far, we are building up a picture of how you would effectively and efficiently store your playbooks, yet we must remember that, throughout this book, we have strongly advocated the authoring of Ansible code as roles wherever possible, as roles can be reused in multiple playbooks. None of the solutions we have discussed actually support role reuse (other than manually copying the code between playbooks), even though we have established a sound methodology for building up our directory structures and processes for running the playbooks.

In the next section, we will look at the specific capabilities of Ansible when it comes to the version control of roles.

Version control of roles in Ansible

Role reuse is an important part of building an efficient, standardized system of playbooks for administrators and engineers to apply. We have given many examples throughout this book—for example, in `Chapter 10`, *Managing Users on Linux*—we proposed a simple role that would add users to a Linux system. To save you referring back, the code is as follows:

```
---

- name: Add required users to Linux servers
  user:
    name: "{{ item.name }}"
    comment: "{{ item.comment }}"
    shell: /bin/bash
    groups: "{{ item.groups }}"
    append: yes
    state: present
  loop:
    - { name: 'johndoe', comment: 'John Doe', groups: 'sudo'}
    - { name: 'janedoe', comment: 'Jane Doe', groups: 'docker'}
```

Given our discussion about role reuse, I'm sure that you can see that the design of this role could be improved. This role has hardcoded user accounts in it, which does not lend itself to reuse at all. However, if the user accounts were specified via an Ansible variable, then this role could be used in any playbook that needed to add a user account to a Linux system. This moves us one step closer to our goal of creating standardized, reusable code.

However, we need to ensure that the code appears in every playbook that requires it. Further, we must also ensure that the version is kept up to date—otherwise, if someone makes an improvement to the code (or fixes a bug or adapts the code for a newer version of Ansible because of some feature deprecation), this will only exist in the modified role—all of the copies will be out of date. If the role is copied to any playbooks, it will become difficult to ensure that they are kept up to date. To achieve this, we clearly need to start storing our roles in our source control system, and in this case, we must store one role per repository (the reasons for this will become apparent as we progress through the following examples).

Once your roles are in your source control system, there are two ways to address the problem of efficient and effective reuse. The first is to make use of Git submodules. This is a Git-specific technology so will not suit you if you are using Subversion or Mercurial, but if you are using Git it is one of two possible solutions.

A Git submodule is basically a reference to another Git repository from within another. Hence, it does not actually contain the code of the submodule—it simply contains a reference to it that can be cloned and updated as required. Suppose that you are writing a playbook to install Apache 2 on a server and you decide that, rather than write your own module, you are going to use Jeff Geerling's Apache 2 role from GitHub (`https://github.com/geerlingguy/ansible-role-apache`):

1. Before you start, you will need to have your playbook directory structure created and checked into your version control system. Then, ensure you have the `roles/` directory in your playbook structure as normal and change to this directory:

   ```
   $ mkdir roles
   $ cd roles
   ```

2. Now, check out the code you want as a submodule, providing the Git tool with a directory name to clone it to—in our case, we'll call it `jeffgeerling.apache2`:

   ```
   $ git submodule add
   https://github.com/geerlingguy/ansible-role-apache.git
   jeffgeerling.apache2
   ```

3. Once this is done, you will notice that you have a new file at the root of your working copy called `.gitmodules`. You will need to add this and the directory created by the submodule `add` command to your repository:

   ```
   $ git add ../.gitmodules jeffgeerling.apache2
   $ git commit -m "Added Apache2 submodule as role"
   $ git push
   ```

   That's all there is to it—you now have this role stored within your playbook directory structure, but as far as Git is concerned, it is stored elsewhere. The whole process should look something like what's shown in the following screenshot:

```
● ● ●                    james@automation-01: ~/test/roles
~/test> mkdir roles
~/test> cd roles
~/test/roles> git submodule add https://github.com/geerlingguy/ansible-role-apach
e.git jeffgeerling.apache2
Cloning into '/home/james/test/roles/jeffgeerling.apache2'...
remote: Enumerating objects: 958, done.
remote: Total 958 (delta 0), reused 0 (delta 0), pack-reused 958
Receiving objects: 100% (958/958), 154.43 KiB | 823.00 KiB/s, done.
Resolving deltas: 100% (499/499), done.
~/test/roles> git status
On branch master
Your branch is up to date with 'origin/master'.

Changes to be committed:
  (use "git reset HEAD <file>..." to unstage)

        new file:   ../.gitmodules
        new file:   jeffgeerling.apache2

~/test/roles> git add ../.gitmodules jeffgeerling.apache2/
~/test/roles> git commit -m "Added Apache2 submodule as role"
[master a86f753] Added Apache2 submodule as role
 2 files changed, 4 insertions(+)
 create mode 100644 .gitmodules
 create mode 160000 roles/jeffgeerling.apache2
~/test/roles> git push
```

To update this submodule at any time, you must change into the directory you created for it earlier and then run a standard `git pull` command. The beauty of this is that, as far as Git is concerned, the submodule is just another repository and so you can run all of the usual subcommands you are used to such as `push`, `pull`, `status`, and so on.

The only thing to add is that, when you clone the playbook directory for the first time from your Git server, although it will be aware of the submodule, it doesn't actually check out the code. Hence, when you clone for the first time, you must run the following commands:

```
$ git clone <your repository URL>
$ cd <your repository name>
$ git submodule init
$ git submodule update
```

From here, you can use the working copy and submodule exactly as described previously.

The other way to solve the problem of role code reuse is to make use of the `ansible-galaxy` tool. We saw `ansible-galaxy` in action in Chapter 2, *Automating Your IT Infrastructure with Ansible,* where we demonstrated it as a way of cloning publicly available roles from the Ansible Galaxy web site (`https://galaxy.ansible.com/`). However, `ansible-galaxy` can also clone roles from a valid Git URL.

Suppose we wanted to achieve exactly what we have just done with the Apache 2 role, but without using Git submodules. Instead, we create a file called `requirements.yml` in the base directory of the playbook structure.

To clone the role we just used, our `requirements.yml` file would need to look like this:

```
---
- src: https://github.com/geerlingguy/ansible-role-apache.git
  scm: git
```

You can, of course, have more than one requirement in this file—just specify them as a standard YAML list. When you have completed this file, you can then download the roles to your working copy using this command:

```
$ ansible-galaxy install -r requirements.yml --roles-path roles
```

This clones the Git repository referenced by the `src` parameter in `requirements.yml` into the `roles/` directory. Note that we do not customize the directory name, so the one from the Git repository is used for the role name (in this case, `ansible-role-apache`). The following screenshot shows an example of this being completed:

```
james@automation-01: ~/test
~/test> cat requirements.yml
---
- src: https://github.com/geerlingguy/ansible-role-apache.git
  scm: git
~/test> ansible-galaxy install -r requirements.yml --roles-path roles
- extracting ansible-role-apache to /home/james/test/roles/ansible-role-apache
- ansible-role-apache was installed successfully
~/test>
```

Unlike the submodules, `ansible-galaxy` does not actually clone the repository as a working copy; hence, you cannot simply change into its directory and run `git pull` command to update it to the latest version. Instead, `requirements.yml` should remain in your working copy, and in the future, to update, you would run the following command:

```
$ ansible-galaxy install -r requirements.yml --roles-path roles --force
```

The `--force` parameter instructs `ansible-galaxy` to download the role even if it is already downloaded, hence overwriting the version you have already installed.

> We have only scratched the surface of what can be achieved with `requirements.yml`—you can download from private repositories, ensure you only ever download a specific Git version, and more—this is left as an exercise for you to investigate.

Hence, you have two completely different yet equally valid ways to efficiently reuse roles by storing them individually in a source control system. By considering everything in this section, including the decision to use AWX or Ansible Tower, you should have a robust and scalable automation architecture built around Ansible.

In the next section, we will address another facet of Ansible that has so far not received a great deal of attention by virtue of our simple example structure, and yet is vital to its operation—the inventory.

Inventories – maintaining a single source of truth

We have worked hard throughout this book to build an automation architecture that implements good practices for your enterprise. For example, when it comes to managing your Ansible playbooks and roles, we have strongly encouraged the use of version control systems and including roles from source control so that there is always a *single source of truth* for your Ansible code.

However, in our examples throughout this book, we have worked with very simple, static inventory files that feature, at most, a handful of hosts. Naturally, your enterprise won't look like this—the whole goal of automation is to be able to handle a large infrastructure of hundreds of machines with ease and grace and to be able to cope with changes in that infrastructure efficiently and effectively.

Most enterprises that begin their automation journey are not starting from scratch—it is anticipated that many who read this book will already have a Linux estate of some size that they need to manage more effectively, and so will already have a list of machines that need automation applying to them.

This completes our problem statement—imagine that you have an estate of Linux servers comprised of hundreds of machines and have built up a scalable automation system using Ansible and AWX/Ansible Tower, with all code stored in version control and roles actively being reused. Why then would you want to manually type out those hundreds of hostnames into a flat-text inventory file?

Further, whenever a new Linux machine is commissioned (or an old one decommissioned)—a not uncommon task in this age of virtualization—imagine having to manually edit that inventory file and ensuring it is in sync with what your estate actually looks like.

In short, this situation is not acceptable. It is not scalable and will very quickly become unmanageable. How can you, to pick one example, be confident that all of the servers in your estate have had the CIS Benchmark applied to them if you are not confident that your inventory contains all your servers to begin with?

Thankfully, Ansible includes a solution to this too, in the form of dynamic inventory script, and we will look at the anatomy of these in the next section.

Working with Ansible dynamic inventories

To keep the examples in this book simple and to focus on the automation code being written, we have made use of the simple `inifile` format of inventory that Ansible supports. However, Ansible can ingest inventory data in JSON format, which can be passed to it by any executable script.

Almost every Linux machine these days will exist within some ecosystem, be it a public cloud provider such as AWS or Azure, a private cloud environment such as OpenStack, or a traditional virtualization environment such as VMware or oVirt. All of these systems already know what their *inventory* is, although they do not use that term as such. For example, if you run a set of Linux virtual machines in Amazon EC2 or OpenStack, both systems know exactly what those machines are and what they are called. Similarly, if you spin them up in VMware or oVirt, the hypervisor managers know what machines are running and what they are called.

In essence, what we are saying is that just about every infrastructure management system already has a kind of inventory that Ansible can use. Our task is to extract that inventory and convert it into the JSON format that Ansible understands so that it can use it.

Thankfully, the developers and contributors involved in the Ansible project have already developed dynamic inventory scripts that cover a wide array of systems. If you look at the project's Ansible repository (`https://github.com/ansible/ansible/tree/devel/contrib/inventory`), you will see all of the currently available inventory scripts. Most of them are written in Python, but you can write it in any language that your operating system can execute—it can even be a shell script if you wish!

In short, if you need a dynamic inventory, there is a good chance that it already exists and you can make use of the existing script. If you are making use of AWX/Ansible Tower, all of these scripts along with their required libraries are all pre-installed, which makes it incredibly easy to get started.

If, however, you are using Ansible in the shell, note that many of the scripts will require additional libraries to function. For example, the `ec2.py` script for producing a dynamic inventory from Amazon EC2 requires the `boto` Python library, which may not be pre-installed. For example, we could download and run the `ec2.py` script by executing these commands:

```
$ wget
https://raw.githubusercontent.com/ansible/ansible/devel/contrib/inventory/e
c2.py
$ chmod +x ec2.py
$ ./ec2.py
```

We would expect the preceding commands to fail because we have not configured the dynamic inventory script with our AWS account data—however, if you perform this without checking the prerequisites (such as the boto library), you will be presented with an error such as this:

```
james@automation-01: ~
~> wget https://raw.githubusercontent.com/ansible/ansible/devel/contrib/inventor
y/ec2.py
--2019-11-18 17:39:54--  https://raw.githubusercontent.com/ansible/ansible/devel
/contrib/inventory/ec2.py
Resolving raw.githubusercontent.com (raw.githubusercontent.com)... 151.101.192.1
33, 151.101.0.133, 151.101.64.133, ...
Connecting to raw.githubusercontent.com (raw.githubusercontent.com)|151.101.192.
133|:443... connected.
HTTP request sent, awaiting response... 200 OK
Length: 73130 (71K) [text/plain]
Saving to: ·ec2.py·

ec2.py         100%  71.42K  --.-KB/s     in 0.1s

2019-11-18 17:39:55 (655 KB/s) - ·ec2.py· saved [73130/73130]

~> chmod +x ec2.py
~> ./ec2.py
Traceback (most recent call last):
  File "./ec2.py", line 164, in <module>
    import boto
ImportError: No module named boto
```

The exact fix for this will be dependent on your operating system—on Ubuntu Server 18.04, I can fix this by running this:

```
$ sudo apt install python-boto
```

On CentOS 7, you will need the EPEL repositories configured, and then you can install it using a command like this:

```
$ sudo yum install python2-boto
```

Each dynamic inventory script will have different pre-requisites—some might not even have any! In addition to the dependencies, you must also configure the script as it will (at a bare minimum) require authentication parameters so that it can query the upstream source for the inventory. You will find that the configuration file is alongside the dynamic inventory script—hence, for our example ec2.py script, you could download the example configuration file using the following command:

```
$ wget
https://raw.githubusercontent.com/ansible/ansible/devel/contrib/inventory/e
c2.ini
```

Both the template configuration file and the comments at the beginning of the dynamic inventory script provide a great deal of documentation and information on how the scripts work and how to make use of them. Be sure to read these when implementing these scripts as it will save you a lot of time when implementing them.

It is not anticipated that everyone reading this book will have an AWS account to test dynamic inventory scripts against, so completing this exercise is left for you.

Finally, it should be noted that, although many dynamic inventory scripts have been provided, there will be systems that do not have a dynamic inventory script available yet. Perhaps you have your own in-house **Configuration Management System** (CMS)—in this instance, as long as you can extract the data from it, you can write your own dynamic inventory plugin. The Ansible project provides you with some guidance and example code to get you started here: `https://docs.ansible.com/ansible/latest/dev_guide/` `developing_inventory.html`.

The beauty of open source software is that you can even contribute it back to the Ansible project so that others may benefit from your work (if you so wish). In short, just as you should always reuse your role code and ensure it is version controlled, so should you make use of dynamic inventories wherever possible.

Before we finish our look at dynamic inventory scripts, we will complete a simple worked example that anyone can try in their environment.

Example – working with the Cobbler dynamic inventory

Cobbler is an open source provisioning system that provides a framework for managing your PXE-based installs. It is embedded in the Spacewalk project (and Red Hat Satellite Server 5.x) and can be used standalone if you require a management framework for your PXE boot environment (rather than managing it by hand as we did in `Chapter 6`, *Custom Builds with PXE Booting*).

Although the actual use of Cobbler is beyond the scope of this book, it serves as an excellent example for our dynamic inventory section of this book because it is extremely easy to get up and running with.

If you are considering the use of Katello for patch management, as discussed in Chapter 9, *Patching with Katello*, note that Katello also provides a robust framework for managing PXE-based installs and it is recommended you investigate this for this purpose so that you are using one tool for both processes. This supports our principle of commonality discussed in Chapter 1, *Building a Standard Operating Environment on Linux*. You would use the foreman.py dynamic inventory script to work with Katello in your environment.

To get started with this example, you will need a demo system that Cobbler is packaged for—at the time of writing, there are no native packages for Ubuntu Server 18.04, so we will install our Cobbler server on CentOS 7. Your dynamic inventory script can be run from an Ubuntu Server machine, though—the only requirement is that it can communicate with your Cobbler server on the network:

1. To get started, install the minimum required Cobbler packages on your CentOS 7 system using the following command:

   ```
   $ sudo yum -y install cobbler cobbler-web
   ```

2. The default configuration for Cobbler should be fine for our simple dynamic inventory test purposes, so we will start the server with this command:

   ```
   $ sudo systemctl start cobblerd.service
   ```

3. Next, we will create distro and profile for our systems—when using Cobbler for actual PXE-based installs, distro describes the operating system and specifies items such as the kernel and initial RAMDisk to be used. These commands should work on your CentOS 7 test system, but be aware that if you don't have these specific kernel files installed, you must change these to reference the kernel you have installed:

   ```
   $ sudo cobbler distro add --name=CentOS --
   kernel=/boot/vmlinuz-3.10.0-957.el7.x86_64 --
   initrd=/boot/initramfs-3.10.0-957.el7.x86_64.img
   $ sudo cobbler profile add --name=webservers --distro=CentOS
   ```

4. It appears that Cobbler does not function with the *out of the box* SELinux policy that runs on CentOS 7—in a production environment, you would modify the policy to support Cobbler correctly. For the sake of this simple demo, you can simply disable SELinux using this command:

```
$ sudo setenforce 0
```

Just don't do this in a production environment!

5. With our prerequisite steps completed, we can now commence adding our actual systems to the Cobbler inventory. We will add two frontend web servers to our `webservers` group using the following commands:

```
$ cobbler system add --name=frontend01 --profile=webservers --dns-
name=frontend01.example.com --interface=eth0
$ cobbler system add --name=frontend02 --profile=webservers --dns-
name=frontend02.example.com --interface=eth0
```

The `--dns-name` parameter should be an actual resolvable DNS name in your test environment for this test to work—I am adding them to `/etc/hosts` on my Ansible server for this test but, again, in a production environment, you would not do this.

6. Cobbler is now set up and has an inventory of two hosts in a group (profile) called `webservers`. Now, we can move back to our Ansible server. On this machine, download the Cobbler dynamic inventory script and its associated configuration file by running this:

```
$ wget
https://raw.githubusercontent.com/ansible/ansible/devel/contrib/inv
entory/cobbler.py
$ wget
https://raw.githubusercontent.com/ansible/ansible/devel/contrib/inv
entory/cobbler.ini
$ chmod +x cobbler.py
```

7. Now, edit the configuration file, `cobbler.ini`—near the top of this file, you will see a few lines that look like this:

```
[cobbler]

host = http://PATH_TO_COBBLER_SERVER/cobbler_api
```

Change the `PATH_TO_COBBLER_SERVER` string to the hostname or IP address of the machine you just installed Cobbler on. That's all there is to it!

8. Now, you can run Ansible and use an ad hoc command to test your dynamic inventory—simply run this:

```
$ ansible webservers -i cobbler.py -m ping
```

You will observe that we are telling Ansible to only perform this action on the `webservers` group from the inventory specified by the `-i` parameter—which, in this case, is our Cobbler dynamic inventory script. If all has gone well, your output should look something like this screenshot:

```
james@automation-01: ~
~> ansible webservers -i cobbler.py -m ping
[DEPRECATION WARNING]: The TRANSFORM_INVALID_GROUP_CHARS settings is set to
allow bad characters in group names by default, this will change, but still be
user configurable on deprecation. This feature will be removed in version 2.10.
Deprecation warnings can be disabled by setting deprecation_warnings=False in
ansible.cfg.
[WARNING]: Invalid characters were found in group names but not replaced, use
-vvvv to see details

frontend01.example.com | SUCCESS => {
    "ansible_facts": {
        "discovered_interpreter_python": "/usr/bin/python"
    },
    "changed": false,
    "ping": "pong"
}
frontend02.example.com | SUCCESS => {
    "ansible_facts": {
        "discovered_interpreter_python": "/usr/bin/python"
    },
    "changed": false,
    "ping": "pong"
}
```

In this case, the deprecation warning is about the output from the Cobbler dynamic inventory script, which suggests it might need updating to work with Ansible 2.10 onward. However, we can see that Ansible can extract the inventory from the Cobbler server and use it for our simple ad hoc command—this would work just as well with a whole playbook!

Play with the Cobbler server; try adding and removing systems and see how Ansible retrieves the up to date inventory each and every time. Using other dynamic inventory scripts can be a little more involved, but it is not complicated provided you refer to the documentation and examples that ship with each. The time spent learning this will more than pay off later in terms of making your life easier and your inventories more accurate.

In the final section of this chapter, we will look a little deeper at ad hoc commands and how they can help you with one-off tasks.

Running one-off tasks with Ansible

In the previous chapter, we used the `ansible webservers -i cobbler.py -m ping` command to test connectivity to all of the servers in the `webservers` group of our dynamic inventory. This type of Ansible command is known as an ad hoc command, and it is typically used to run a single Ansible module against an inventory, with a set of parameters.

Throughout this book, we have encouraged the use of full playbooks and roles for all Ansible tasks—and for good reason! If you frequently run commands without storing the code in some shape or form, it will soon become very difficult, if not impossible, to know who ran what and when they ran it. Indeed, if you have looked into AWX/Ansible Tower, you will see that it does not even support ad hoc Ansible commands—running them is not aligned with the principles of auditability and role-based access control that underpin this product.

The example `ping` command we have looked at is the same as writing a playbook that looks like this:

```
---
- hosts: webservers
  gather_facts: no

  tasks:
    - ping:
```

The question is, then, why would you want to learn about ad hoc commands in Ansible? The answer often comes about for one-off maintenance tasks. The beauty of Ansible is that once you have implemented it throughout your infrastructure (and set up authentication, inventories, and so on), it has access to all of your servers.

For example, suppose you need to distribute an emergency patch to a set of systems by copying a file across. There are several ways you could solve this problem, including these:

- Write an Ansible playbook (and/or reusable role) to copy the file
- Copy across the file manually using `scp` or a similar tool
- Execute an ad hoc Ansible command

Of these three options, the first is almost certainly going to be inefficient in an emergency scenario. The manual copying using `scp` is perfectly valid but is inefficient, especially when you have gone to the trouble of setting up Ansible.

In an ad hoc command, you can use any module that you can use in a playbook or role. You can specify the same arguments too, only they are formatted a little differently as we specify them on the command line rather than in a YAML file.

Let's suppose an error has been found on the front page of our web server, and we urgently need to copy across a new version that has the fix in it. The ad hoc command to run this might look like this:

```
$ ansible webservers -i inventory -m copy -a "src=frontpage.html
dest=/var/www/html/frontpage.html" --become
```

Let's break that command down—the group and inventory script are specified just as before, but this time, we have the following:

`-m copy`	Tells Ansible to use the `copy` module for the ad hoc command
`-a "..."`	Provides the parameters or arguments for the module
`src=frontpage.html`	The `src` parameter, which tells the copy module where to obtain the file from on the Ansible server
`dest=/var/www/html/frontpage.html`	The `dest` parameter, which tells the copy module where to write the file on the destination server
`--become`	Tells Ansible to `become` root (that is, sudo)

When you run this command, you will note that the output is quite different from the `ansible-playbook` command. Nonetheless, the files are faithfully copied to all specified hosts in the inventory without you needing to write an entire playbook. The following screenshot shows an example of the output from this command:

```
● ● ●                              james@automation-01: ~
~> ansible webservers -i inventory -m copy -a "src=frontpage.html dest=/var/www/
html/frontpage.html" --become
frontend02.example.com | CHANGED => {
    "ansible_facts": {
        "discovered_interpreter_python": "/usr/bin/python"
    },
    "changed": true,
    "checksum": "e0410b4ed767a812e27a1efa04ac94a444a2a625",
    "dest": "/var/www/html/frontpage.html",
    "gid": 0,
    "group": "root",
    "md5sum": "6041cbd4d15f314b8662307845322adc",
    "mode": "0644",
    "owner": "root",
    "secontext": "system_u:object_r:httpd_sys_content_t:s0",
    "size": 28,
    "src": "/home/james/.ansible/tmp/ansible-tmp-1574269058.8-176850757288154/so
urce",
    "state": "file",
    "uid": 0
}
frontend01.example.com | CHANGED => {
    "ansible_facts": {
        "discovered_interpreter_python": "/usr/bin/python"
    },
```

What is doubly useful about these ad hoc commands is that not only is the file copied to all hosts specified without writing an entire playbook, but that the output from the command shows all of the return values from the module that you launched—copy, in this case. This is incredibly useful in playbook and role development as you might want to register the output of a particular task into a variable, and using an ad hoc command such as this shows you what this variable would contain.

For example, say that you wanted to actually perform the preceding task in a role instead of an ad hoc command, and register the results of this task in a variable called filecopy. The main.yml file in the role tasks/ directory might look like this:

```
---
- name: Copy across new web server front page
  copy:
    src: "frontpage.html"
    dest: "/var/www/html/frontpage.html"
  register: filecopy
```

We know from our ad hoc command that `filecopy` will be a dictionary containing several useful items, including `changed` and `size`. Hence, we could easily perform some conditional processing on these in a later task—for example, perhaps running another related task with the following clause:

```
when: filecopy.changed == true
```

Of course, if you needed to just run a raw shell command, you could do that too using the shell command—a simple example is shown as follows:

```
$ ansible webservers -i inventory -m shell -a "echo test > /tmp/test"
```

This, of course, is a contrived example, but it demonstrates to you how you could run an identical shell command across all of the servers in an Ansible inventory with relative ease. You can even inject variables into the module arguments using the format now familiar to you from your role and playbook development, as in this example:

```
$ ansible webservers -i inventory -m shell -a "echo Hello from {{
inventory_hostname }} > /tmp/test && cat /tmp/test"
```

The output of this specific command should look something like the following screenshot—see how the `shell` module returns the output from the command within the Ansible output—this is incredibly powerful and would, for example, enable you to gather information from all of the machines in an inventory with ease:

```
james@automation-01: ~

~> ansible webservers -i inventory -m shell -a "echo Hello from {{ inventory_hos
tname }} > /tmp/test && cat /tmp/test"
frontend01.example.com | CHANGED | rc=0 >>
Hello from frontend01.example.com

frontend02.example.com | CHANGED | rc=0 >>
Hello from frontend02.example.com
```

Hence, you could use Ansible ad hoc commands to perform a quick audit of your systems or to check the value of a specific setting across a set of servers.

Another place where ad hoc commands are valuable is in testing Jinja2 expressions. We have come across these a few times in the book, and when developing a playbook or role, the last thing you want to do is run through an entire play, only to discover that one of your Jinja2 expressions was wrong. Ad hoc commands enable you to easily and rapidly test these on the command line.

Say, for example, you want to develop a Jinja2 expression to put into a playbook that returns the uppercase value of a variable called vmname if it is defined, and otherwise, return the keyword all in lowercase. This would be useful in defining a host pattern for use in a playbook workflow, for example. This is not a trivial Jinja2 expression, and so rather than testing it within a playbook, let's figure it out on the command line. What we would do is print the Jinja2 expression using a debug msg, and then set the vmname variable using the -e flag. Hence, we might run this:

```
$ ansible localhost -m debug -a "msg={% if vmname is defined %}{{ vmname |
upper }}{% else %}all{% endif %}" -e vmname=test

$ ansible localhost -m debug -a "msg={% if vmname is defined %}{{ vmname |
upper }}{% else %}all{% endif %}"
```

The following screenshot shows this in action:

```
james@automation-01: ~
~> ansible localhost -m debug -a "msg={% if vmname is defined %}{{ vmname | uppe
r }}{% else %}all{% endif %}" -e vmname=test
localhost | SUCCESS => {
    "msg": "TEST"
}
~> ansible localhost -m debug -a "msg={% if vmname is defined %}{{ vmname | uppe
r }}{% else %}all{% endif %}"
localhost | SUCCESS => {
    "msg": "all"
}
```

As you can see from the preceding screenshot, the commands produce the desired output when vmname is set and undefined, and so we can copy this into our playbook or role and proceed with confidence!

That concludes our chapter on tips and tricks—it is hoped that these final words will help you with implementing a highly reliable and scalable Linux automation infrastructure based upon Ansible in your enterprise.

Summary

Effective automation in an enterprise setting goes beyond writing Ansible playbooks and roles—it is all about maintaining single sources of truth so that you can always have confidence in your automation processes. It is also about leveraging your chosen tool for as many purposes as possible, including assisting you with playbook and role development, and in helping you with one-off tasks that do not necessarily warrant a playbook (although this is discouraged as it removes some of the auditing capability offered by playbook development and effective use of AWX/Ansible Tower).

In this chapter, you learned how to make effective use of version control to maintain a history of your Linux environment. You then gained hands-on experience in using dynamic inventories for Ansible to prevent discrepancies in deployments and to ensure that both your inventories and playbooks can be trusted. Finally, you learned how to handle one-off tasks using Ansible and even assist your own playbook development.

That concludes our book on Linux automation in the enterprise—I hope that you have found it valuable and that it will assist you on your own journey of effective automation in a large scale setting.

Questions

1. What is Ansible Galaxy?
2. Why is it important to use version control for your playbooks and especially your roles?
3. List two ways in which you can include role code from a separate Git repository within your own Git project.
4. Why is it important to use dynamic inventories where possible?
5. What language(s) should you write your dynamic inventory scripts in if writing your own?
6. Where would you find the documentation on requirements and configuration examples for the dynamic inventory scripts shipped with Ansible?
7. What is an ad hoc Ansible command?
8. List two ways in which ad hoc commands can help you with playbook and role development.
9. How can you run an arbitrary shell command across a group of Linux servers using an Ansible ad hoc command?

Further reading

- To explore the effective use of Git for version control of your playbooks, especially when it comes to branching and merging, please refer to *Git Best Practices Guide* by *Eric Pidoux* (`https://www.packtpub.com/gb/application-development/git-best-practices-guide`)

- For an in-depth understanding of Ansible, please refer to *Mastering Ansible, 3rd Edition* by *James Freeman* and *Jesse Keating* (`https://www.packtpub.com/gb/virtualization-and-cloud/mastering-ansible-third-edition`)

Assessments

Chapter 1 - Building a Standard Operating Environment on Linux

1. Standard Operating Environment.
2. There are many reasons, but commonly enterprises will have Linux machines in service for many years (often whether they originally planned to or not!). An operation system falling out of support and not having security patches available is a big problem for most enterprises, and so Linux distributions should be chosen accordingly.
3. Yes, absolutely—the standards are there to serve as a guideline and to prevent things from getting chaotic, but they are not intended to be so rigid that they hamper progress or innovation.
4. Possible answers might include the following:
    - The speed at which new machines can be brought up for scaling purposes
    - Confidence in those machines that they will work the same as the current ones
    - The reliability of the machines brought into service
5. Possible answers might include the following:
    - High levels of confidence in the environment amongst all staff members
    - Supports automation of tasks
    - Consistency reduces the possibility of an application working in one environment and failing in another
6. As all the machines across the enterprise are the same (or at least broadly similar), staff can manage a large environment with a relatively small amount of knowledge, as all machines should be built the same way, to the same standards, and all applications should be deployed in the same way.
7. SOEs ensure the consistency of machine builds, which will include security hardening—the environment will also be built to known standards, which should have redundant services disabled (reducing the attack surface) and a well-understood patching strategy.

Chapter 2 - Automating Your IT Infrastructure with Ansible

1. Ansible is an open source automation platform used for running tasks across an inventory of servers. It differs from a simple shell script in that it will (when using native modules) only attempt to make changes when they are required (hence resulting in a consistent state), and it offers native support for remote connections to other machines (using SSH on Linux) and encryption of sensitive data and makes use of highly readable, self-documenting code.
2. An Ansible inventory is simply a list of servers against which an Ansible playbook is to be run.
3. Ansible has built-in features to make it easy to reuse roles—hence, a single role might find application in several playbooks. Conversely, if the code is written in a single large playbook, the only way to reuse the code in a different playbook is to copy and paste, which is both cumbersome and difficult to keep track of (especially when the code is changed in one place).
4. Jinja2.
5. Yes—Ansible has a strict and well-documented variable precedence order.
6. Employing templates will always result in a deployed file that looks the same on all machines. Using search and replace can be tricky, and simple changes to the target file on one machine can break the search pattern in all but the most meticulously designed regular expressions.
7. Ansible facts can be used to tell Ansible useful information, such as which operating system it is running on—hence, playbooks can be coded to perform different actions on a CentOS and Ubuntu host (for example, using `yum` on CentOS and `apt` on Ubuntu).

Chapter 3 - Streamlining Infrastructure Management with AWX

1. AWX stores credentials in a manner that is not easily reversible, even to administrators—as a result, it prevents those running automation tasks from accessing secure credentials and making use of them in another context.

2. If two people are working from a set of playbooks, how can you ensure they are consistent? Equally, how can you ensure that you understand the changes that have been made in your playbooks, especially when issues arise? Good version control strategies address these and many more challenges.

3. AWX has all of the dynamic inventory scripts provided as part of the Ansible project built in, along with all supporting libraries. They can be configured through the AWX user interface, and so can be considered to *work out of the box*, whereas additional work is required to use them on the command line.

4. A project is a logical grouping of playbooks—it might be a single directory on a filesystem or a repository in a version control system such as Git.

5. A template is analogous to the `ansible-playbook` command, along with all its switches and parameters, which you might run on the command line.

6. This is visible in the **Job History** pane for each job in the user interface—every job has the Git commit hash stored along with other valuable information about the task that was run.

7. The AWX server itself houses some very sensitive data, including the database, which contains reversibly encrypted credentials. Also, it is possible to run playbooks from a known path on the local filesystem of the AWX host and so, to enforce version control usage, it is important that as few people as possible have access to this server.

8. AWX has a built-in scheduler that can run playbooks at a time of your choosing (either as a one-off or regularly).

Chapter 4 - Deployment Methodologies

1. A Docker container is built from code—commonly a `Dockerfile`—and as a result, you can be confident of what a Docker container will look like when it is built. An SOE is also built programmatically, and so all builds in the SOE should look the same (perhaps allowing for minor differences when deploying on different platforms).

2. The MariaDB service takes up disk space, which although seemingly small, would waste a lot of storage if deployed hundreds of times. It also means you need to ensure it is disabled when it is not needed, which is not a necessary check if it is not installed at all.

3. Build the image off the most minimal set of packages possible. Don't include anything that isn't needed across all (or at least 90% of) machines. Clean up the image (for example, sysprep) before completing the build process.

4. If a password gets compromised, you will have to change it across all deployed machines as the password will be replicated from the original image. This may require an audit to ensure all machines that were deployed with this password are found and addressed.

5. Create the standard operating system image with a `syslog` file that includes the correct parameters to send logging information to a centralized logging server. Check and enforce this configuration regularly with Ansible.

6. If your requirements are highly specialized (perhaps a very specific set of package versions is required for one of your applications), you might choose to build your own. You would also do this if you had special security requirements, or perhaps for some reason, you don't have confidence/trust in the publicly available image.

7. Deploy the SSH configuration file with Ansible using a Jinja2 template to ensure consistency across all machines.

Chapter 5 - Using Ansible to Build Virtual Machine Templates for Deployment

1. Sysprep removes all redundant information from the image so it is clean when it is deployed. This might include system logs, bash history files, SSH host identification keys, MAC addresses in udev rules—anything that should not be deployed a hundred times across the enterprise.

2. Whenever you need to know something about the underlying system—perhaps the IP address, the operating system, or the disk geometry.

3. Ideally, create a Jinja2 template and deploy it with Ansible using the `template` module.

4. `get_url`.

5. You would write two tasks, one that uses the `apt` module, and one that uses the `yum` module. Each task should have a `when` clause and check the Ansible Facts to ensure it runs the correct task on the corresponding operating system.

6. To ensure it was not corrupted when you downloaded it and to ensure it has not been tampered with (for example, malicious software injected).

7. The roles can be reused to audit, validate, and enforce configuration across the enterprise once the template has been deployed.

Chapter 6 - Custom Builds with PXE Booting

1. Pre-eXecution Environment.
2. A DHCP server and a TFTP server—commonly, another service is required for serving larger volumes of data; this might be a web, FTP, or NFS server.
3. Check the download site for the distribution you are using or the ISO contents—there is normally a specific folder containing the kernel and RAMDisk images for network booting.
4. An installation where no user interaction is required at all and the end result is a fully installed and configured machine.
5. A kickstart file is specific to Red Hat-derivative operating systems such as CentOS and RHEL, whereas a pre-seed file is used on Debian derivatives such as Ubuntu.
6. To execute custom scripts or actions that cannot be performed earlier in the unattended installation.
7. Legacy BIOS PXE booting and UEFI network booting require different binary files for the boot process—hence, these must be separated and served appropriately according to the machine type.
8. There are multiple ways—the easiest if using automated partitioning is to provide a statement such as this:

```
d-i partman-auto/choose_recipe select home
```

Chapter 7 - Configuration Management with Ansible

1. Commonly, these might be `replace` and `lineinfile`.
2. In brief, a template file is created that contains a mix of plaintext (which will be replicated as is) and valid Jinja2 expressions, which will be parsed and turned into the appropriate text when the template is deployed. These might be simple variable substitutions or more complex constructs such as `for` loops or `if..then..else` statements.
3. Many Linux configurations are now split across multiple files, and it is possible for someone to accidentally (or maliciously) override your configuration in another file that gets included later on.

4. Regular expressions can easily be broken if not carefully designed—for example, a Linux service might accept a configuration directive if there is whitespace before it; however, if your regular expression does not take account of this, it might overlook valid configuration directives, which need changing.

5. It is simply deployed as is—almost akin to the `copy` module in Ansible.

6. Make use of the `validate` parameter with the `template` module.

7. Run Ansible in check mode—if the playbook and roles are well written, any reported `changed` results means that the configuration has deviated from the desired state and might need to be addressed.

Chapter 8 - Enterprise Repository Management with Pulp

1. Pulp repositories can be version controlled (through snapshots taken in time). They are also disk space-efficient and do not duplicate packages across mirrors.

2. Linux repositories change on a very regular basis, and a machine patched on Monday may not look like a machine patched on Tuesday. This can, in worst-case scenarios, impact testing results.

3. Pulp 2.x requires a message broker and a MongoDB database to run.

4. `/var/lib/mongodb` should be 10 GB or more in size. `/var/lib/pulp` should be sized according to the repositories you want to mirror. They should be created on the XFS filesystem.

5. At the simplest possible level, you could create a repository file in `/etc/yum.repos.d` and point it at the appropriate path on the Pulp server (as documented in Chapter 8, *Enterprise Repository Management with Pulp*). It is also possible to configure the Pulp Consumer for this task.

6. The Pulp Consumer only works on RPM-based systems, and so if you use this in a mixed CentOS and Ubuntu environment (for example), you will have a differing approach between your Ubuntu and CentOS hosts. Using Ansible for patching works for both system types and ensures consistency in your approach, which makes life simpler for those who manage the environment.

7. No, it does not. You would run `pulp-admin orphan remove --all`.

Chapter 9 - Patching with Katello

1. Katello offers a rich web-based user interface, filtering for repository creation, the concept of life cycle environments (for example, development and production), and a whole other set of features.

2. A Product is a collection of supported files in Katello—it might be a mirror of an RPM repository, some manually uploaded files, a collection of Puppet manifests, or a DEB repository mirror.

3. A content view is a version-controlled snapshot of a set of Products as defined in the answer to *question 2*. In the context used in this book, it is a version-controlled set of repositories.

4. Yes, it can.

5. You would create one `Lifecycle Environment` for each distinct environment in your enterprise—for example, `Development`, `Testing`, `Staging`, and `Production`. Hence, you can have a different version of a Content View associated with each environment, allowing `Development` to test the most bleeding-edge packages, whilst `Production` receives the most stable, tested ones.

6. A `Publish` operation created a new version of a content view—this is not associated with any of your `Lifecycle Environments` at this stage. A `Promote` operation associates the published version with a `Lifecycle Environment`.

7. When you are ready to test/deploy that version of the repository content in the environment you are promoting to (for example, new version of packages to `Development`).

Chapter 10 - Managing Users on Linux

1. They provide an emergency route into the server in case of failure of the directory service.

2. The `user` module.

3. Run an ad hoc Ansible command and use the `password_hash` filter to generate the hash, as in this example:

```
$ ansible localhost -i localhost, -m debug -a "msg={{ 'secure123' |
password_hash('sha512') }}"
```

4. The `realmd` package.

5. Create a template to match the file on the group of servers, and then write a role/playbook with a task to deploy the template. Run the playbook in check mode and if `changed` status results occur, then the templated file differs from the configuration on the servers.

6. If you get a directive wrong in `sudoers`, the worst-case scenario is you will lock yourself out of becoming `root` on your server (hence preventing you from fixing the problem). Validating the file helps to prevent this.

7. A directory service can audit logins, manage password complexity, lock accounts centrally either on demand or as a result of too many failed login attempts.

8. This depends on your business requirements and existing architecture. A business with a Microsoft infrastructure will almost certainly already have Microsoft Active Directory, whilst a business running purely on Linux will not need to introduce Windows Server and so should consider FreeIPA.

Chapter 11 - Database Management

1. Ansible provides a self-documenting way of deploying both the software and database content—coupled with a tool such as AWX, it ensures you have an audit trail of who made what changes and when.

2. Create the configuration file as a template and deploy it using the template across all servers. Where configurations are split across multiple files, either ensure that all files are managed by Ansible or remove the `include` statement from the files to ensure parameters cannot be accidentally overridden.

3. Ansible performs all its operations on the database machine using SSH—hence, there is no need to open your database server to the network to manage it.

4. You would use the `shell` module when the native module you need cannot perform the operation you require. For example, older versions of Ansible could do most things on PostgreSQL, but couldn't perform a full vacuum. This has now been rectified but serves as an example - the `shell` module is your solution when you either do not have a native Ansible module that addresses your requirements, or where one exists but the task you are performing is outside its capabilities.

5. Ansible, especially when coupled with AWX, provides an audit trail and ensures that you can track what operations were performed and when. You can also schedule routine operations in AWX.

6. You would create a role or playbook and use the `shell` module to call one of the native PostgreSQL backup tools such as `pg_basebackup` or `pg_dump`.

7. `mysql_user`.

8. PostgreSQL has more native modules supporting it in Ansible than any other database platform.

Chapter 12 - Performing Routine Maintenance with Ansible

1. The `df` command can be provided with a path and it will work out the mount point on which that path lives and give you the free disk space. Ansible Facts provide disk usage statistics, but only by mount point, and so you must figure out which mount point your path lives on.

2. The `find` module is used to locate files.

3. Changes to configuration files might get made accidentally, maliciously, or as a result of an emergency change to fix an issue. In all cases, it is important to identify the changes and ensure that they are either removed or the playbooks updated to reflect the new configuration (especially when they were made to resolve an issue).

4. You could use the `template` module or `copy` module to copy over the file and run Ansible in check mode. You could also checksum the file and see whether that matches a known value.

5. Use the `service` module in a task with the appropriate parameters.

6. Jinja2 provides the filtering as well as templating in Ansible.

7. Use the split operator on the variable—for example, `{{ item.split(,) }}`.

8. If you change all of the server content in one go, you might accidentally take the whole service offline—it is better to take a small number of servers out of service at a time, make and validate the changes, and then reintroduce them.

9. Set `max_fail_percentage` to an appropriate value for your environment to stop the play if more than a given percentage of failures occur.

Chapter 13 - Using CIS Benchmarks

1. They provide a standardized, industry-agreed way to secure Linux servers.
2. Yes, it does.
3. A level 1 benchmark is not expected to have an impact on day-to-day operations of your server. A level 2 benchmark is and so should be implemented with care.
4. Scored benchmarks are expected to be crucial to all systems, whereas benchmarks that are not scored are expected to be applied to only some systems (for example, wireless network adapter configuration hardening will only apply to a subset of machines—hence, this should not affect the score of all machines).
5. This is normally provided in the benchmark document but often involves using the `grep` utility within the script to check for the configuration settings in a given file and reporting back on whether it was found or not.
6. Possible answers include the following:
    * Pattern matching can be an imprecise science, and you must be careful of false positives and indeed false negatives!
    * Shell scripts are not normally state-aware and care must be taken not to write the same configuration out each time the script is run, even if it is the same as before.
    * Shell scripts are difficult to read, especially when they become large, and so can be difficult to manage and maintain.
7. Shell scripts are not very readable, and as the number of security requirements to implement increases, so does the size of the script, in the end becoming something that no-one would be able to manage.
8. Pipe the shell script into an SSH session opened with the remote server.
9. This enables the path to be altered easily in case the script needs to be repurposed—for example, some key system binaries live in different paths on Ubuntu and CentOS systems.
10. In general, it is best to run scripts at the lowest privilege level possible, only elevating for specific tasks that require this. Also, `sudo` is sometimes configured to require a Terminal session, and this can prevent running an entire script under sudo when you pipe it into an SSH session.

Chapter 14 - CIS Hardening with Ansible

1. The modules wrap up a whole set of shell scripting functionality, including the conditionals that would be required to ensure that the script only makes changes when required and can report back on whether the change was made and whether it was successful.
2. There are several ways—you can run the entire playbook with the `--limit` parameter set, or you can use the `when` clause within the playbook to ensure that the tasks only run on given hostnames.
3. Name your tasks after the benchmark (including the number) so you can easily identify what they are for. Also, include the level and scoring detail to make it easy to interpret and audit results from playbook runs.
4. Tag the tasks as `level1` and `level2` accordingly, and then run the playbook with the `--tags level1` parameter.
5. The `--tags` parameter only runs tasks with the tags specified, whereas the `--skip-tags` parameters runs all tasks except those specified.
6. The CIS Benchmarks are very large in size, and there is no point in reinventing the wheel, especially with open source code as you can audit the playbooks before you use them to ensure they are secure and meet your requirements.
7. It tells Ansible to run in check mode, which means that no changes are performed, but Ansible will try to predict which changes would have been made if it had been run in its normal mode.
8. No—the `shell` module can't support check mode because it is impossible to know what command someone may have passed to it in a playbook.

Chapter 15 - Auditing Security Policy with OpenSCAP

1. Security Content Automation Protocol.
2. SCAP policies can audit your systems against a given standard - for example the CIS Benchmarks discussed in this book, or the **PCI-DSS (Payment Card Industry - Data Security Standard)** requirements. There are many pre-written policies available, and with open source tools such as OpenSCAP, you can write your own policies with your own requirements. This is valuable to the enterprise in being able to run audits against Linux servers and ensure they remain compliant with a chosen standard.
3. You would most likely the OpenSCAP Daemon for this purpose.

4. At a fundamental level, the OVAL file contains the low level system checks the scanning engine should perform. The XCCDF file references the OVAL file (in fact it cannot be used without it) contains amongst other definitions, profiles which make use of scan definitions to audit against known policies (for example, PCI-DSS), and code to generate human readable reports from the scan output.

5. In some environments, the vendor might only provide you with support if you use their policy files. An example of this is Red Hat Enterprise Linux 7, where Red Hat state that they will only support you if you use the SSG policies available from their own repos.

6. SCAP policies are highly specific to the operating system they are running on. Although in many scenarios, CentOS 7 and RHEL 7 can be treated as the same, there are fundamental differences. SCAP takes account of this and ensures that it differentiates between operating systems, even CentOS 7 and RHEL 7, and as such it will mark many if not all of the RHEL 7 audits as `notapplicable` when they are run against CentOS 7. The same would be true if a CentOS 7 specific policy was run against a RHEL 7 host.

7. Yes you can - a command such as the following would generate an HTML report from an XML results file: `sudo oscap xccdf generate report --output /var/www/html/reportoscapd.html /var/lib/oscapd/results/1/1/results.xml`

8. You must have set up passwordless (key based) SSH access to the server you wish to scan. It must also have passwordless sudo access unless you are using the root account over SSH (not recommended).

Chapter 16 - Tips and Tricks

1. Ansible Galaxy is a publicly available repository of Ansible roles for you to reuse or develop as you wish. It is also a place where you can share the roles you have created.

2. Playbooks and roles are bound to change over time, but there will always be times where it is a requirement to understand what happened historically. Roles especially are designed to be reused, and so it is important they are centrally version controlled so that all playbooks that make use of them are sure they are using the correct version role.

3. Possible answers include the following:
    - Use a `requirements.yml` file to specify the role URLs in a repository and install them with `ansible-galaxy`.
    - Add them to your `roles/` directory as Git submodules.

4. Especially in cloud computing, the servers you have deployed will change constantly. Ansible only knows what to automate from its inventory file, so it is vital that the inventory file is up to date or servers may get missed. Making use of dynamic inventories ensures the inventory is always up to date as the latest inventory is always dynamically generated.

5. You can write them in any language provided the output is in the correct JSON format for Ansible. Most are written in Python.

6. Look in the comments at the beginning of the dynamic inventory script itself or the accompanying configuration file.

7. It is a command that can run a single Ansible module once without the need to write an entire playbook.

8. Possible answers include the following:
    - They can help you to test and develop Jinja2 filter expressions without having to run an entire playbook.
    - They can help you to test out module functionality before you commit it to playbook or role code.

9. Run an Ansible ad hoc command using the shell module (-m shell) and pass the shell command in the arguments of the module (-a "ls -la /tmp").

Other Books You May Enjoy

If you enjoyed this book, you may be interested in these other books by Packt:

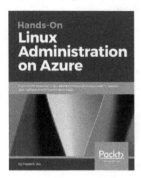

Hands-On Linux Administration on Azure

Frederik Vos

ISBN: 978-1-78913-096-6

- Understand why Azure is the ideal solution for your open source workloads
- Master essential Linux skills and learn to find your way around the Linux environment
- Deploy Linux in an Azure environment
- Use configuration management to manage Linux in Azure
- Manage containers in an Azure environment
- Enhance Linux security and use Azure's identity management systems
- Automate deployment with Azure Resource Manager (ARM) and Powershell
- Employ Ansible to manage Linux instances in an Azure cloud environment

Hands-On Linux for Architects
Denis Salamanca, Esteban Flores

ISBN: 978-1-78953-410-8

- Study the basics of infrastructure design and the steps involved
- Expand your current design portfolio with Linux-based solutions
- Discover open source software-based solutions to optimize your architecture
- Understand the role of high availability and fault tolerance in a resilient design
- Identify the role of containers and how they improve your continuous integration and continuous deployment pipelines
- Gain insights into optimizing and making resilient and highly available designs by applying industry best practices

Leave a review - let other readers know what you think

Please share your thoughts on this book with others by leaving a review on the site that you bought it from. If you purchased the book from Amazon, please leave us an honest review on this book's Amazon page. This is vital so that other potential readers can see and use your unbiased opinion to make purchasing decisions, we can understand what our customers think about our products, and our authors can see your feedback on the title that they have worked with Packt to create. It will only take a few minutes of your time, but is valuable to other potential customers, our authors, and Packt. Thank you!

Index

Trivial File Transfer Protocol (TFTP) 150